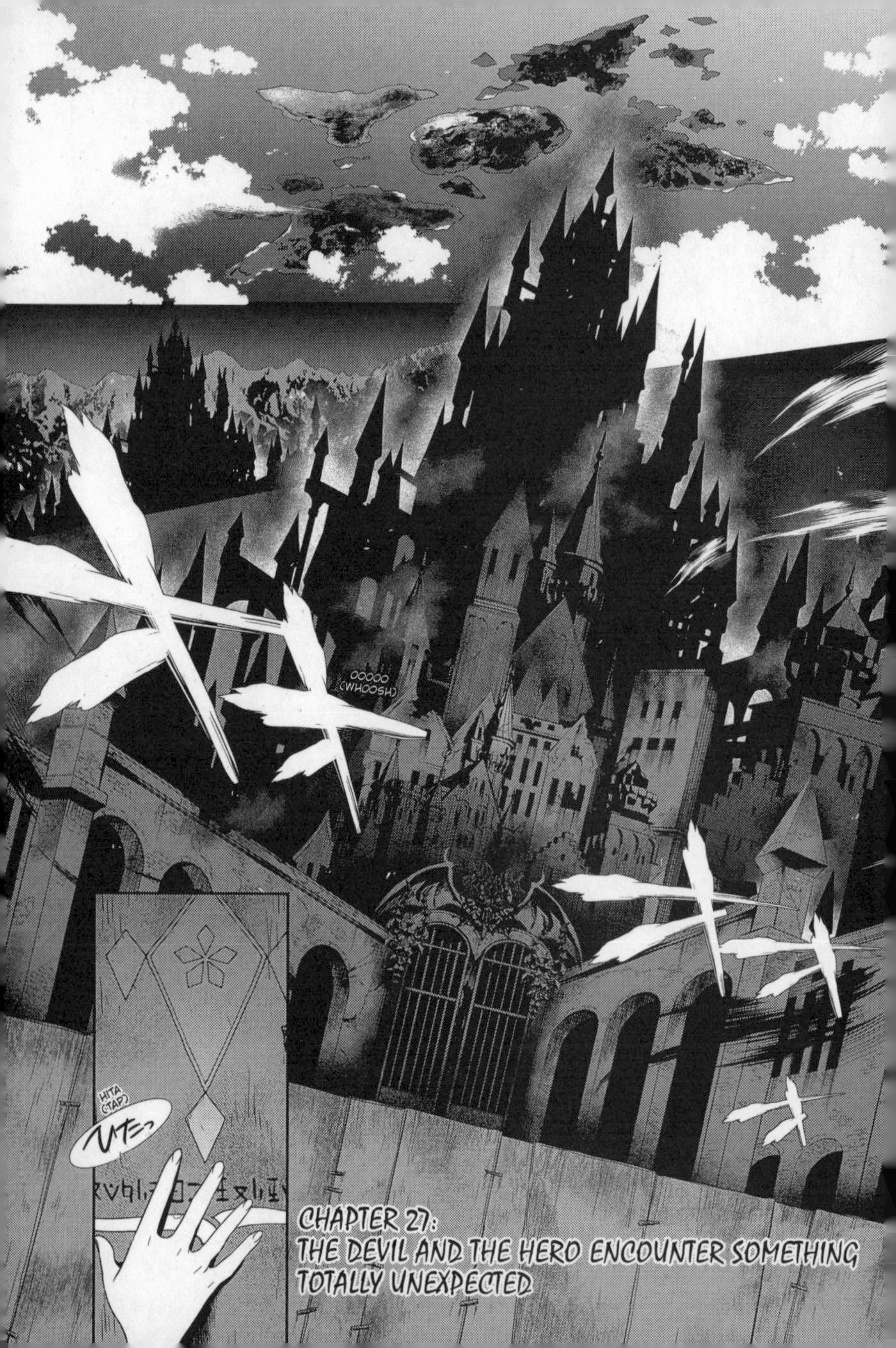
OOOOO (WHOOSH)
HITA (TAP)
CHAPTER 27:
THE DEVIL AND THE HERO ENCOUNTER SOMETHING TOTALLY UNEXPECTED

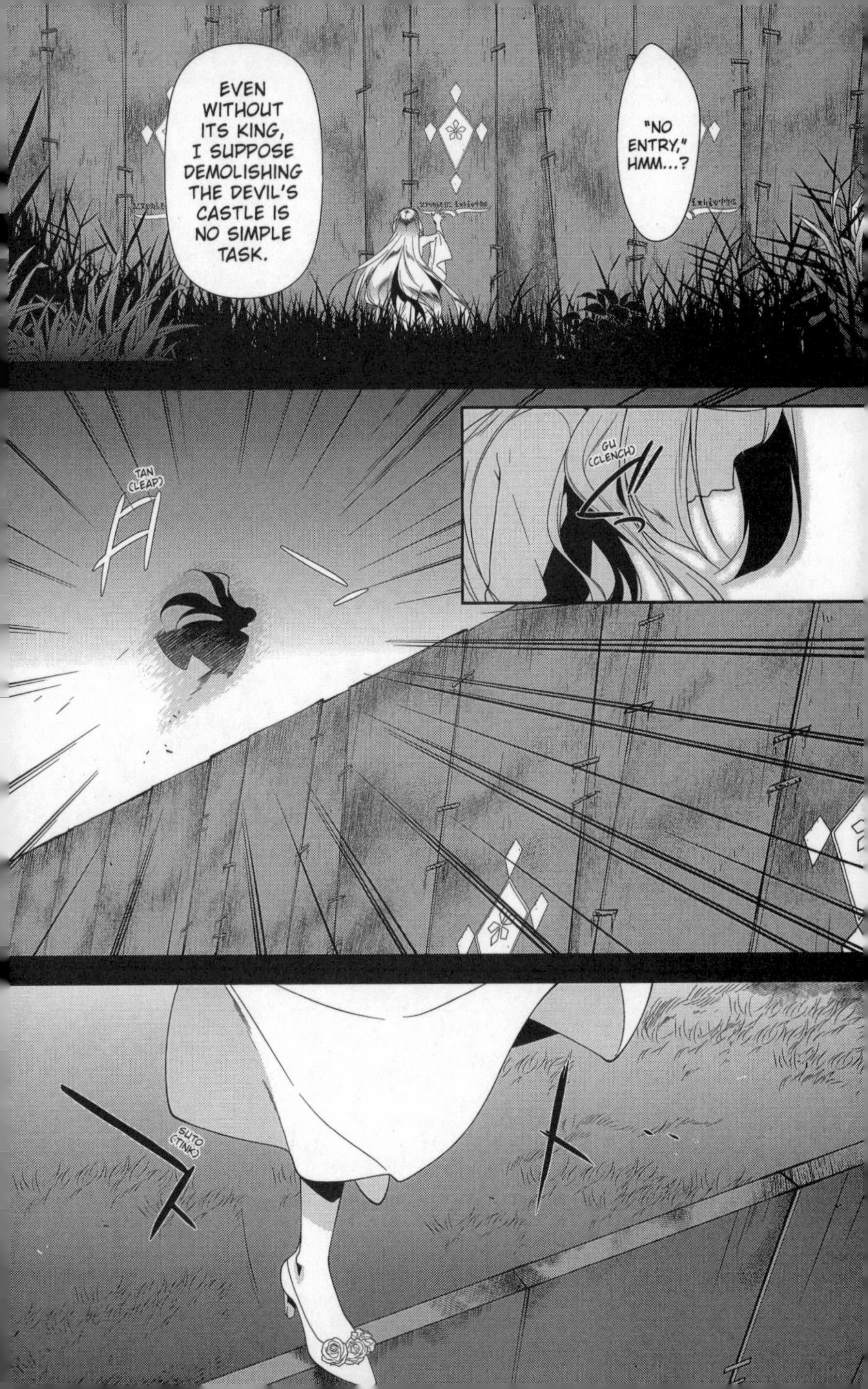
"NO ENTRY," HMM...?
EVEN WITHOUT ITS KING, I SUPPOSE DEMOLISHING THE DEVIL'S CASTLE IS NO SIMPLE TASK.
GU (CLENCH)
TAN (LEAP)
SUTO (TINK)

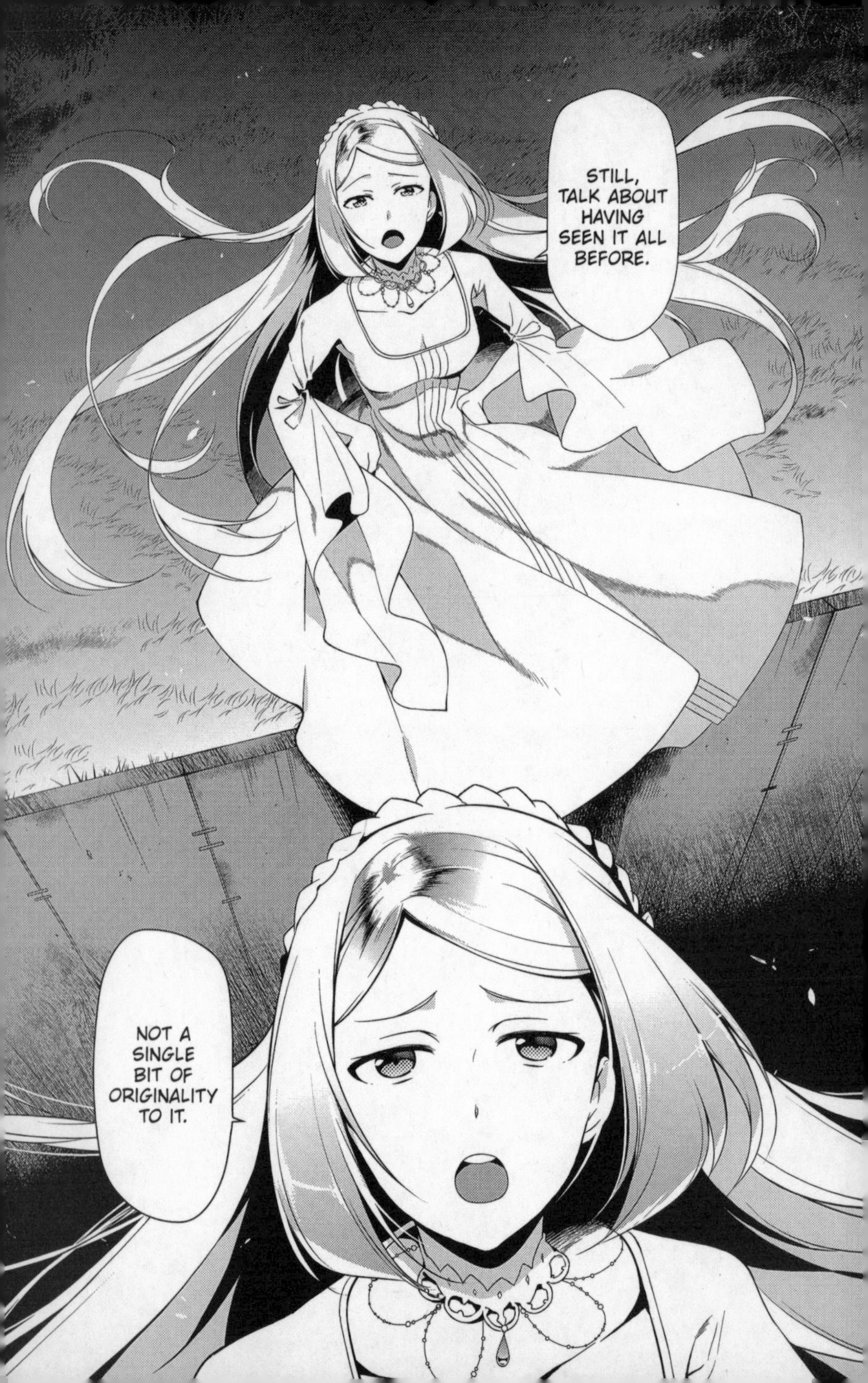
STILL, TALK ABOUT HAVING SEEN IT ALL BEFORE.
NOT A SINGLE BIT OF ORIGINALITY TO IT.

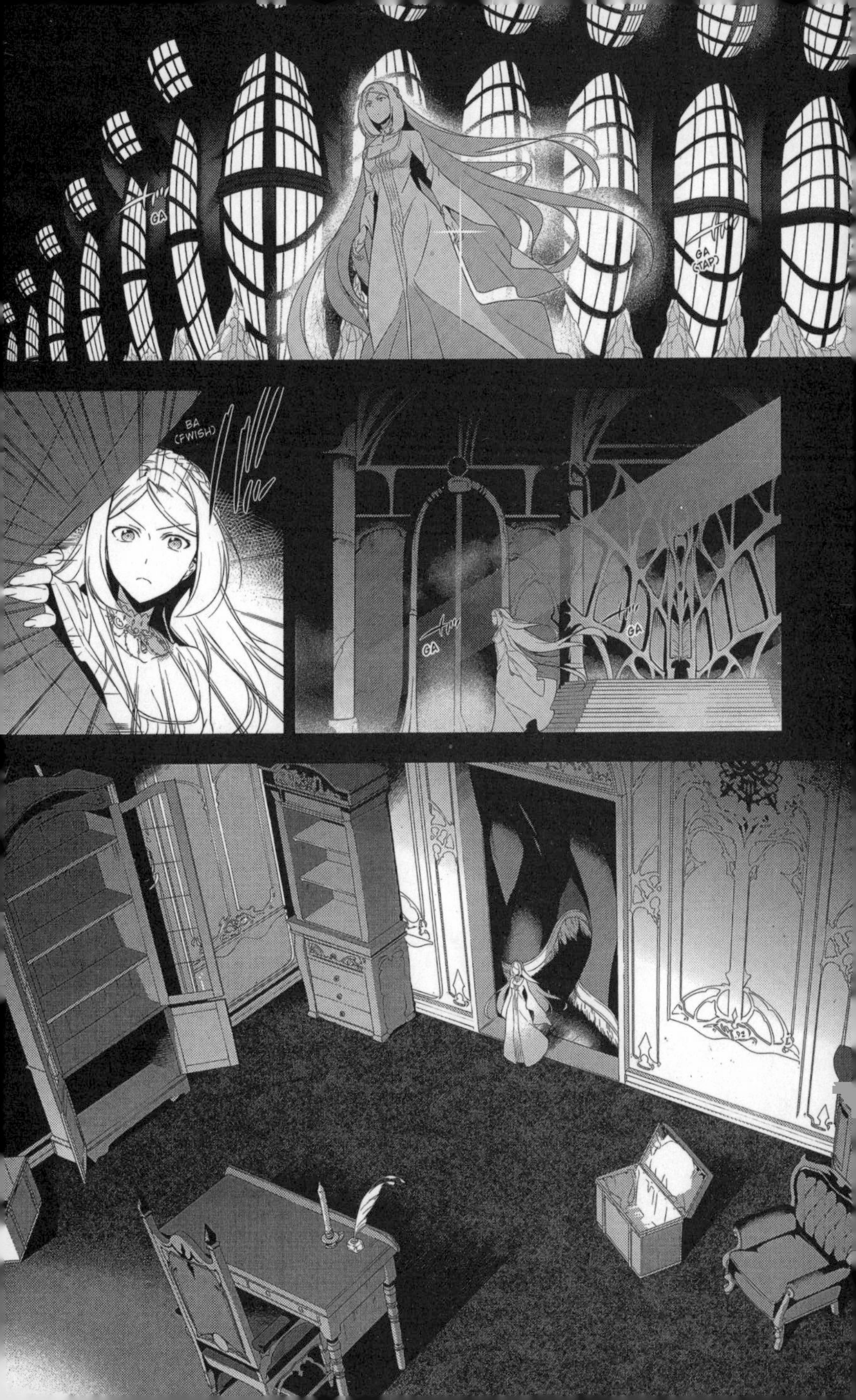
GA
(TAP)
GA
GA
GA
BA
(FWISH)

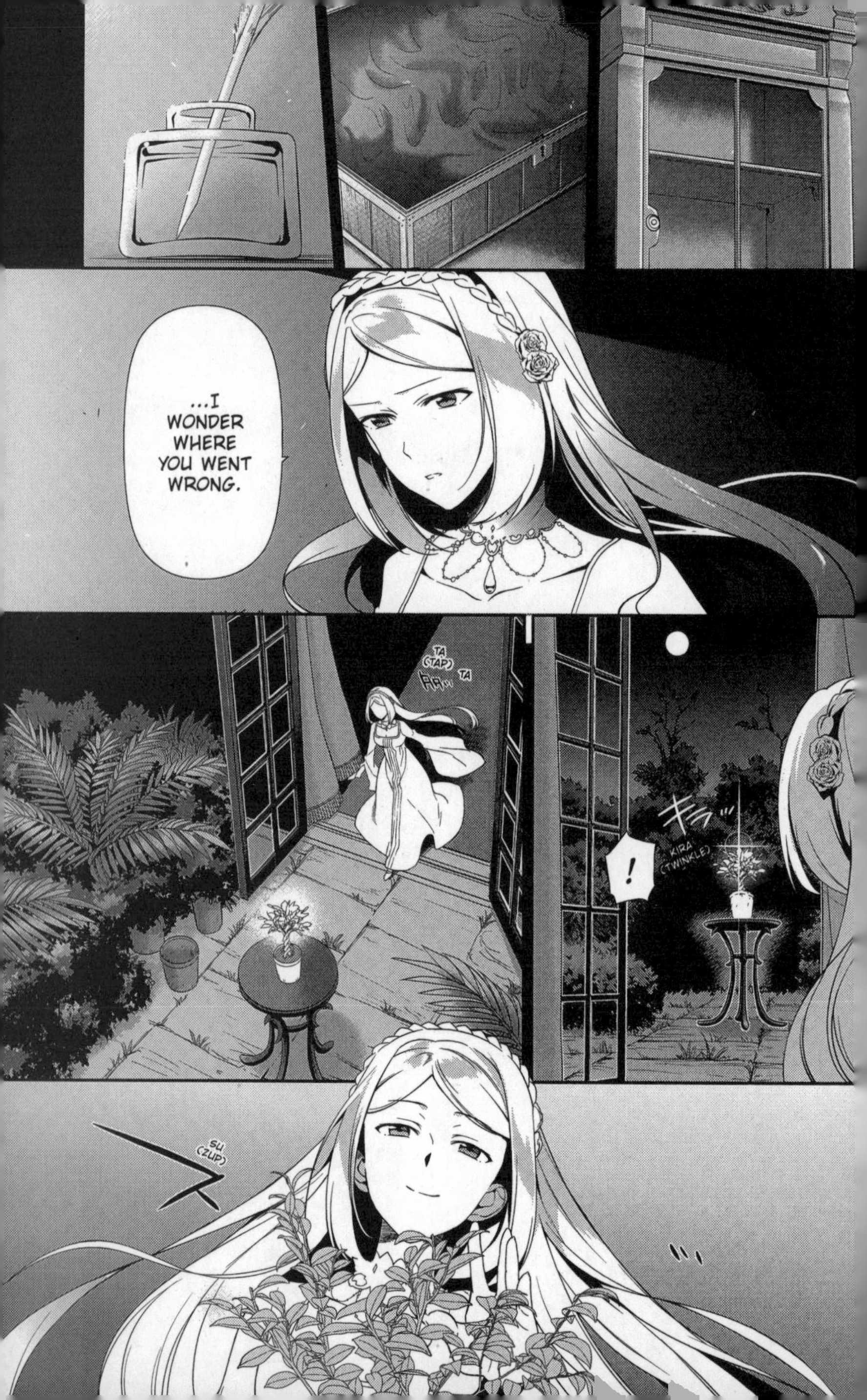
...I WONDER WHERE YOU WENT WRONG.
キラッ
KIRA (TWINKLE)
!
TA (TAP) TA
SU (ZUP)

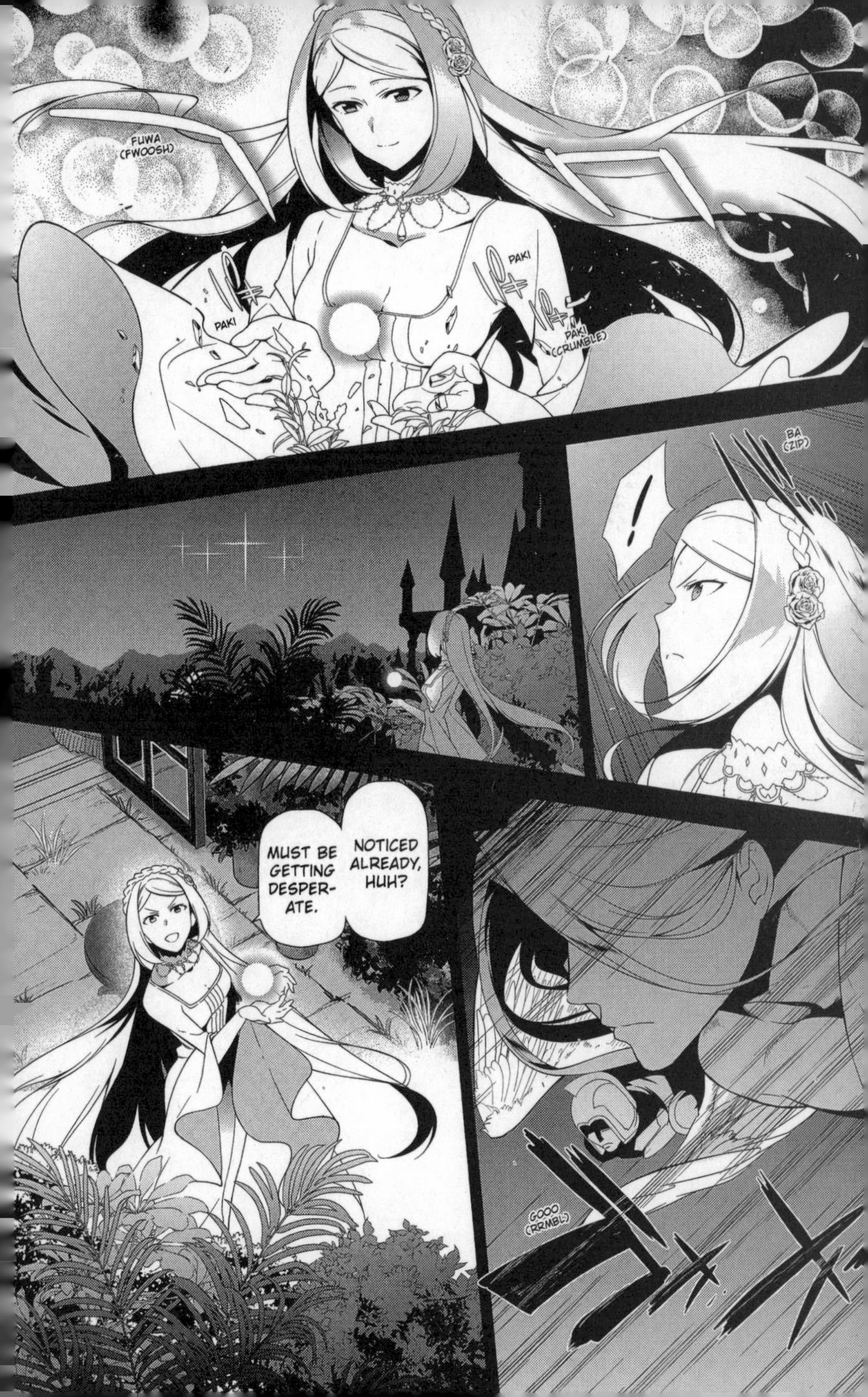
FUWA (FWOOSH)
PAKI
PAKI (CRUMBLE)
PAKI
BA (ZIP)
!
GOOO (RRMBL)
NOTICED ALREADY, HUH?
MUST BE GETTING DESPER-ATE.

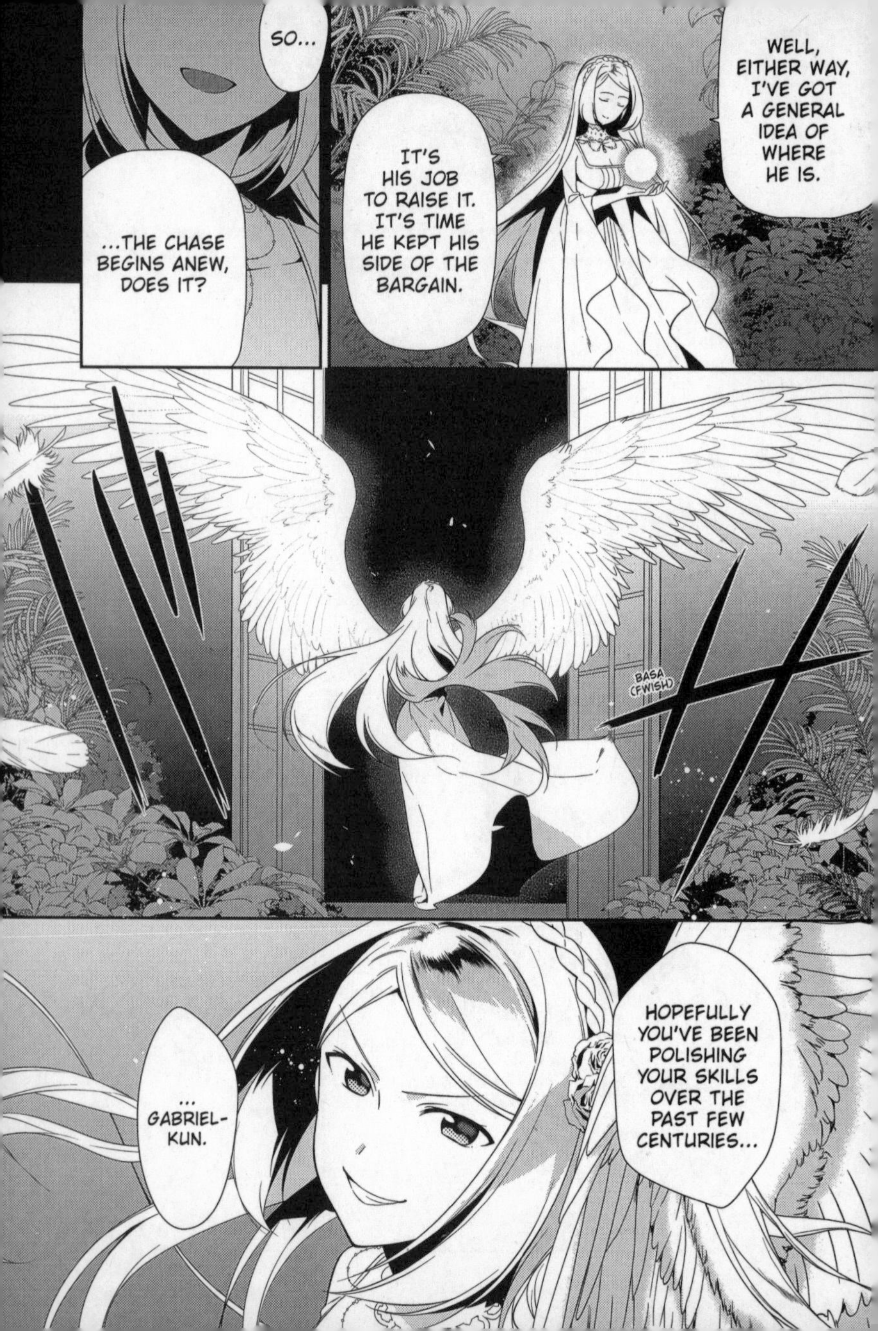
WELL, EITHER WAY, I'VE GOT A GENERAL IDEA OF WHERE HE IS.
IT'S HIS JOB TO RAISE IT. IT'S TIME HE KEPT HIS SIDE OF THE BARGAIN.
SO...
...THE CHASE BEGINS ANEW, DOES IT?
BASA (FWISH)
HOPEFULLY YOU'VE BEEN POLISHING YOUR SKILLS OVER THE PAST FEW CENTURIES...
...GABRIEL-KUN.

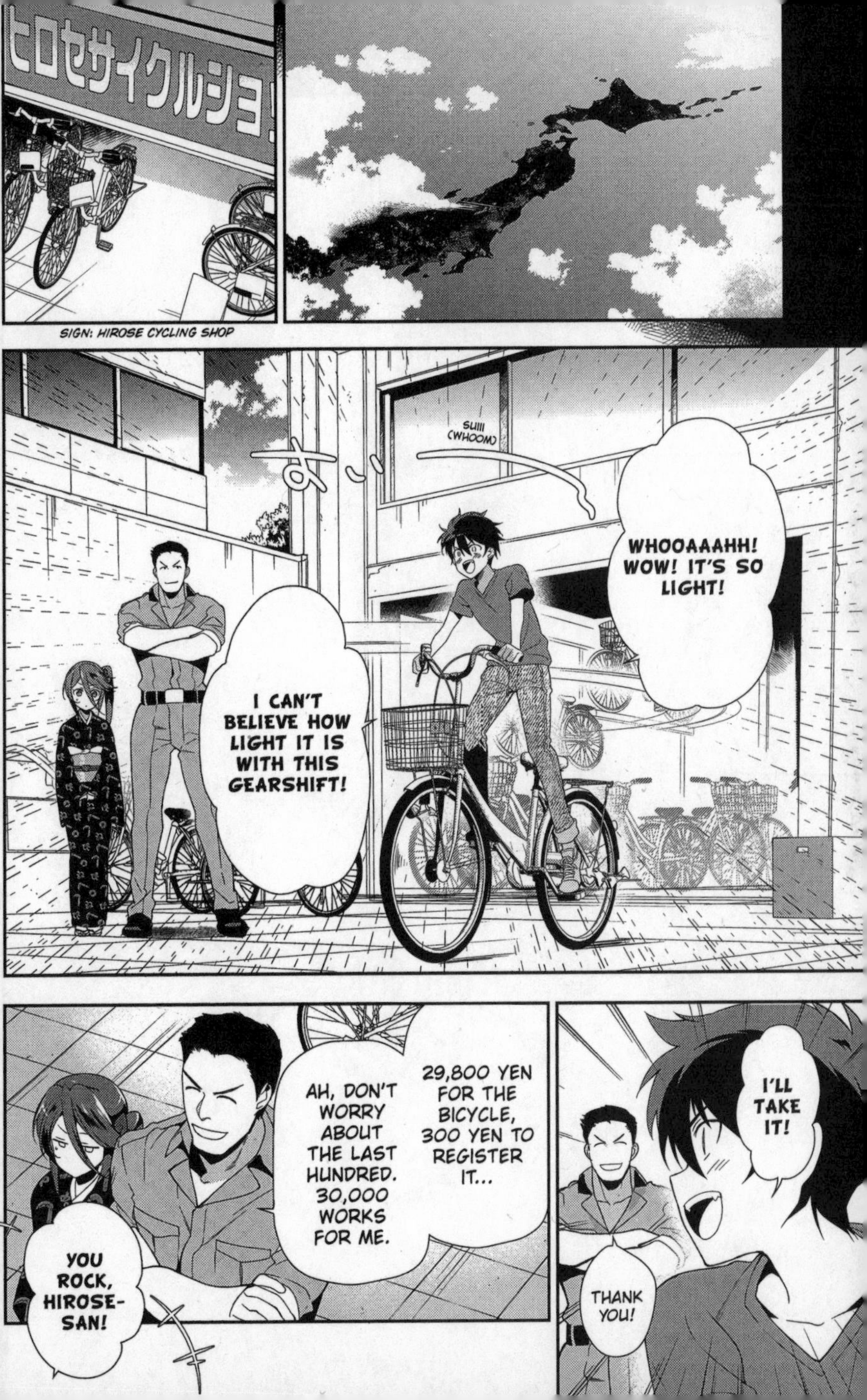
ヒロセサイクルショ
SIGN: HIROSE CYCLING SHOP
すい〜
SUIII (WHOOM)
WHOOAAAHH! WOW! IT'S SO LIGHT!
I CAN'T BELIEVE HOW LIGHT IT IS WITH THIS GEARSHIFT!
I'LL TAKE IT!
THANK YOU!
29,800 YEN FOR THE BICYCLE, 300 YEN TO REGISTER IT...
AH, DON'T WORRY ABOUT THE LAST HUNDRED. 30,000 WORKS FOR ME.
YOU ROCK, HIROSE-SAN!

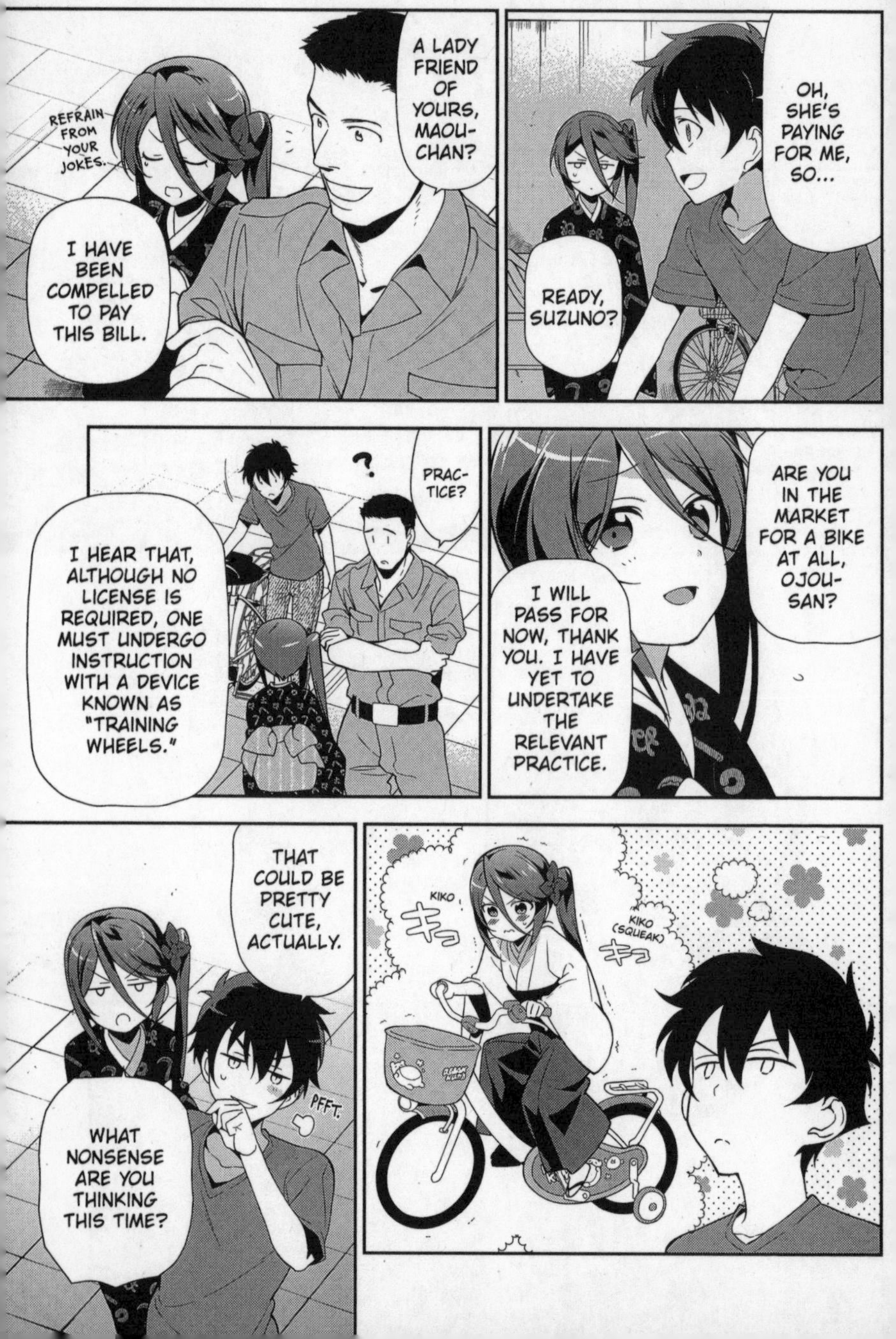
OH, SHE'S PAYING FOR ME, SO...
READY, SUZUNO?
A LADY FRIEND OF YOURS, MAOU-CHAN?
REFRAIN FROM YOUR JOKES.
I HAVE BEEN COMPELLED TO PAY THIS BILL.
ARE YOU IN THE MARKET FOR A BIKE AT ALL, OJOU-SAN?
I WILL PASS FOR NOW, THANK YOU. I HAVE YET TO UNDERTAKE THE RELEVANT PRACTICE.
PRAC-TICE?
I HEAR THAT, ALTHOUGH NO LICENSE IS REQUIRED, ONE MUST UNDERGO INSTRUCTION WITH A DEVICE KNOWN AS "TRAINING WHEELS."
KIKO (SQUEAK)
KIKO
THAT COULD BE PRETTY CUTE, ACTUALLY.
PFFT.
WHAT NONSENSE ARE YOU THINKING THIS TIME?

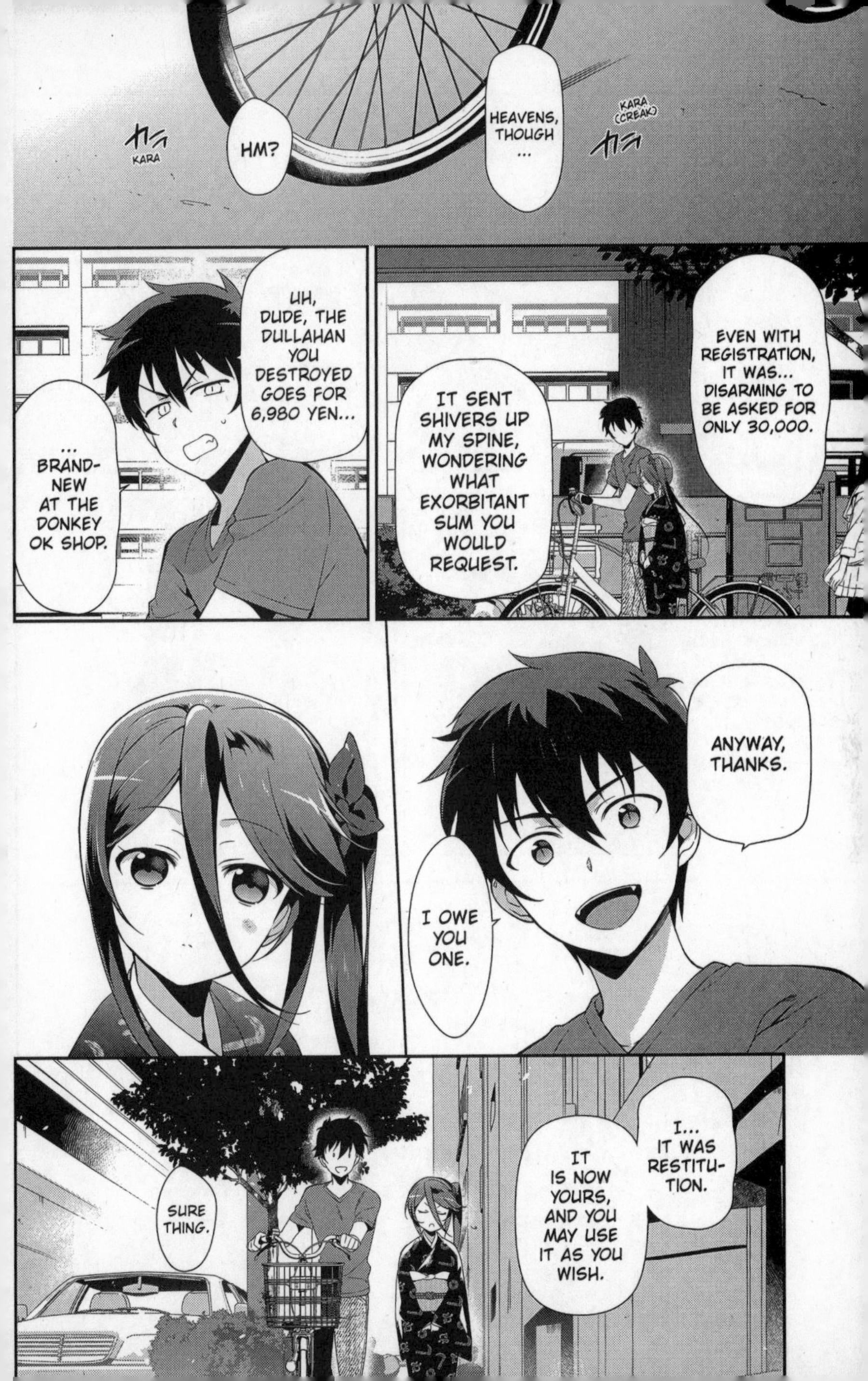
KARA (CREAK)
HEAVENS, THOUGH ...
HM?
KARA
EVEN WITH REGISTRATION, IT WAS... DISARMING TO BE ASKED FOR ONLY 30,000.
IT SENT SHIVERS UP MY SPINE, WONDERING WHAT EXORBITANT SUM YOU WOULD REQUEST.
UH, DUDE, THE DULLAHAN YOU DESTROYED GOES FOR 6,980 YEN...
... BRAND-NEW AT THE DONKEY OK SHOP.
ANYWAY, THANKS.
I OWE YOU ONE.
I... IT WAS RESTITU-TION.
IT IS NOW YOURS, AND YOU MAY USE IT AS YOU WISH.
SURE THING.

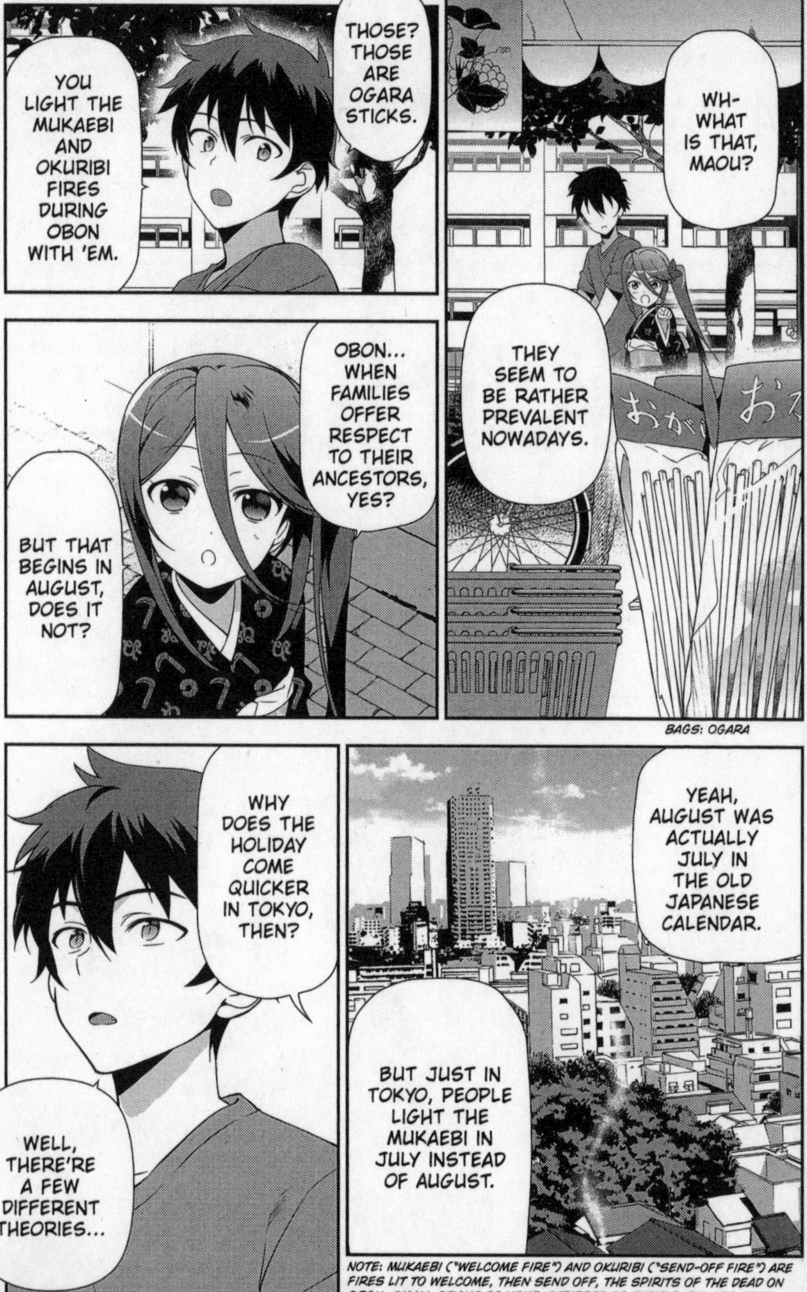
WH-WHAT IS THAT, MAOU?
THEY SEEM TO BE RATHER PREVALENT NOWADAYS.
THOSE? THOSE ARE OGARA STICKS.
YOU LIGHT THE MUKAEBI AND OKURIBI FIRES DURING OBON WITH 'EM.
OBON... WHEN FAMILIES OFFER RESPECT TO THEIR ANCESTORS, YES?
BUT THAT BEGINS IN AUGUST, DOES IT NOT?
YEAH, AUGUST WAS ACTUALLY JULY IN THE OLD JAPANESE CALENDAR.
BUT JUST IN TOKYO, PEOPLE LIGHT THE MUKAEBI IN JULY INSTEAD OF AUGUST.
WHY DOES THE HOLIDAY COME QUICKER IN TOKYO, THEN?
WELL, THERE'RE A FEW DIFFERENT THEORIES...

BAGS: OGARA

NOTE: MUKAEBI ("WELCOME FIRE") AND OKURIBI ("SEND-OFF FIRE") ARE FIRES LIT TO WELCOME, THEN SEND OFF, THE SPIRITS OF THE DEAD ON OBON. SMALL STICKS OF HEMP, STRIPPED OF THEIR BARK, ARE OFTEN USED AS FUEL.

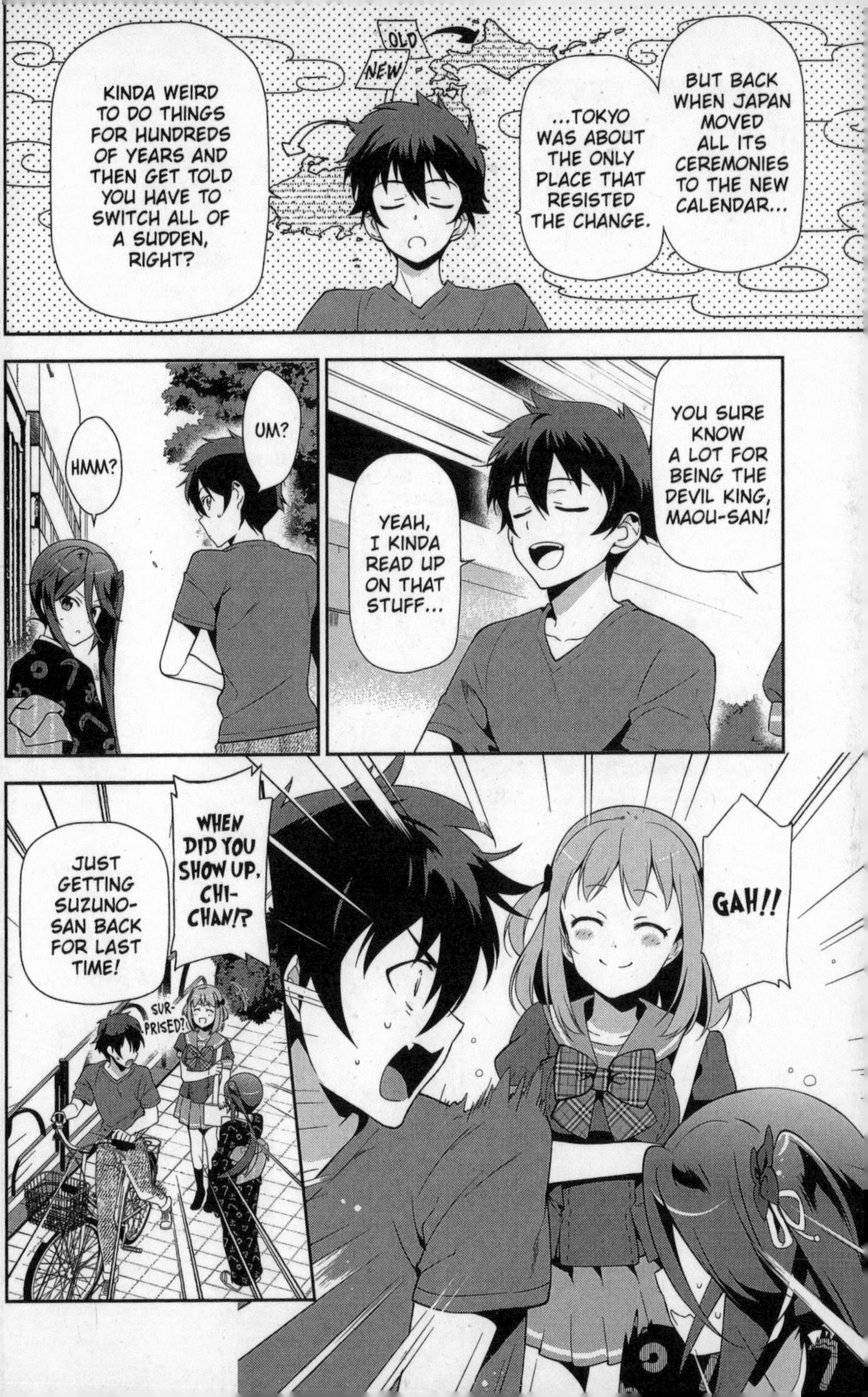
OLD
NEW
BUT BACK WHEN JAPAN MOVED ALL ITS CEREMONIES TO THE NEW CALENDAR...
...TOKYO WAS ABOUT THE ONLY PLACE THAT RESISTED THE CHANGE.
KINDA WEIRD TO DO THINGS FOR HUNDREDS OF YEARS AND THEN GET TOLD YOU HAVE TO SWITCH ALL OF A SUDDEN, RIGHT?
YOU SURE KNOW A LOT FOR BEING THE DEVIL KING, MAOU-SAN!
YEAH, I KINDA READ UP ON THAT STUFF...
UM?
HMM?
GAH!!
WHEN DID YOU SHOW UP, CHI-CHAN!?
JUST GETTING SUZUNO-SAN BACK FOR LAST TIME!
SUR-PRISED?

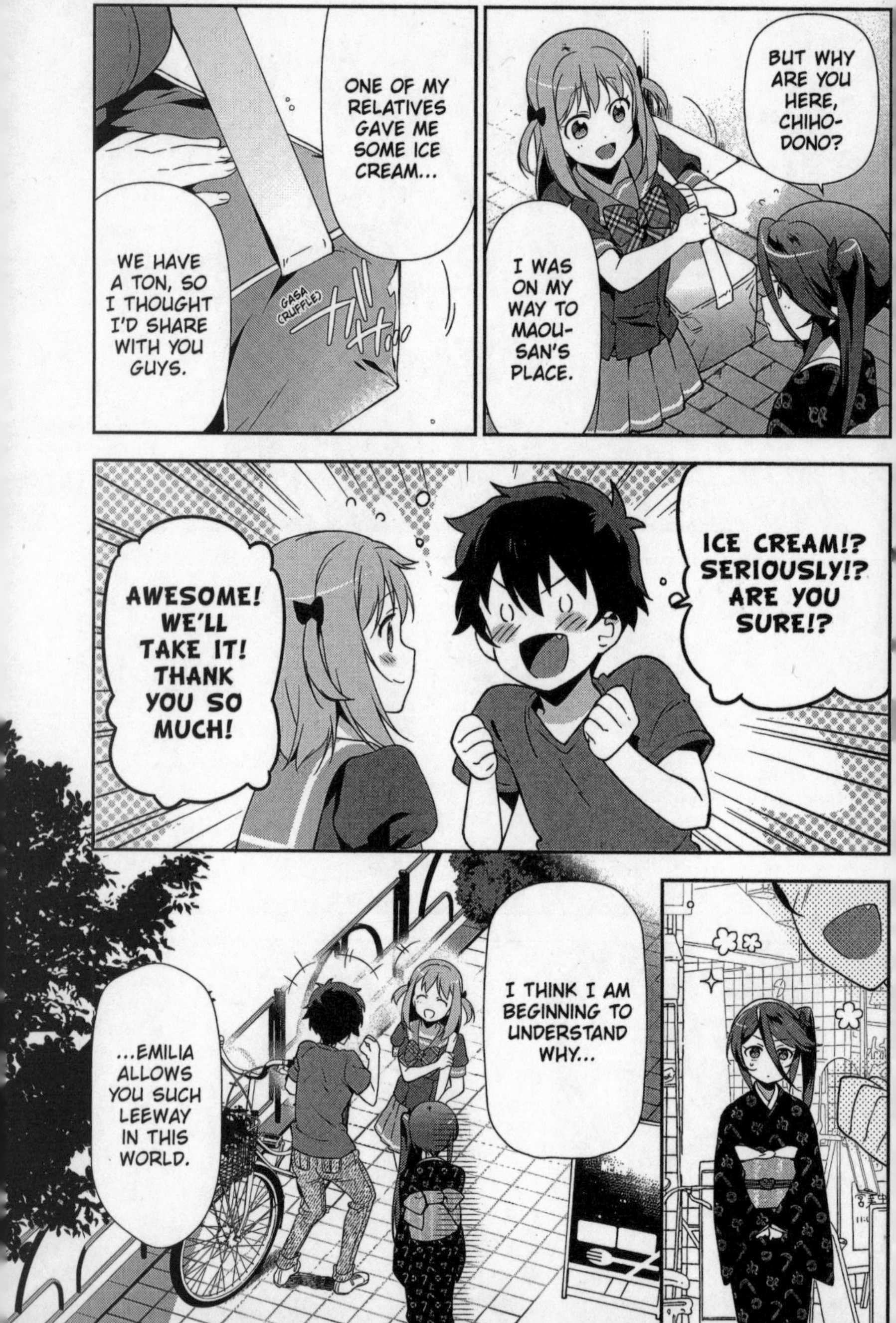
BUT WHY ARE YOU HERE, CHIHO-DONO?
I WAS ON MY WAY TO MAOU-SAN'S PLACE.
ONE OF MY RELATIVES GAVE ME SOME ICE CREAM...
GASA (RUFFLE)
WE HAVE A TON, SO I THOUGHT I'D SHARE WITH YOU GUYS.
ICE CREAM!? SERIOUSLY!? ARE YOU SURE!?
AWESOME! WE'LL TAKE IT! THANK YOU SO MUCH!
I THINK I AM BEGINNING TO UNDERSTAND WHY...
...EMILIA ALLOWS YOU SUCH LEEWAY IN THIS WORLD.

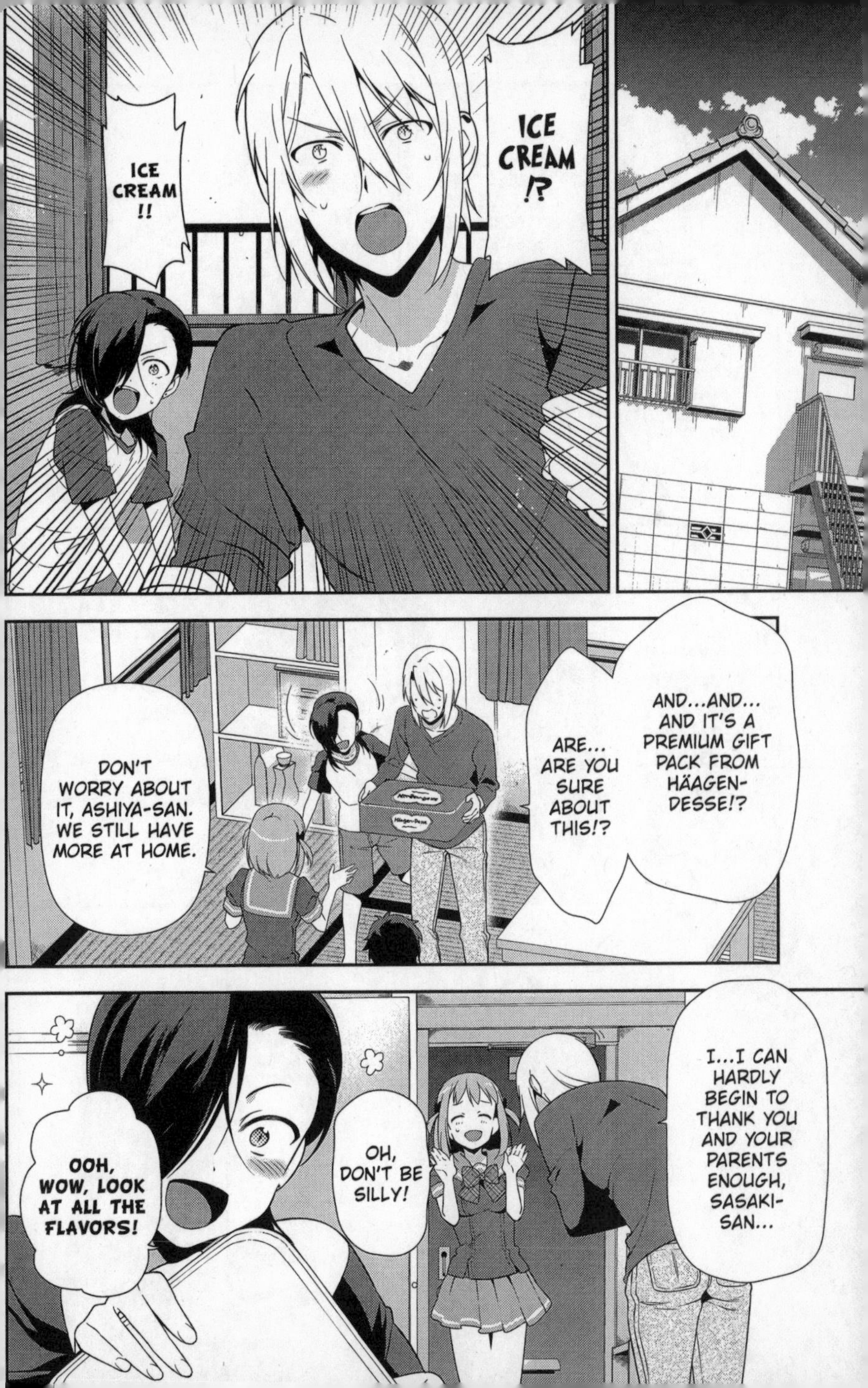
ICE CREAM!?
ICE CREAM!!
AND...AND... AND IT'S A PREMIUM GIFT PACK FROM HÄAGEN-DESSE!?
ARE... ARE YOU SURE ABOUT THIS!?
DON'T WORRY ABOUT IT, ASHIYA-SAN. WE STILL HAVE MORE AT HOME.
I...I CAN HARDLY BEGIN TO THANK YOU AND YOUR PARENTS ENOUGH, SASAKI-SAN...
OH, DON'T BE SILLY!
OOH, WOW, LOOK AT ALL THE FLAVORS!

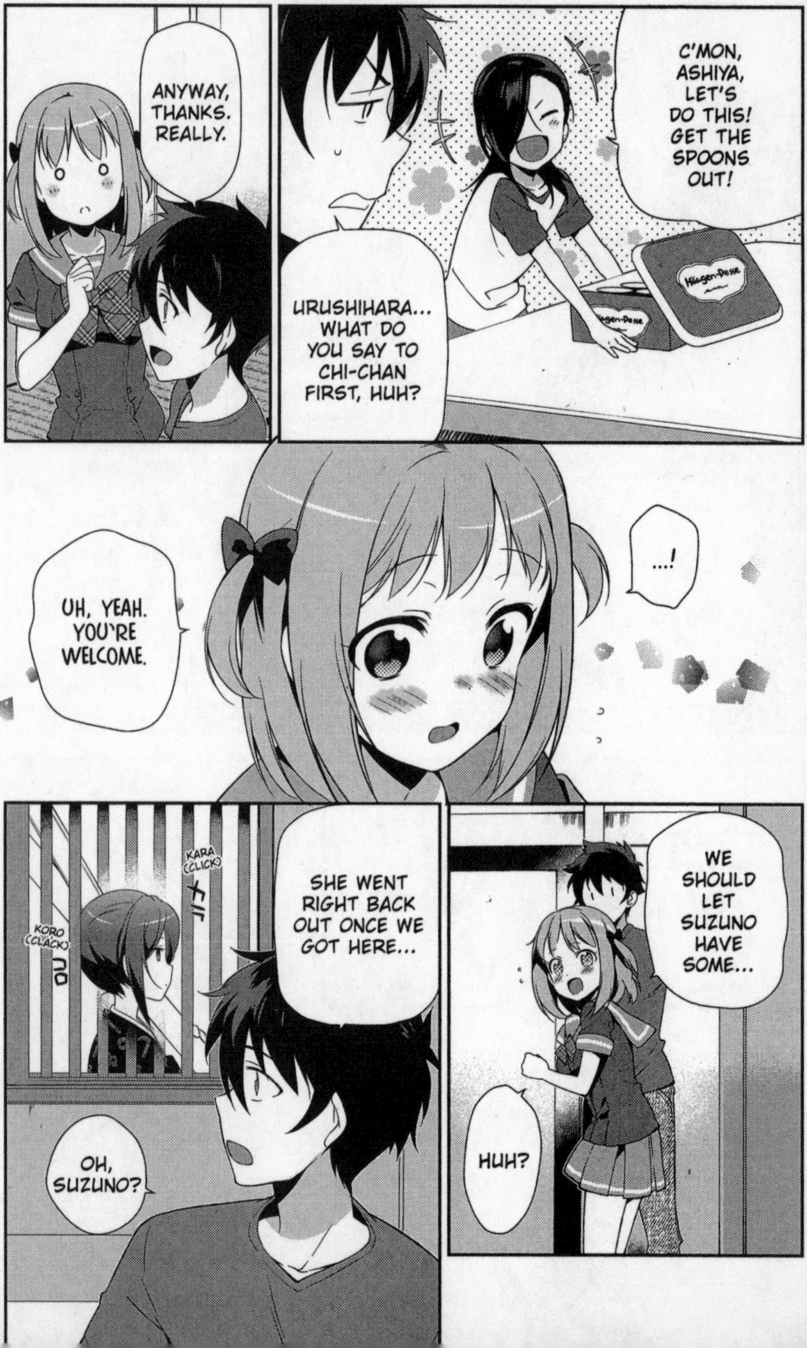
C'MON, ASHIYA, LET'S DO THIS! GET THE SPOONS OUT!
URUSHIHARA... WHAT DO YOU SAY TO CHI-CHAN FIRST, HUH?
ANYWAY, THANKS. REALLY.
...!
UH, YEAH. YOU'RE WELCOME.
WE SHOULD LET SUZUNO HAVE SOME...
HUH?
SHE WENT RIGHT BACK OUT ONCE WE GOT HERE...
KARA (CLICK)
KORO (CLACK)
OH, SUZUNO?

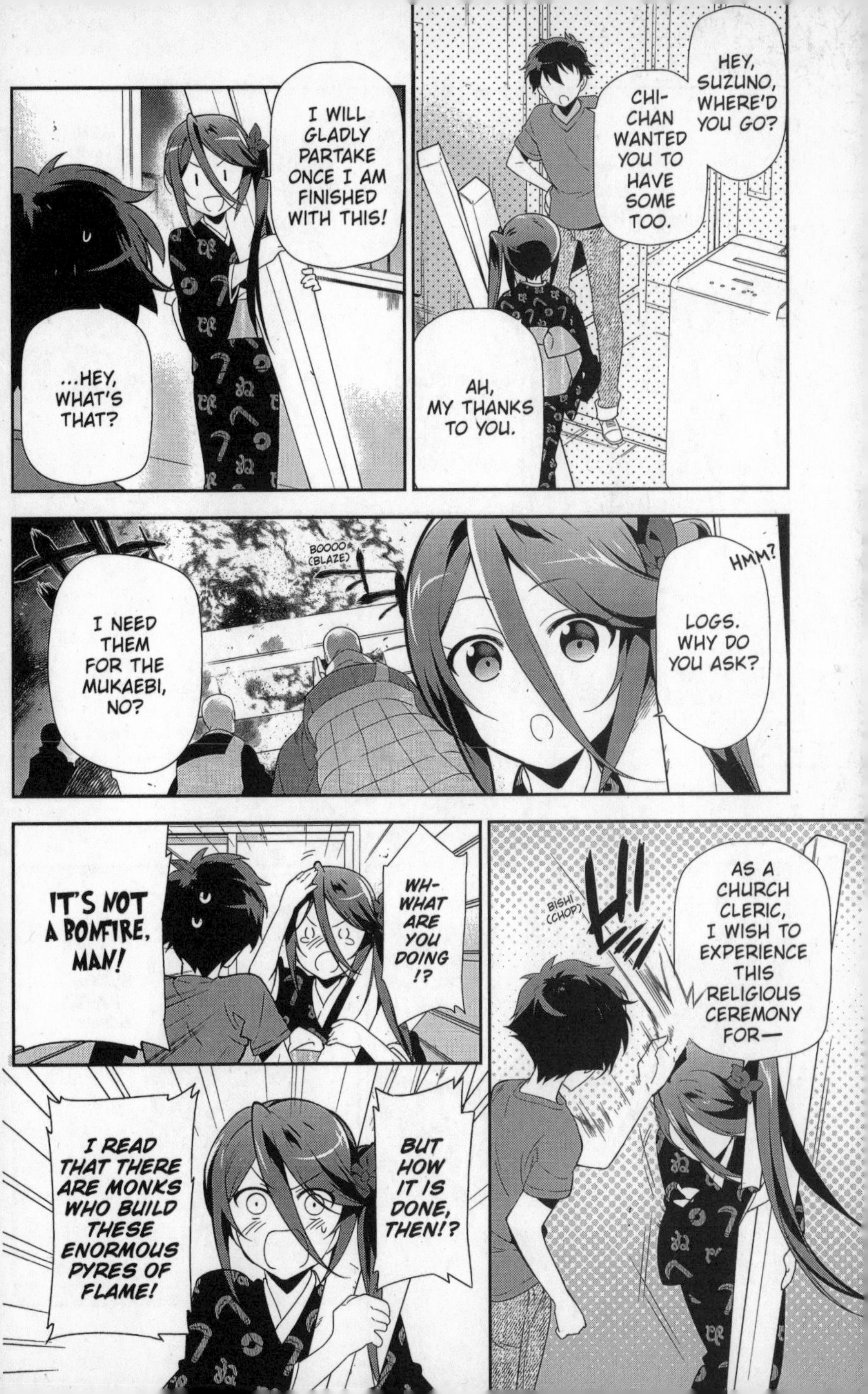
HEY, SUZUNO, WHERE'D YOU GO?
CHI-CHAN WANTED YOU TO HAVE SOME TOO.
AH, MY THANKS TO YOU.
I WILL GLADLY PARTAKE ONCE I AM FINISHED WITH THIS!
...HEY, WHAT'S THAT?
HMM?
LOGS. WHY DO YOU ASK?
BOOOO (BLAZE)
I NEED THEM FOR THE MUKAEBI, NO?
AS A CHURCH CLERIC, I WISH TO EXPERIENCE THIS RELIGIOUS CEREMONY FOR—
BISHI (CHOP)
WH-WHAT ARE YOU DOING!?
IT'S NOT A BONFIRE, MAN!
BUT HOW IT IS DONE, THEN!?
I READ THAT THERE ARE MONKS WHO BUILD THESE ENORMOUS PYRES OF FLAME!

ASHIYA.
SA (ZIP)
PACHIN (SNAP)
YES, MY LIEGE.
A DISH ...?
THIS IS A HOUROKU, A CLAY PAN.
YOU CAN BUY ALL THIS STUFF AT THE HUNDRED-YEN STORE. THEY THROW IN THE NEWSPAPER FOR FREE.
THEN YOU PUT THIS ON A FLAT SURFACE...
KOTO (PLOP)
JIJI (FRIZZ)
JI
PACHI
PACHI (CRACKLE)
...TA-DA! THAT'S THE EASIEST WAY TO LIGHT A MUKAEBI.
... WHAT?

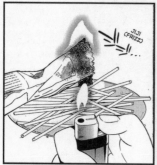

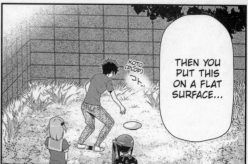

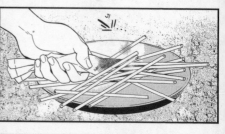

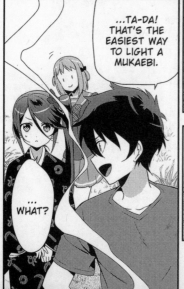

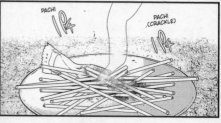

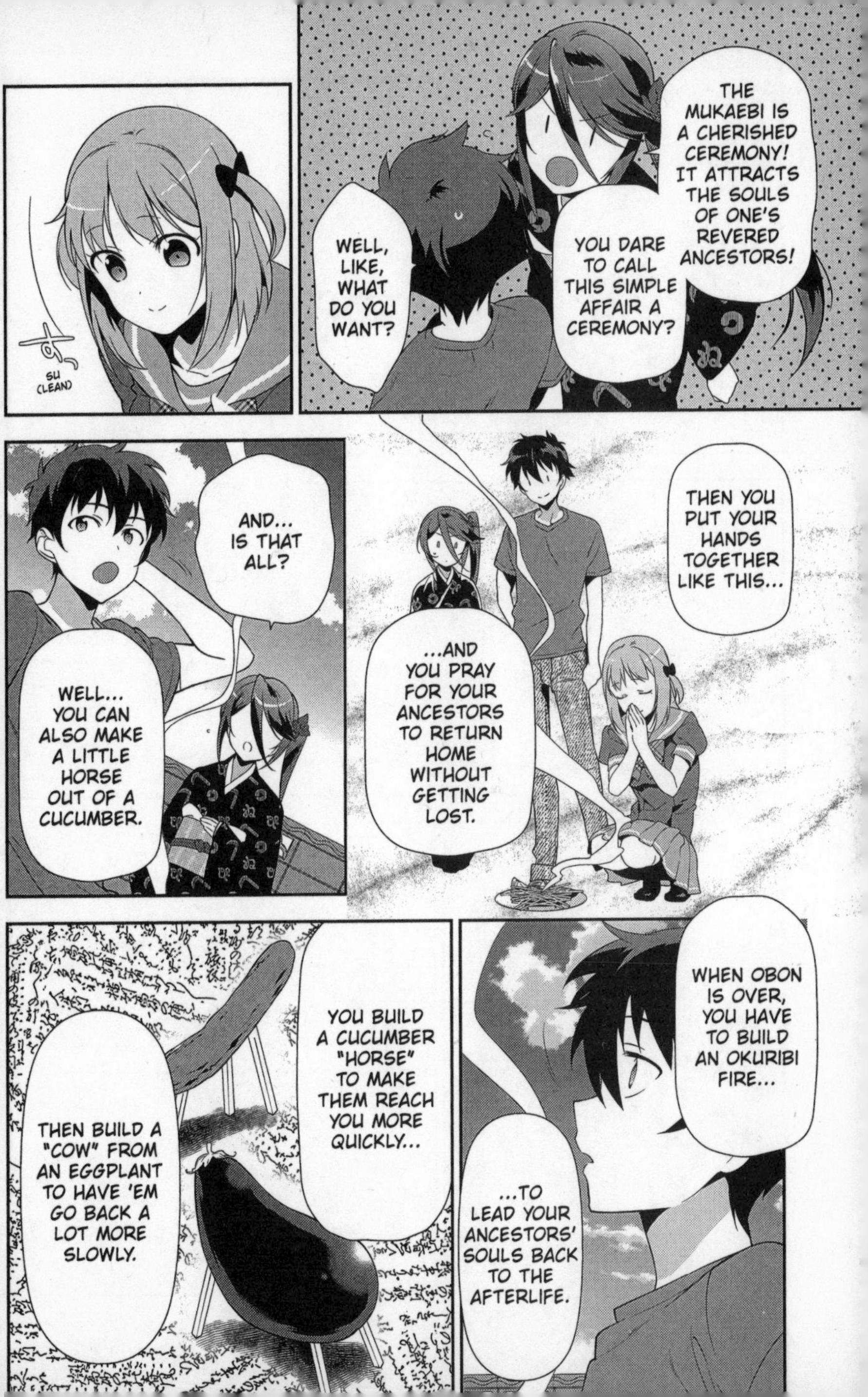
THE MUKAEBI IS A CHERISHED CEREMONY! IT ATTRACTS THE SOULS OF ONE'S REVERED ANCESTORS!
YOU DARE TO CALL THIS SIMPLE AFFAIR A CEREMONY?
WELL, LIKE, WHAT DO YOU WANT?
すっ
SU (LEAN)
THEN YOU PUT YOUR HANDS TOGETHER LIKE THIS...
...AND YOU PRAY FOR YOUR ANCESTORS TO RETURN HOME WITHOUT GETTING LOST.
AND... IS THAT ALL?
WELL... YOU CAN ALSO MAKE A LITTLE HORSE OUT OF A CUCUMBER.
WHEN OBON IS OVER, YOU HAVE TO BUILD AN OKURIBI FIRE...
...TO LEAD YOUR ANCESTORS' SOULS BACK TO THE AFTERLIFE.
YOU BUILD A CUCUMBER "HORSE" TO MAKE THEM REACH YOU MORE QUICKLY...
THEN BUILD A "COW" FROM AN EGGPLANT TO HAVE 'EM GO BACK A LOT MORE SLOWLY.

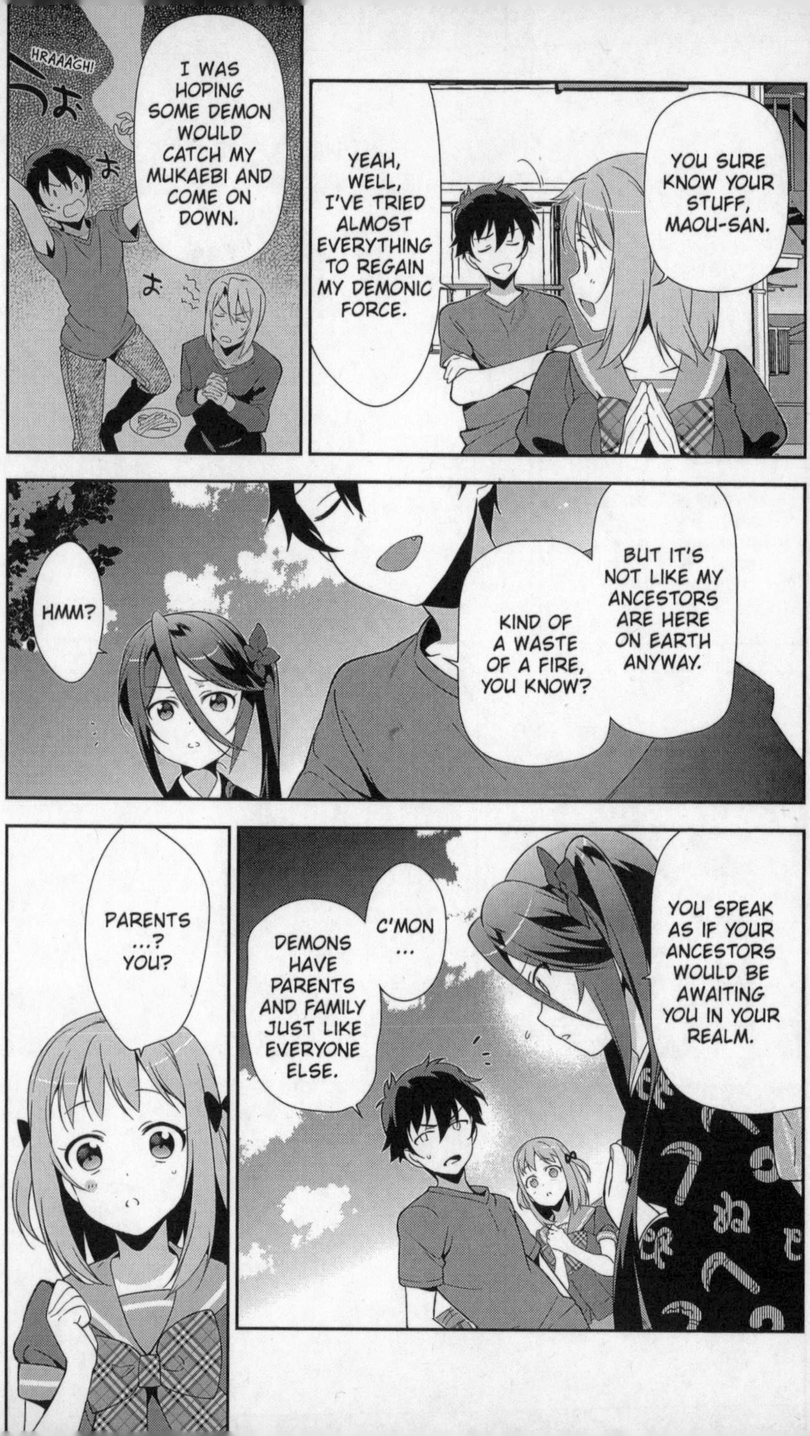
YOU SURE KNOW YOUR STUFF, MAOU-SAN.
YEAH, WELL, I'VE TRIED ALMOST EVERYTHING TO REGAIN MY DEMONIC FORCE.
HRAAAGH!
I WAS HOPING SOME DEMON WOULD CATCH MY MUKAEBI AND COME ON DOWN.
BUT IT'S NOT LIKE MY ANCESTORS ARE HERE ON EARTH ANYWAY.
KIND OF A WASTE OF A FIRE, YOU KNOW?
HMM?
YOU SPEAK AS IF YOUR ANCESTORS WOULD BE AWAITING YOU IN YOUR REALM.
C'MON...
DEMONS HAVE PARENTS AND FAMILY JUST LIKE EVERYONE ELSE.
PARENTS...? YOU?

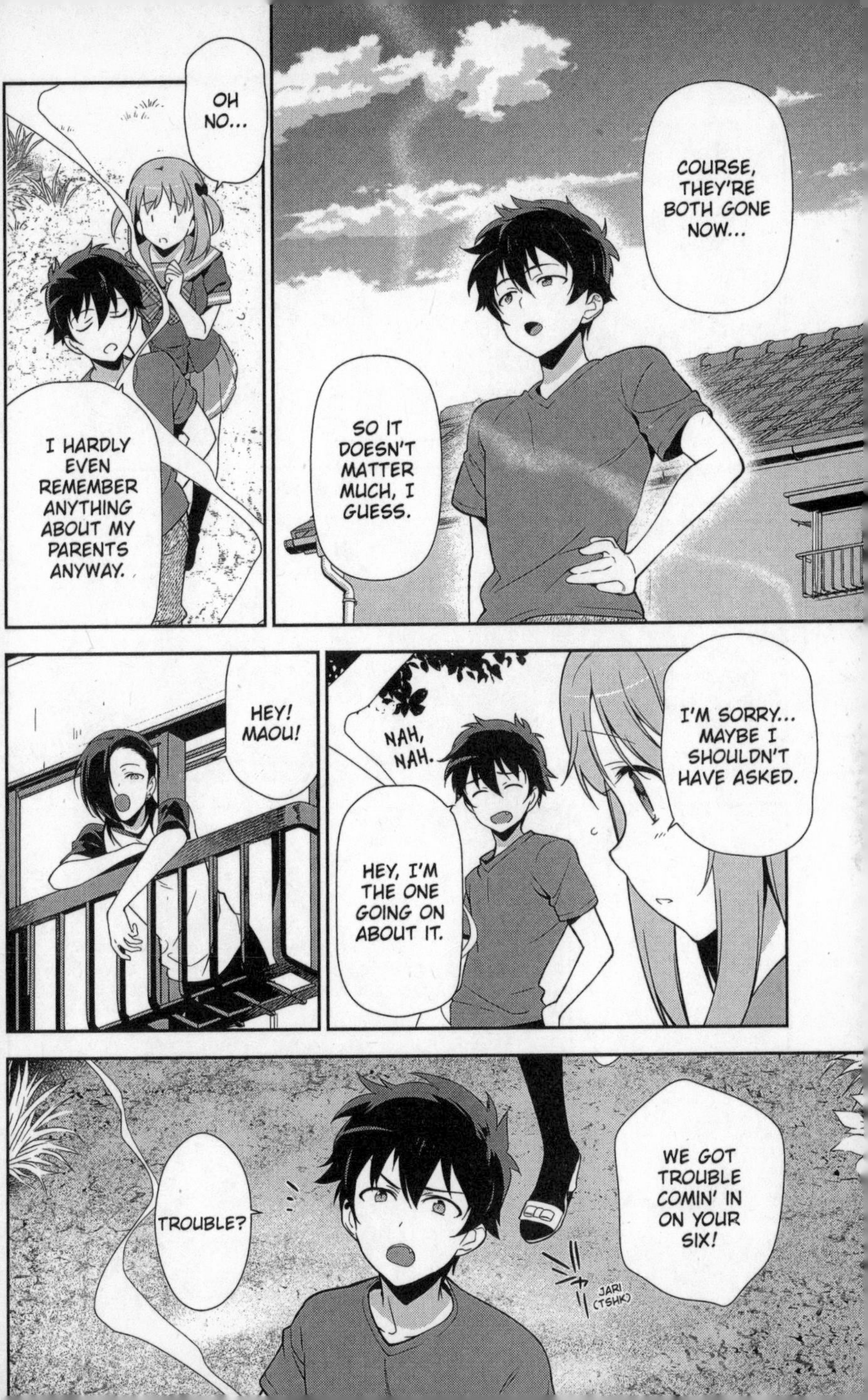
COURSE, THEY'RE BOTH GONE NOW...
SO IT DOESN'T MATTER MUCH, I GUESS.
OH NO...
I HARDLY EVEN REMEMBER ANYTHING ABOUT MY PARENTS ANYWAY.
I'M SORRY... MAYBE I SHOULDN'T HAVE ASKED.
NAH, NAH.
HEY, I'M THE ONE GOING ON ABOUT IT.
HEY! MAOU!
WE GOT TROUBLE COMIN' IN ON YOUR SIX!
JARI (TSHK)
TROUBLE?

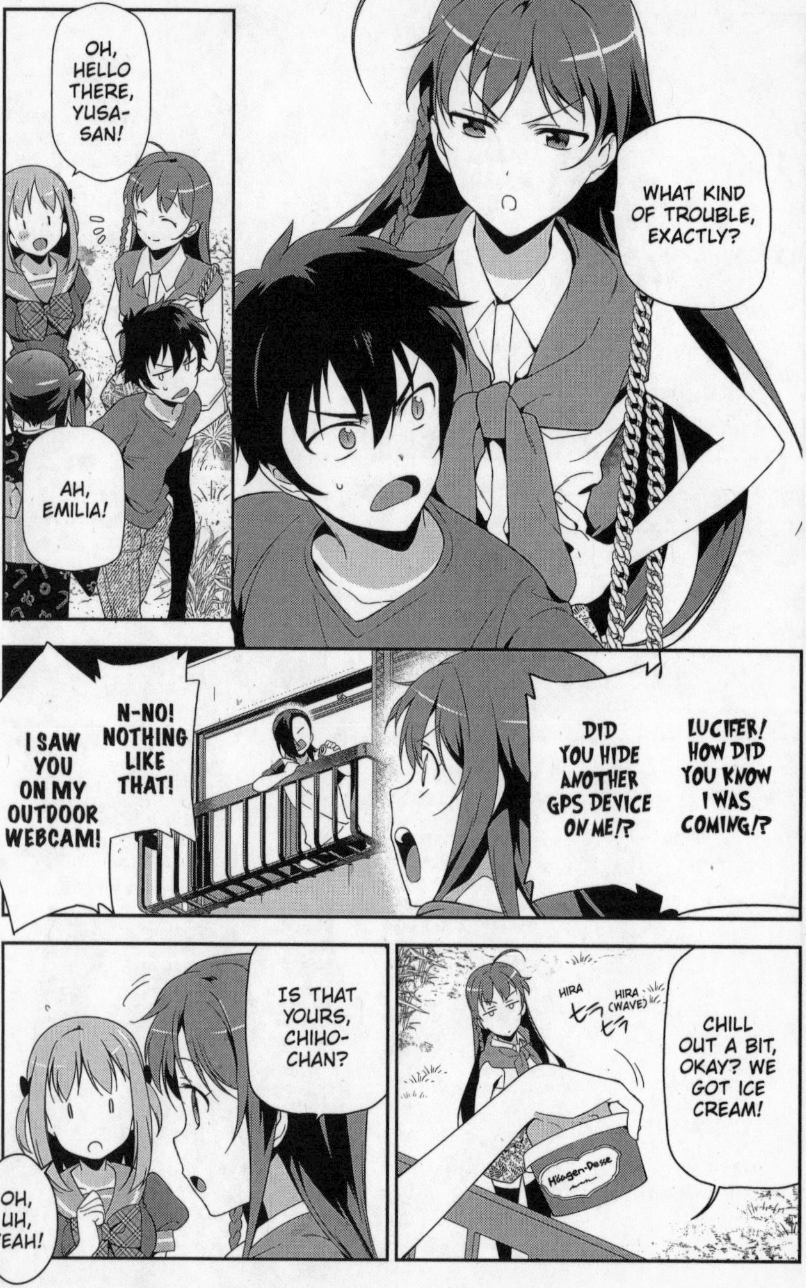
WHAT KIND OF TROUBLE, EXACTLY?
OH, HELLO THERE, YUSA-SAN!
AH, EMILIA!
LUCIFER! HOW DID YOU KNOW I WAS COMING!?
DID YOU HIDE ANOTHER GPS DEVICE ON ME!?
N-NO! NOTHING LIKE THAT!
I SAW YOU ON MY OUTDOOR WEBCAM!
HIRA HIRA (WAVE)
CHILL OUT A BIT, OKAY? WE GOT ICE CREAM!
IS THAT YOURS, CHIHO-CHAN?
OH, UH, YEAH!

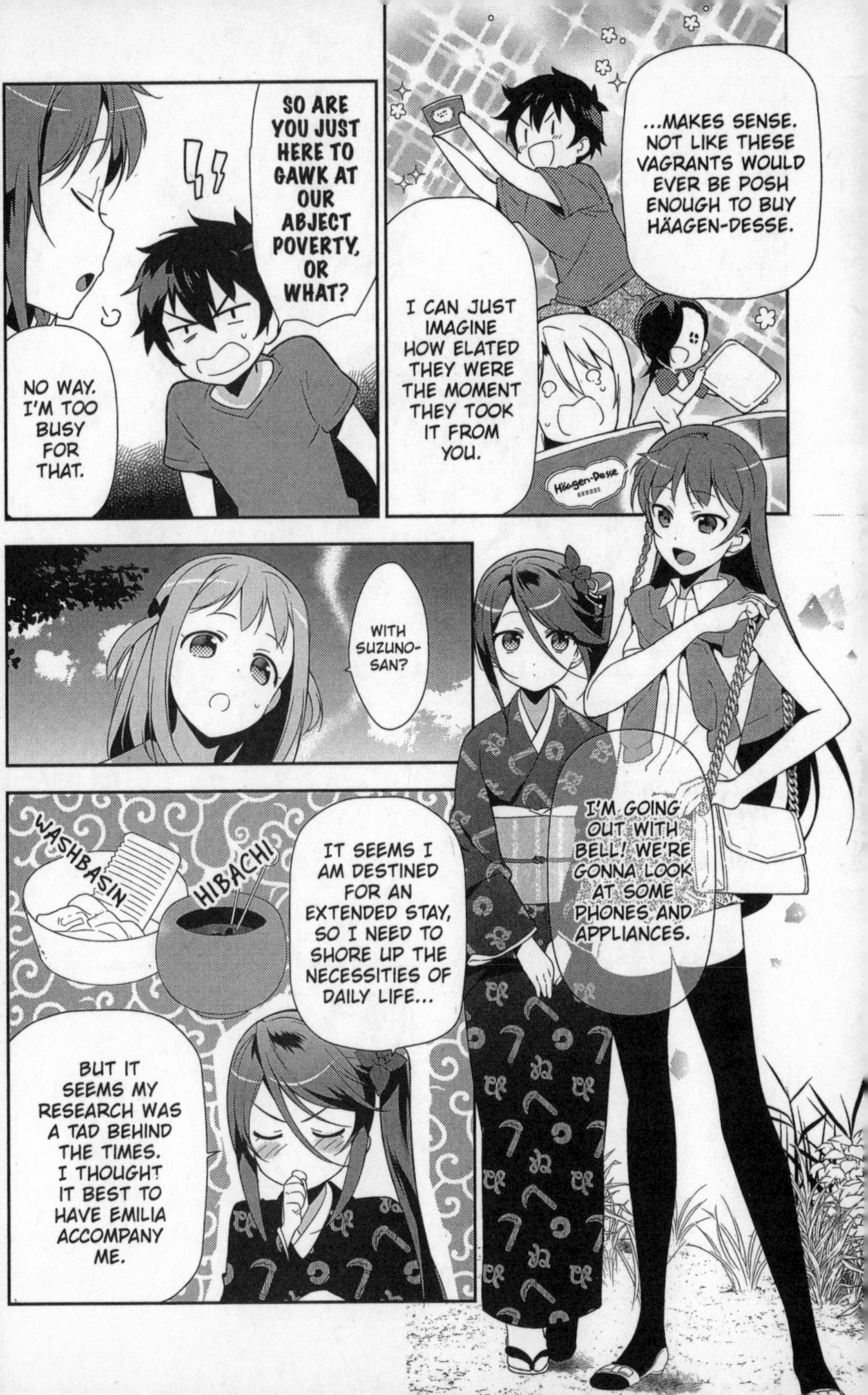
...MAKES SENSE. NOT LIKE THESE VAGRANTS WOULD EVER BE POSH ENOUGH TO BUY HÄAGEN-DESSE.
I CAN JUST IMAGINE HOW ELATED THEY WERE THE MOMENT THEY TOOK IT FROM YOU.
Häagen-Desse
SO ARE YOU JUST HERE TO GAWK AT OUR ABJECT POVERTY, OR WHAT?
NO WAY. I'M TOO BUSY FOR THAT.
I'M GOING OUT WITH BELL! WE'RE GONNA LOOK AT SOME PHONES AND APPLIANCES.
WITH SUZUNO-SAN?
IT SEEMS I AM DESTINED FOR AN EXTENDED STAY, SO I NEED TO SHORE UP THE NECESSITIES OF DAILY LIFE...
HIBACHI
WASHBASIN
BUT IT SEEMS MY RESEARCH WAS A TAD BEHIND THE TIMES. I THOUGHT IT BEST TO HAVE EMILIA ACCOMPANY ME.

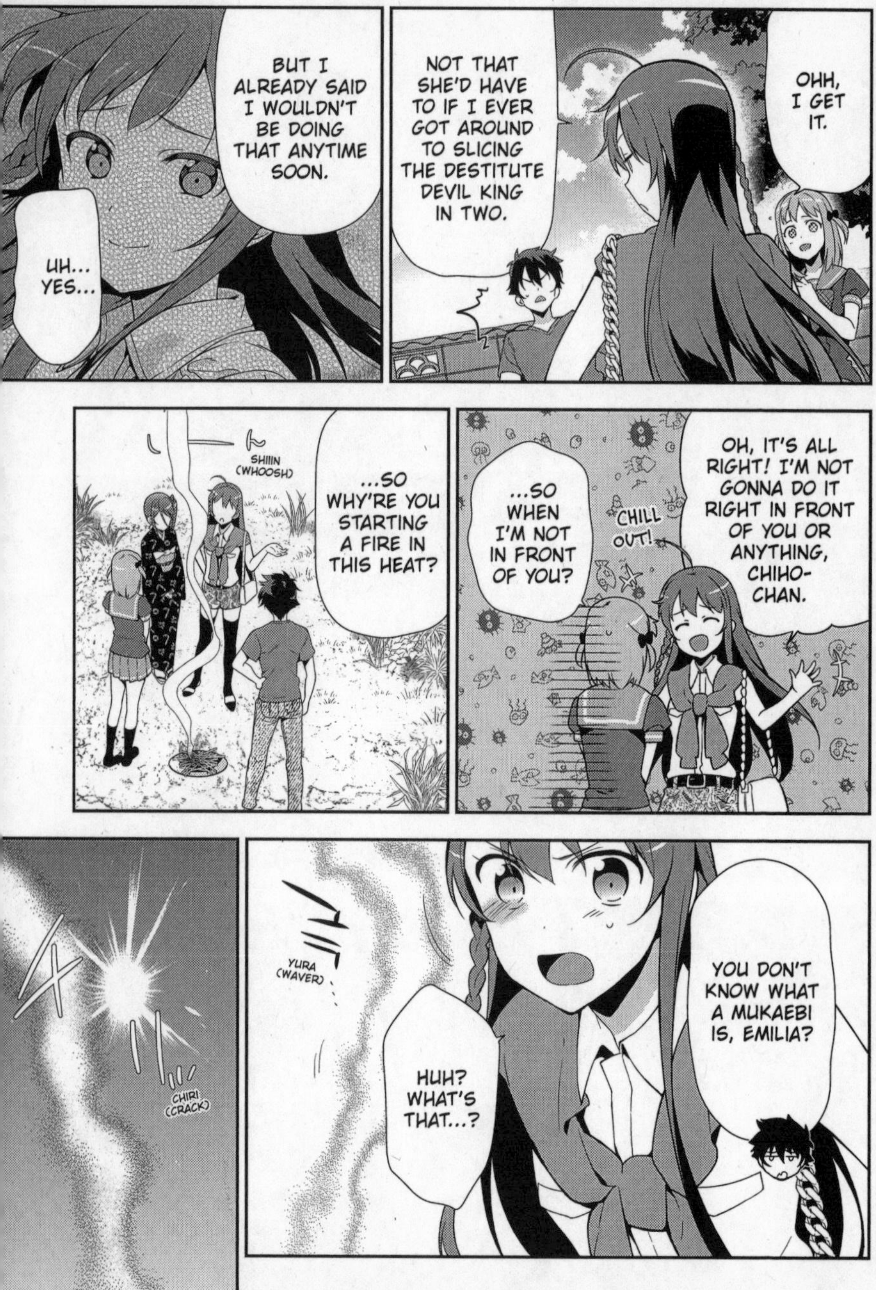
OHH, I GET IT.
NOT THAT SHE'D HAVE TO IF I EVER GOT AROUND TO SLICING THE DESTITUTE DEVIL KING IN TWO.
BUT I ALREADY SAID I WOULDN'T BE DOING THAT ANYTIME SOON.
UH... YES...
OH, IT'S ALL RIGHT! I'M NOT GONNA DO IT RIGHT IN FRONT OF YOU OR ANYTHING, CHIHO-CHAN.
CHILL OUT!
...SO WHEN I'M NOT IN FRONT OF YOU?
...SO WHY'RE YOU STARTING A FIRE IN THIS HEAT?
SHIIIN (WHOOSH)
YOU DON'T KNOW WHAT A MUKAEBI IS, EMILIA?
HUH? WHAT'S THAT...?
YURA (WAVER)
CHIRI (CRACK)

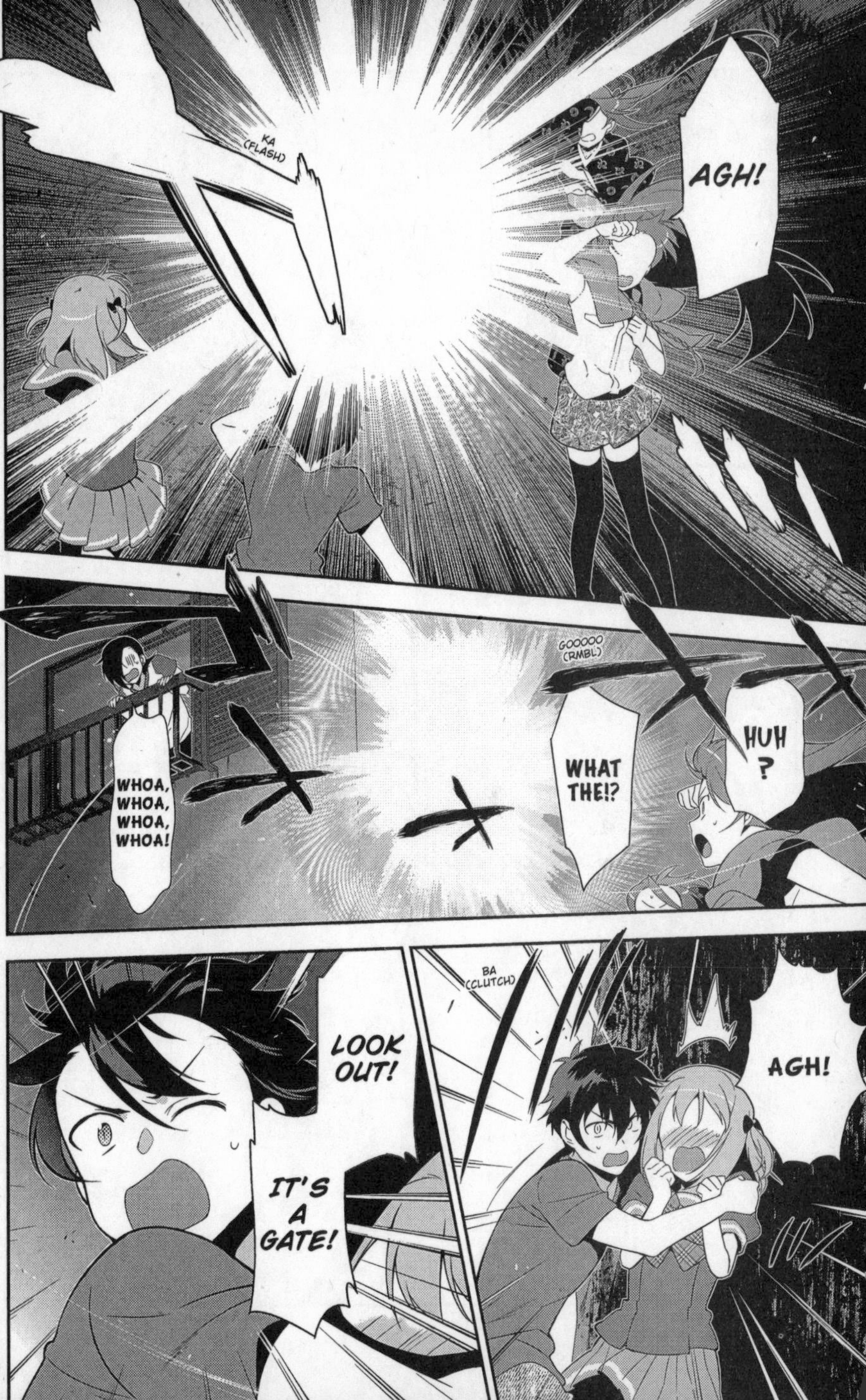
AGH!
KA (FLASH)
HUH ?
WHAT THE!?
GOOOOO (RMBL)
WHOA, WHOA, WHOA, WHOA!
AGH!
BA (CLUTCH)
LOOK OUT!
IT'S A GATE!

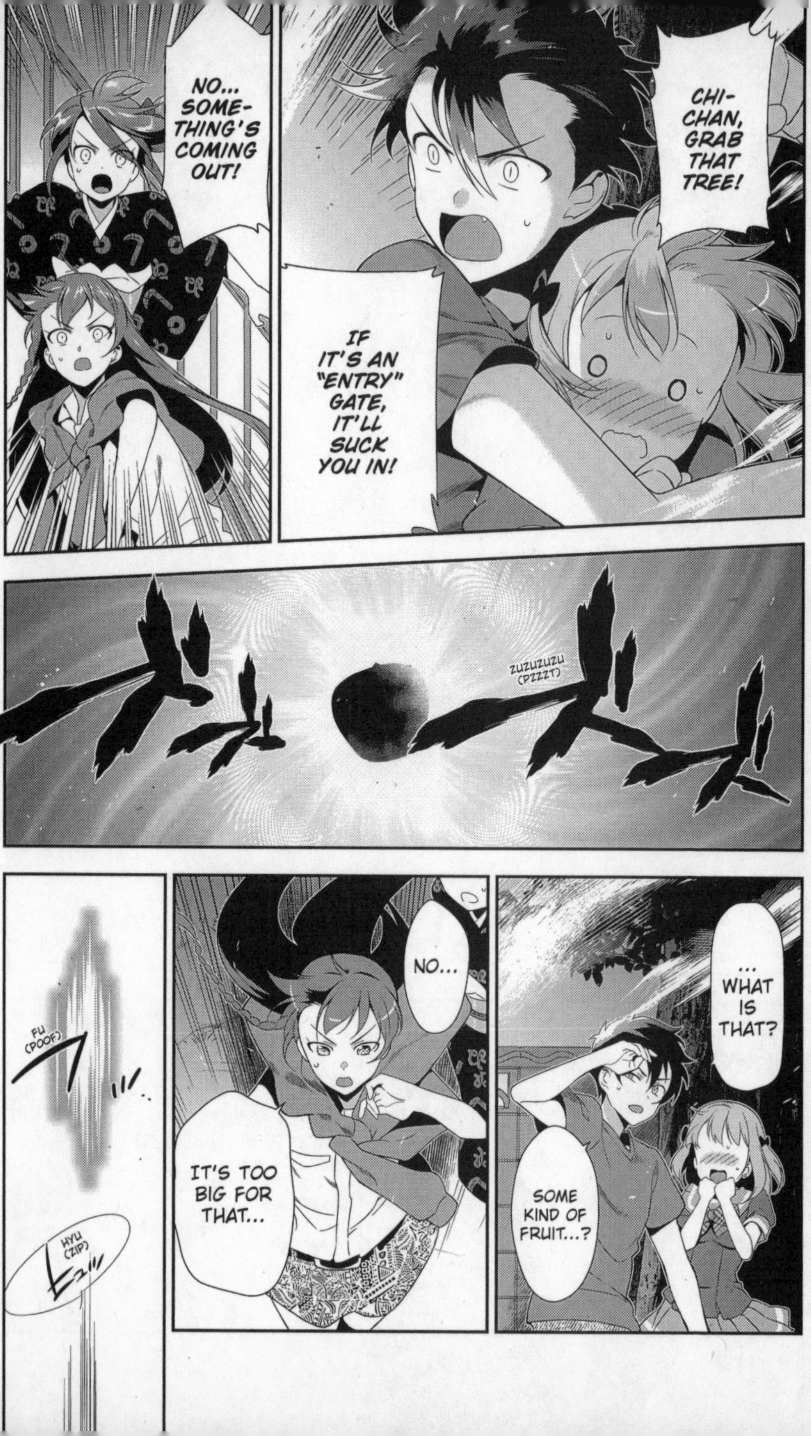
CHI-CHAN, GRAB THAT TREE!
IF IT'S AN "ENTRY" GATE, IT'LL SUCK YOU IN!
NO... SOME-THING'S COMING OUT!
ZUZUZUZU (PZZZT)
... WHAT IS THAT?
SOME KIND OF FRUIT...?
NO...
IT'S TOO BIG FOR THAT...
FU (POOF)
HYU (ZIP)

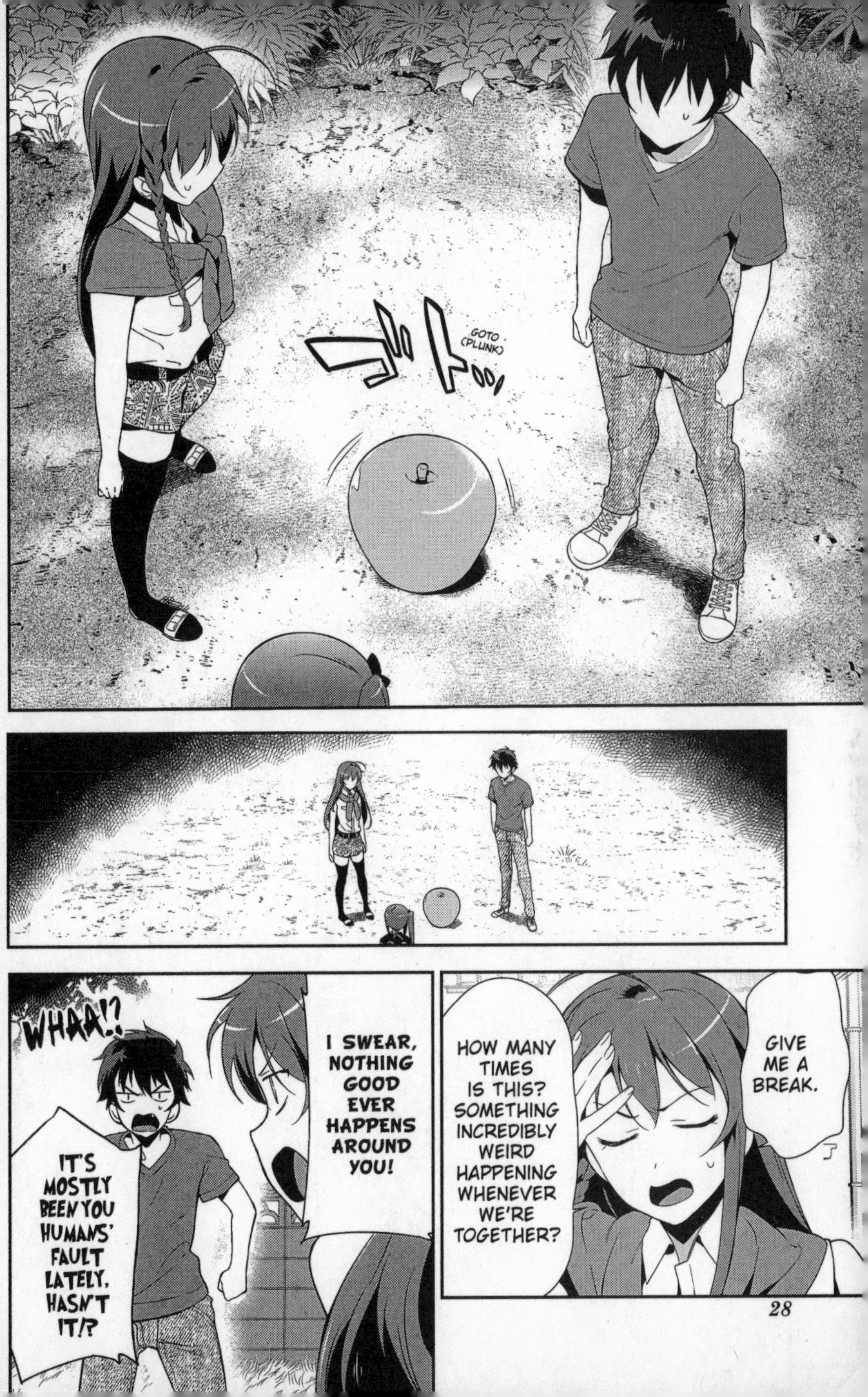
GOTO
(PLUNK)
GIVE ME A BREAK.
HOW MANY TIMES IS THIS? SOMETHING INCREDIBLY WEIRD HAPPENING WHENEVER WE'RE TOGETHER?
I SWEAR, NOTHING GOOD EVER HAPPENS AROUND YOU!
WHAA!?
IT'S MOSTLY BEEN YOU HUMANS' FAULT LATELY, HASN'T IT!?

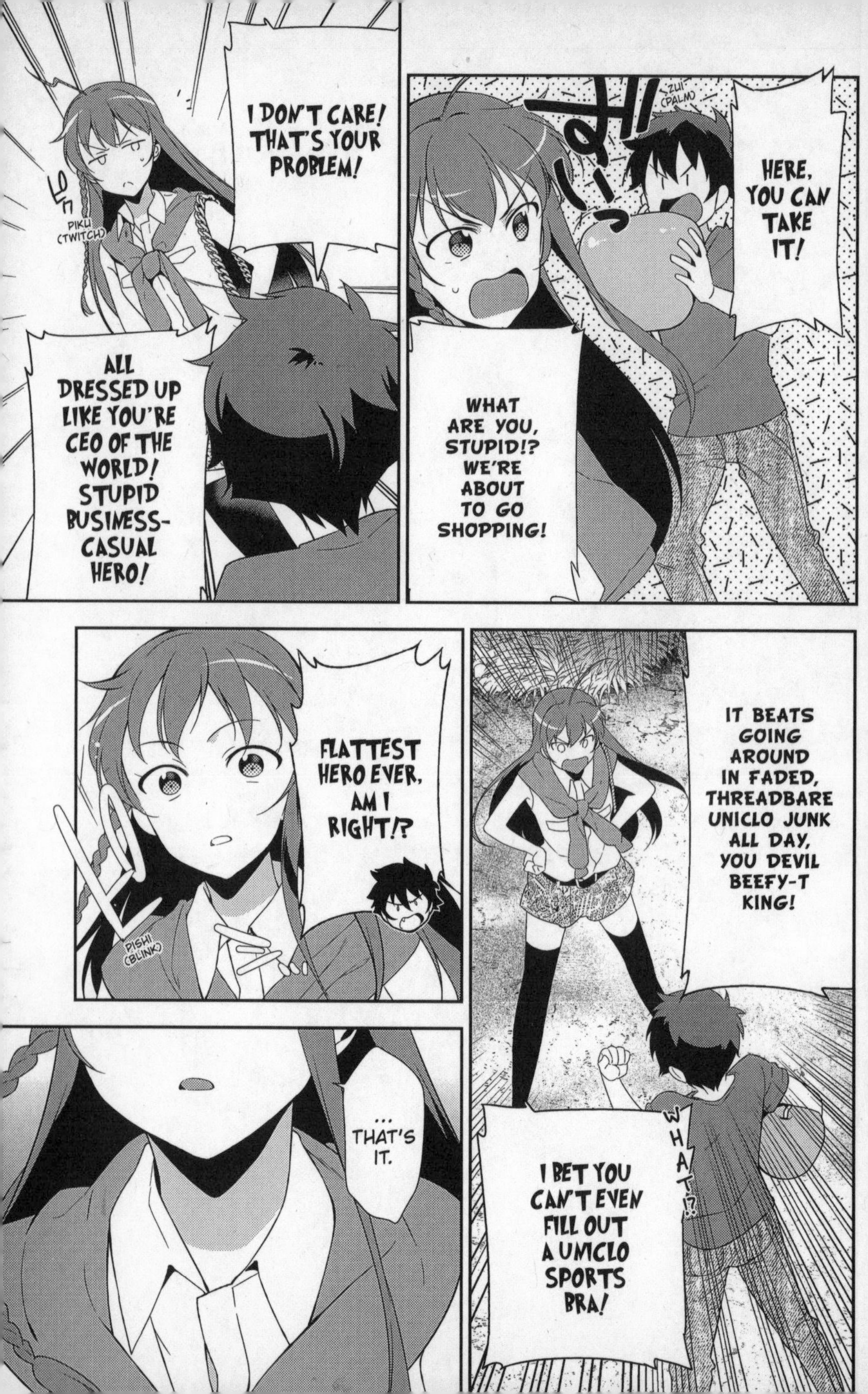
ZUI (PALM)
HERE, YOU CAN TAKE IT!
WHAT ARE YOU, STUPID!? WE'RE ABOUT TO GO SHOPPING!
I DON'T CARE! THAT'S YOUR PROBLEM!
PIKU (TWITCH)
ALL DRESSED UP LIKE YOU'RE CEO OF THE WORLD! STUPID BUSINESS-CASUAL HERO!
IT BEATS GOING AROUND IN FADED, THREADBARE UNICLO JUNK ALL DAY, YOU DEVIL BEEFY-T KING!
I BET YOU CAN'T EVEN FILL OUT A UNICLO SPORTS BRA!
WHAT!?
FLATTEST HERO EVER, AM I RIGHT!?
PISHI (BLINK)
... THAT'S IT.

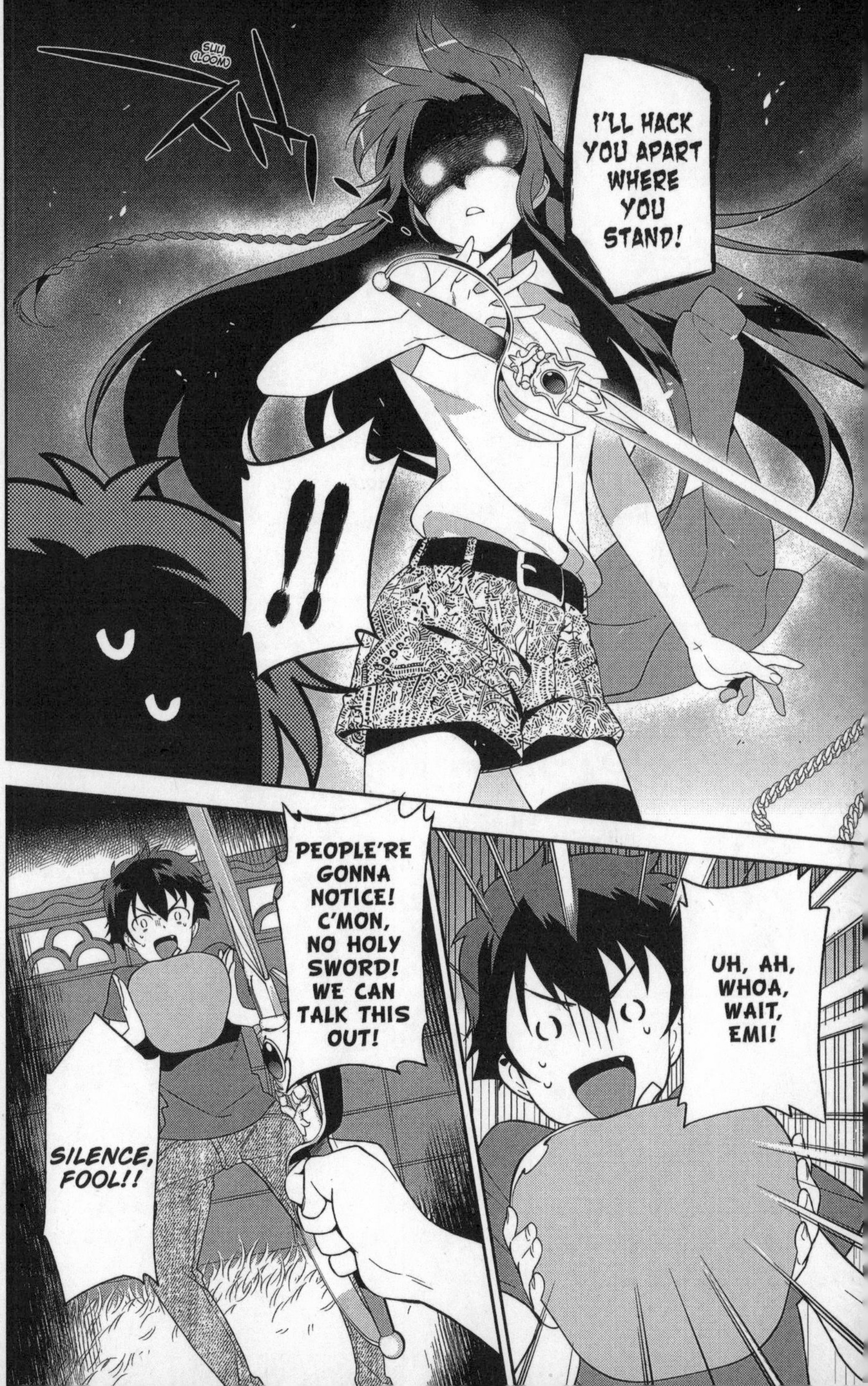
SUU (LOOM)
I'LL HACK YOU APART WHERE YOU STAND!
!!
UH, AH, WHOA, WAIT, EMI!
PEOPLE'RE GONNA NOTICE! C'MON, NO HOLY SWORD! WE CAN TALK THIS OUT!
SILENCE, FOOL!!

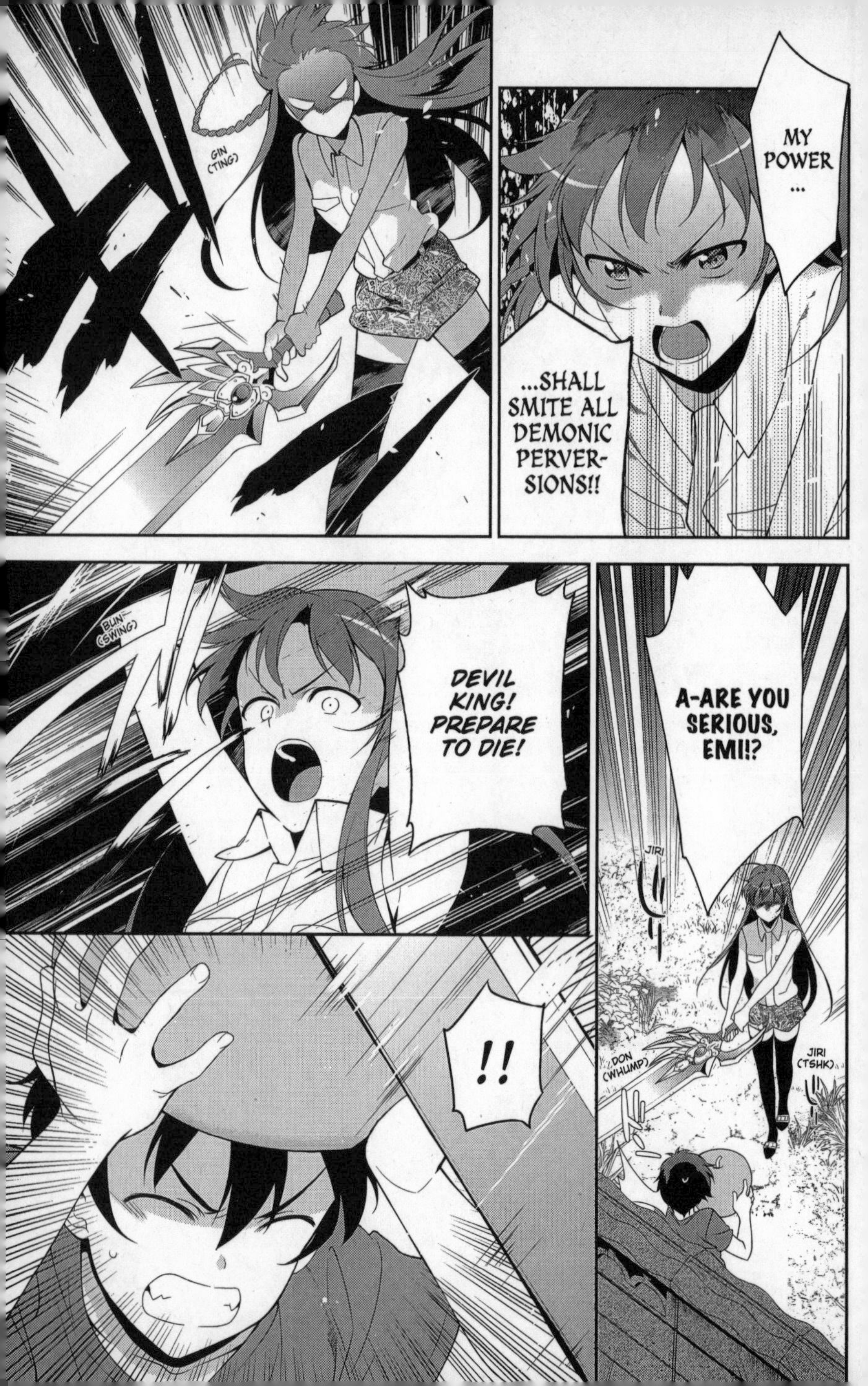
MY POWER ...
...SHALL SMITE ALL DEMONIC PERVER-SIONS!!
GIN (TING)
A-ARE YOU SERIOUS, EMI!?
JIRI
JIRI (TSHK)
DON (WHUMP)
BUN (SWING)
DEVIL KING! PREPARE TO DIE!
!!

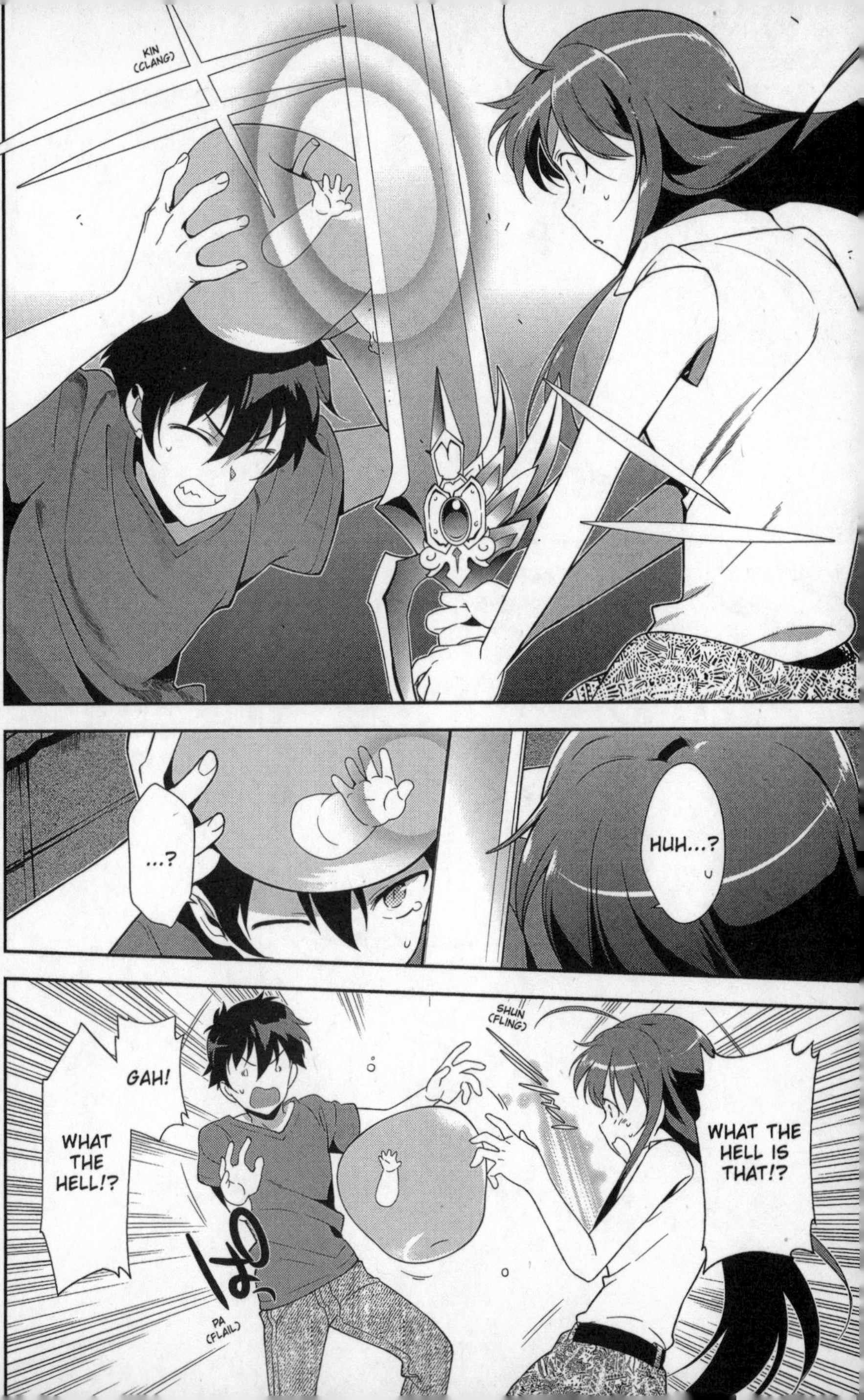
KIN
(CLANG)
HUH...?
...?
SHUN
(FLING)
WHAT THE HELL IS THAT!?
GAH!
WHAT THE HELL!?
PA
(FLAIL)

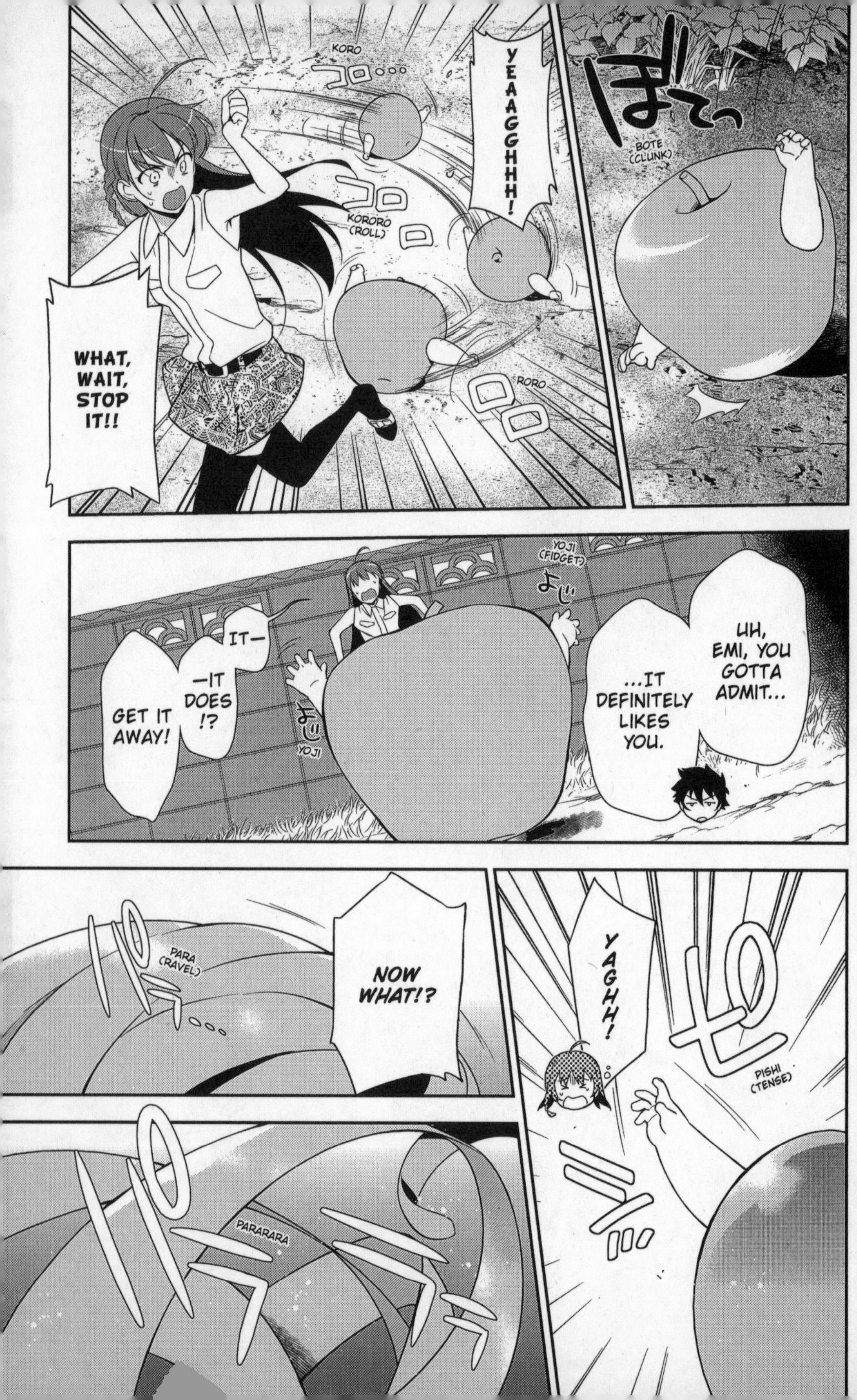
BOTE (CLUNK)
YEAAGGHHH!
KORO
KOROROO (ROLL)
RORO
WHAT, WAIT, STOP IT!!
UH, EMI, YOU GOTTA ADMIT...
...IT DEFINITELY LIKES YOU.
YOJI (FIDGET)
IT—
—IT DOES!?
GET IT AWAY!
YOJI
YAGHH!
PISHI (TENSE)
NOW WHAT!?
PARA (RAVEL)
PARARARA

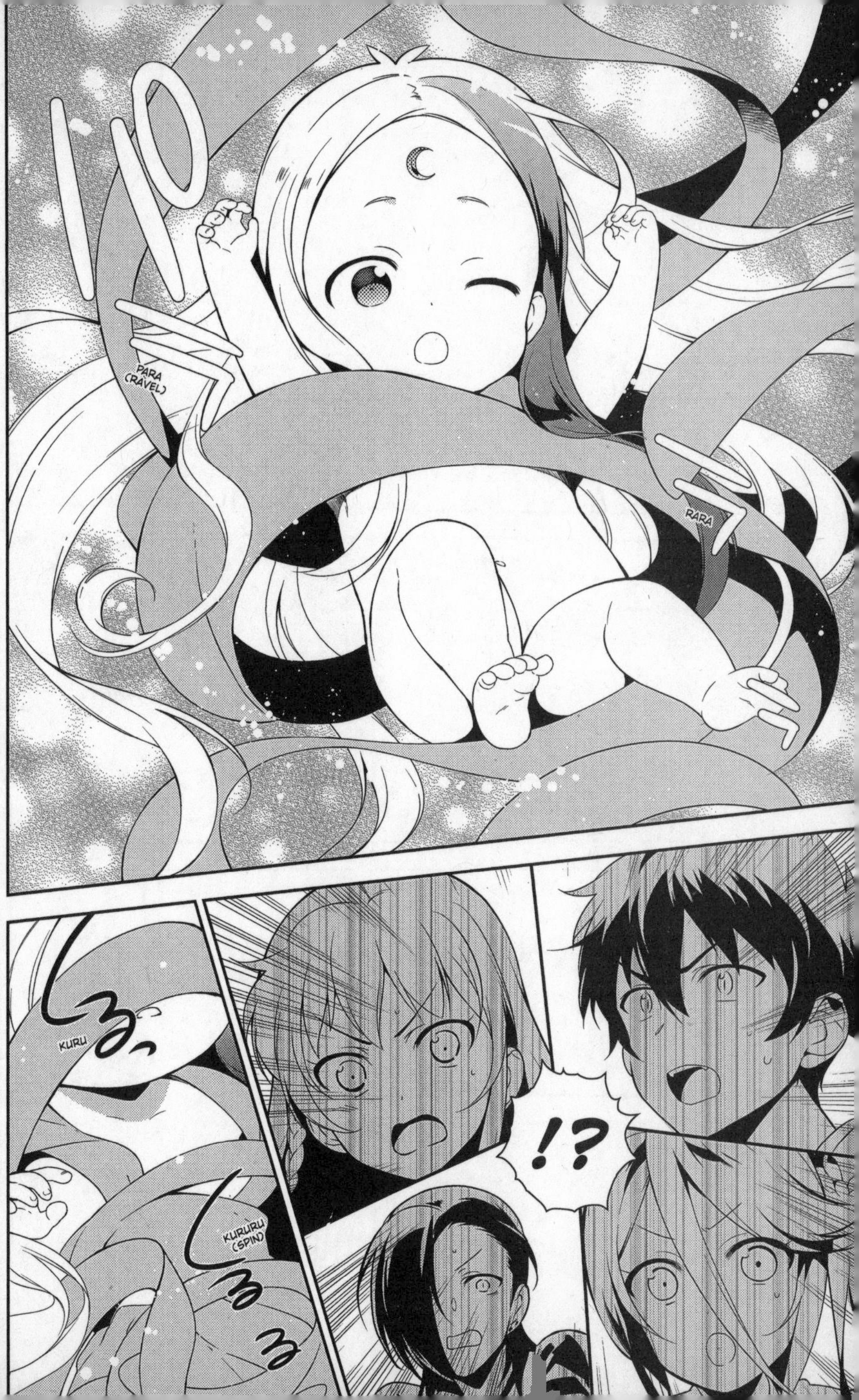
PARA (RAVEL)
RARA
!?
KURU
KURURU (SPIN)

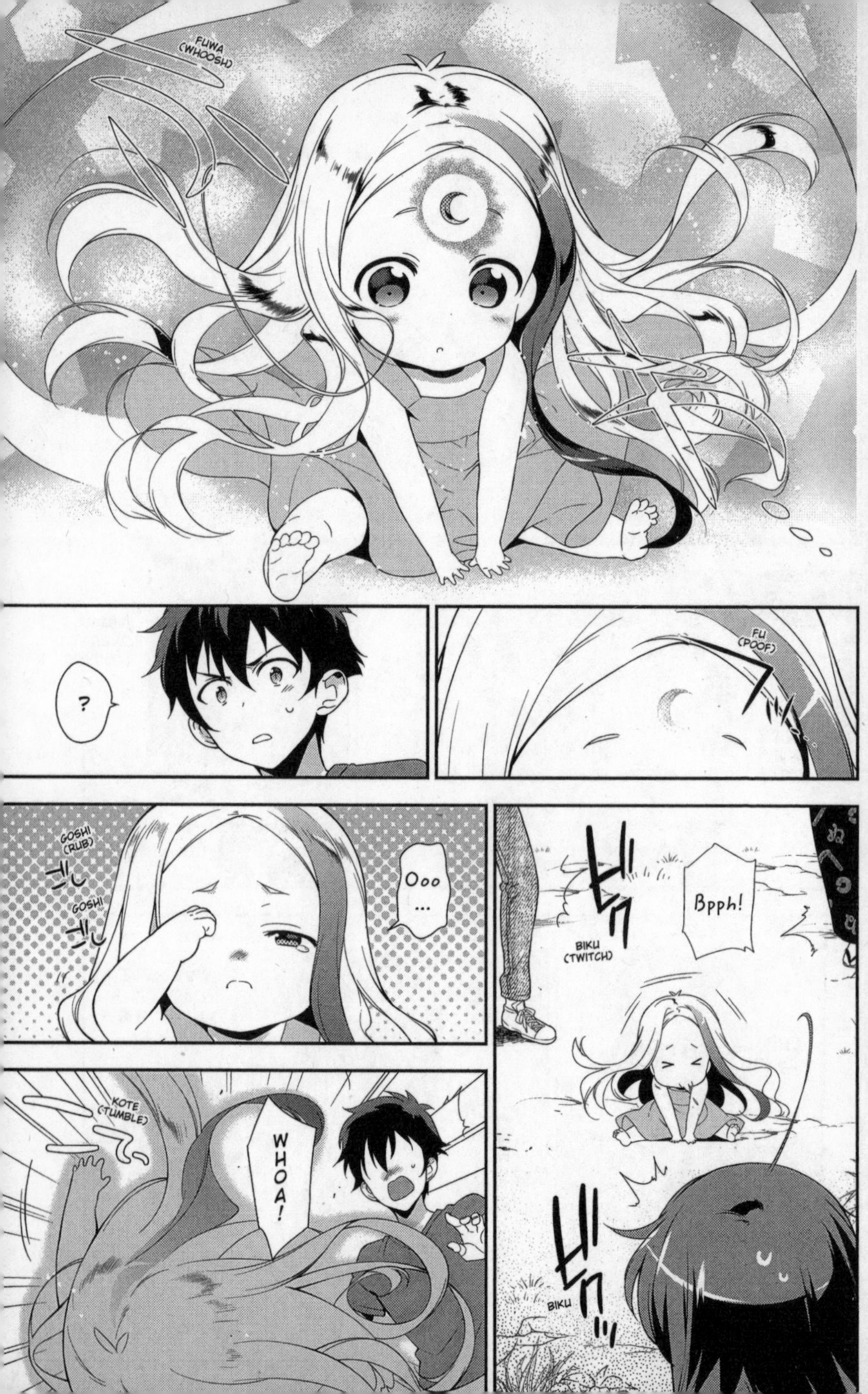
FUWA (WHOOSH)
FU (POOF)
?
Bpph!
BIKU (TWITCH)
BIKU
Ooo ...
GOSHI (RUB)
GOSHI
WHOA!
KOTE (TUMBLE)

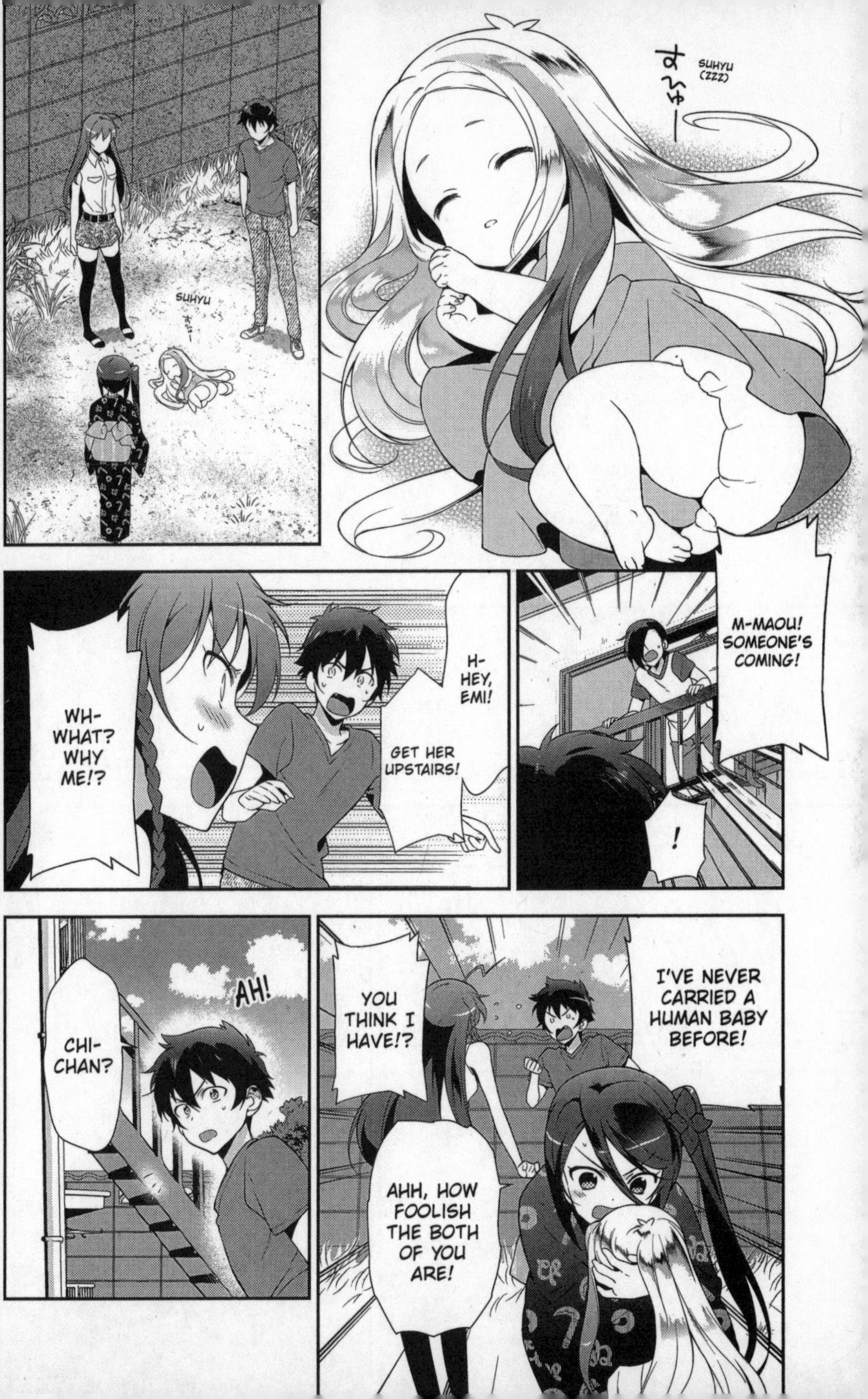
すひゅー
SUHYU (ZZZ)
SUHYU
M-MAOU! SOMEONE'S COMING!
!
H-HEY, EMI!
GET HER UPSTAIRS!
WH-WHAT? WHY ME!?
I'VE NEVER CARRIED A HUMAN BABY BEFORE!
YOU THINK I HAVE!?
AHH, HOW FOOLISH THE BOTH OF YOU ARE!
AH!
CHI-CHAN?

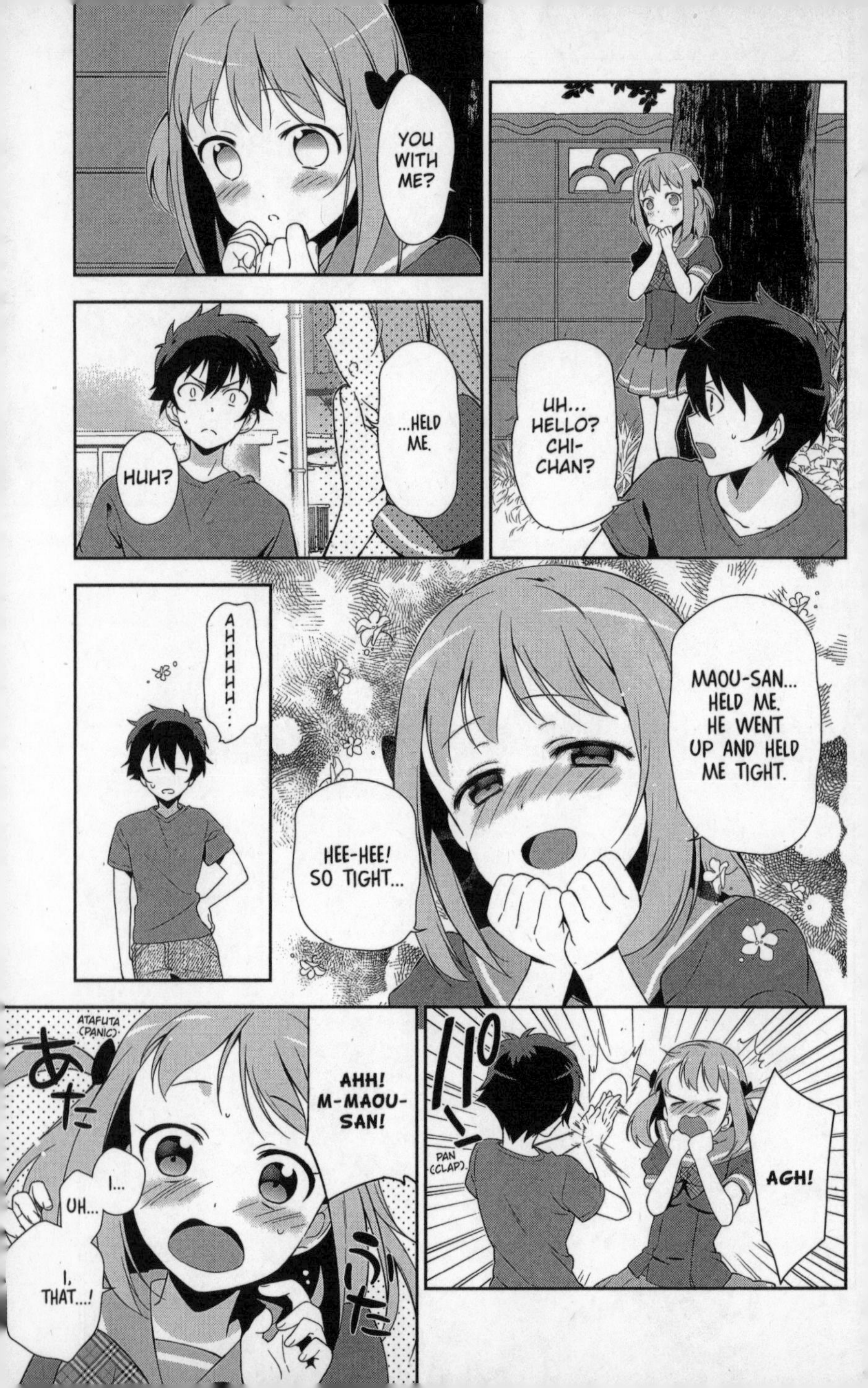
UH... HELLO? CHI-CHAN?
YOU WITH ME?
...HELD ME.
HUH?
MAOU-SAN... HELD ME. HE WENT UP AND HELD ME TIGHT.
HEE-HEE! SO TIGHT...
AHHHHH...
AGH!
PAN (CLAP)
AHH! M-MAOU-SAN!
ATAFUTA (PANIC)
I... UH...
I, THAT...!

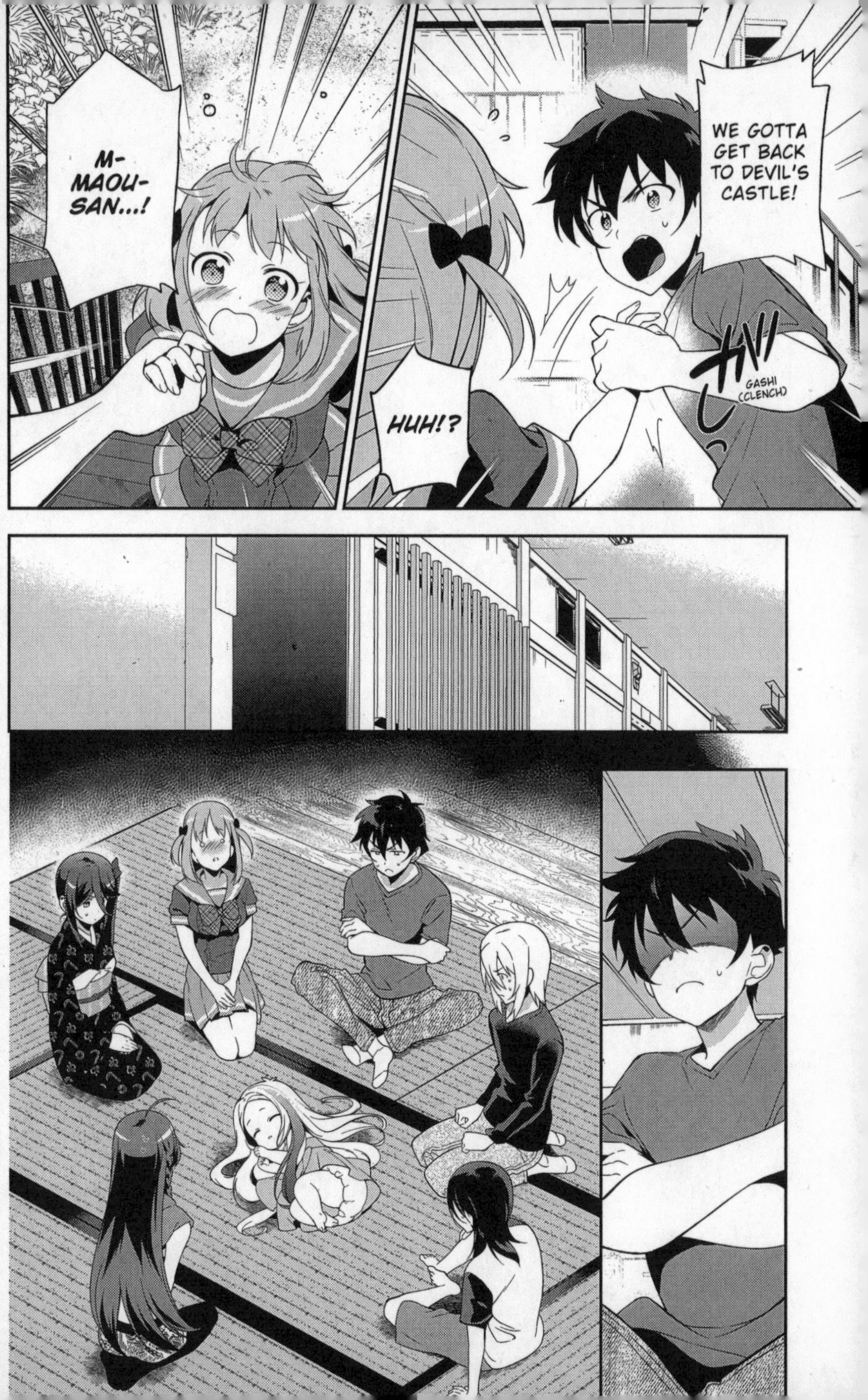
WE GOTTA GET BACK TO DEVIL'S CASTLE!
GASHI (CLENCH)
HUH!?
M-MAOU-SAN...!

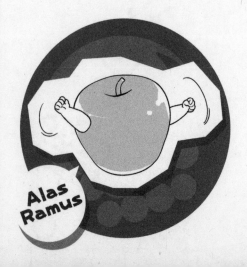

Alas
Ramus

THE DEVIL IS A PART-TIMER!

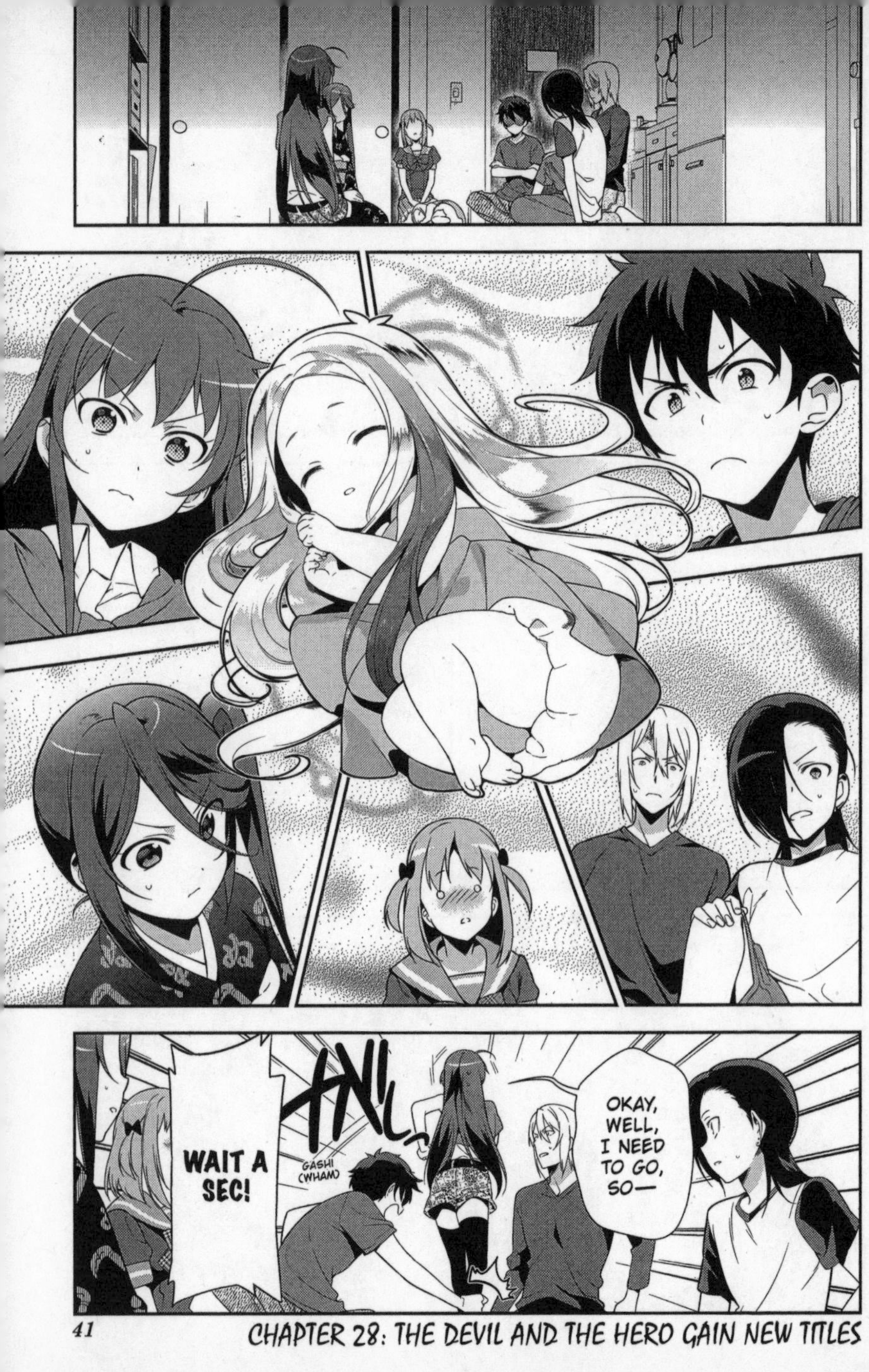
OKAY, WELL, I NEED TO GO, SO—
GASHI (WHAM)
WAIT A SEC!

CHAPTER 28: THE DEVIL AND THE HERO GAIN NEW TITLES

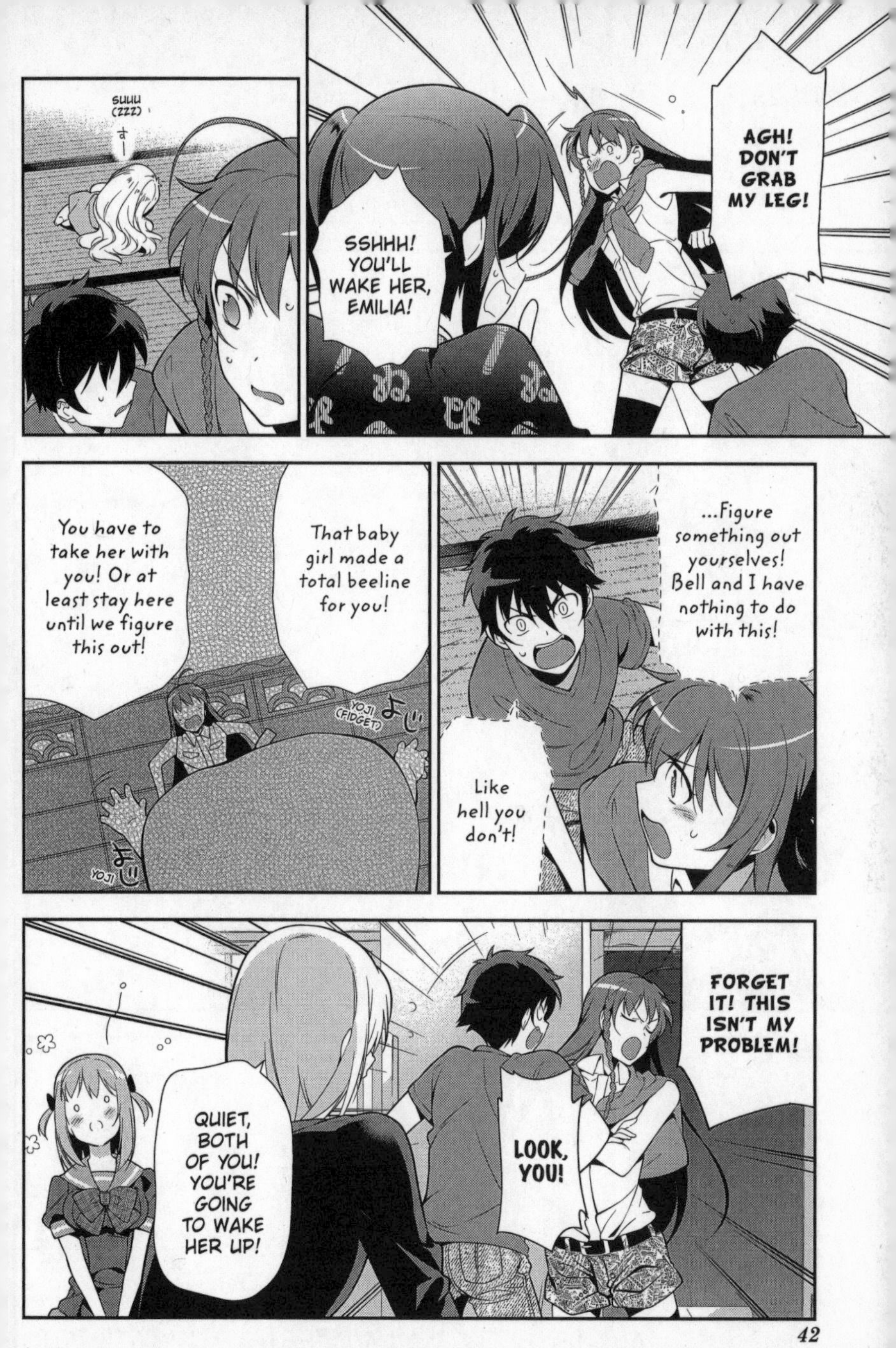
AGH! DON'T GRAB MY LEG!
SSHHH! YOU'LL WAKE HER, EMILIA!
SUUU (ZZZ)
すー
...Figure something out yourselves! Bell and I have nothing to do with this!
Like hell you don't!
That baby girl made a total beeline for you!
You have to take her with you! Or at least stay here until we figure this out!
YOJI (FIDGET) よじ
よじ YOJI
FORGET IT! THIS ISN'T MY PROBLEM!
LOOK, YOU!
QUIET, BOTH OF YOU! YOU'RE GOING TO WAKE HER UP!

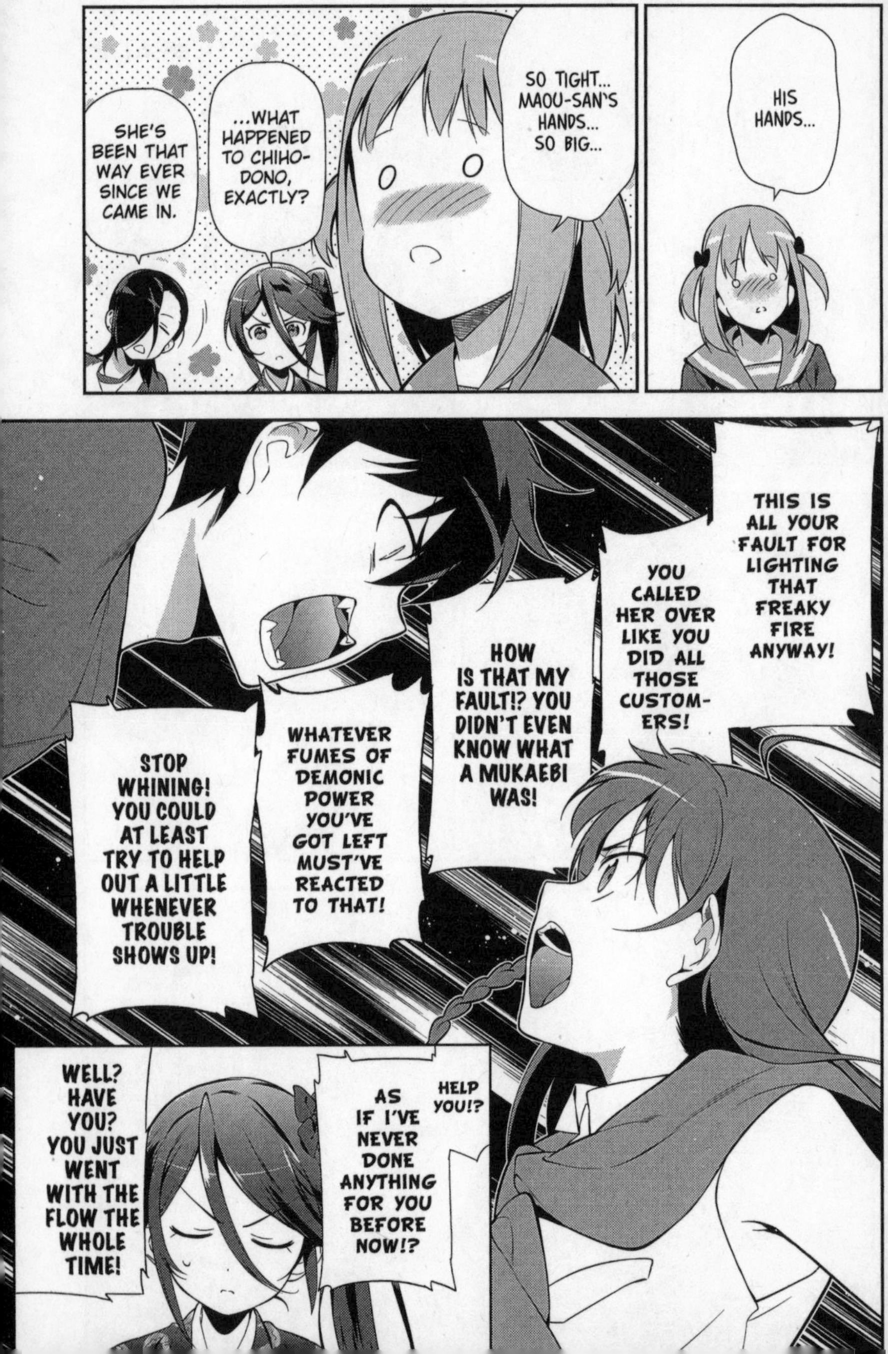
HIS HANDS...
SO TIGHT... MAOU-SAN'S HANDS... SO BIG...
...WHAT HAPPENED TO CHIHO-DONO, EXACTLY?
SHE'S BEEN THAT WAY EVER SINCE WE CAME IN.
THIS IS ALL YOUR FAULT FOR LIGHTING THAT FREAKY FIRE ANYWAY!
YOU CALLED HER OVER LIKE YOU DID ALL THOSE CUSTOMERS!
HOW IS THAT MY FAULT!? YOU DIDN'T EVEN KNOW WHAT A MUKAEBI WAS!
WHATEVER FUMES OF DEMONIC POWER YOU'VE GOT LEFT MUST'VE REACTED TO THAT!
STOP WHINING! YOU COULD AT LEAST TRY TO HELP OUT A LITTLE WHENEVER TROUBLE SHOWS UP!
HELP YOU!?
AS IF I'VE NEVER DONE ANYTHING FOR YOU BEFORE NOW!?
WELL? HAVE YOU? YOU JUST WENT WITH THE FLOW THE WHOLE TIME!

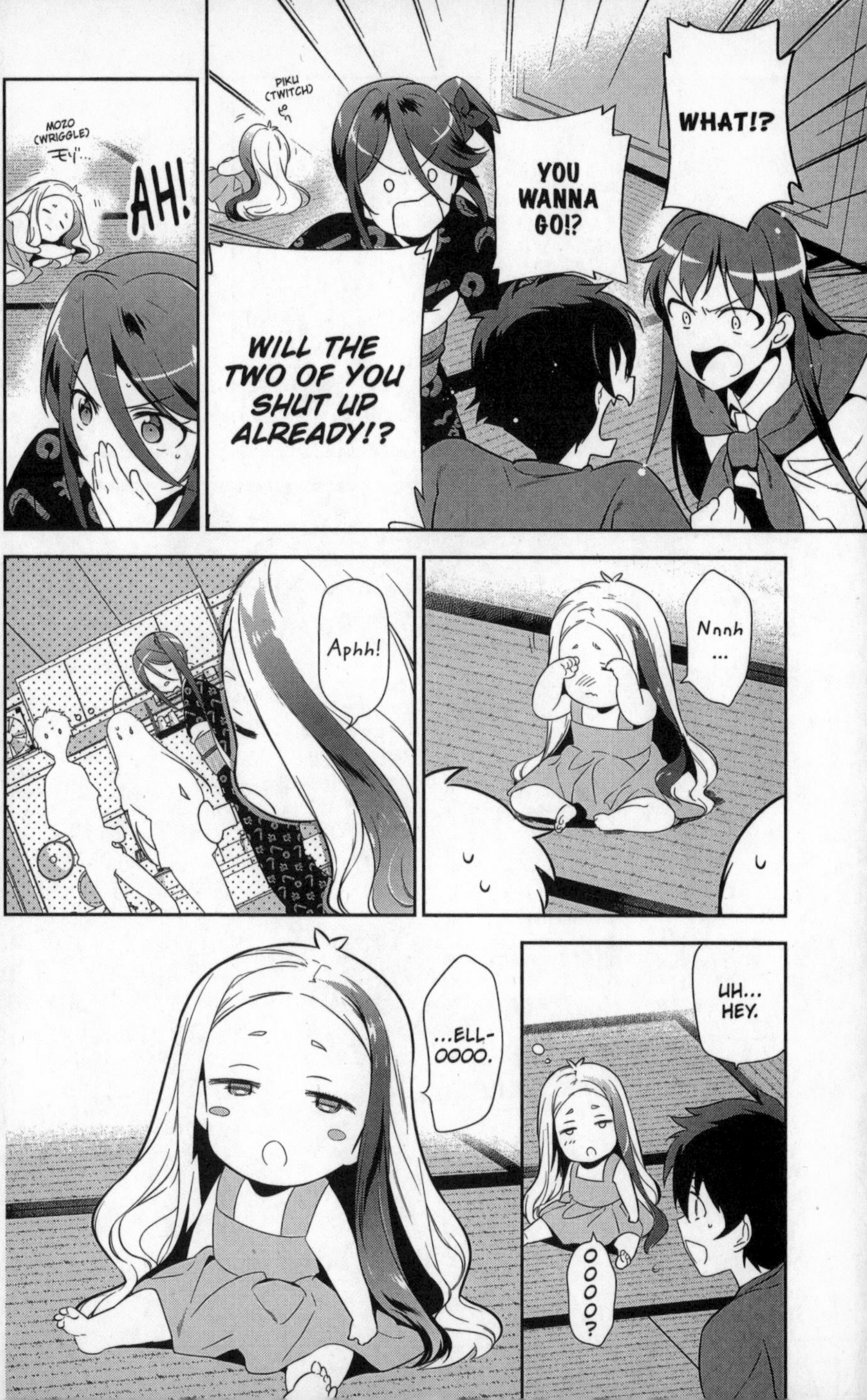
WHAT!?
YOU WANNA GO!?
PIKU (TWITCH)
WILL THE TWO OF YOU SHUT UP ALREADY!?
MOZO (WRIGGLE)
AH!
Nnnh ...
Aphh!
UH... HEY.
OOOO?
...ELL-OOOO.

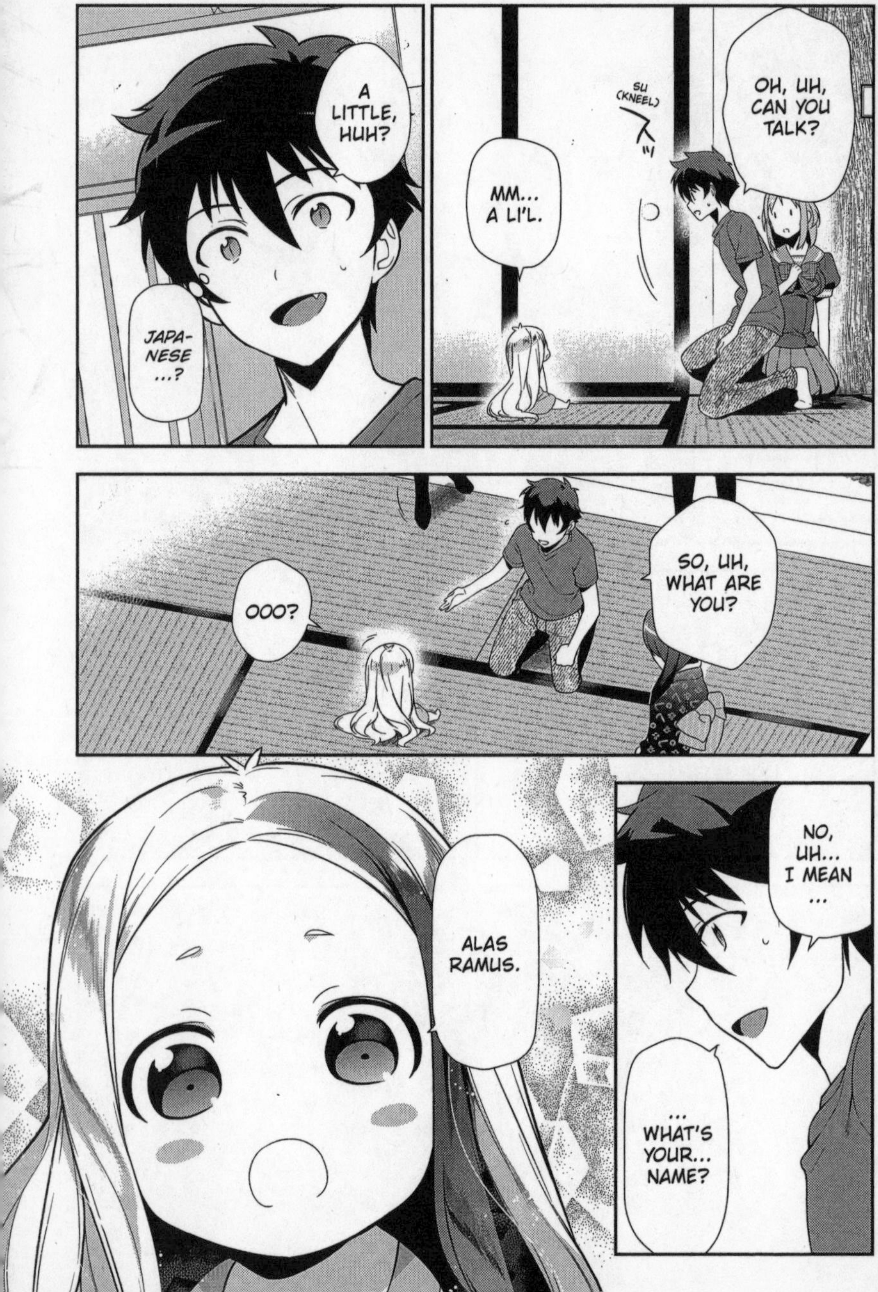
OH, UH, CAN YOU TALK?
SU (KNEEL)
MM... A LI'L.
A LITTLE, HUH?
JAPA-NESE ...?
SO, UH, WHAT ARE YOU?
OOO?
NO, UH... I MEAN ...
... WHAT'S YOUR... NAME?
ALAS RAMUS.

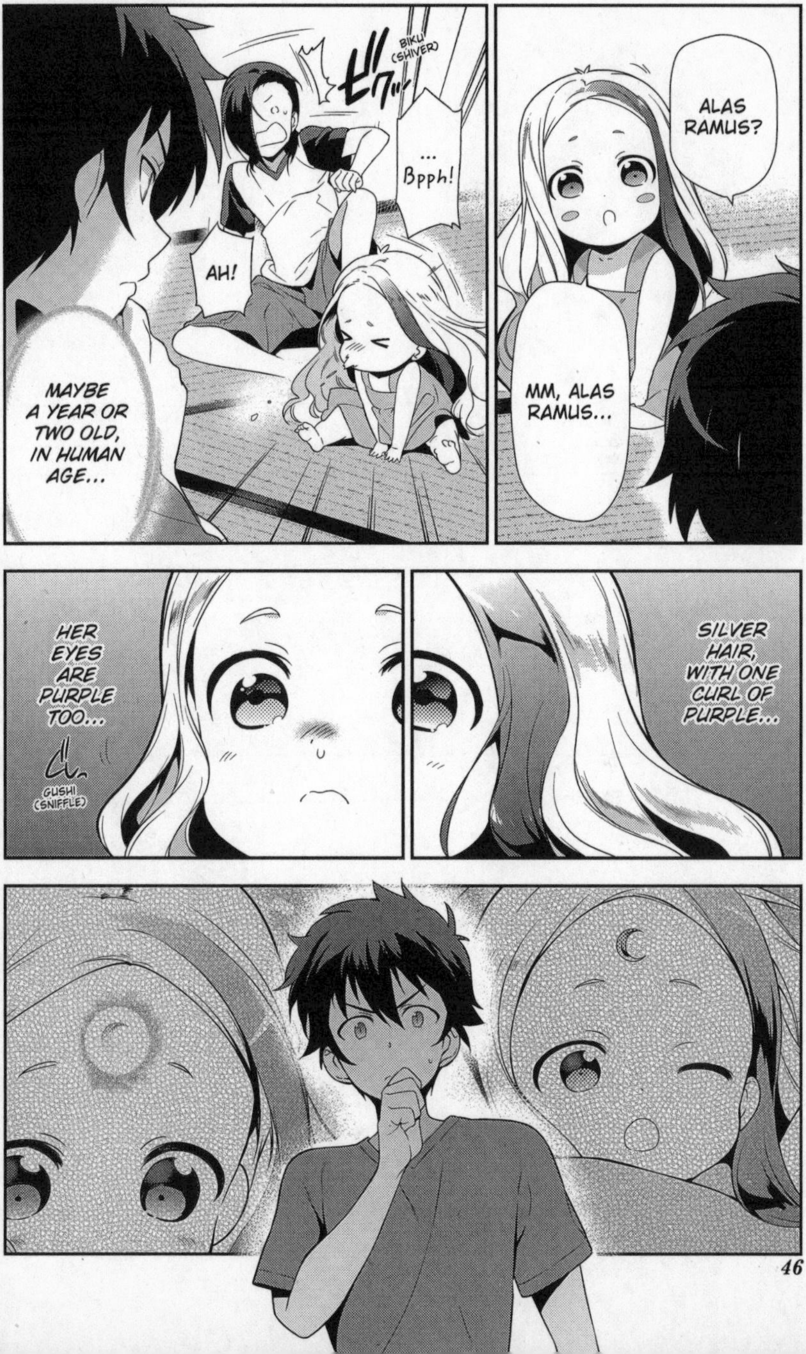
ALAS RAMUS?
MM, ALAS RAMUS...
BIKU (SHIVER)
... Bpph!
AH!
MAYBE A YEAR OR TWO OLD, IN HUMAN AGE...
SILVER HAIR, WITH ONE CURL OF PURPLE...
HER EYES ARE PURPLE TOO...
GUSHI (SNIFFLE)

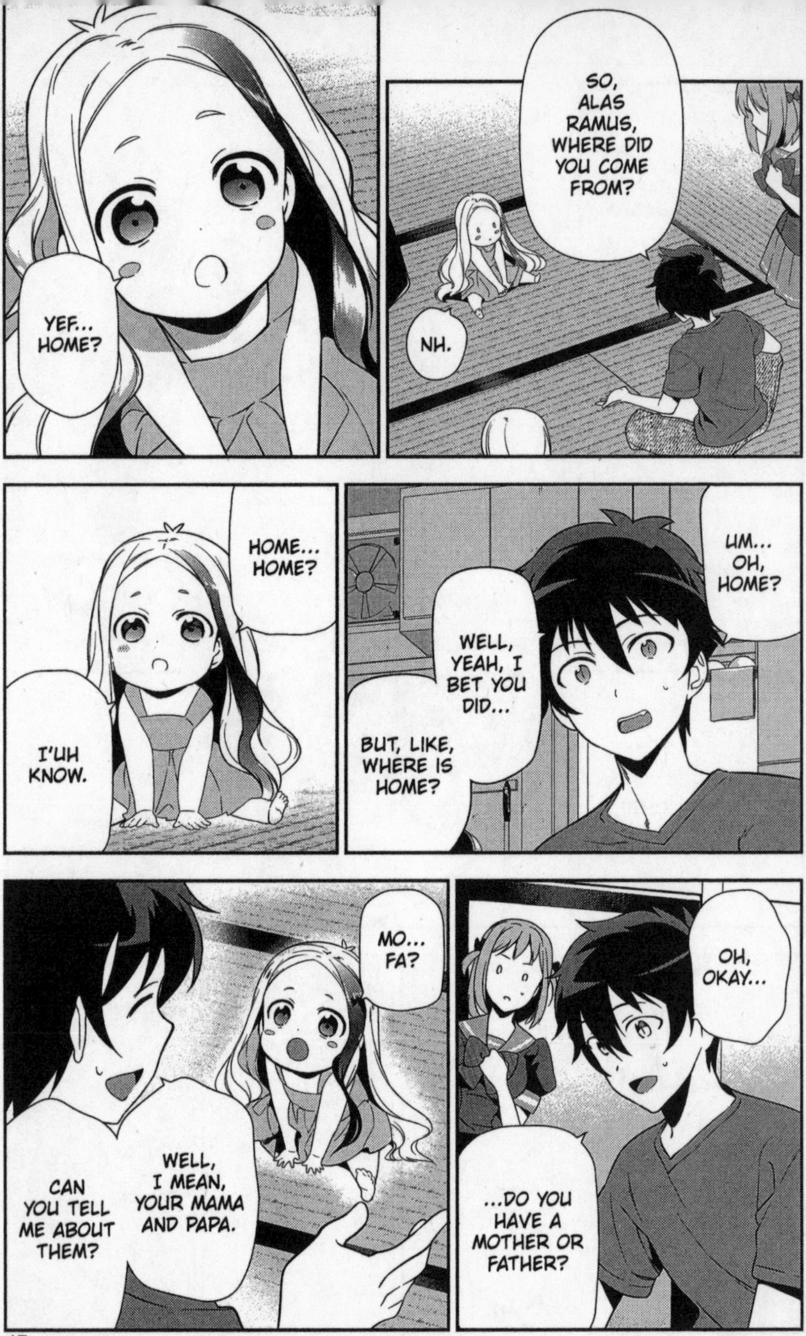
SO, ALAS RAMUS, WHERE DID YOU COME FROM?
NH.
YEF... HOME?
UM... OH, HOME?
WELL, YEAH, I BET YOU DID...
BUT, LIKE, WHERE IS HOME?
HOME... HOME?
I'UH KNOW.
OH, OKAY...
...DO YOU HAVE A MOTHER OR FATHER?
MO... FA?
WELL, I MEAN, YOUR MAMA AND PAPA.
CAN YOU TELL ME ABOUT THEM?

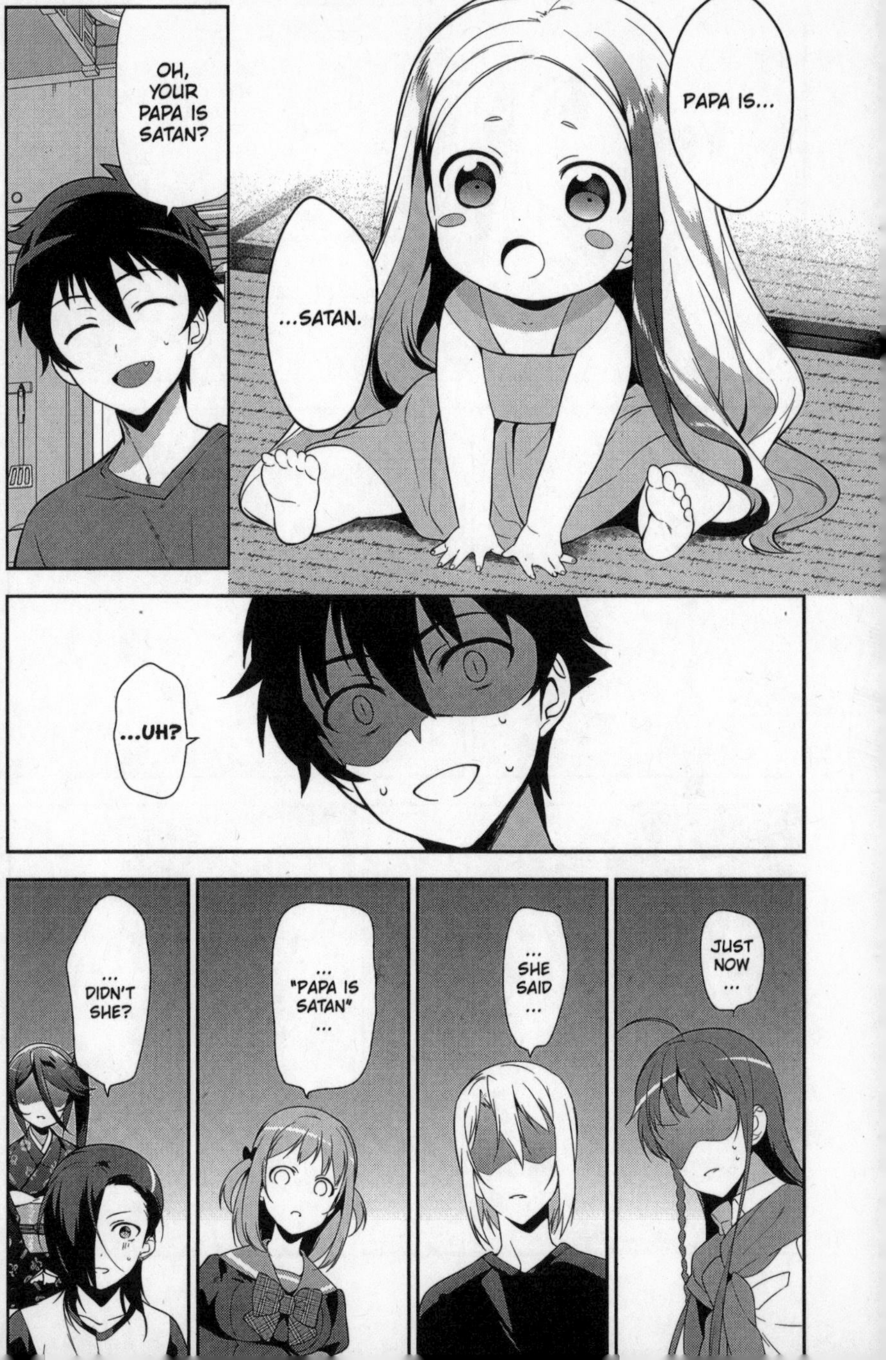
PAPA IS...
...SATAN.
OH, YOUR PAPA IS SATAN?
...UH?
JUST NOW ...
... SHE SAID ...
... "PAPA IS SATAN" ...
... DIDN'T SHE?

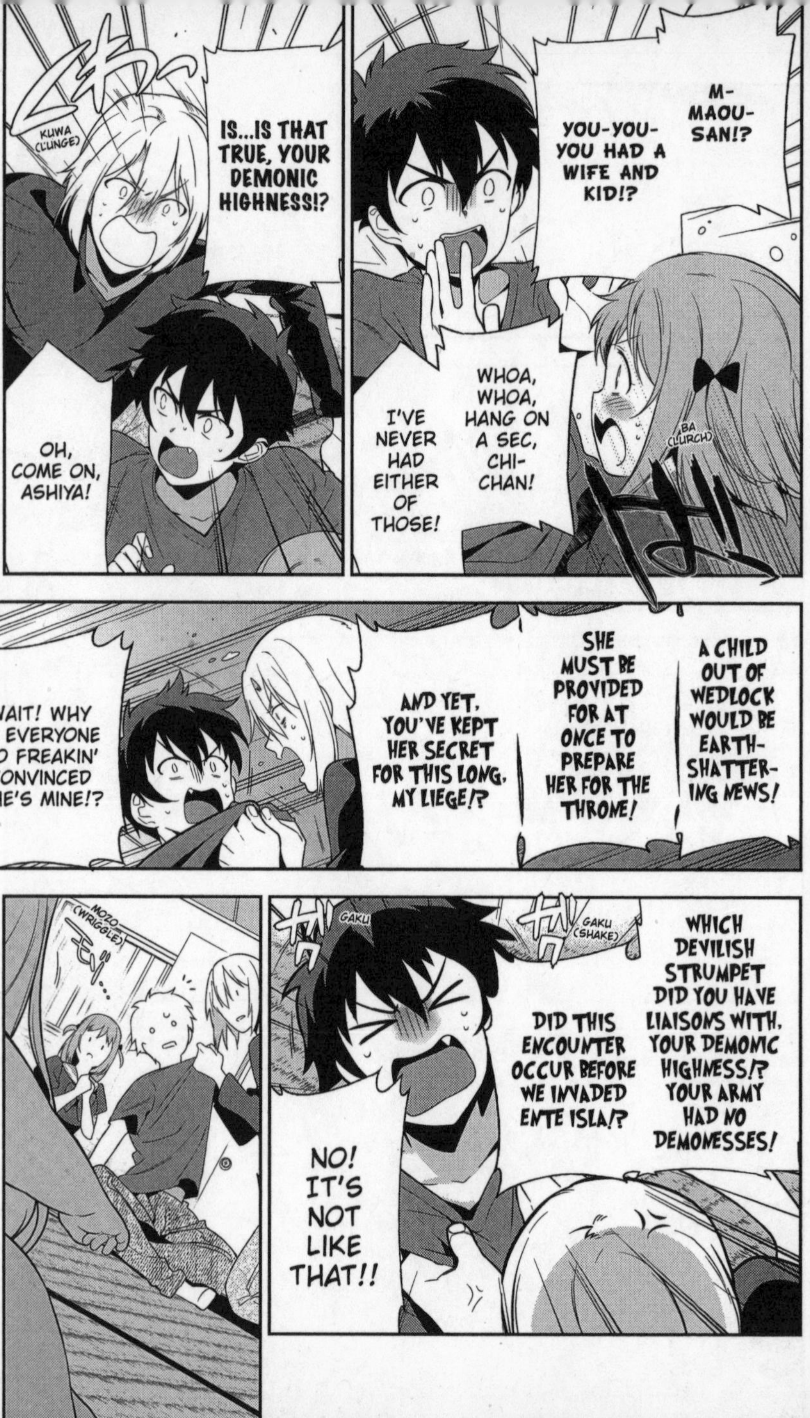
M-MAOU-SAN!?
YOU-YOU-YOU HAD A WIFE AND KID!?
BA (LURCH)
WHOA, WHOA, HANG ON A SEC, CHI-CHAN!
I'VE NEVER HAD EITHER OF THOSE!
KUWA (LUNGE)
IS...IS THAT TRUE, YOUR DEMONIC HIGHNESS!?
OH, COME ON, ASHIYA!
A CHILD OUT OF WEDLOCK WOULD BE EARTH-SHATTERING NEWS!
SHE MUST BE PROVIDED FOR AT ONCE TO PREPARE HER FOR THE THRONE!
AND YET, YOU'VE KEPT HER SECRET FOR THIS LONG, MY LIEGE!?
WAIT! WHY IS EVERYONE SO FREAKIN' CONVINCED SHE'S MINE!?
GAKU (SHAKE)
GAKU
WHICH DEVILISH STRUMPET DID YOU HAVE LIAISONS WITH, YOUR DEMONIC HIGHNESS!? YOUR ARMY HAD NO DEMONESSES!
DID THIS ENCOUNTER OCCUR BEFORE WE INVADED ENTE ISLA!?
NO! IT'S NOT LIKE THAT!!
MOZO (WRIGGLE)

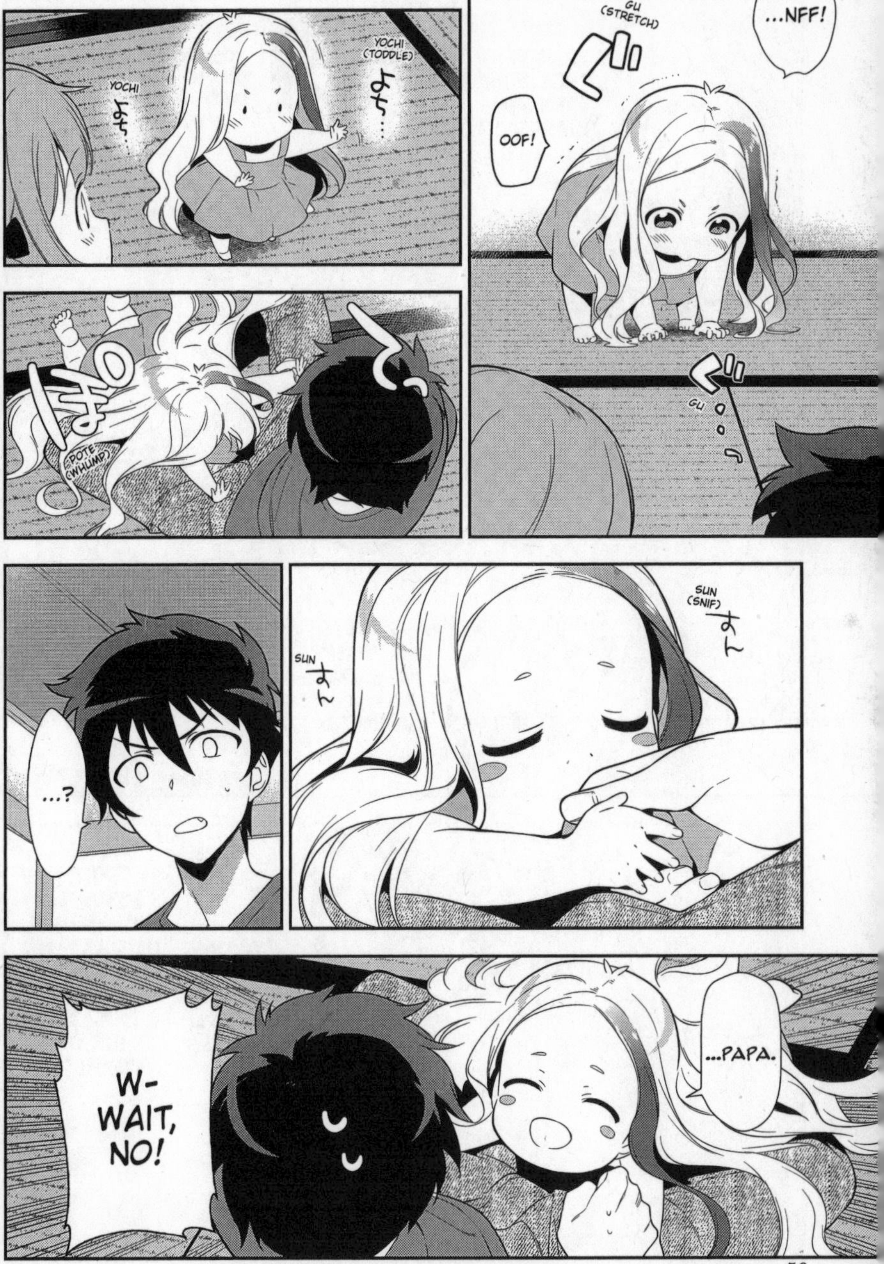
...NFF!
GU (STRETCH)
OOF!
GU
YOCHI (TODDLE)
YOCHI
POTE (WHUMP)
SUN (SNIF)
SUN
...?
...PAPA.
W-WAIT, NO!

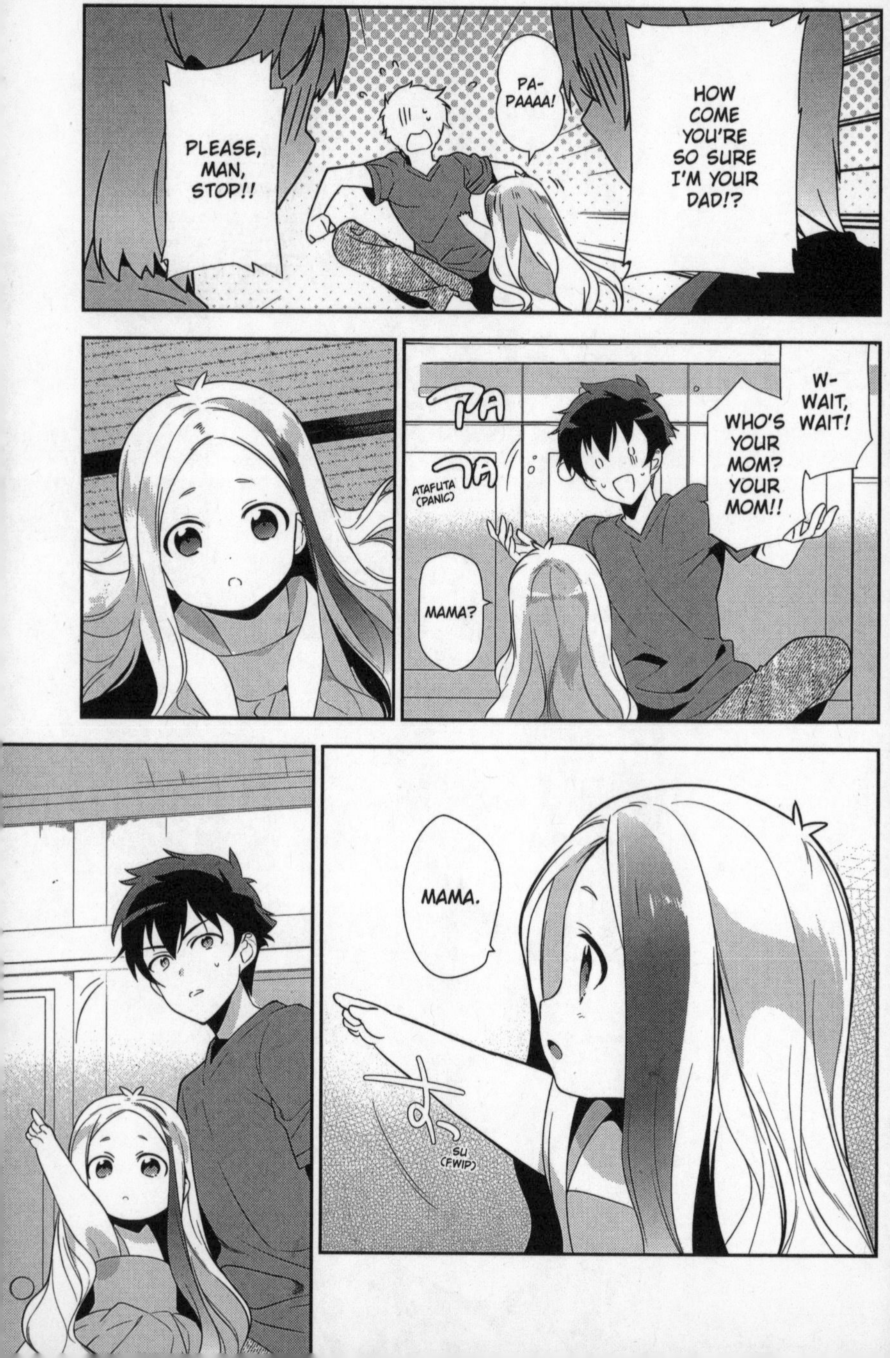
HOW COME YOU'RE SO SURE I'M YOUR DAD!?
PA-PAAAA!
PLEASE, MAN, STOP!!
W-WAIT, WAIT!
WHO'S YOUR MOM? YOUR MOM!!
ATAFUTA (PANIC)
MAMA?
MAMA.
SU (FWIP)

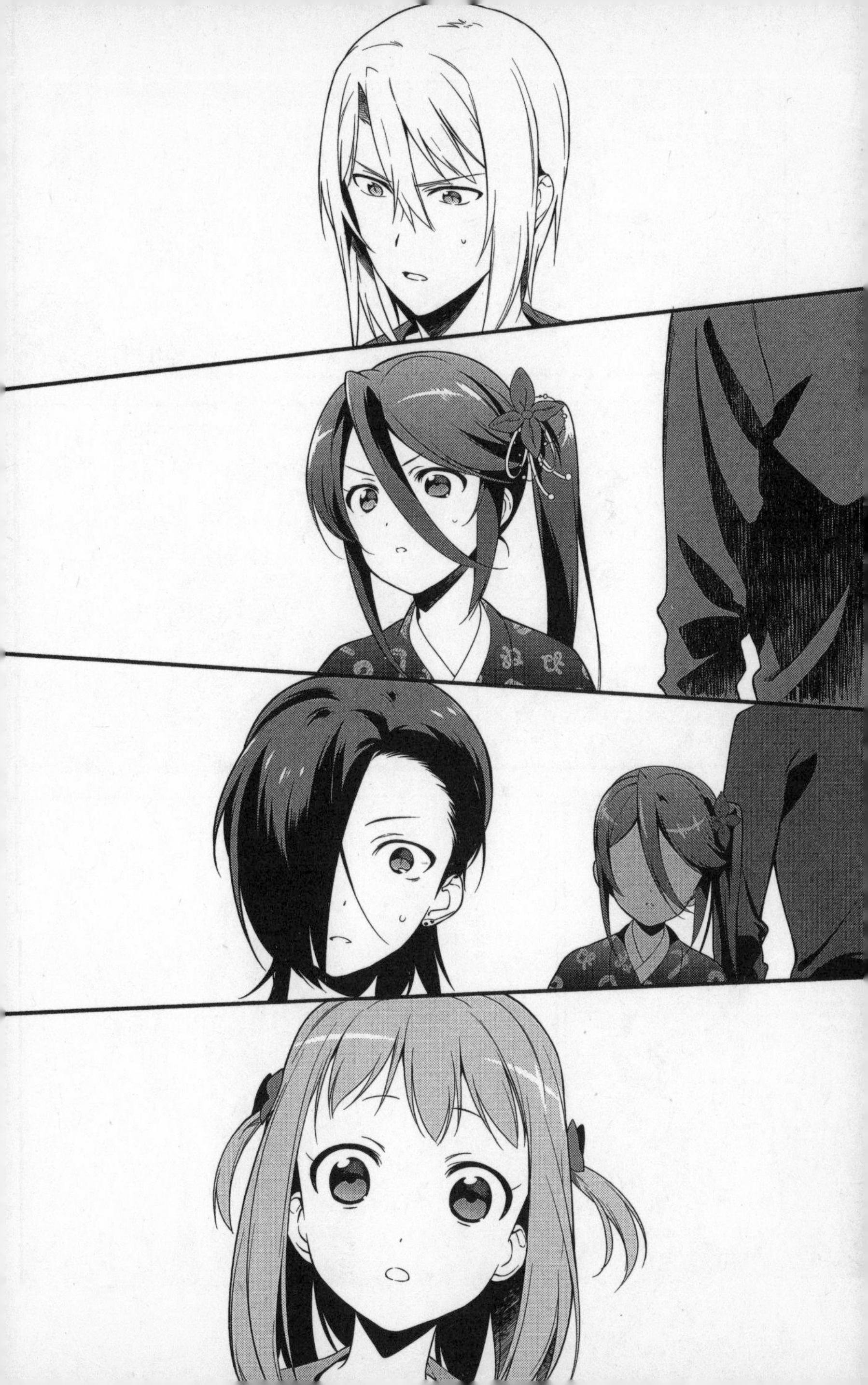

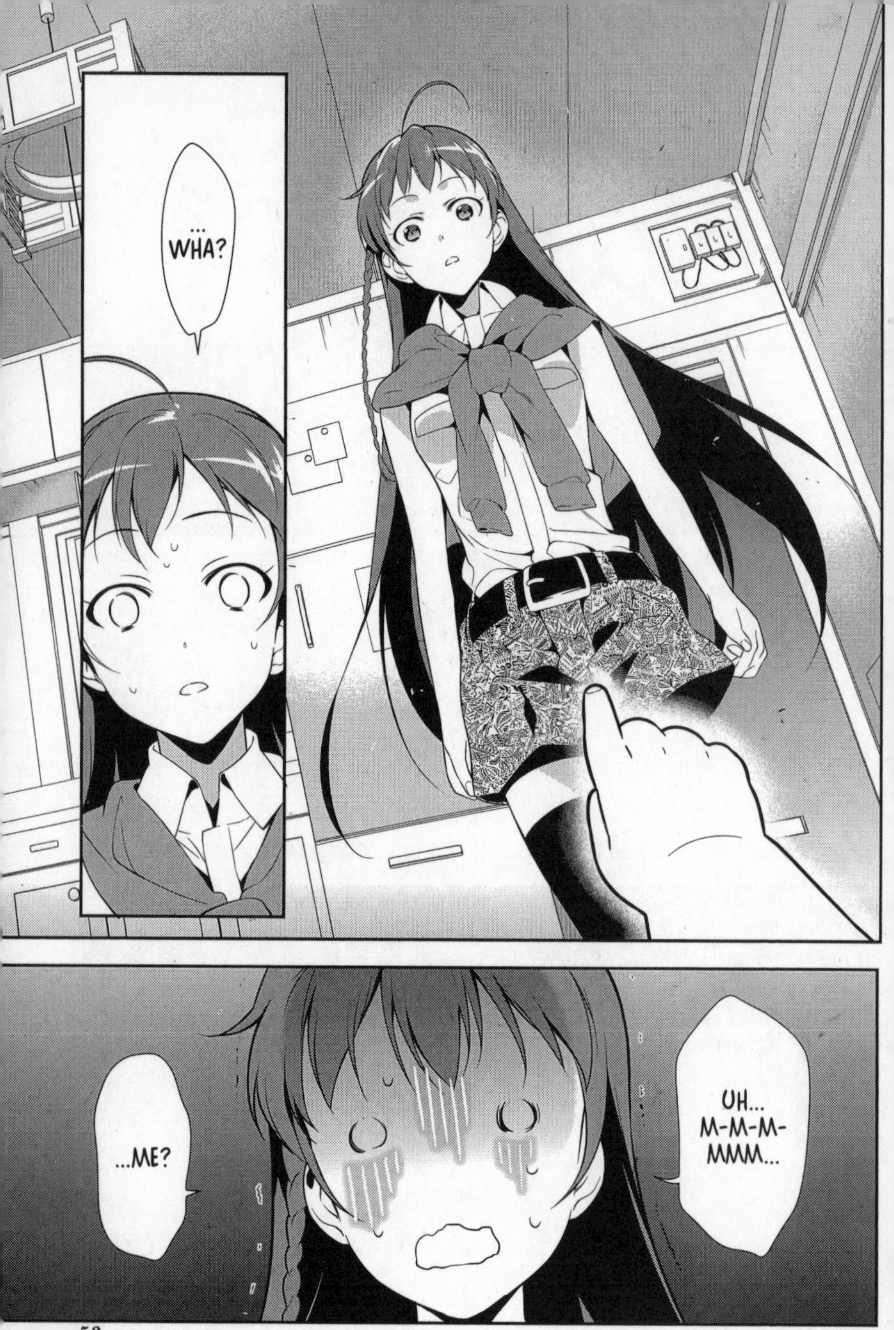
...WHA?
UH... M-M-M-MMM...
...ME?

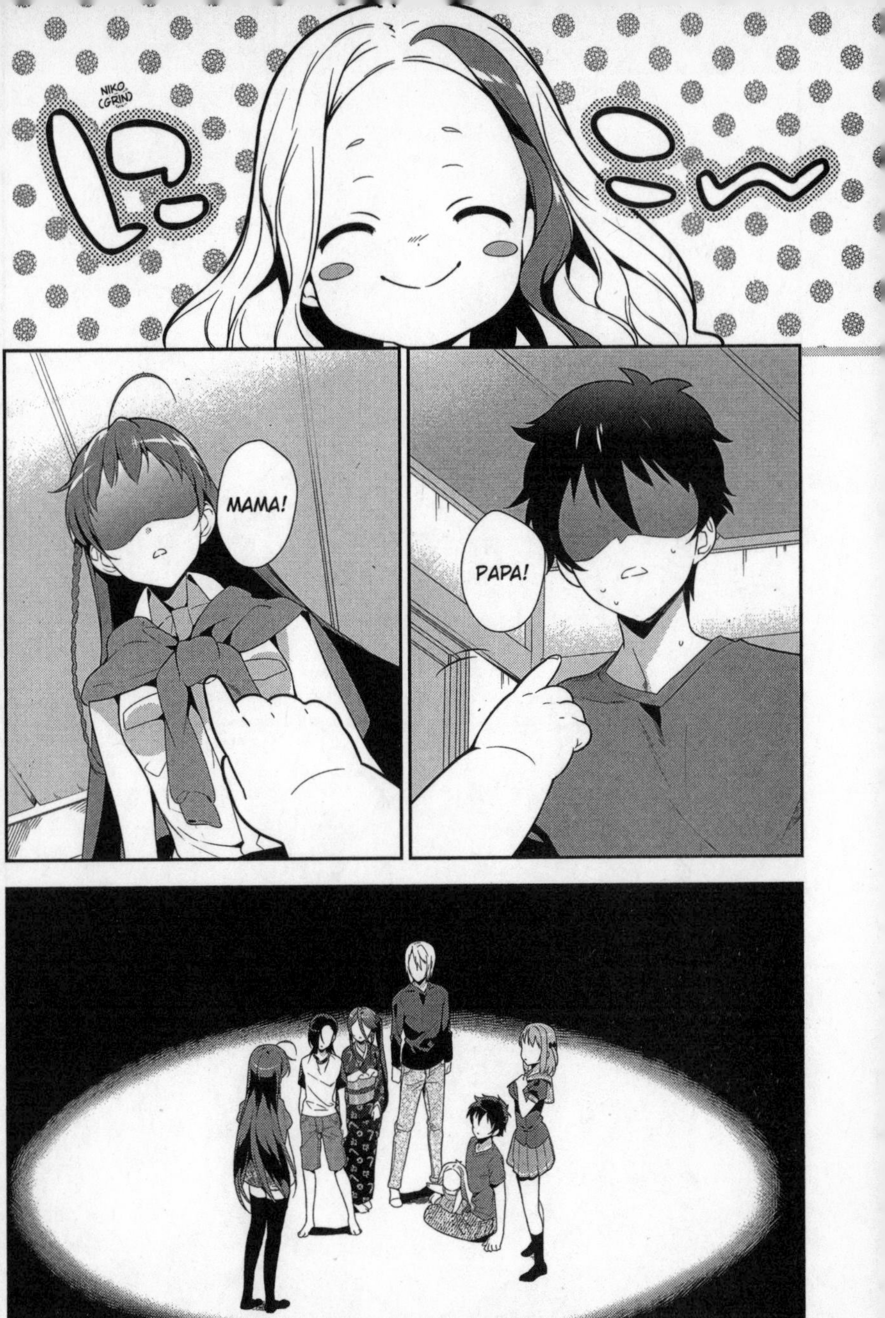
NIKO (GRIN)
PAPA!
MAMA!

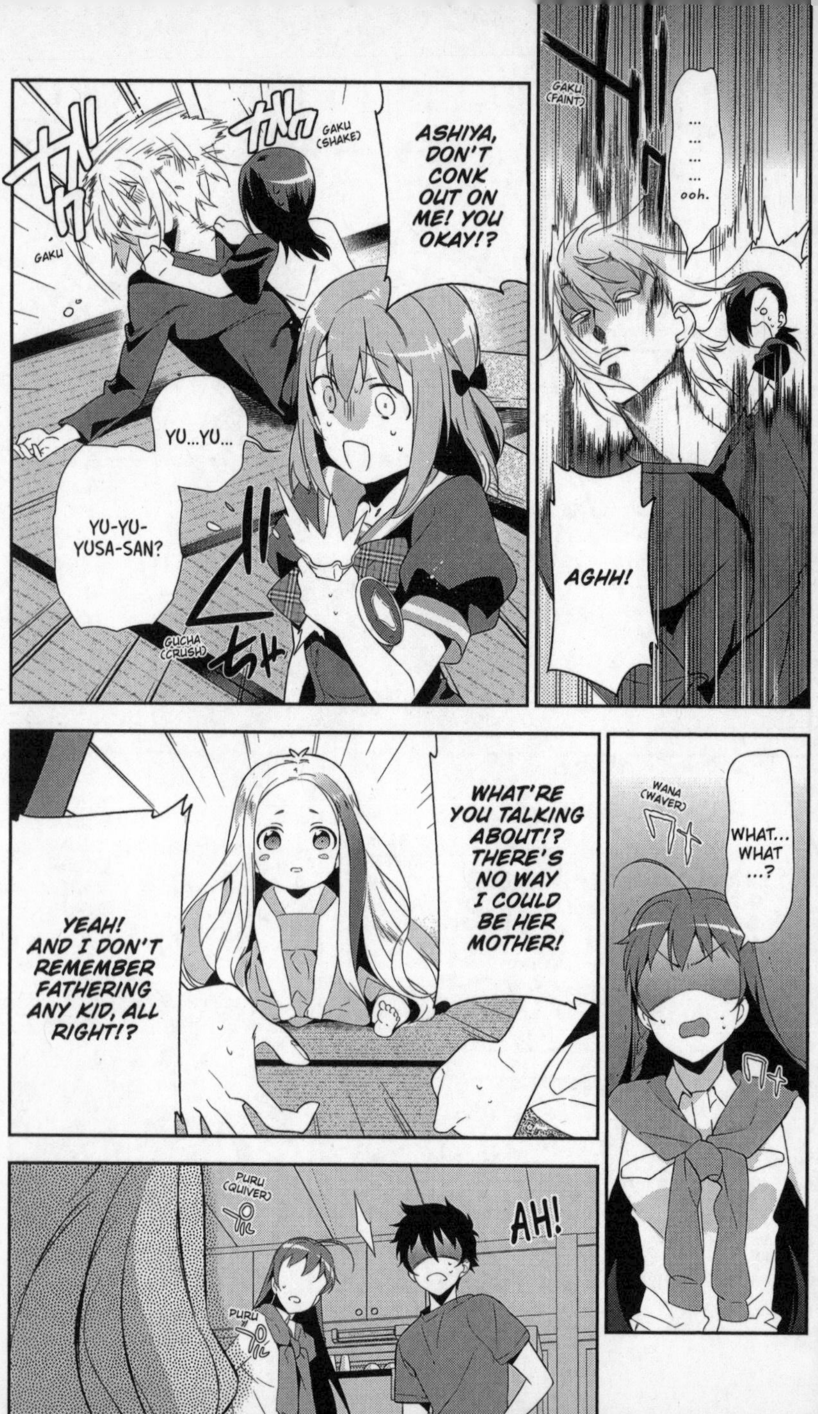
GAKU (FAINT)
... ... ooh.
AGHH!
GAKU (SHAKE)
ASHIYA, DON'T CONK OUT ON ME! YOU OKAY!?
GAKU
YU...YU...
YU-YU-YUSA-SAN?
GUCHA (CRUSH)
WANA (WAVER)
WHAT... WHAT ...?
WHAT'RE YOU TALKING ABOUT!? THERE'S NO WAY I COULD BE HER MOTHER!
YEAH! AND I DON'T REMEMBER FATHERING ANY KID, ALL RIGHT!?
PURU (QUIVER)
AH!
PURU

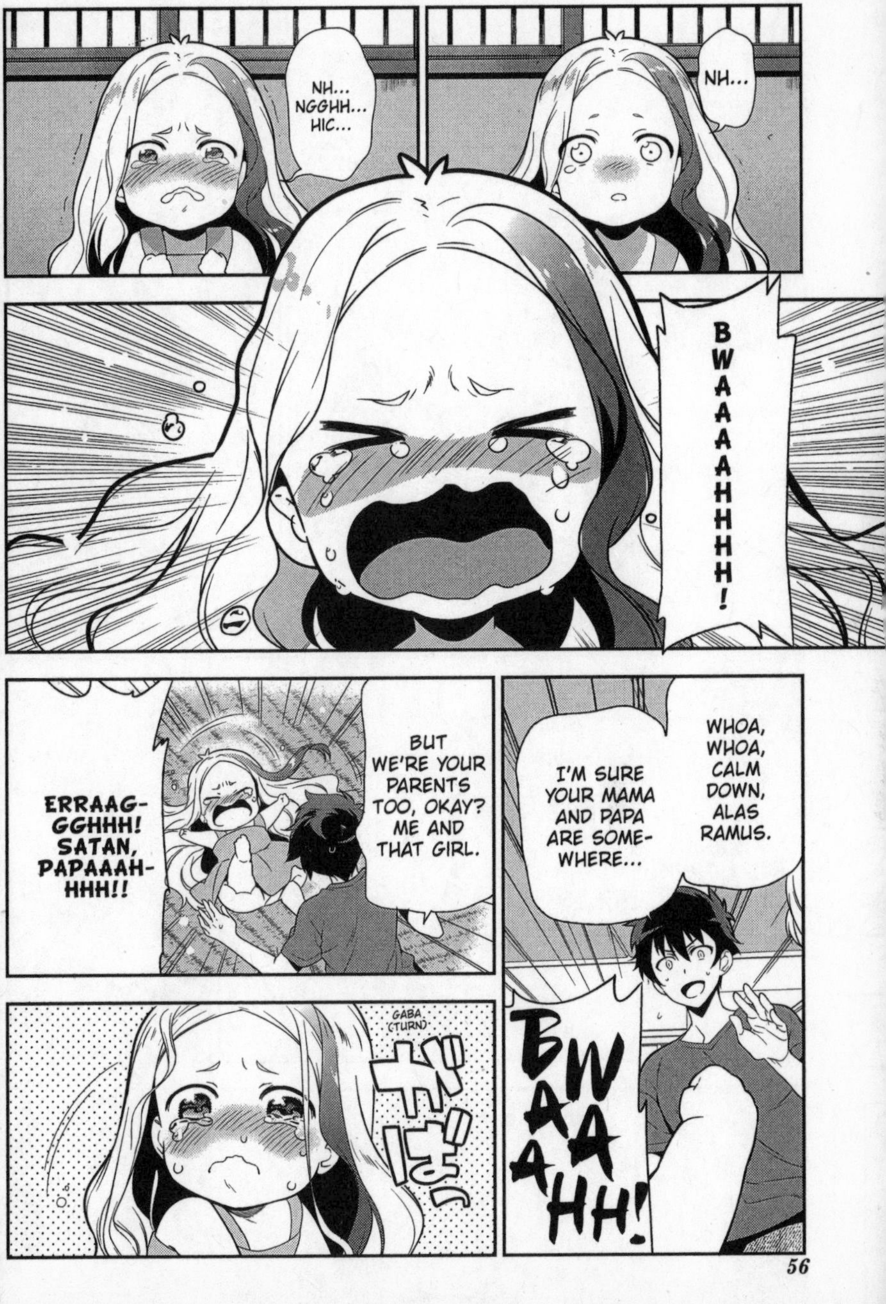
NH...
NH... NGGHH... HIC...
BWAAAAAAHHHHH!
WHOA, WHOA, CALM DOWN, ALAS RAMUS.
I'M SURE YOUR MAMA AND PAPA ARE SOME-WHERE...
BWAAAAHH!
BUT WE'RE YOUR PARENTS TOO, OKAY? ME AND THAT GIRL.
ERRAAG-GGHHH! SATAN, PAPAAAH-HHH!!
GABA (TURN)

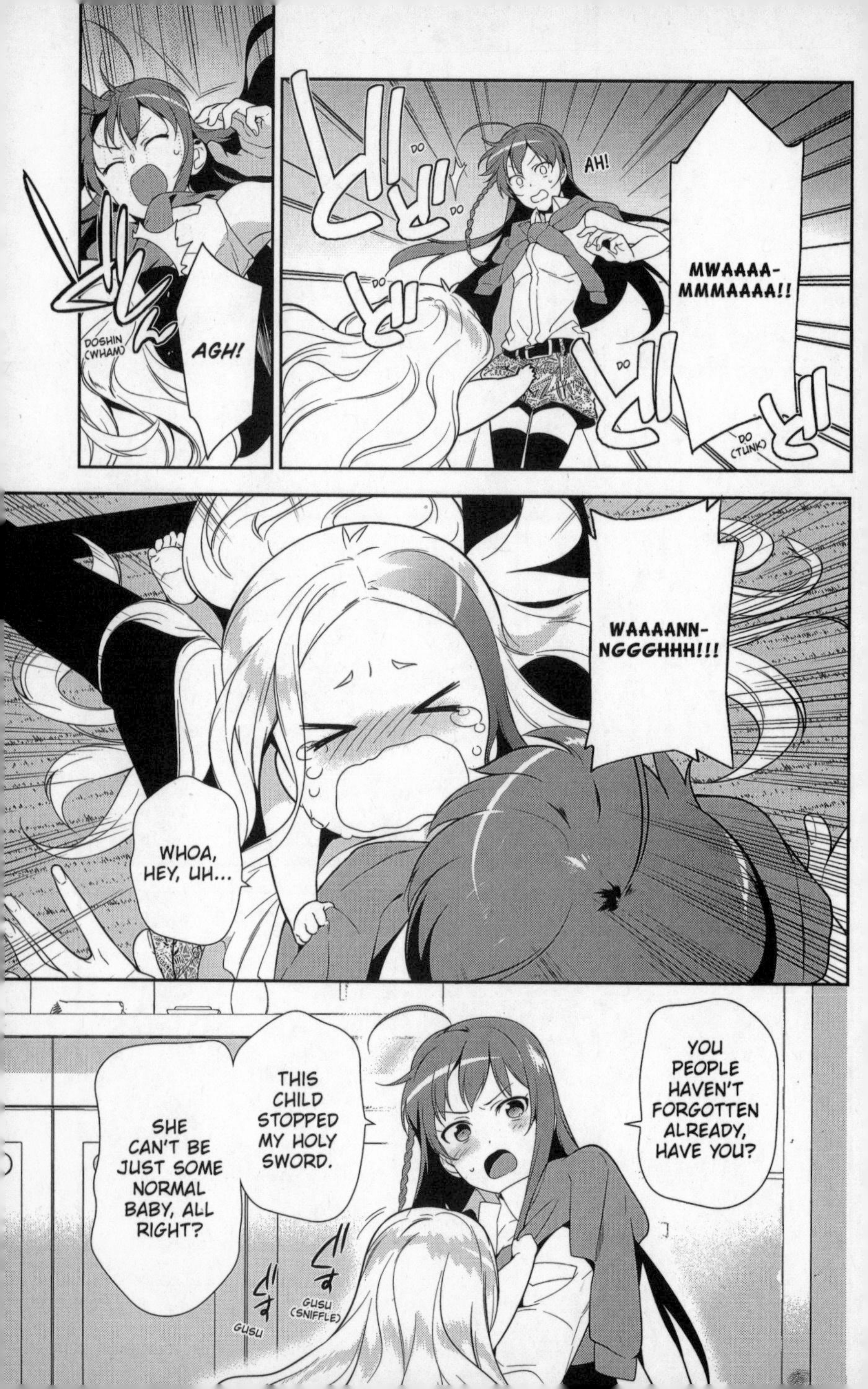
MWAAAA-MMMAAAA!!
DO (TUNK)
DO
AH!
DO
DO
DO
AGH!
DOSHIN (WHAM)
WAAAANN-NGGGHHH!!!
WHOA, HEY, UH...
YOU PEOPLE HAVEN'T FORGOTTEN ALREADY, HAVE YOU?
THIS CHILD STOPPED MY HOLY SWORD.
SHE CAN'T BE JUST SOME NORMAL BABY, ALL RIGHT?
GUSU (SNIFFLE)
GUSU

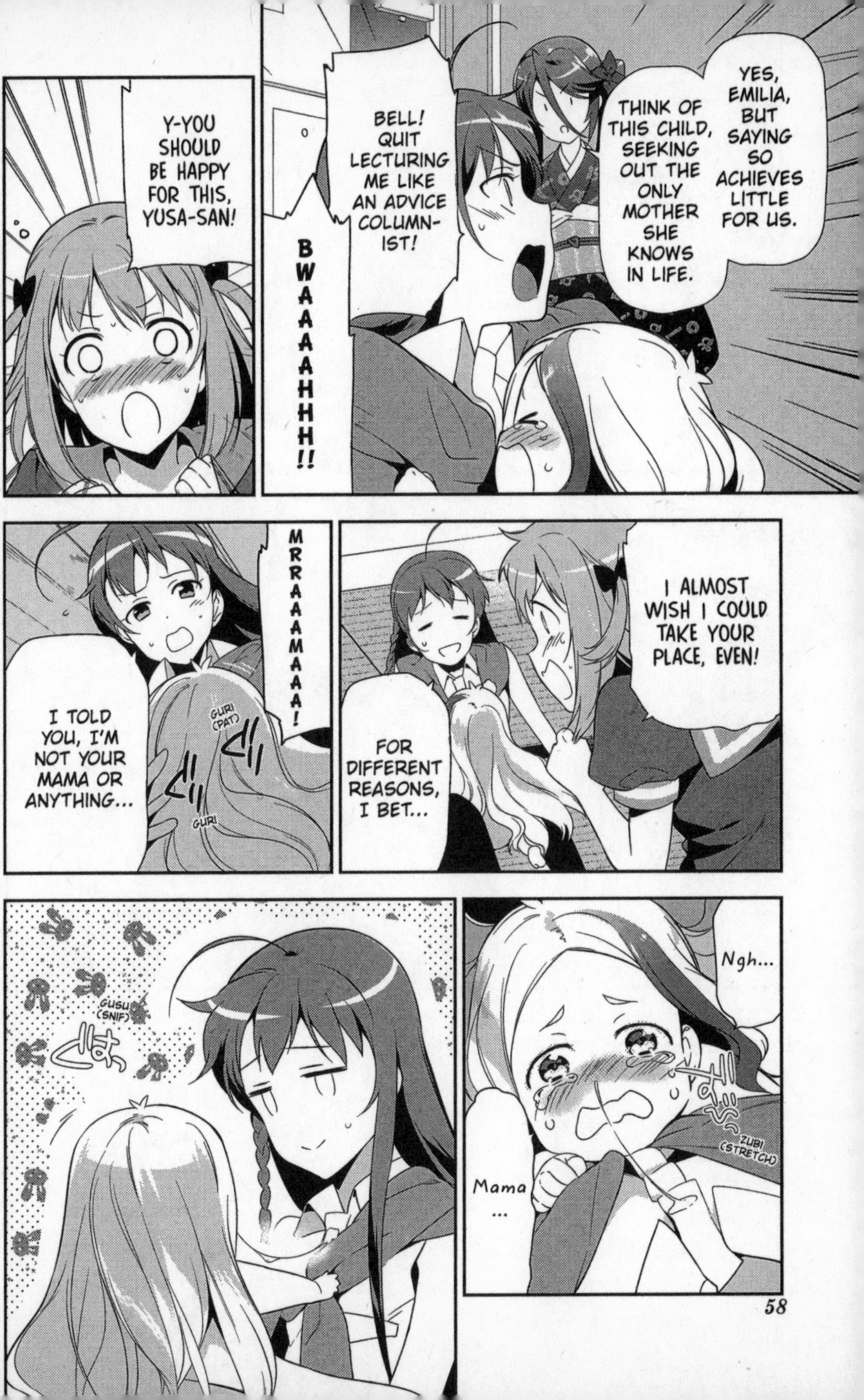

YES, EMILIA, BUT SAYING SO ACHIEVES LITTLE FOR US.
THINK OF THIS CHILD, SEEKING OUT THE ONLY MOTHER SHE KNOWS IN LIFE.
BELL! QUIT LECTURING ME LIKE AN ADVICE COLUMN-IST!
BWAAAAAAHHHH!!
Y-YOU SHOULD BE HAPPY FOR THIS, YUSA-SAN!
I ALMOST WISH I COULD TAKE YOUR PLACE, EVEN!
FOR DIFFERENT REASONS, I BET...
MRRAAAAMAAAA!
GURI (PAT)
GURI
I TOLD YOU, I'M NOT YOUR MAMA OR ANYTHING...
Ngh...
ZUBI (STRETCH)
Mama ...
GUSU (SNIF)

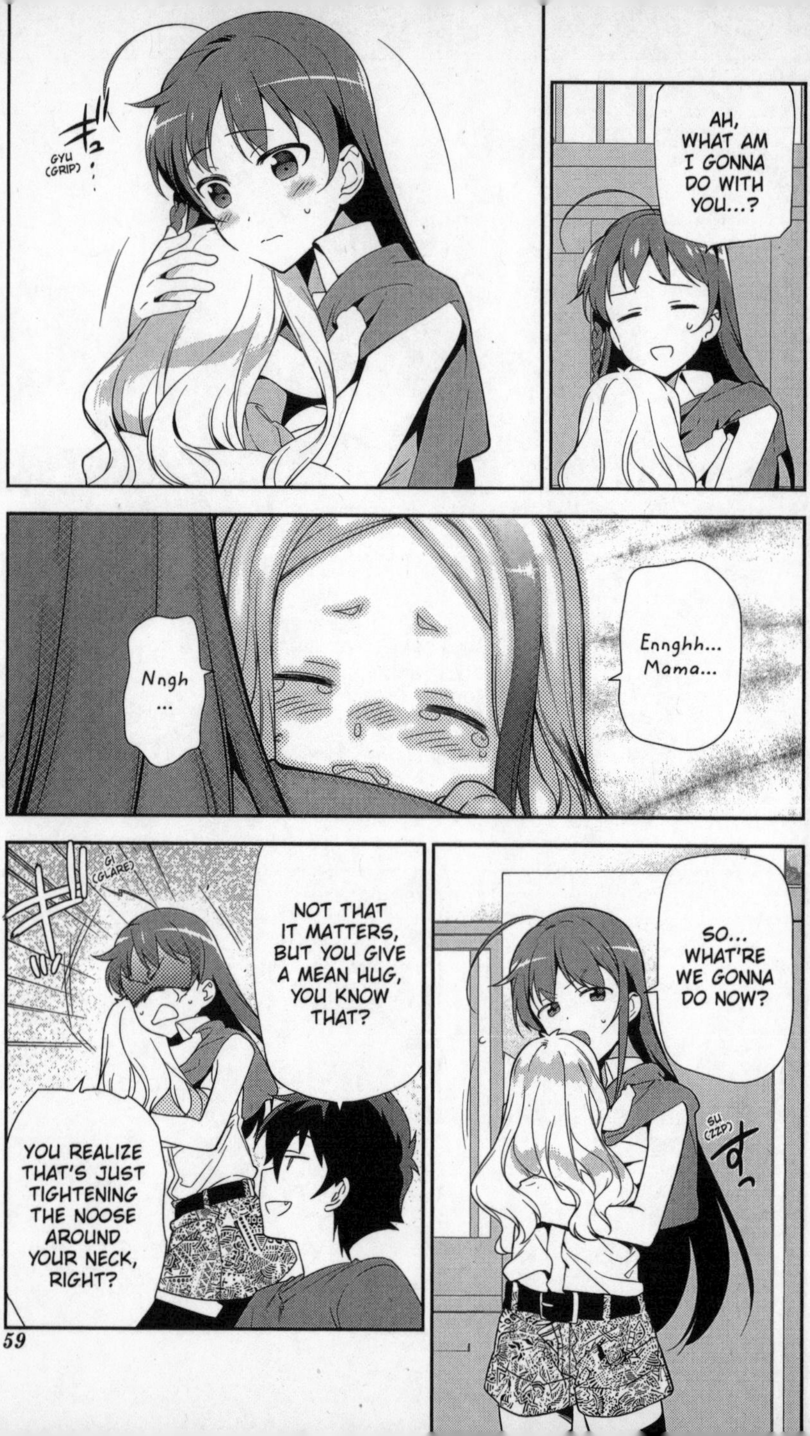
AH, WHAT AM I GONNA DO WITH YOU...?
GYU (GRIP)
Ennghh... Mama...
Nngh ...
SO... WHAT'RE WE GONNA DO NOW?
SU (ZZP)
NOT THAT IT MATTERS, BUT YOU GIVE A MEAN HUG, YOU KNOW THAT?
GI (GLARE)
YOU REALIZE THAT'S JUST TIGHTENING THE NOOSE AROUND YOUR NECK, RIGHT?

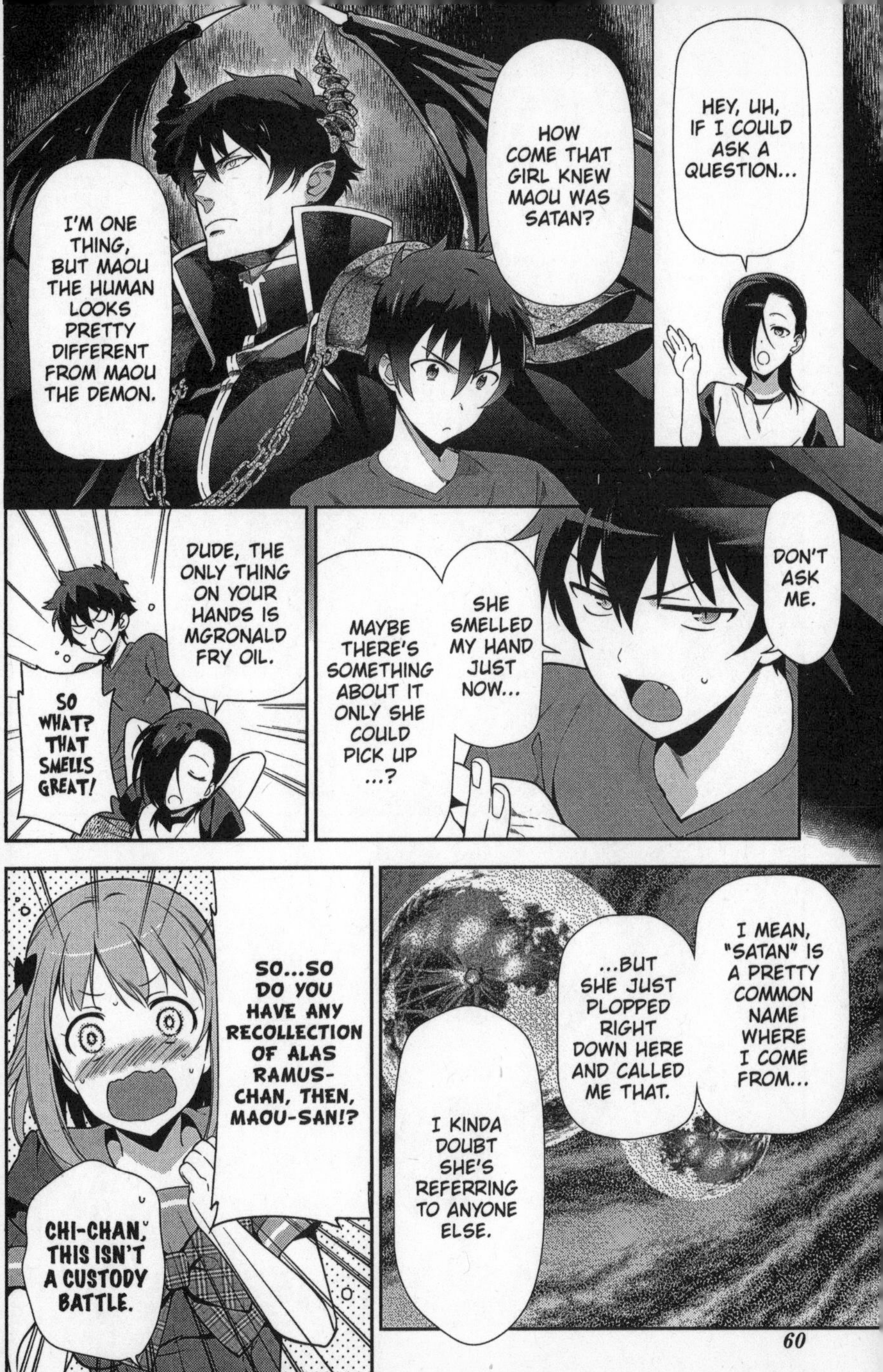
HEY, UH, IF I COULD ASK A QUESTION...
HOW COME THAT GIRL KNEW MAOU WAS SATAN?
I'M ONE THING, BUT MAOU THE HUMAN LOOKS PRETTY DIFFERENT FROM MAOU THE DEMON.
DON'T ASK ME.
SHE SMELLED MY HAND JUST NOW...
MAYBE THERE'S SOMETHING ABOUT IT ONLY SHE COULD PICK UP ...?
DUDE, THE ONLY THING ON YOUR HANDS IS MGRONALD FRY OIL.
SO WHAT? THAT SMELLS GREAT!
I MEAN, "SATAN" IS A PRETTY COMMON NAME WHERE I COME FROM...
...BUT SHE JUST PLOPPED RIGHT DOWN HERE AND CALLED ME THAT.
I KINDA DOUBT SHE'S REFERRING TO ANYONE ELSE.
SO...SO DO YOU HAVE ANY RECOLLECTION OF ALAS RAMUS-CHAN, THEN, MAOU-SAN!?
CHI-CHAN, THIS ISN'T A CUSTODY BATTLE.

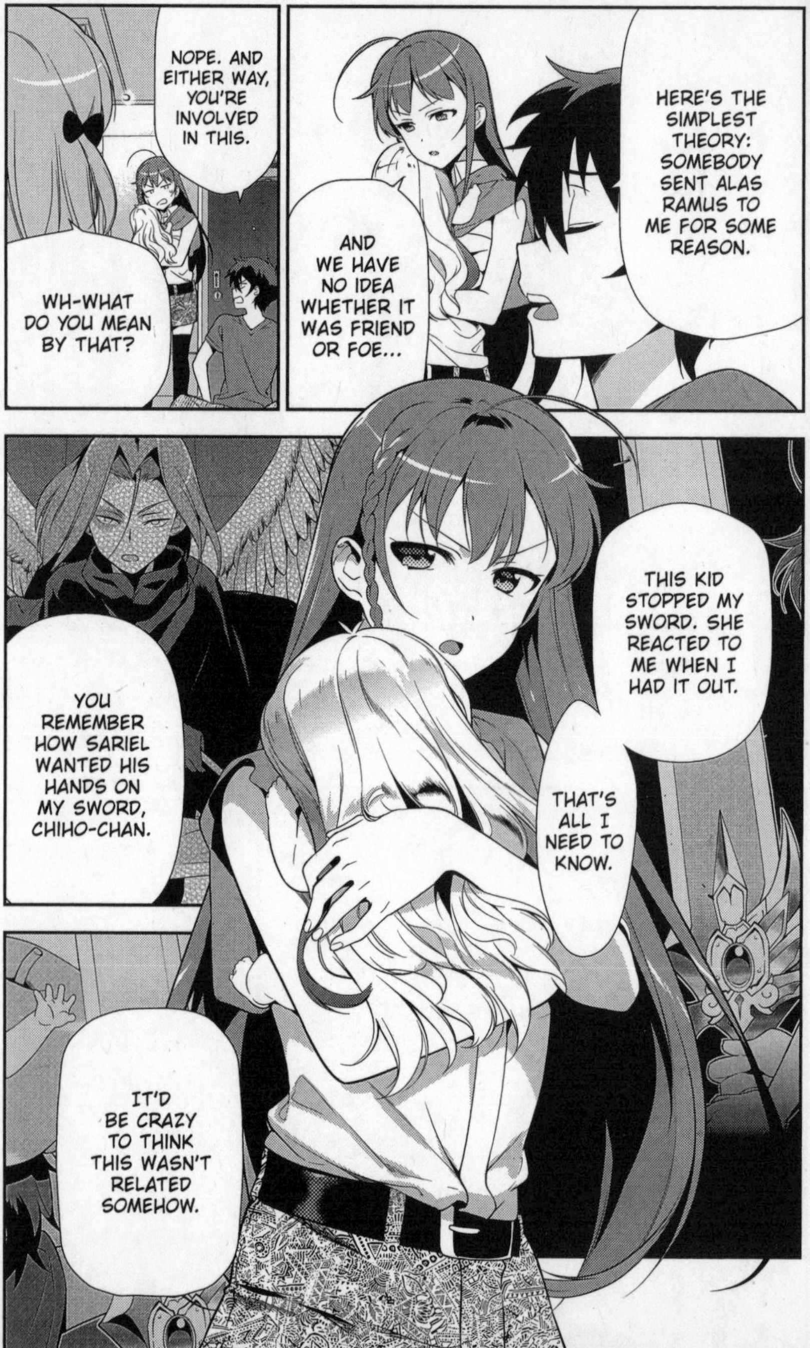
HERE'S THE SIMPLEST THEORY: SOMEBODY SENT ALAS RAMUS TO ME FOR SOME REASON.
AND WE HAVE NO IDEA WHETHER IT WAS FRIEND OR FOE...
NOPE. AND EITHER WAY, YOU'RE INVOLVED IN THIS.
WH-WHAT DO YOU MEAN BY THAT?
THIS KID STOPPED MY SWORD. SHE REACTED TO ME WHEN I HAD IT OUT.
THAT'S ALL I NEED TO KNOW.
YOU REMEMBER HOW SARIEL WANTED HIS HANDS ON MY SWORD, CHIHO-CHAN.
IT'D BE CRAZY TO THINK THIS WASN'T RELATED SOMEHOW.

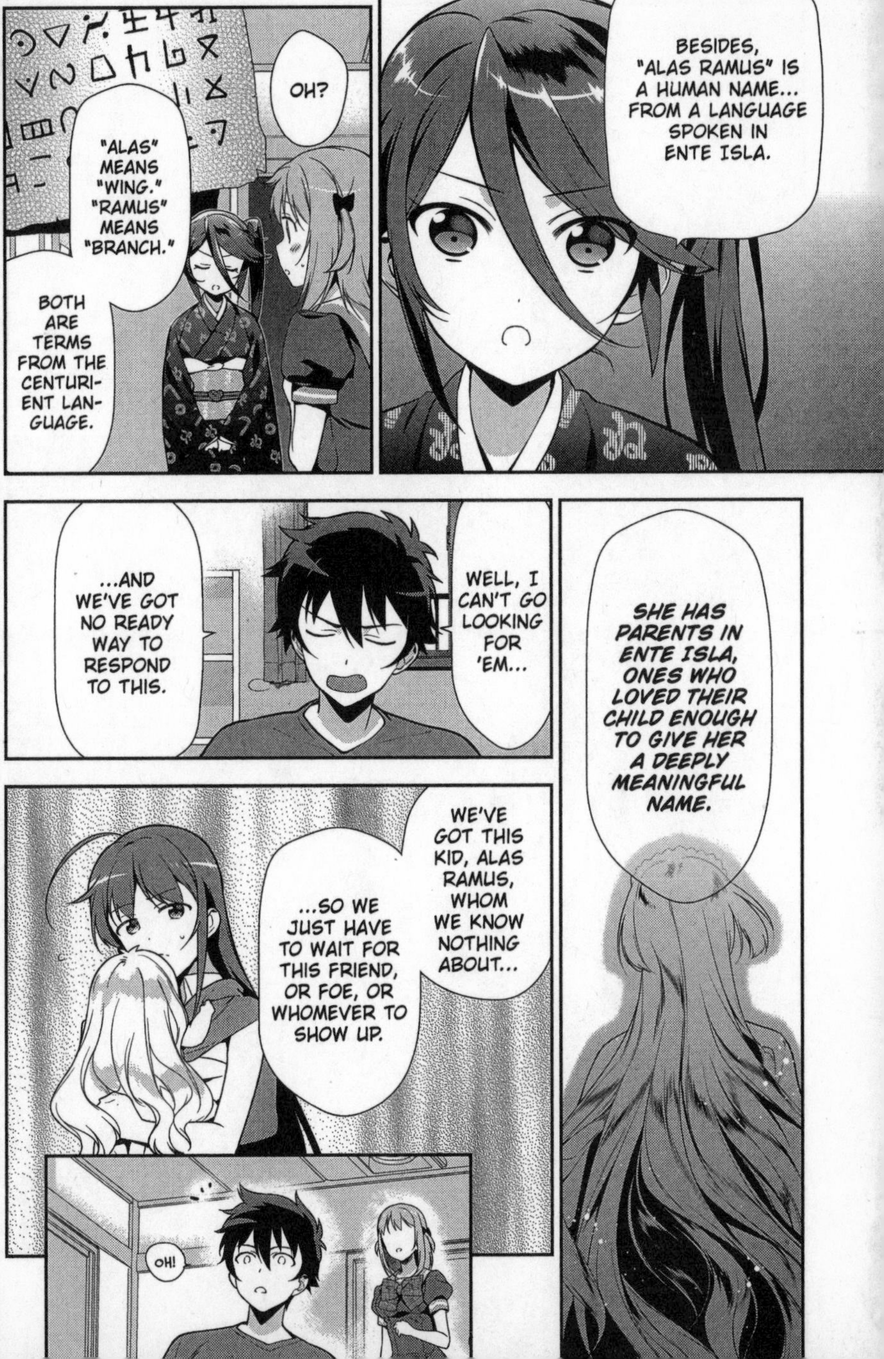
BESIDES, "ALAS RAMUS" IS A HUMAN NAME... FROM A LANGUAGE SPOKEN IN ENTE ISLA.
OH?
"ALAS" MEANS "WING." "RAMUS" MEANS "BRANCH."
BOTH ARE TERMS FROM THE CENTURI-ENT LAN-GUAGE.
SHE HAS PARENTS IN ENTE ISLA, ONES WHO LOVED THEIR CHILD ENOUGH TO GIVE HER A DEEPLY MEANINGFUL NAME.
WELL, I CAN'T GO LOOKING FOR 'EM...
...AND WE'VE GOT NO READY WAY TO RESPOND TO THIS.
WE'VE GOT THIS KID, ALAS RAMUS, WHOM WE KNOW NOTHING ABOUT...
...SO WE JUST HAVE TO WAIT FOR THIS FRIEND, OR FOE, OR WHOMEVER TO SHOW UP.
OH!

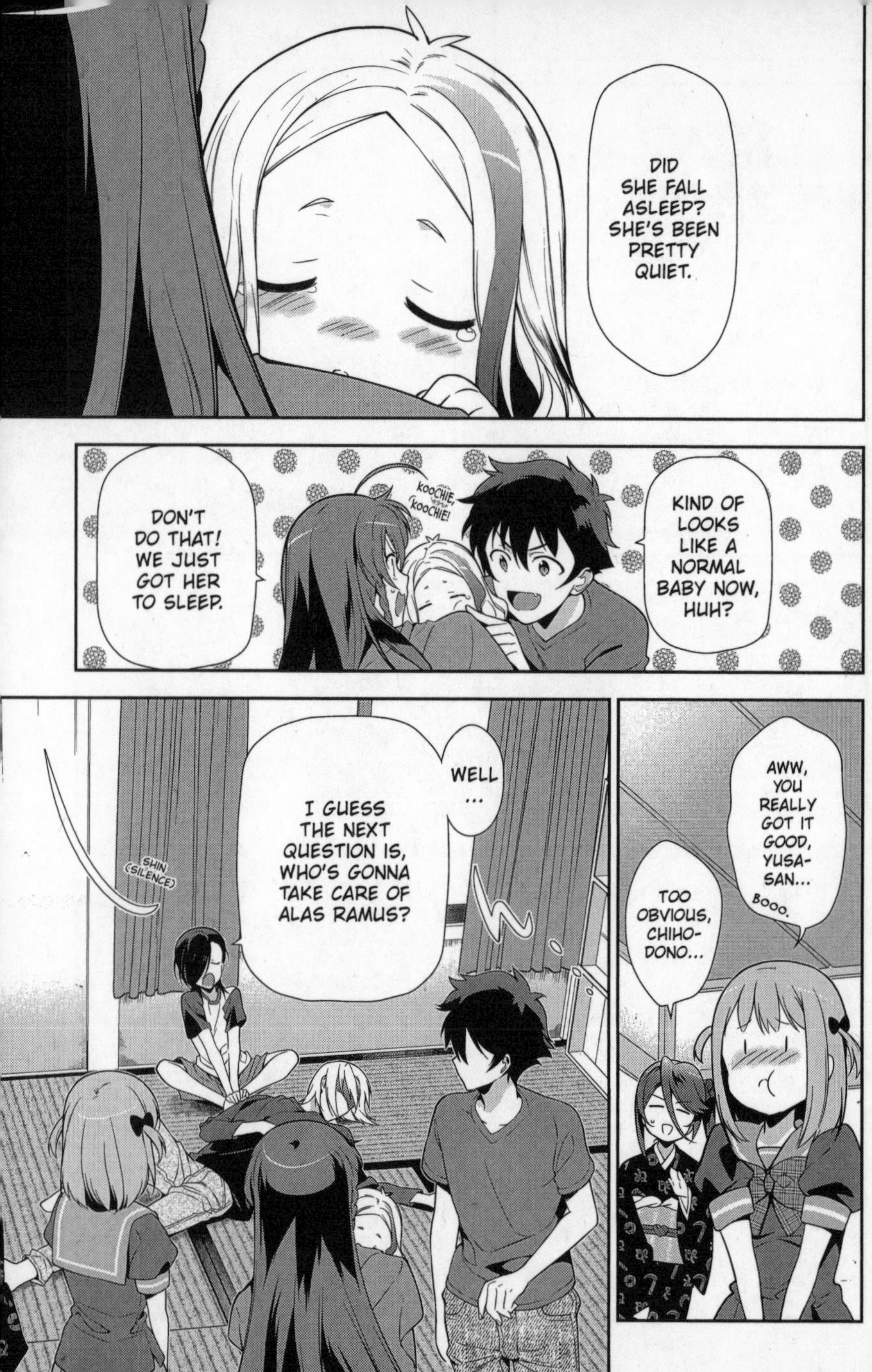
DID SHE FALL ASLEEP? SHE'S BEEN PRETTY QUIET.
KIND OF LOOKS LIKE A NORMAL BABY NOW, HUH?
KOOCHIE, KOOCHIE!
DON'T DO THAT! WE JUST GOT HER TO SLEEP.
AWW, YOU REALLY GOT IT GOOD, YUSA-SAN...
BOOO.
TOO OBVIOUS, CHIHO-DONO...
WELL ...
I GUESS THE NEXT QUESTION IS, WHO'S GONNA TAKE CARE OF ALAS RAMUS?
SHIN (SILENCE)

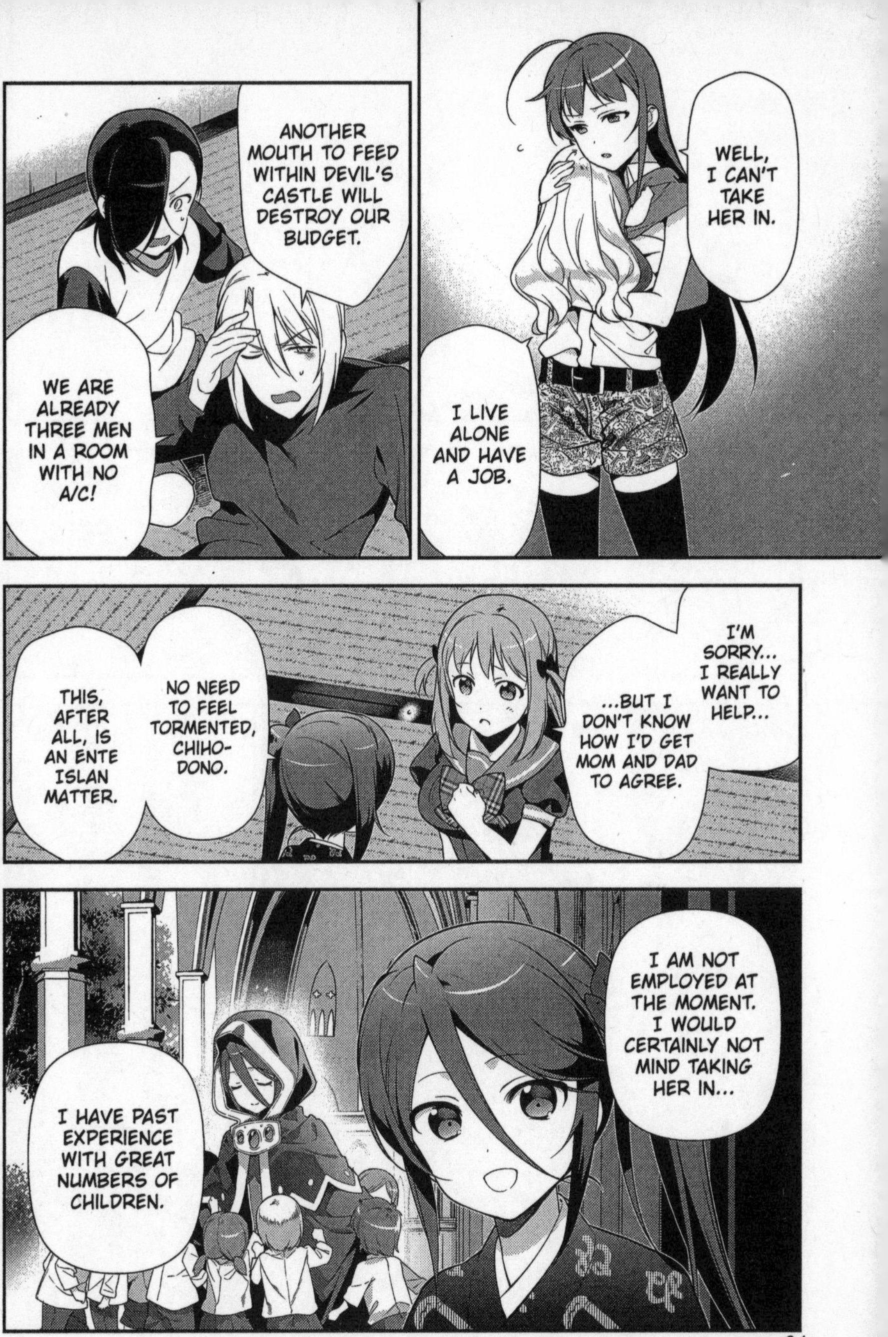
WELL, I CAN'T TAKE HER IN.
I LIVE ALONE AND HAVE A JOB.
ANOTHER MOUTH TO FEED WITHIN DEVIL'S CASTLE WILL DESTROY OUR BUDGET.
WE ARE ALREADY THREE MEN IN A ROOM WITH NO A/C!
I'M SORRY... I REALLY WANT TO HELP...
...BUT I DON'T KNOW HOW I'D GET MOM AND DAD TO AGREE.
NO NEED TO FEEL TORMENTED, CHIHO-DONO.
THIS, AFTER ALL, IS AN ENTE ISLAN MATTER.
I AM NOT EMPLOYED AT THE MOMENT. I WOULD CERTAINLY NOT MIND TAKING HER IN...
I HAVE PAST EXPERIENCE WITH GREAT NUMBERS OF CHILDREN.

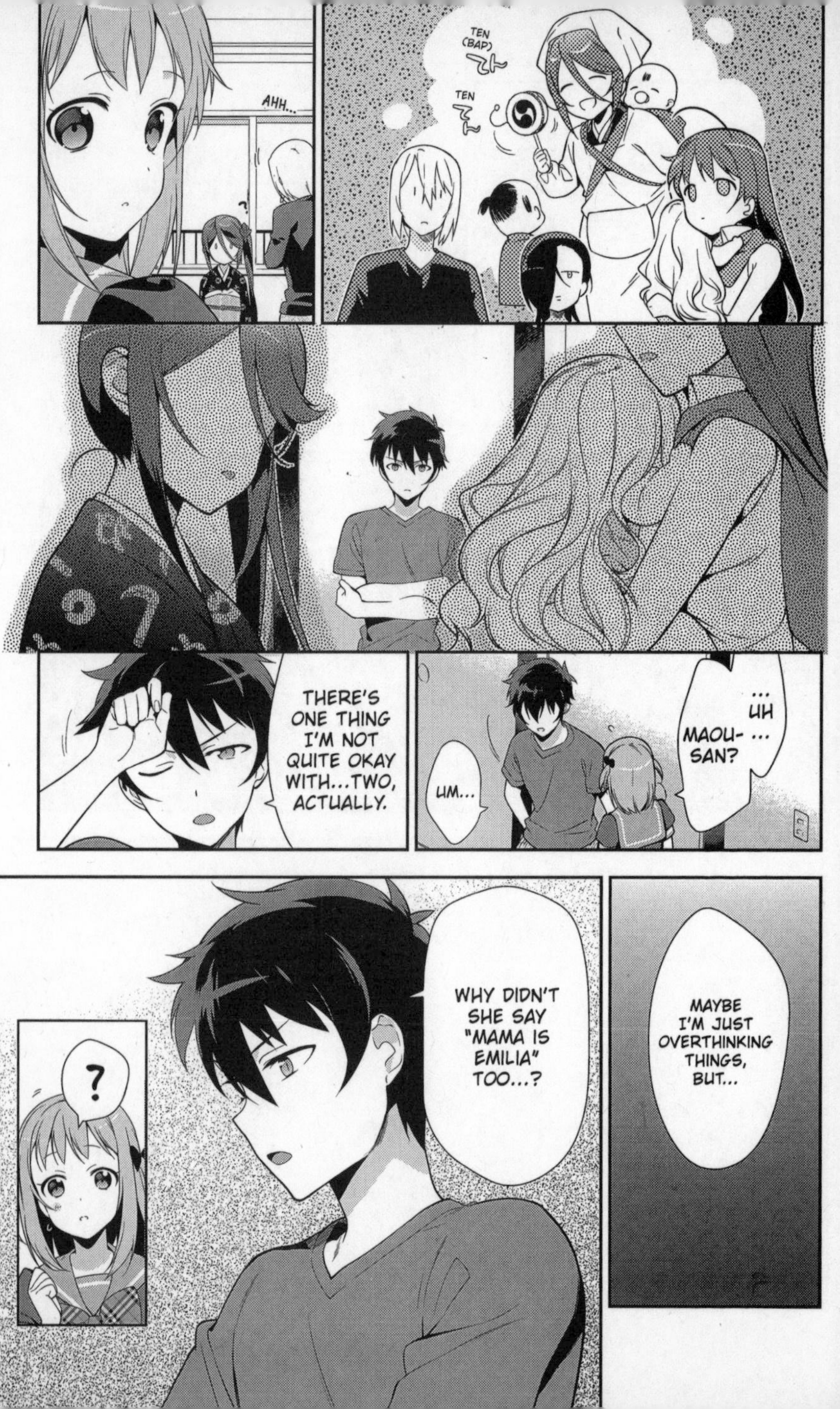
TEN (BAP) てん
TEN てん
AHH...
... UH ... MAOU-SAN?
UM...
THERE'S ONE THING I'M NOT QUITE OKAY WITH...TWO, ACTUALLY.
MAYBE I'M JUST OVERTHINKING THINGS, BUT...
WHY DIDN'T SHE SAY "MAMA IS EMILIA" TOO...?
?

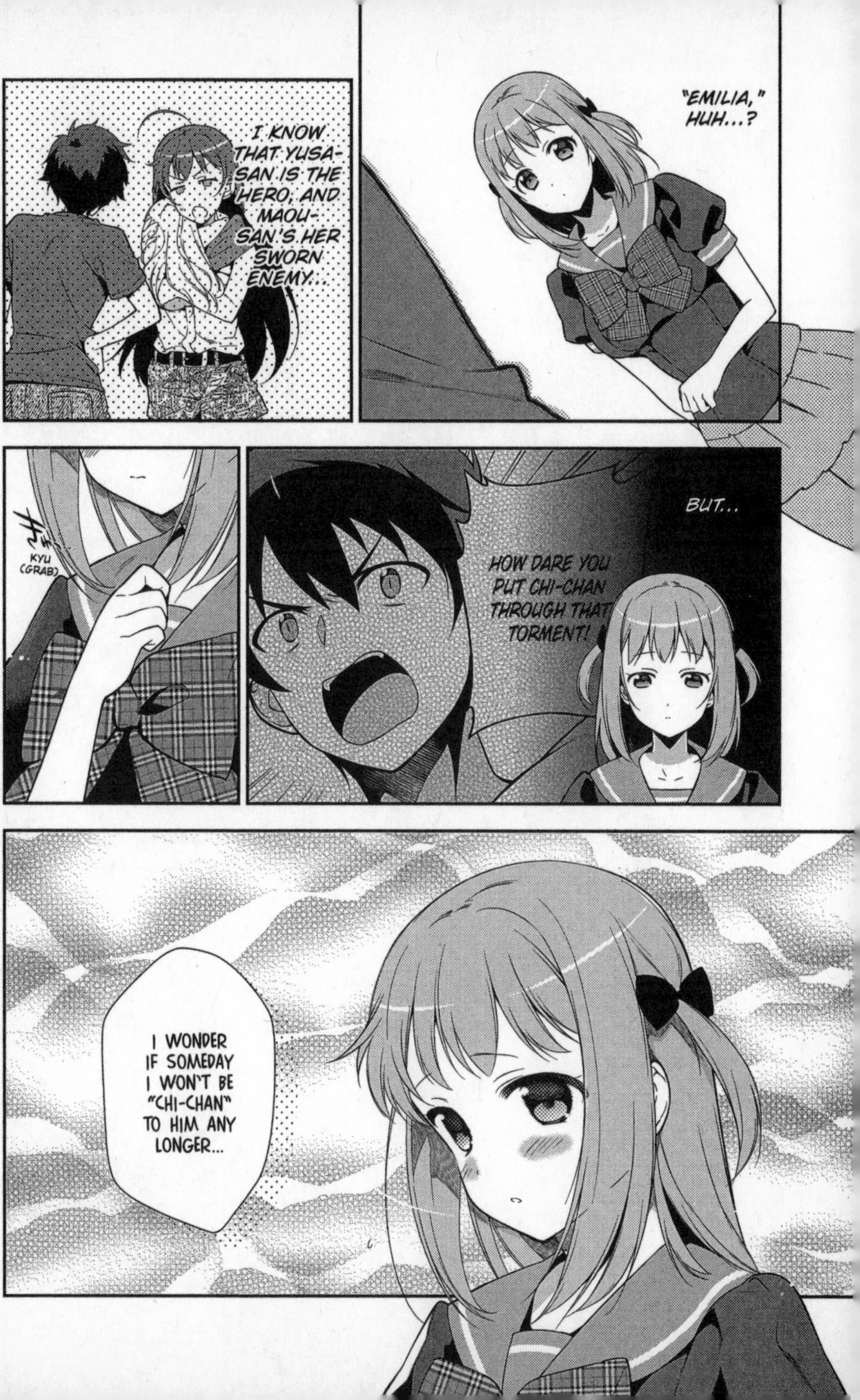
"EMILIA," HUH...?
I KNOW THAT YUSA-SAN IS THE HERO, AND MAOU-SAN'S HER SWORN ENEMY...
BUT...
HOW DARE YOU PUT CHI-CHAN THROUGH THAT TORMENT!
KYU (GRAB)
I WONDER IF SOMEDAY I WON'T BE "CHI-CHAN" TO HIM ANY LONGER...

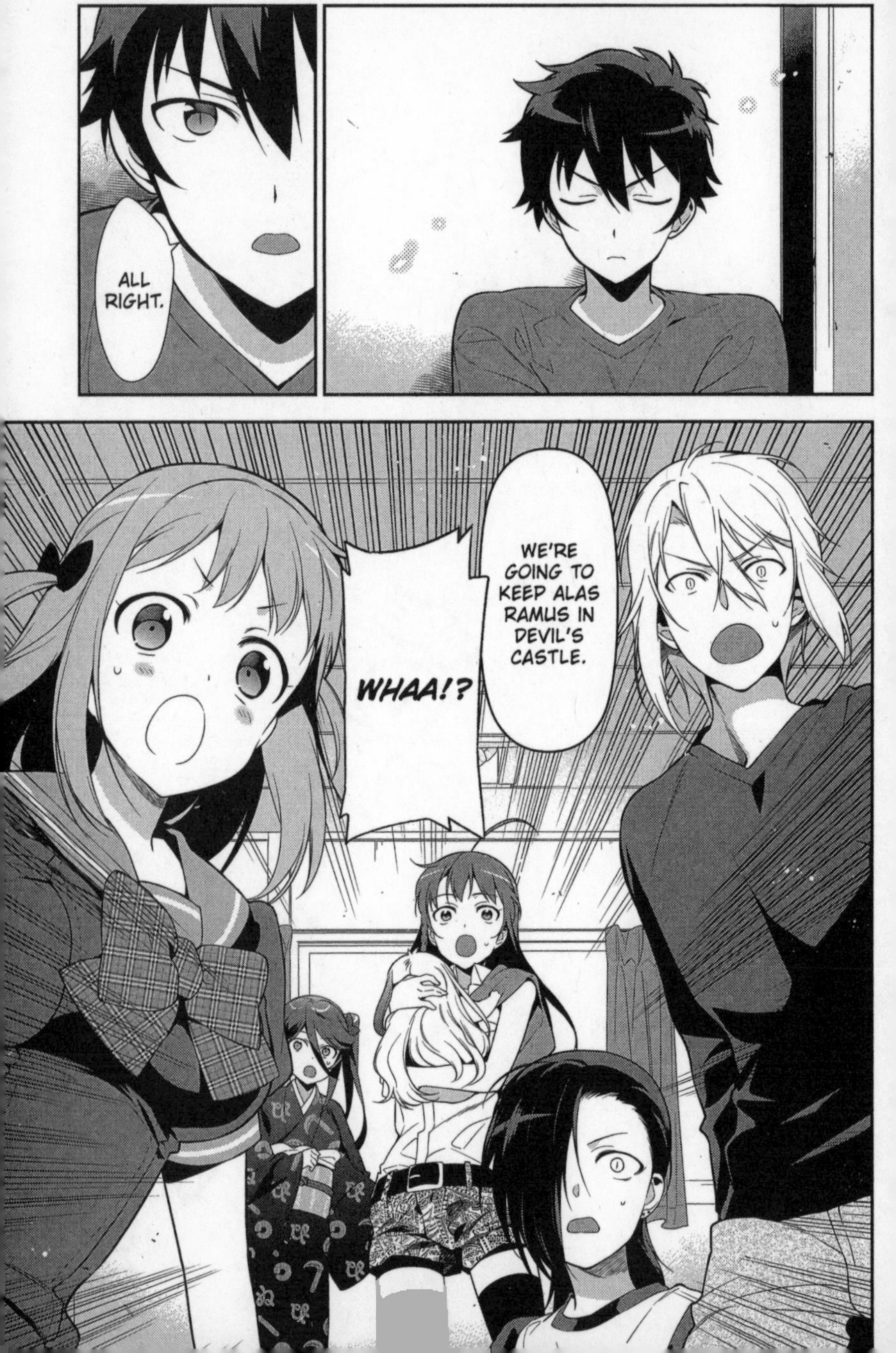
ALL RIGHT.
WE'RE GOING TO KEEP ALAS RAMUS IN DEVIL'S CASTLE.
WHAA!?

THE DEVIL IS A PART-TIMER!

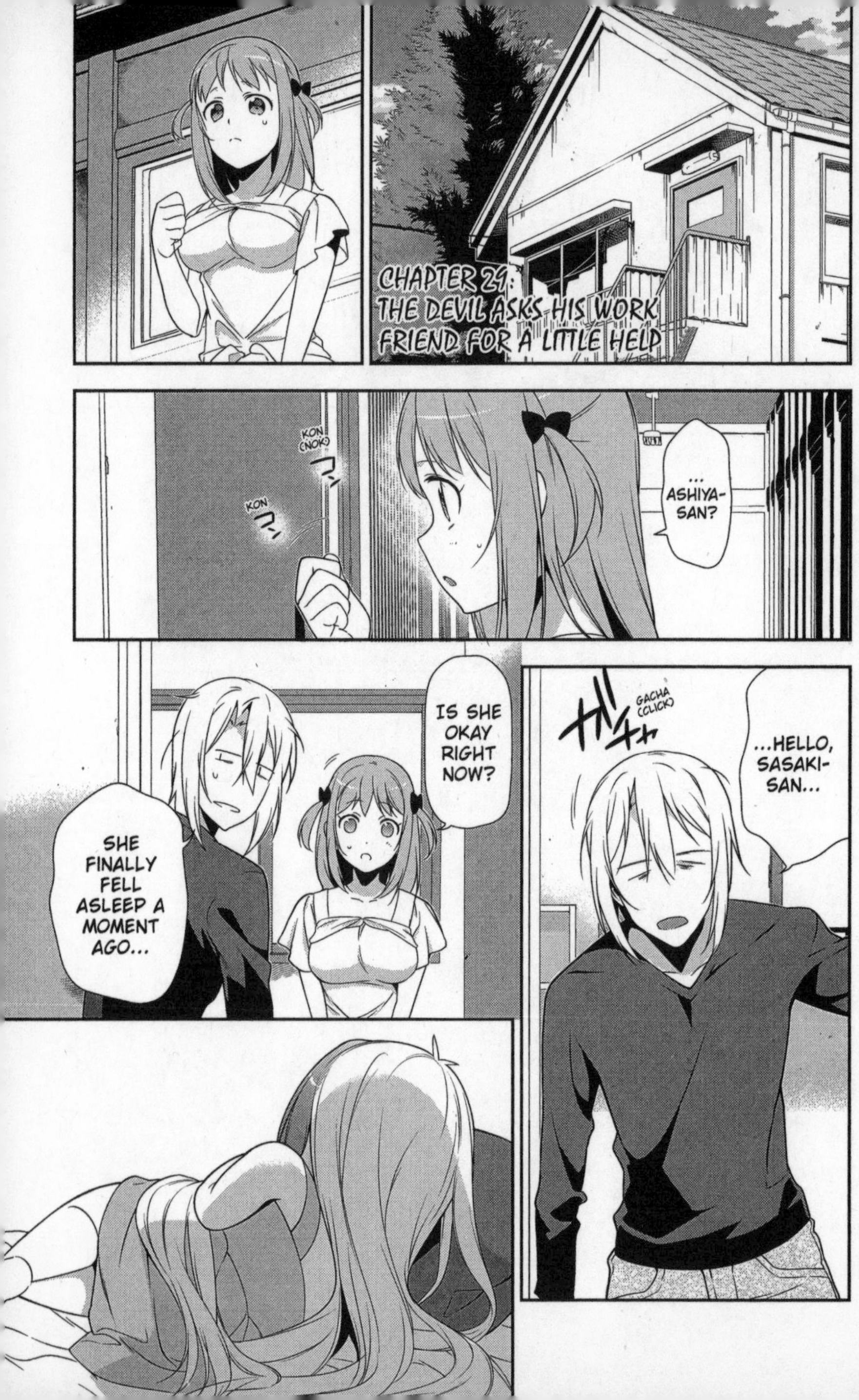
CHAPTER 29: THE DEVIL ASKS HIS WORK FRIEND FOR A LITTLE HELP
... ASHIYA-SAN?
KON (NOK)
KON
GACHA (CLICK)
...HELLO, SASAKI-SAN...
IS SHE OKAY RIGHT NOW?
SHE FINALLY FELL ASLEEP A MOMENT AGO...

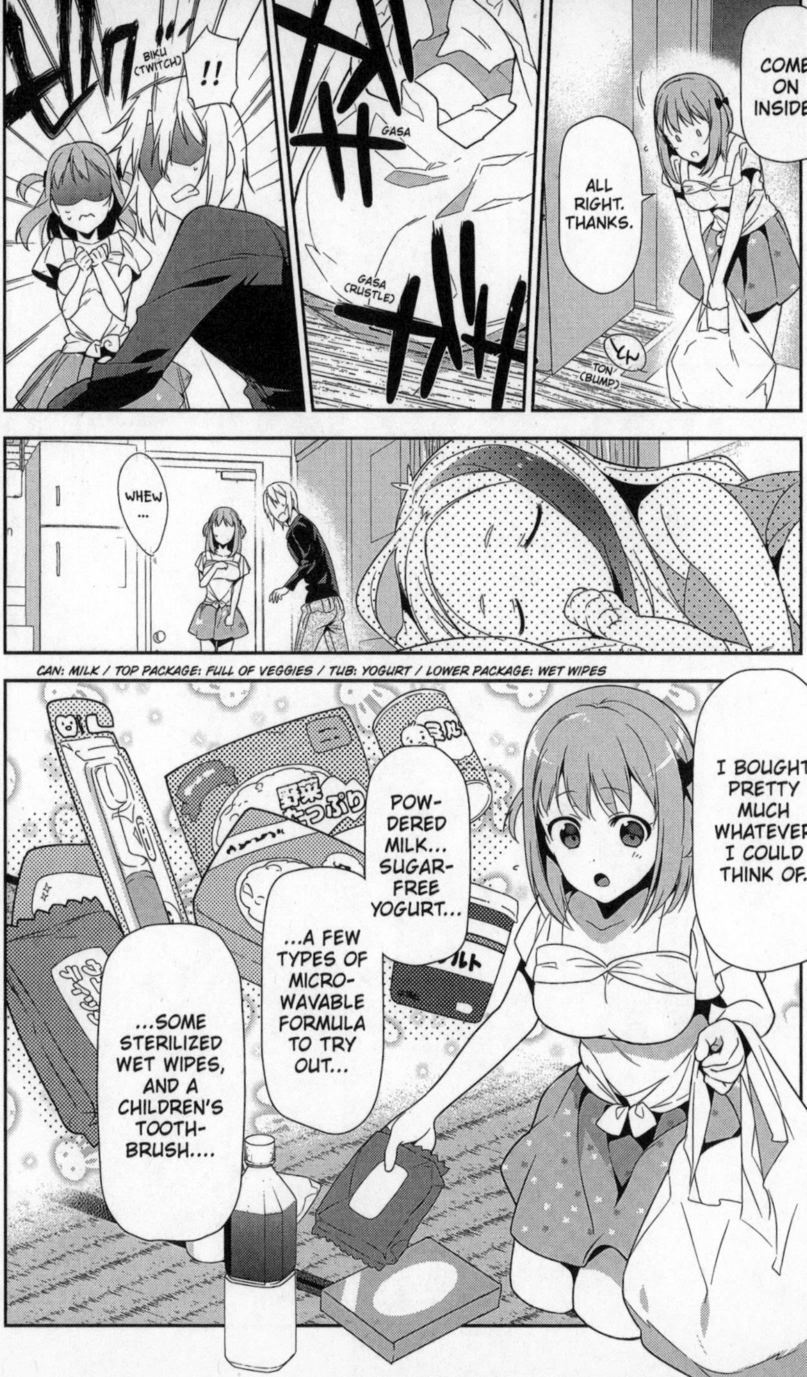
COME ON INSIDE.
ALL RIGHT. THANKS.
とん
TON (BUMP)
GASA
GASA (RUSTLE)
BIKU (TWITCH)
!!
WHEW...
CAN: MILK / TOP PACKAGE: FULL OF VEGGIES / TUB: YOGURT / LOWER PACKAGE: WET WIPES
I BOUGHT PRETTY MUCH WHATEVER I COULD THINK OF.
POW-DERED MILK... SUGAR-FREE YOGURT...
...A FEW TYPES OF MICRO-WAVABLE FORMULA TO TRY OUT...
...SOME STERILIZED WET WIPES, AND A CHILDREN'S TOOTH-BRUSH....

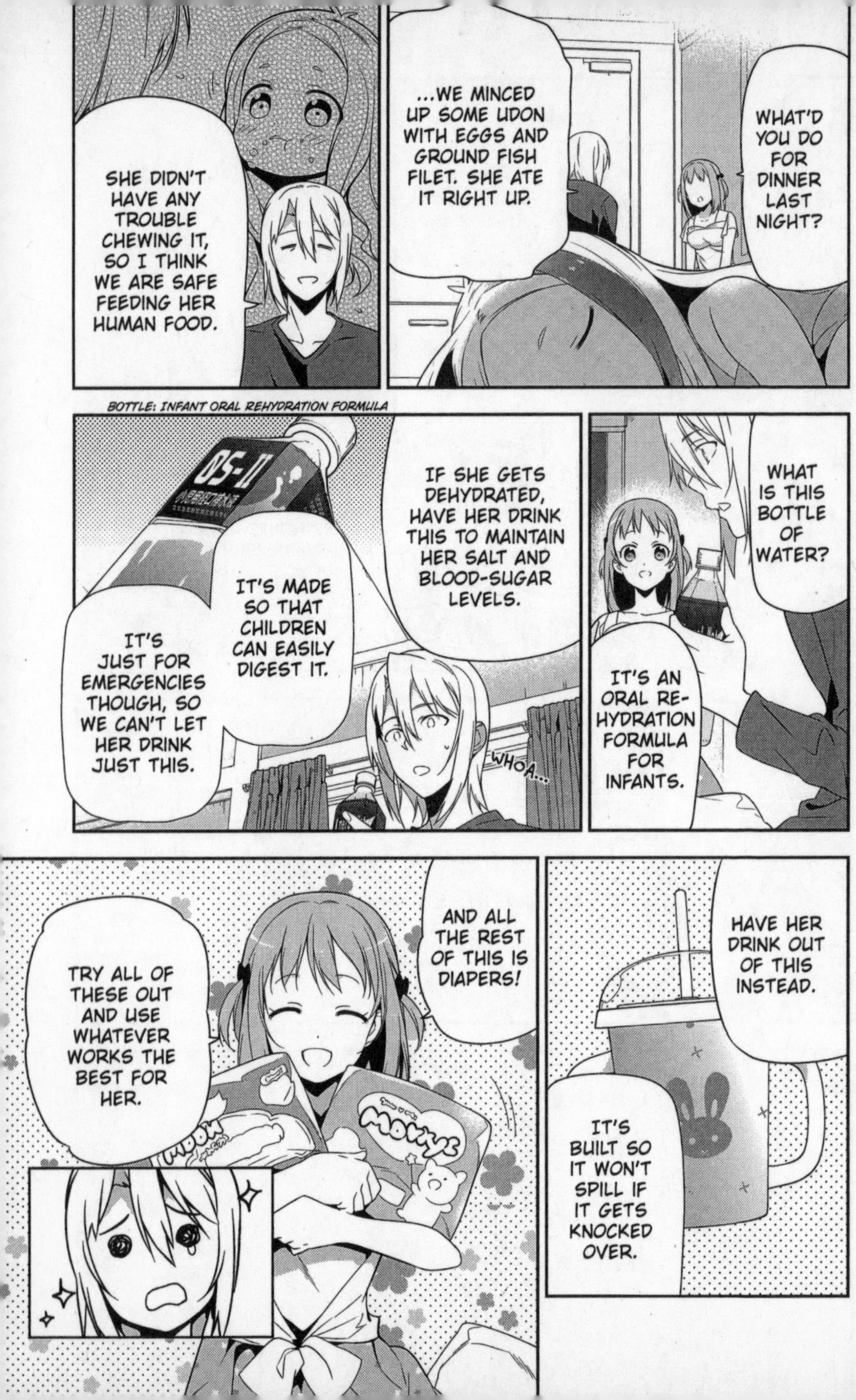
WHAT'D YOU DO FOR DINNER LAST NIGHT?
...WE MINCED UP SOME UDON WITH EGGS AND GROUND FISH FILET. SHE ATE IT RIGHT UP.
SHE DIDN'T HAVE ANY TROUBLE CHEWING IT, SO I THINK WE ARE SAFE FEEDING HER HUMAN FOOD.
BOTTLE: INFANT ORAL REHYDRATION FORMULA
WHAT IS THIS BOTTLE OF WATER?
IT'S AN ORAL RE-HYDRATION FORMULA FOR INFANTS.
IF SHE GETS DEHYDRATED, HAVE HER DRINK THIS TO MAINTAIN HER SALT AND BLOOD-SUGAR LEVELS.
IT'S MADE SO THAT CHILDREN CAN EASILY DIGEST IT.
IT'S JUST FOR EMERGENCIES THOUGH, SO WE CAN'T LET HER DRINK JUST THIS.
WHOA...
HAVE HER DRINK OUT OF THIS INSTEAD.
IT'S BUILT SO IT WON'T SPILL IF IT GETS KNOCKED OVER.
AND ALL THE REST OF THIS IS DIAPERS!
TRY ALL OF THESE OUT AND USE WHATEVER WORKS THE BEST FOR HER.

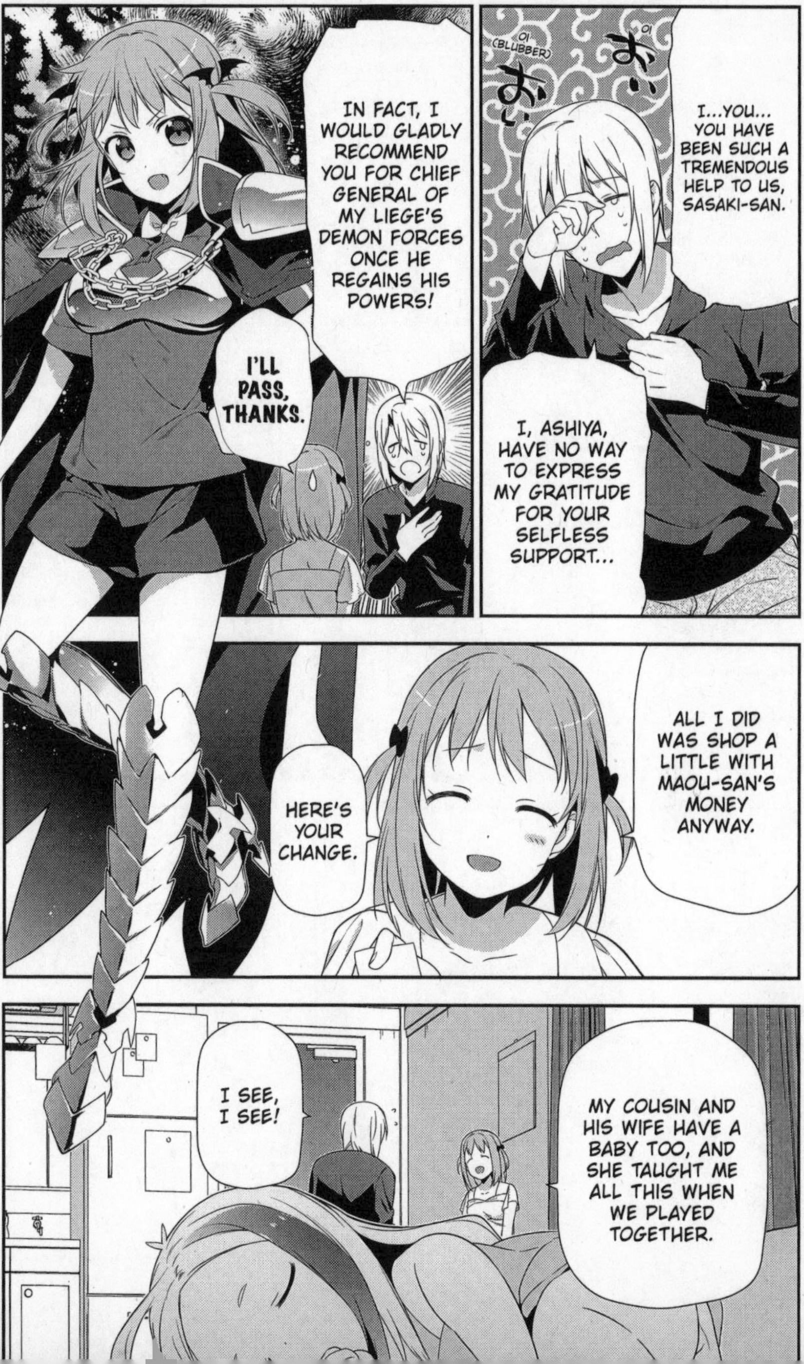
OI (BLUBBER) OI
I...YOU... YOU HAVE BEEN SUCH A TREMENDOUS HELP TO US, SASAKI-SAN.
I, ASHIYA, HAVE NO WAY TO EXPRESS MY GRATITUDE FOR YOUR SELFLESS SUPPORT...
IN FACT, I WOULD GLADLY RECOMMEND YOU FOR CHIEF GENERAL OF MY LIEGE'S DEMON FORCES ONCE HE REGAINS HIS POWERS!
I'LL PASS, THANKS.
ALL I DID WAS SHOP A LITTLE WITH MAOU-SAN'S MONEY ANYWAY.
HERE'S YOUR CHANGE.
MY COUSIN AND HIS WIFE HAVE A BABY TOO, AND SHE TAUGHT ME ALL THIS WHEN WE PLAYED TOGETHER.
I SEE, I SEE!

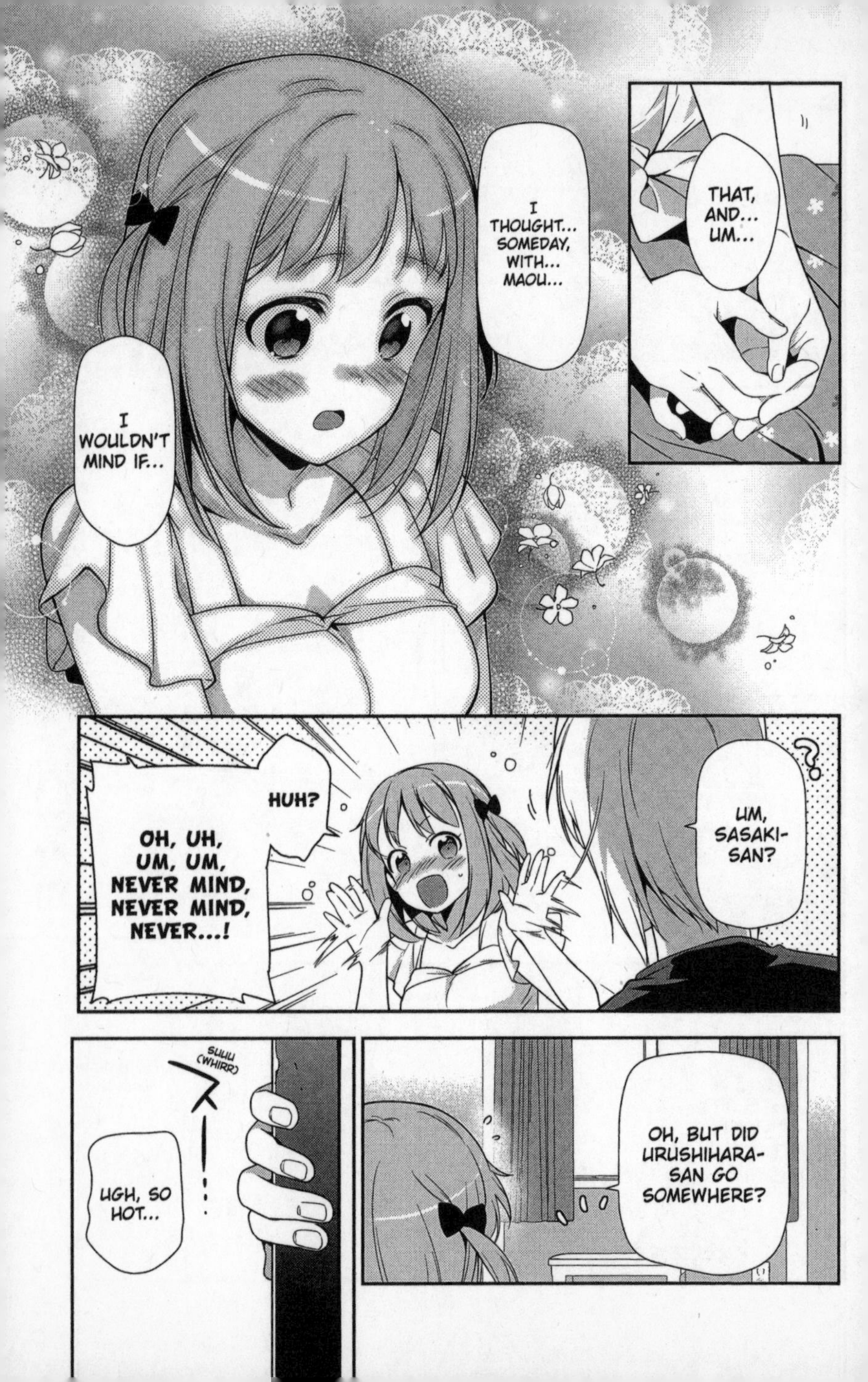
THAT, AND... UM...
I THOUGHT... SOMEDAY, WITH... MAOU...
I WOULDN'T MIND IF...
UM, SASAKI-SAN?
HUH?
OH, UH, UM, UM, NEVER MIND, NEVER MIND, NEVER...!
OH, BUT DID URUSHIHARA-SAN GO SOMEWHERE?
SUUU (WHIRR)
UGH, SO HOT...

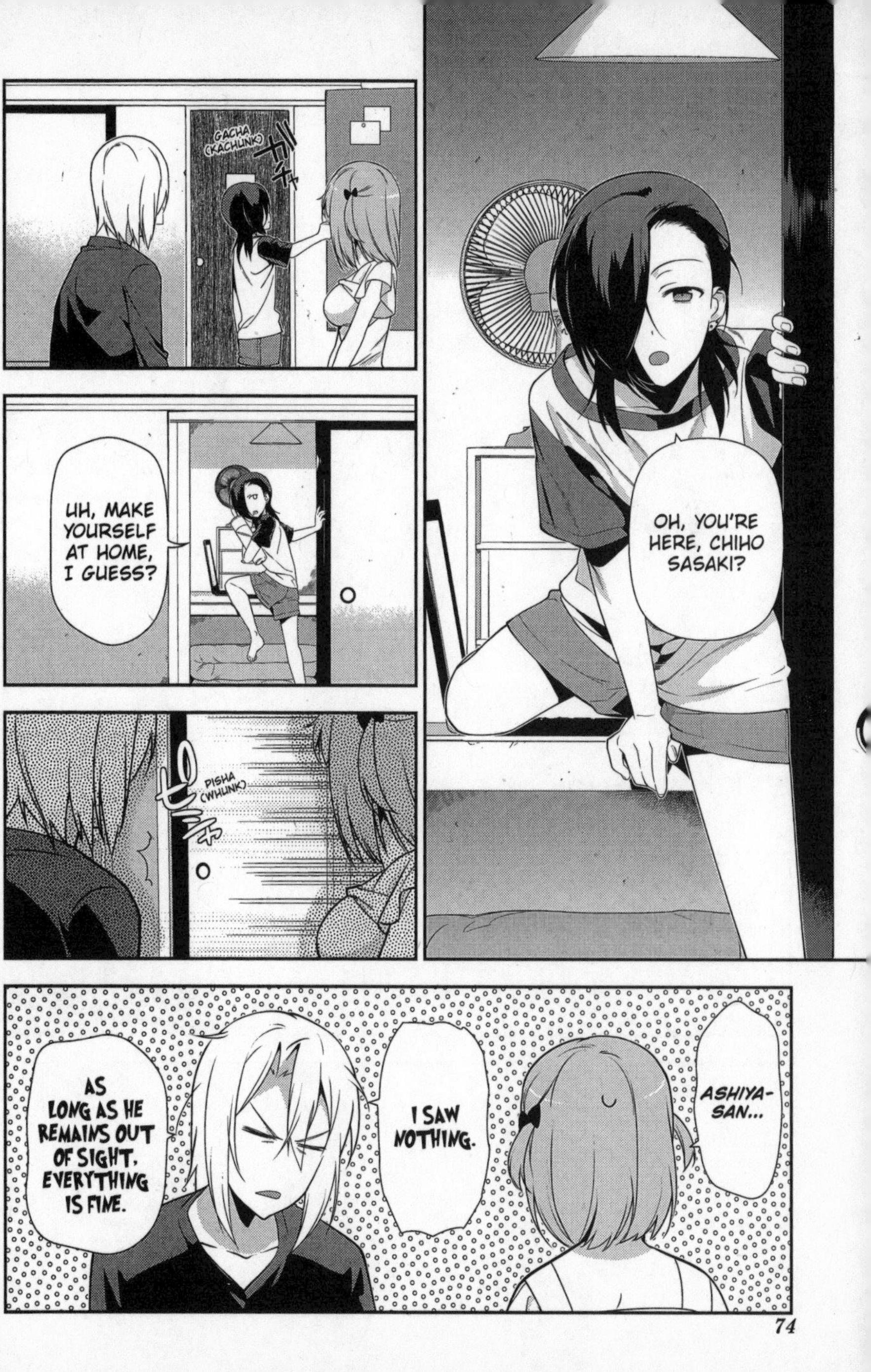
OH, YOU'RE HERE, CHIHO SASAKI?
GACHA (KACHUNK)
UH, MAKE YOURSELF AT HOME, I GUESS?
PISHA (WHUNK)
ASHIYA-SAN...
I SAW NOTHING.
AS LONG AS HE REMAINS OUT OF SIGHT, EVERYTHING IS FINE.

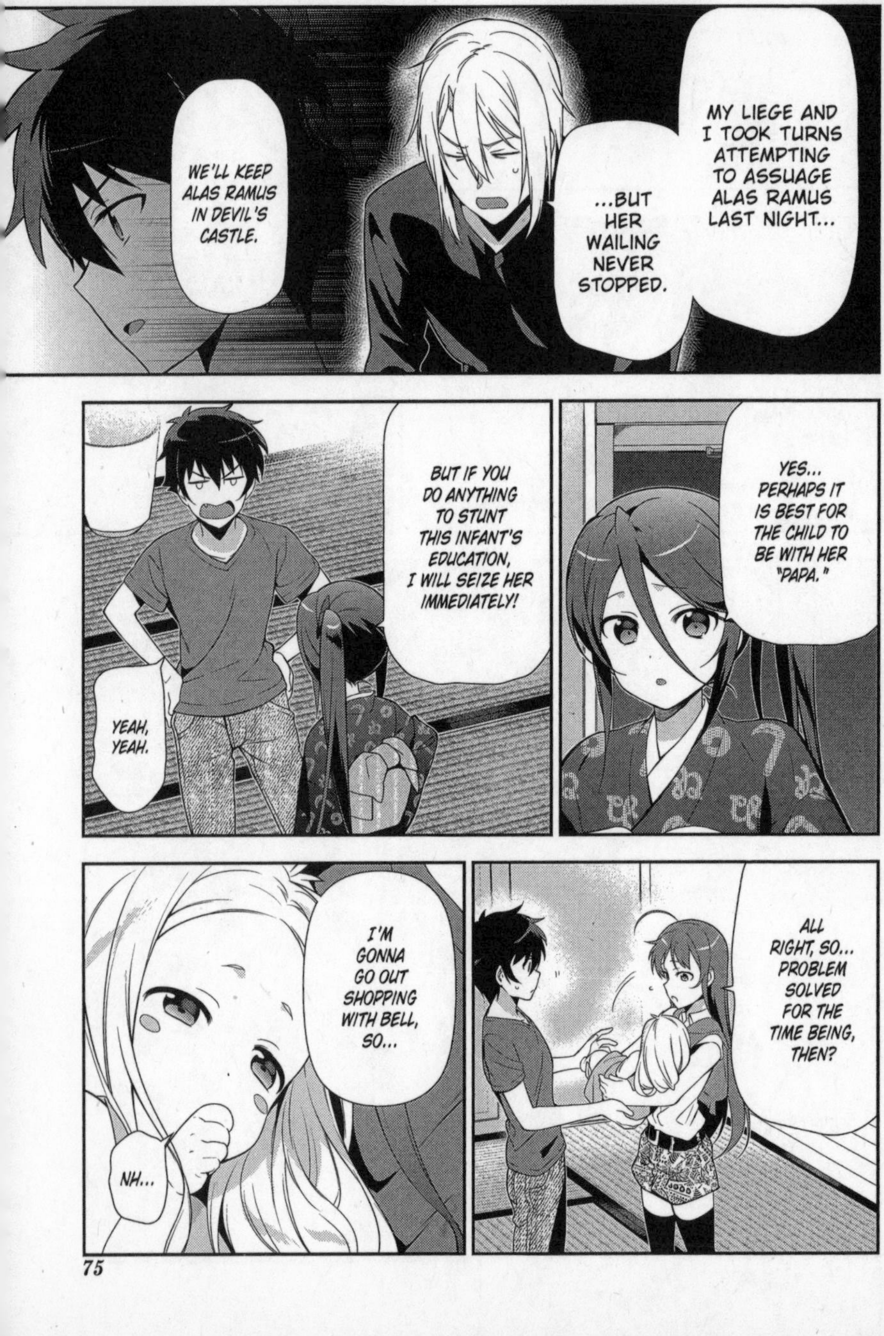
MY LIEGE AND I TOOK TURNS ATTEMPTING TO ASSUAGE ALAS RAMUS LAST NIGHT...
...BUT HER WAILING NEVER STOPPED.
WE'LL KEEP ALAS RAMUS IN DEVIL'S CASTLE.
YES... PERHAPS IT IS BEST FOR THE CHILD TO BE WITH HER "PAPA."
BUT IF YOU DO ANYTHING TO STUNT THIS INFANT'S EDUCATION, I WILL SEIZE HER IMMEDIATELY!
YEAH, YEAH.
ALL RIGHT, SO... PROBLEM SOLVED FOR THE TIME BEING, THEN?
I'M GONNA GO OUT SHOPPING WITH BELL, SO...
NH...

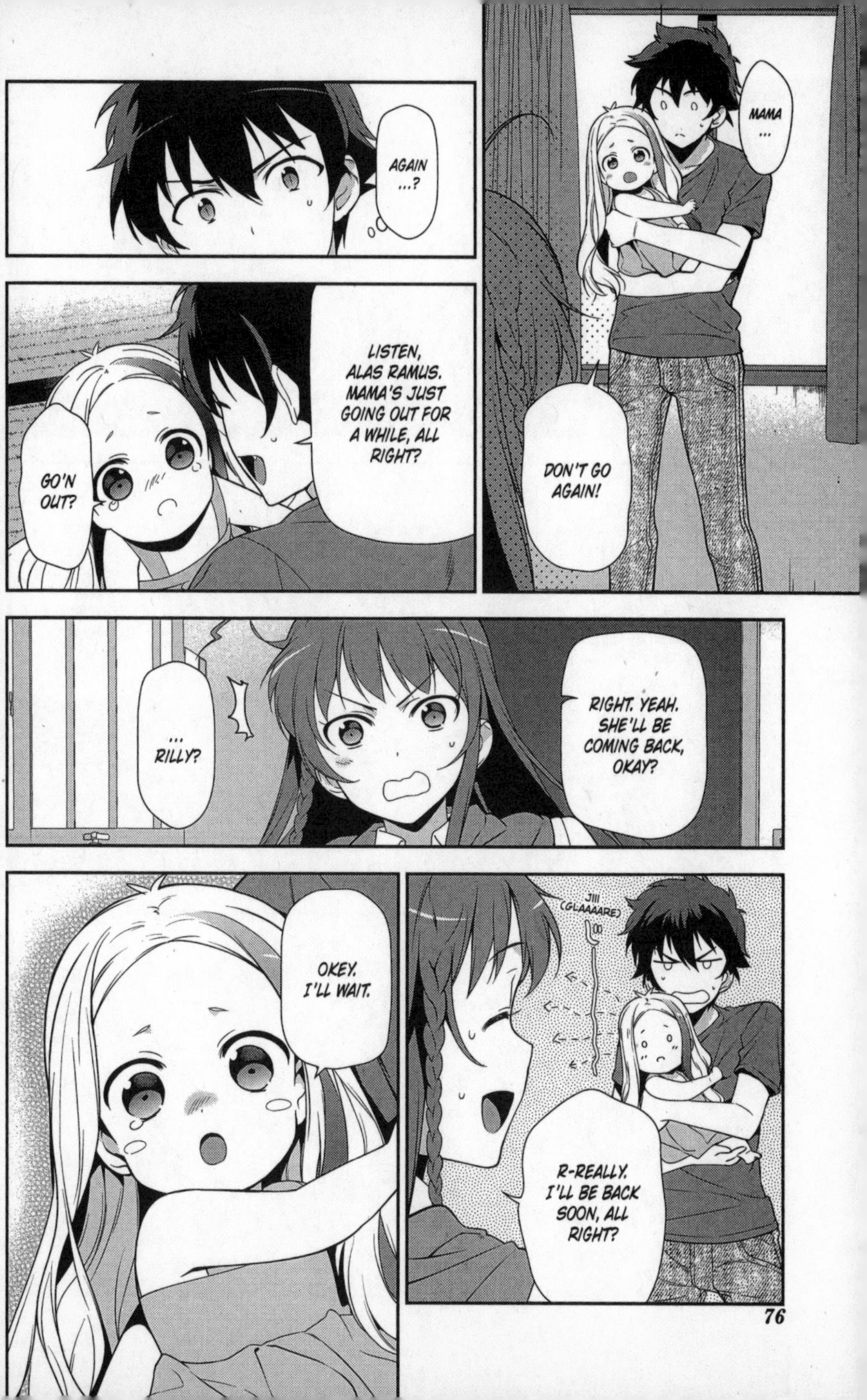
MAMA ...
DON'T GO AGAIN!
AGAIN ...?
LISTEN, ALAS RAMUS. MAMA'S JUST GOING OUT FOR A WHILE, ALL RIGHT?
GO'N OUT?
RIGHT. YEAH. SHE'LL BE COMING BACK, OKAY?
... RILLY?
JIII (GLAAAARE)
R-REALLY. I'LL BE BACK SOON, ALL RIGHT?
OKEY. I'LL WAIT.

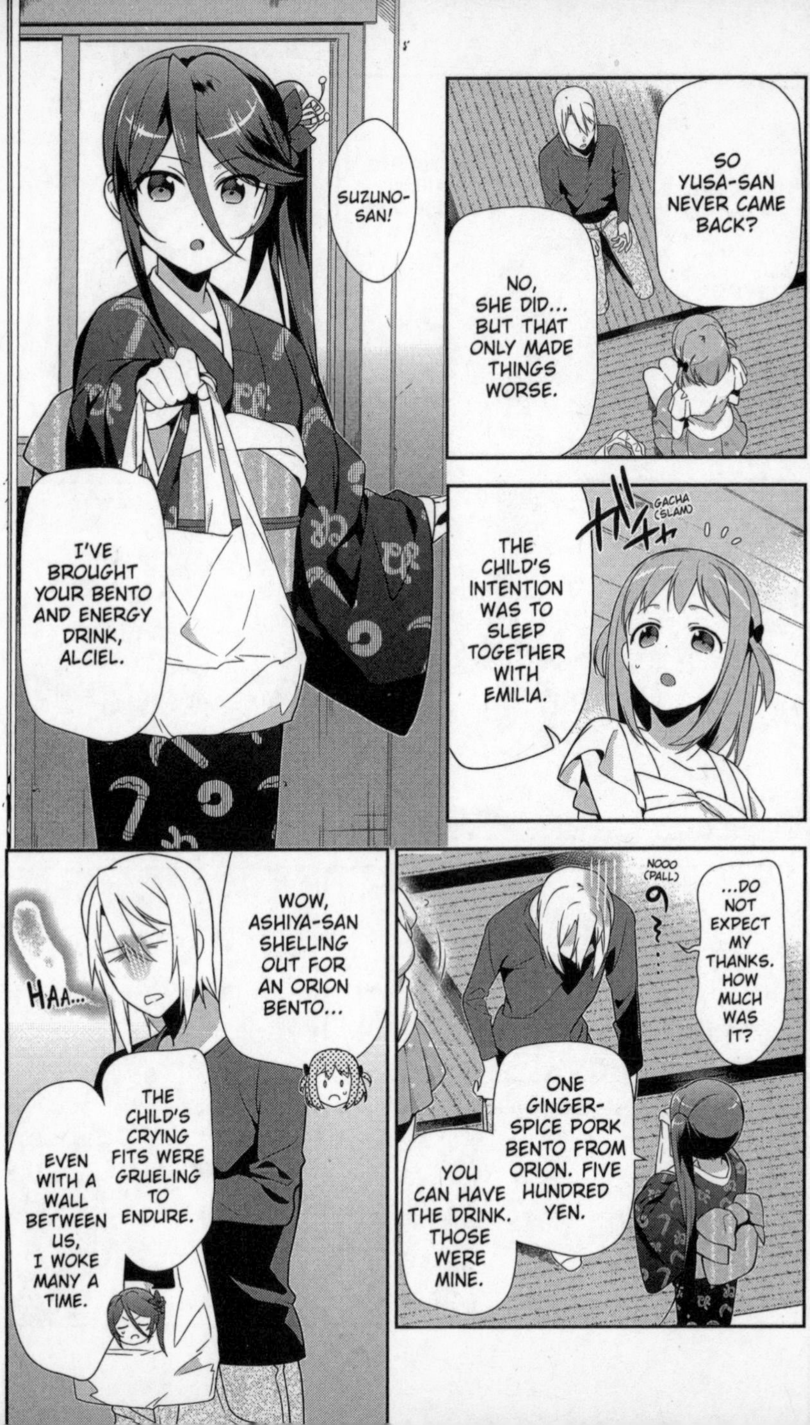

SO YUSA-SAN NEVER CAME BACK?
NO, SHE DID... BUT THAT ONLY MADE THINGS WORSE.
GACHA (SLAM)
THE CHILD'S INTENTION WAS TO SLEEP TOGETHER WITH EMILIA.
SUZUNO-SAN!
I'VE BROUGHT YOUR BENTO AND ENERGY DRINK, ALCIEL.
...DO NOT EXPECT MY THANKS. HOW MUCH WAS IT?
NOOO (PALL)
ONE GINGER-SPICE PORK BENTO FROM ORION. FIVE HUNDRED YEN.
YOU CAN HAVE THE DRINK. THOSE WERE MINE.
WOW, ASHIYA-SAN SHELLING OUT FOR AN ORION BENTO...
HAA...
THE CHILD'S CRYING FITS WERE GRUELING TO ENDURE.
EVEN WITH A WALL BETWEEN US, I WOKE MANY A TIME.

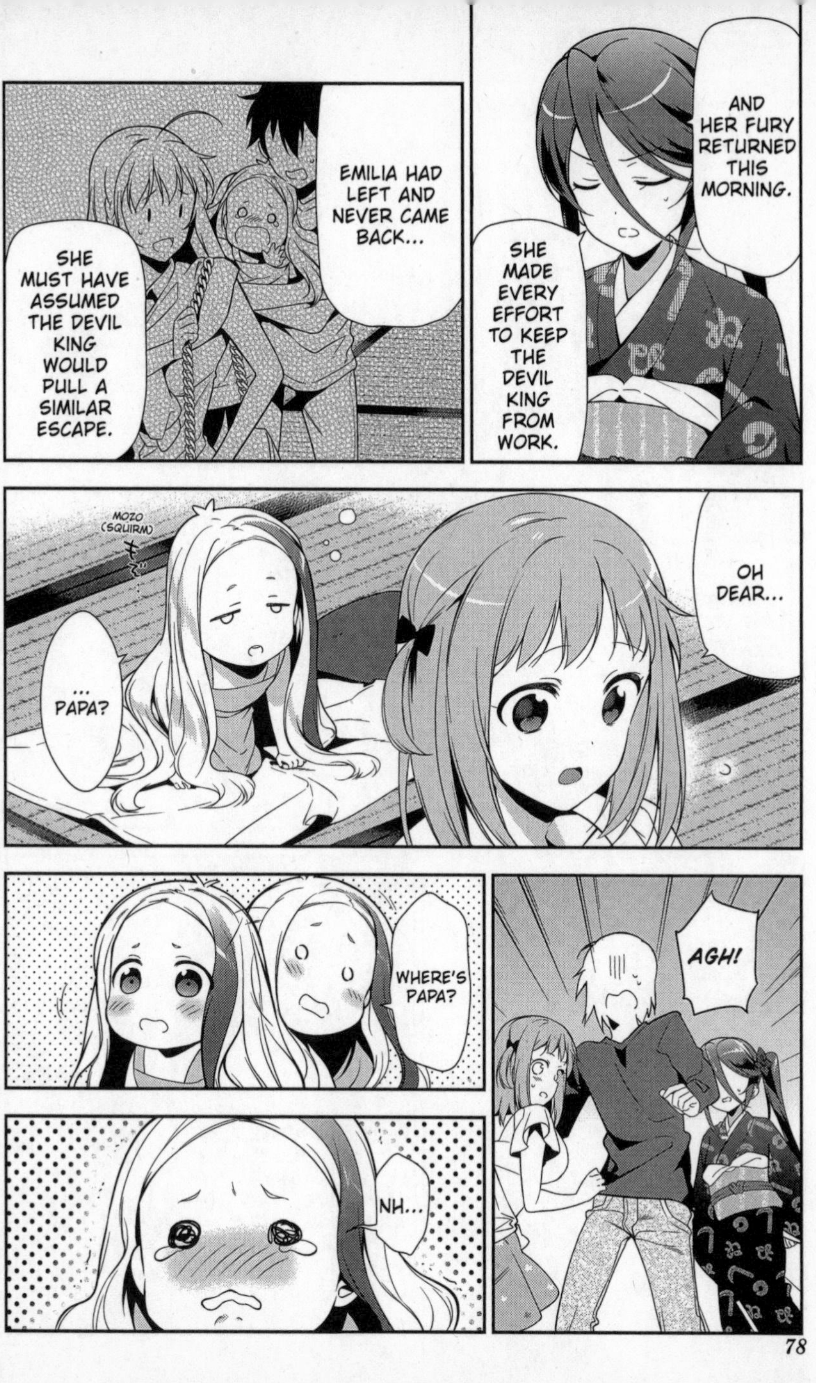
AND HER FURY RETURNED THIS MORNING.
SHE MADE EVERY EFFORT TO KEEP THE DEVIL KING FROM WORK.
EMILIA HAD LEFT AND NEVER CAME BACK...
SHE MUST HAVE ASSUMED THE DEVIL KING WOULD PULL A SIMILAR ESCAPE.
OH DEAR...
MOZO (SQUIRM)
... PAPA?
AGH!
WHERE'S PAPA?
NH...

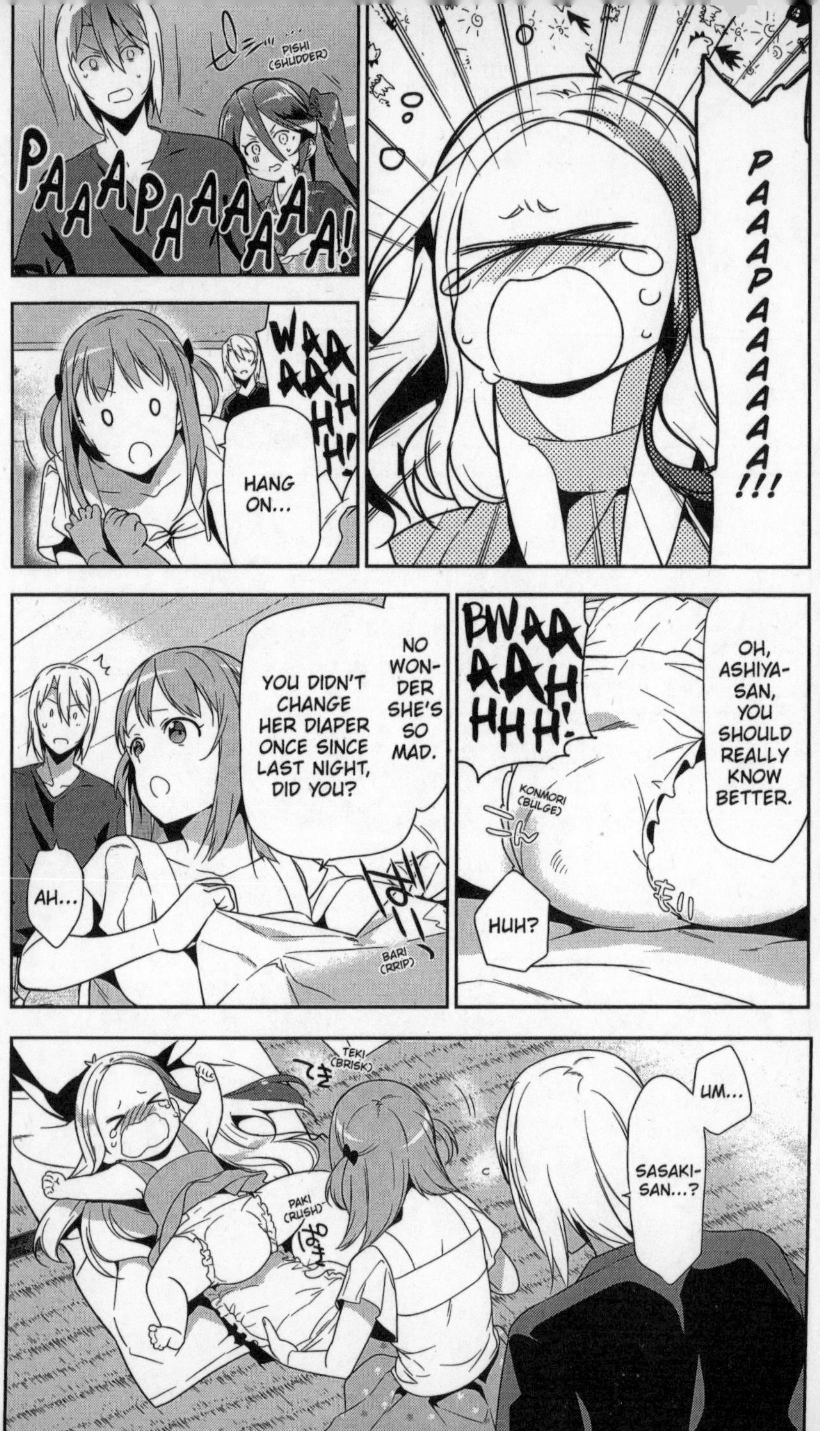
PAAAPAAAAAAA!!!
PISHI (SHUDDER)
PAAAPAAAAAAA!
WAAAAAHHHH!
HANG ON...
BWAAAAHHHH!
OH, ASHIYA-SAN, YOU SHOULD REALLY KNOW BETTER.
KONMORI (BULGE)
HUH?
NO WON-DER SHE'S SO MAD.
YOU DIDN'T CHANGE HER DIAPER ONCE SINCE LAST NIGHT, DID YOU?
AH...
BARI (RRIP)
UM...
SASAKI-SAN...?
TEKI (BRISK)
PAKI (RUSH)

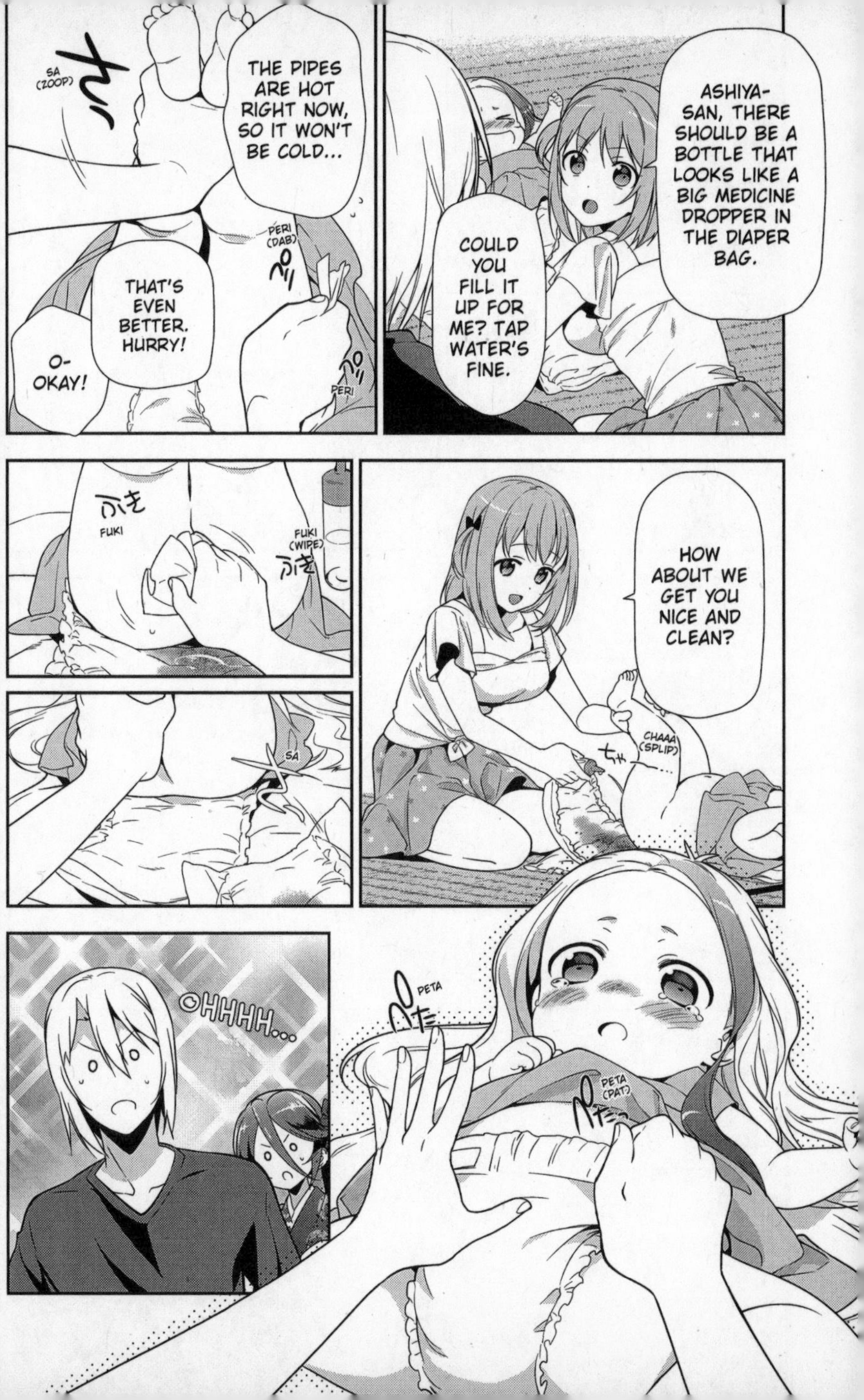
ASHIYA-SAN, THERE SHOULD BE A BOTTLE THAT LOOKS LIKE A BIG MEDICINE DROPPER IN THE DIAPER BAG.
COULD YOU FILL IT UP FOR ME? TAP WATER'S FINE.
SA (ZOOP)
THE PIPES ARE HOT RIGHT NOW, SO IT WON'T BE COLD...
PERI (DAB)
THAT'S EVEN BETTER. HURRY!
O-OKAY!
PERI
HOW ABOUT WE GET YOU NICE AND CLEAN?
CHAAA (SPLIP)
ふき
FUKI (WIPE)
ふき
FUKI
SA
PETA
PETA (PAT)
OHHHH...

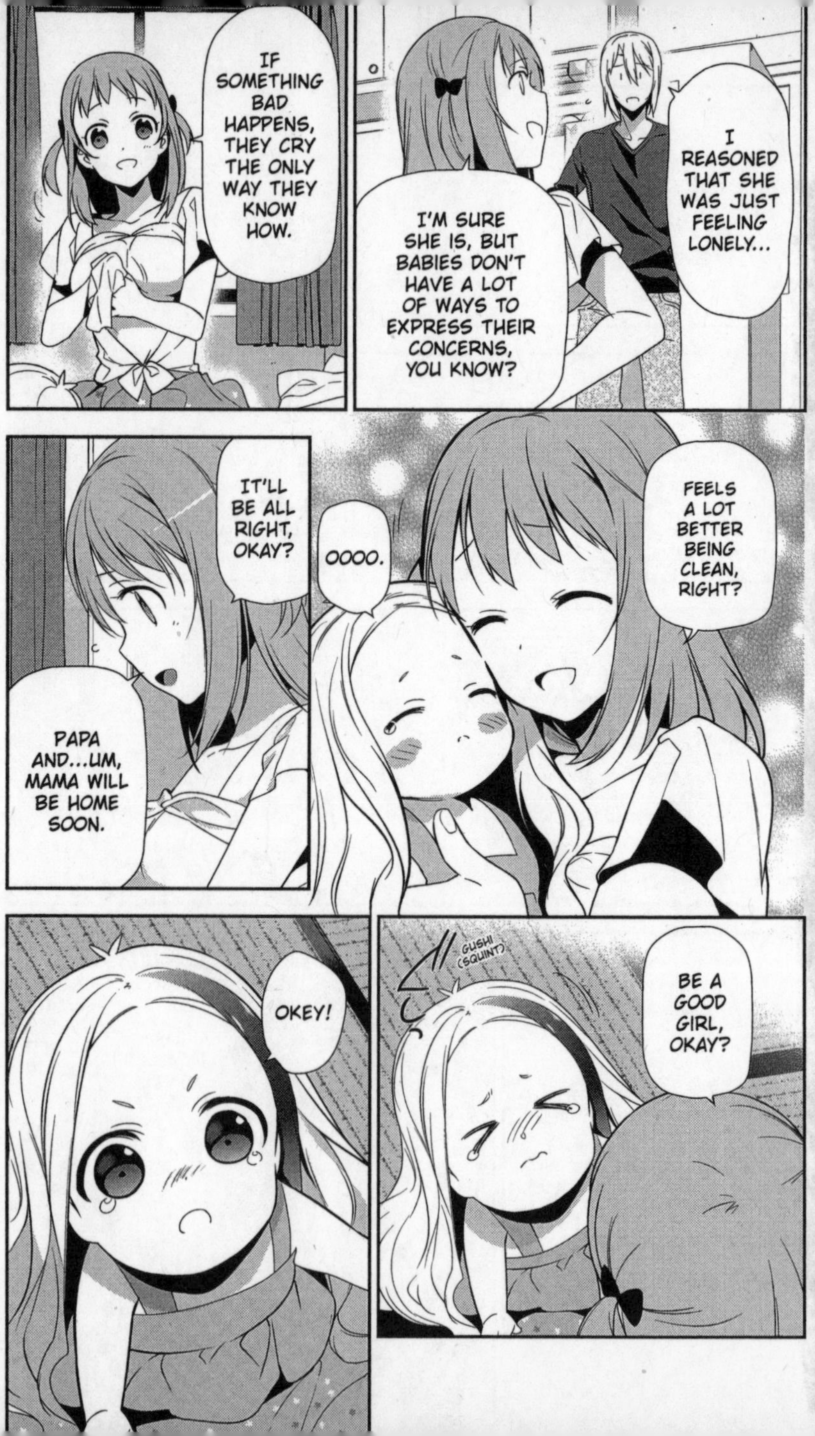
I REASONED THAT SHE WAS JUST FEELING LONELY...
I'M SURE SHE IS, BUT BABIES DON'T HAVE A LOT OF WAYS TO EXPRESS THEIR CONCERNS, YOU KNOW?
IF SOMETHING BAD HAPPENS, THEY CRY THE ONLY WAY THEY KNOW HOW.
FEELS A LOT BETTER BEING CLEAN, RIGHT?
OOOO.
IT'LL BE ALL RIGHT, OKAY?
PAPA AND...UM, MAMA WILL BE HOME SOON.
BE A GOOD GIRL, OKAY?
GUSHI (SQUINT)
OKEY!

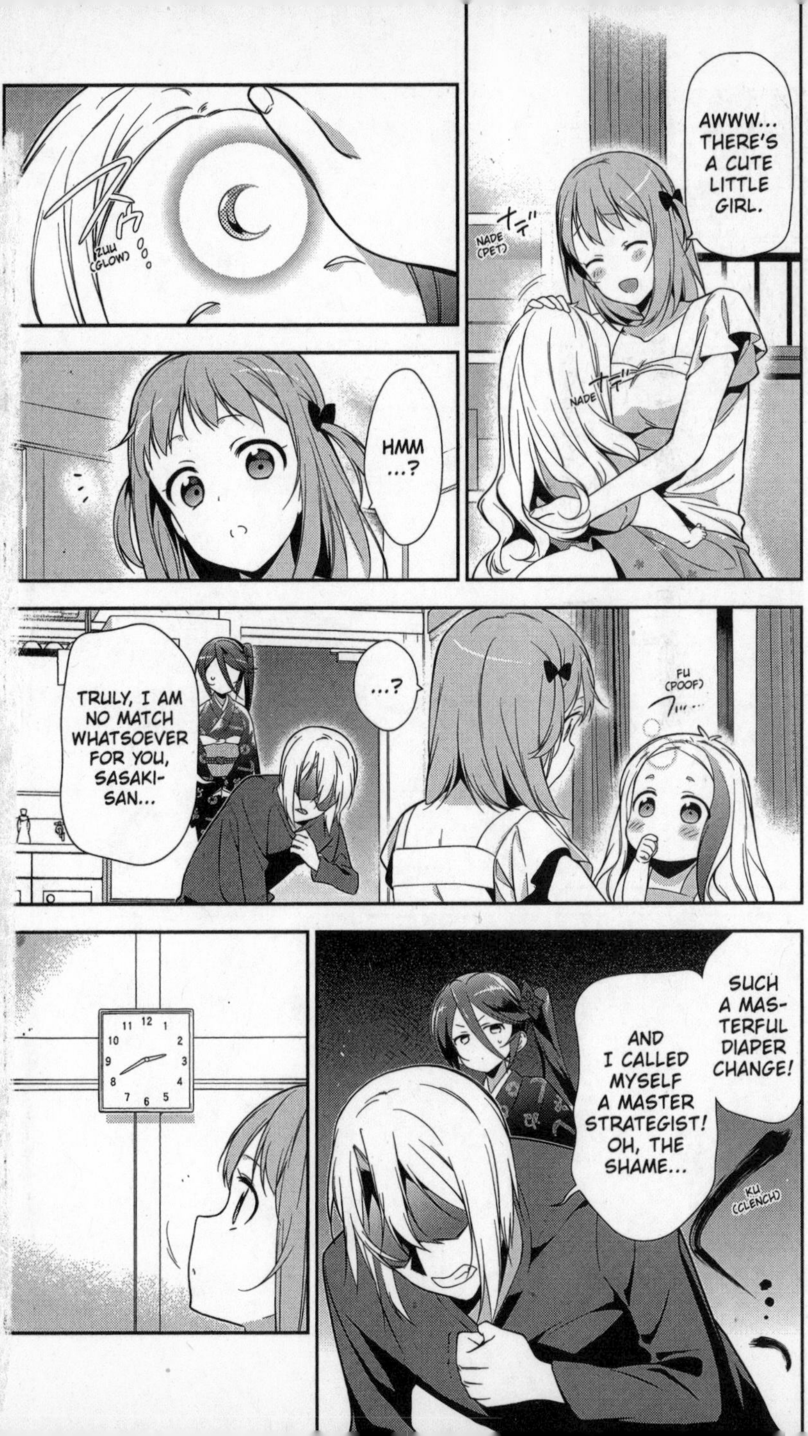
AWWW... THERE'S A CUTE LITTLE GIRL.
NADE (PET)
NADE
ZUU (GLOW)
HMM ...?
...
FU (POOF)
...?
TRULY, I AM NO MATCH WHATSOEVER FOR YOU, SASAKI-SAN...
SUCH A MAS-TERFUL DIAPER CHANGE!
AND I CALLED MYSELF A MASTER STRATEGIST! OH, THE SHAME...
KU (CLENCH)
...
...

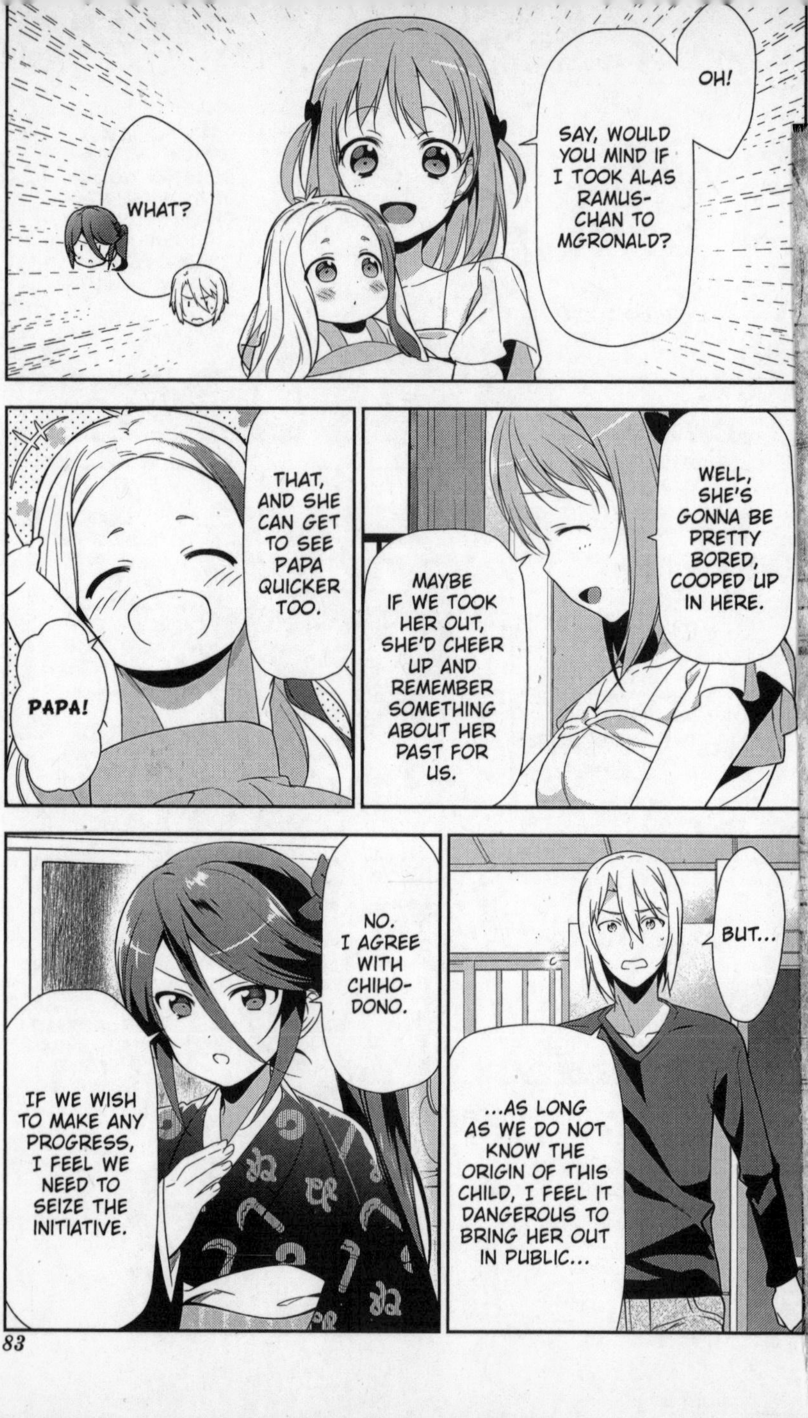
OH!
SAY, WOULD YOU MIND IF I TOOK ALAS RAMUS-CHAN TO MGRONALD?
WHAT?
WELL, SHE'S GONNA BE PRETTY BORED, COOPED UP IN HERE.
MAYBE IF WE TOOK HER OUT, SHE'D CHEER UP AND REMEMBER SOMETHING ABOUT HER PAST FOR US.
THAT, AND SHE CAN GET TO SEE PAPA QUICKER TOO.
PAPA!
BUT...
...AS LONG AS WE DO NOT KNOW THE ORIGIN OF THIS CHILD, I FEEL IT DANGEROUS TO BRING HER OUT IN PUBLIC...
NO. I AGREE WITH CHIHO-DONO.
IF WE WISH TO MAKE ANY PROGRESS, I FEEL WE NEED TO SEIZE THE INITIATIVE.

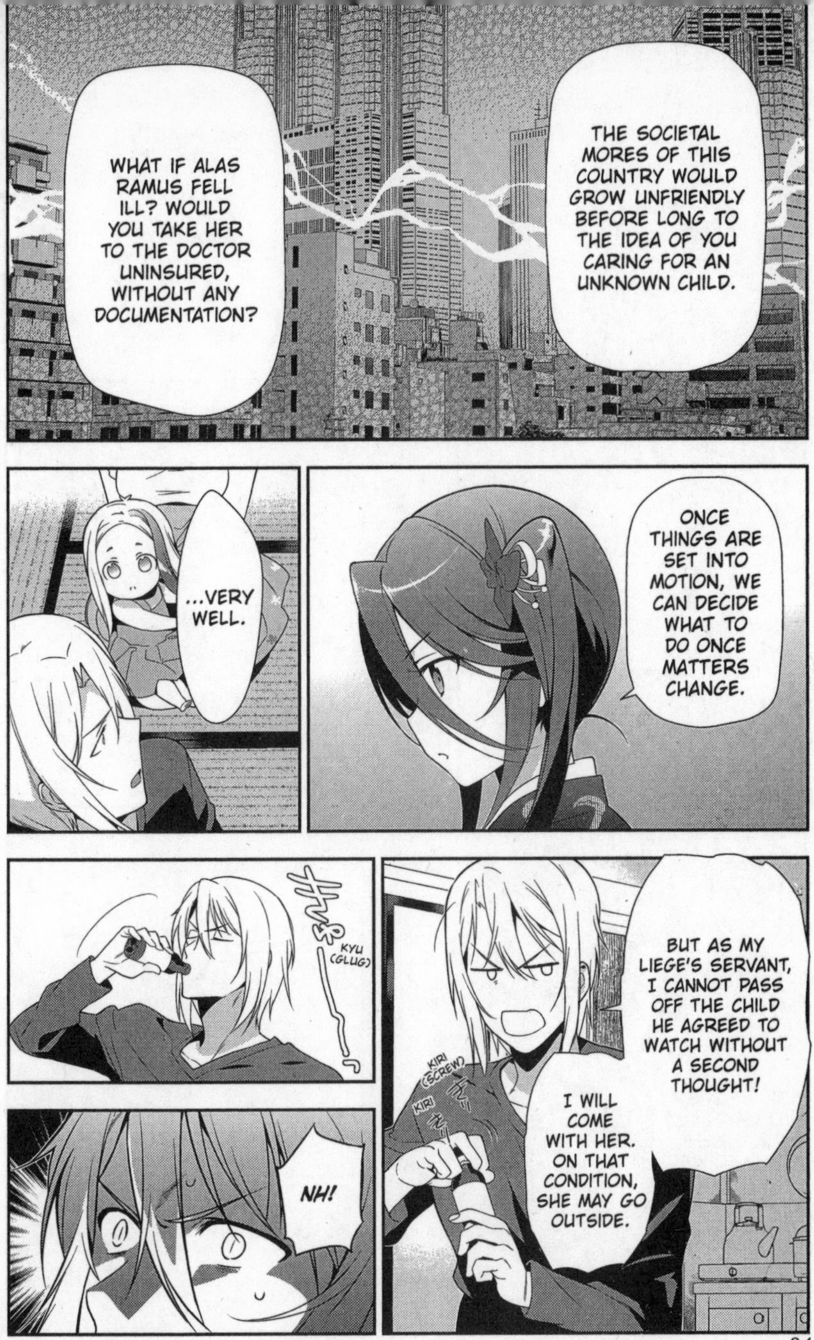
THE SOCIETAL MORES OF THIS COUNTRY WOULD GROW UNFRIENDLY BEFORE LONG TO THE IDEA OF YOU CARING FOR AN UNKNOWN CHILD.
WHAT IF ALAS RAMUS FELL ILL? WOULD YOU TAKE HER TO THE DOCTOR UNINSURED, WITHOUT ANY DOCUMENTATION?
ONCE THINGS ARE SET INTO MOTION, WE CAN DECIDE WHAT TO DO ONCE MATTERS CHANGE.
...VERY WELL.
BUT AS MY LIEGE'S SERVANT, I CANNOT PASS OFF THE CHILD HE AGREED TO WATCH WITHOUT A SECOND THOUGHT!
KIRI (SCREW)
KIRI
I WILL COME WITH HER. ON THAT CONDITION, SHE MAY GO OUTSIDE.
KYU (GLUG)
NH!

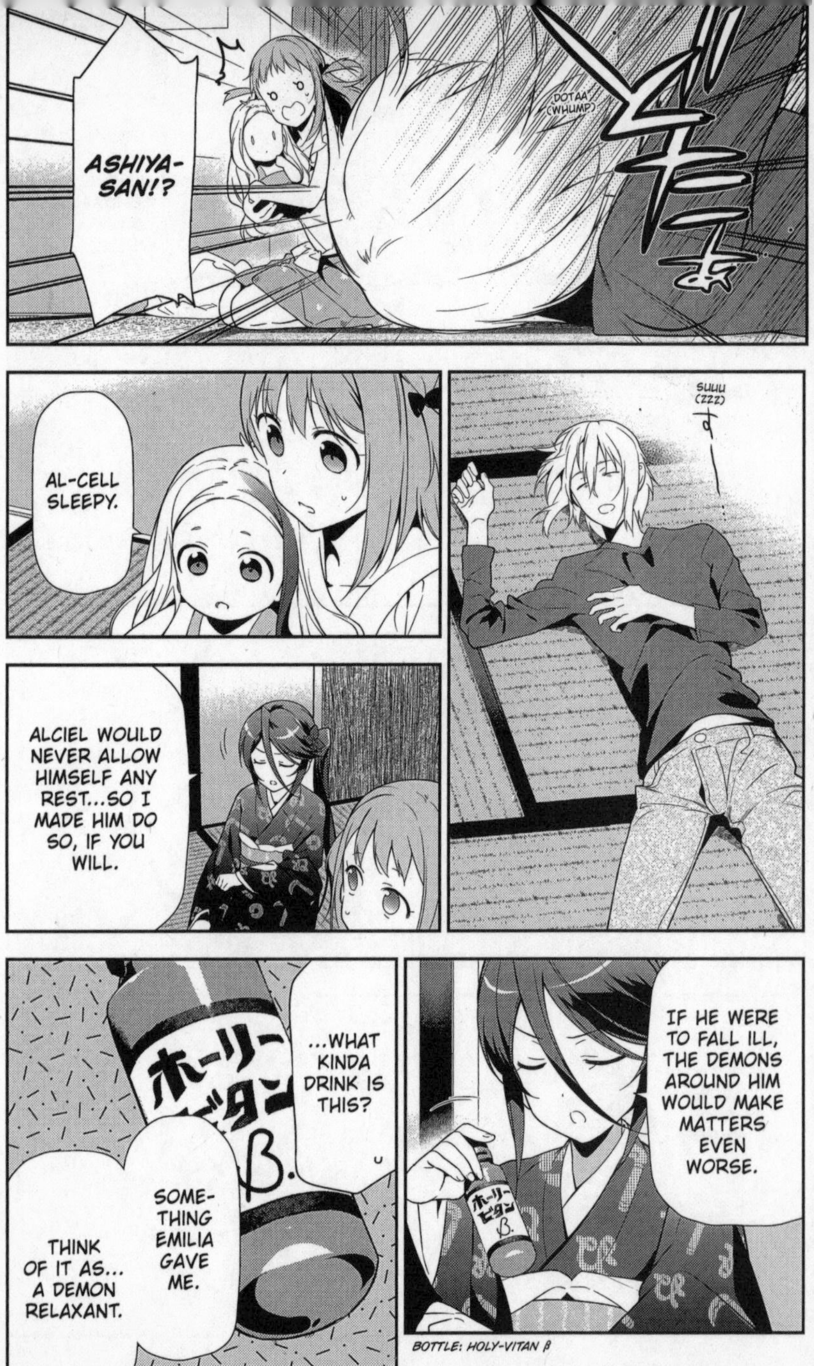
DOTAA (WHUMP)
ASHIYA-SAN!?
SUUU (ZZZ)
AL-CELL SLEEPY.
ALCIEL WOULD NEVER ALLOW HIMSELF ANY REST...SO I MADE HIM DO SO, IF YOU WILL.
IF HE WERE TO FALL ILL, THE DEMONS AROUND HIM WOULD MAKE MATTERS EVEN WORSE.
...WHAT KINDA DRINK IS THIS?
SOME-THING EMILIA GAVE ME.
THINK OF IT AS... A DEMON RELAXANT.
BOTTLE: HOLY-VITAN β

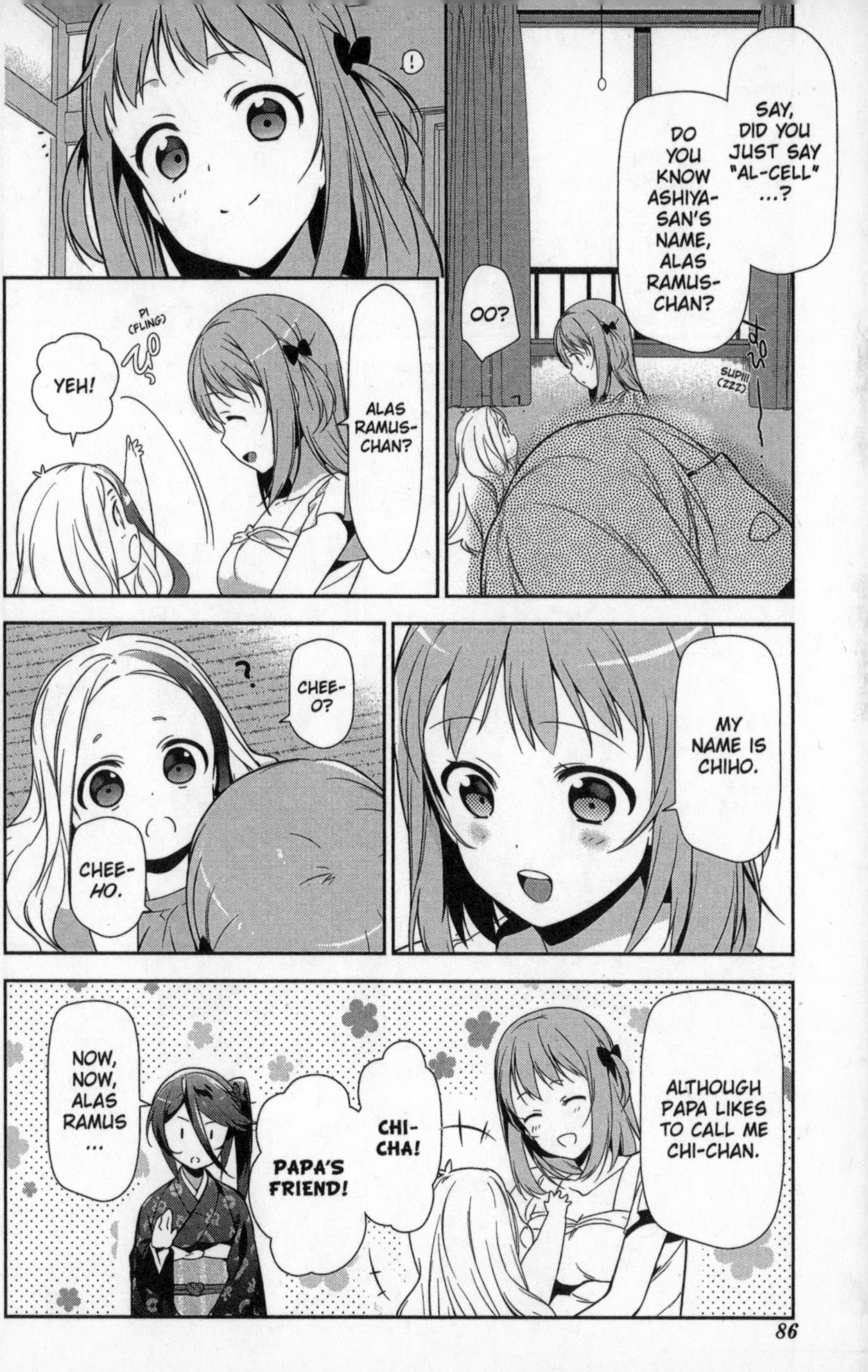
SAY, DID YOU JUST SAY "AL-CELL" ...?
DO YOU KNOW ASHIYA-SAN'S NAME, ALAS RAMUS-CHAN?
OO?
SUPIII (ZZZ)
!
ALAS RAMUS-CHAN?
PI (FLING)
YEH!
MY NAME IS CHIHO.
CHEE-O?
?
CHEE-HO.
ALTHOUGH PAPA LIKES TO CALL ME CHI-CHAN.
CHI-CHA!
PAPA'S FRIEND!
NOW, NOW, ALAS RAMUS ...

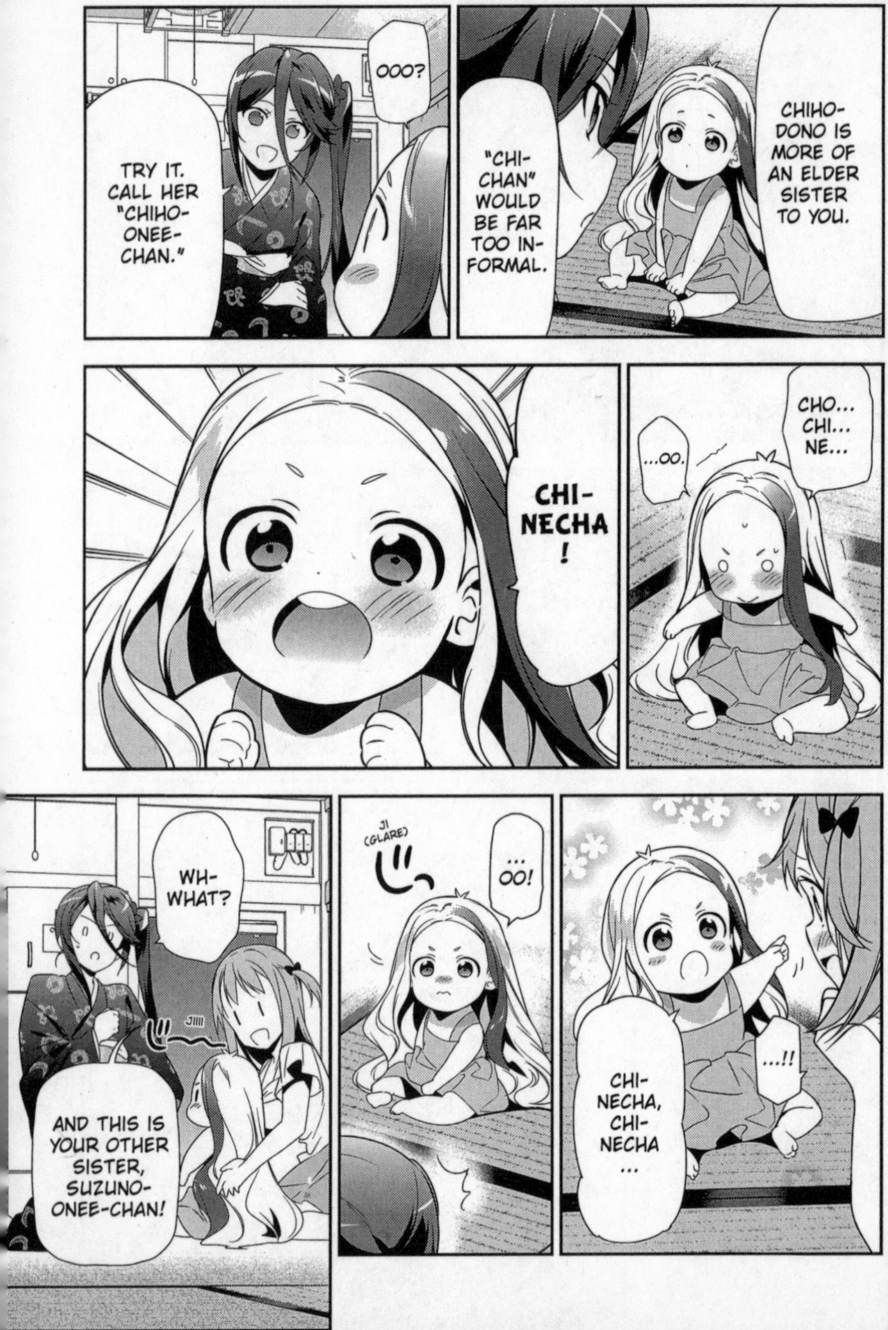
CHIHO-DONO IS MORE OF AN ELDER SISTER TO YOU.
"CHI-CHAN" WOULD BE FAR TOO INFORMAL.
OOO?
TRY IT. CALL HER "CHIHO-ONEE-CHAN."
CHO... CHI... NE...
...OO.
CHI-NECHA!
...!!
CHI-NECHA, CHI-NECHA...
...OO!
JI (GLARE)
WH-WHAT?
JIIII
AND THIS IS YOUR OTHER SISTER, SUZUNO-ONEE-CHAN!

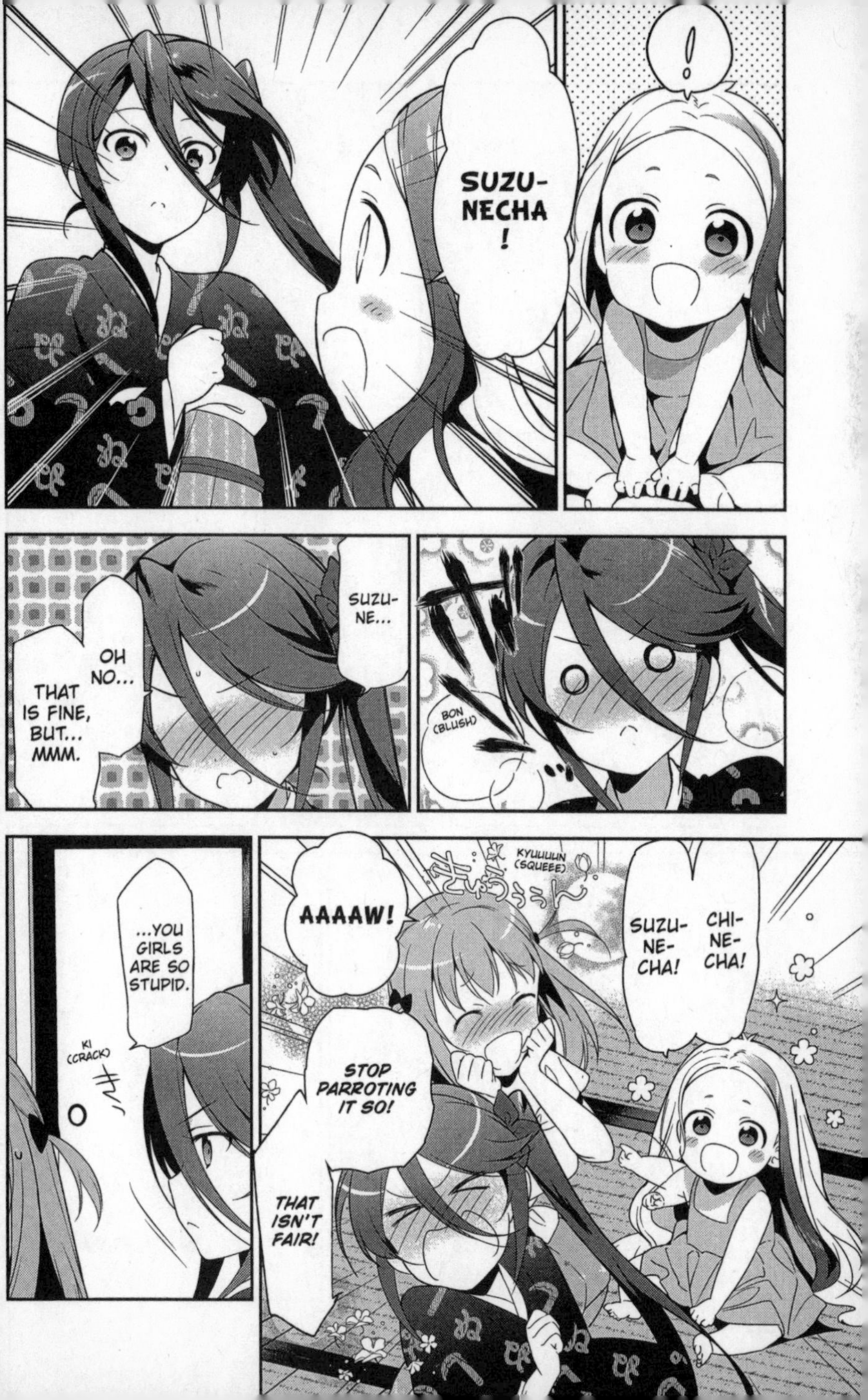
!
SUZU-NECHA!
BON (BLUSH)
SUZU-NE...
OH NO...
THAT IS FINE, BUT... MMM.
CHI-NE-CHA!
SUZU-NE-CHA!
KYUUUUN (SQUEEE)
AAAAW!
STOP PARROTING IT SO!
THAT ISN'T FAIR!
...YOU GIRLS ARE SO STUPID.
KI (CRACK)

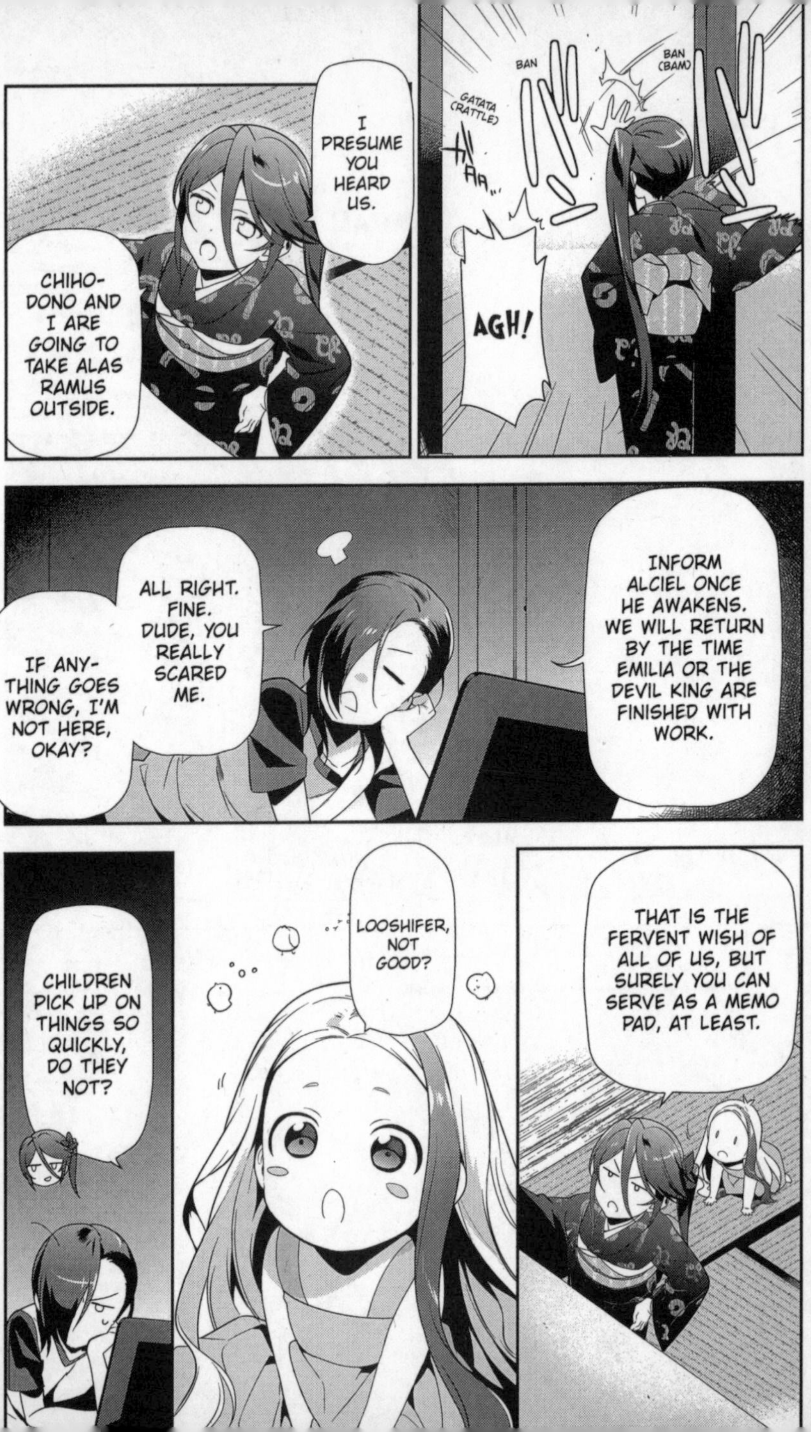
BAN
BAN (BAM)
GATATA (RATTLE)
AGH!
I PRESUME YOU HEARD US.
CHIHO-DONO AND I ARE GOING TO TAKE ALAS RAMUS OUTSIDE.
INFORM ALCIEL ONCE HE AWAKENS. WE WILL RETURN BY THE TIME EMILIA OR THE DEVIL KING ARE FINISHED WITH WORK.
ALL RIGHT. FINE. DUDE, YOU REALLY SCARED ME.
IF ANY-THING GOES WRONG, I'M NOT HERE, OKAY?
THAT IS THE FERVENT WISH OF ALL OF US, BUT SURELY YOU CAN SERVE AS A MEMO PAD, AT LEAST.
LOOSHIFER, NOT GOOD?
CHILDREN PICK UP ON THINGS SO QUICKLY, DO THEY NOT?

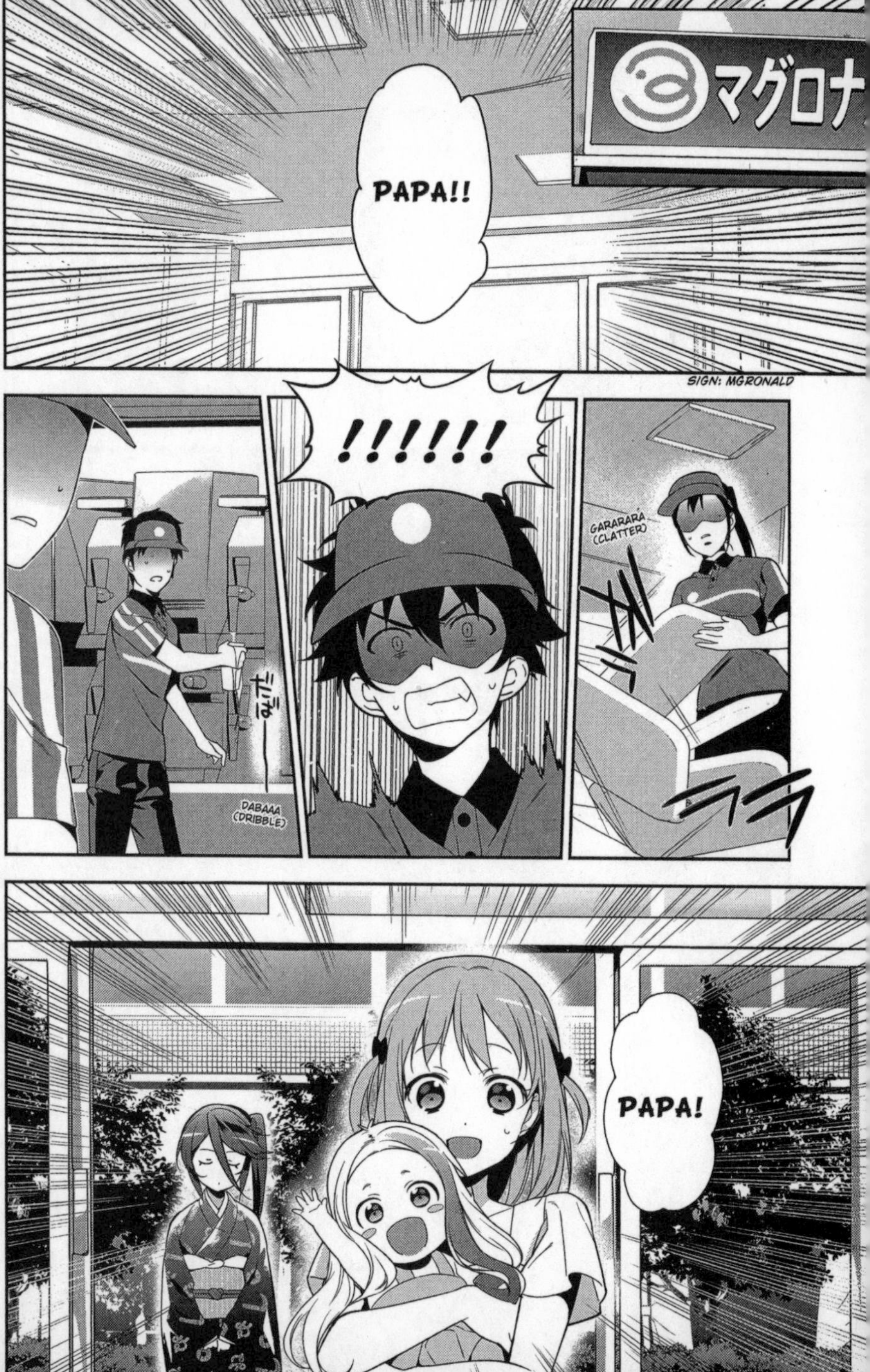
マグロナ
PAPA!!
SIGN: MGRONALD
GARARARA (CLATTER)
!!!!!!
DABAAA (DRIBBLE)
PAPA!

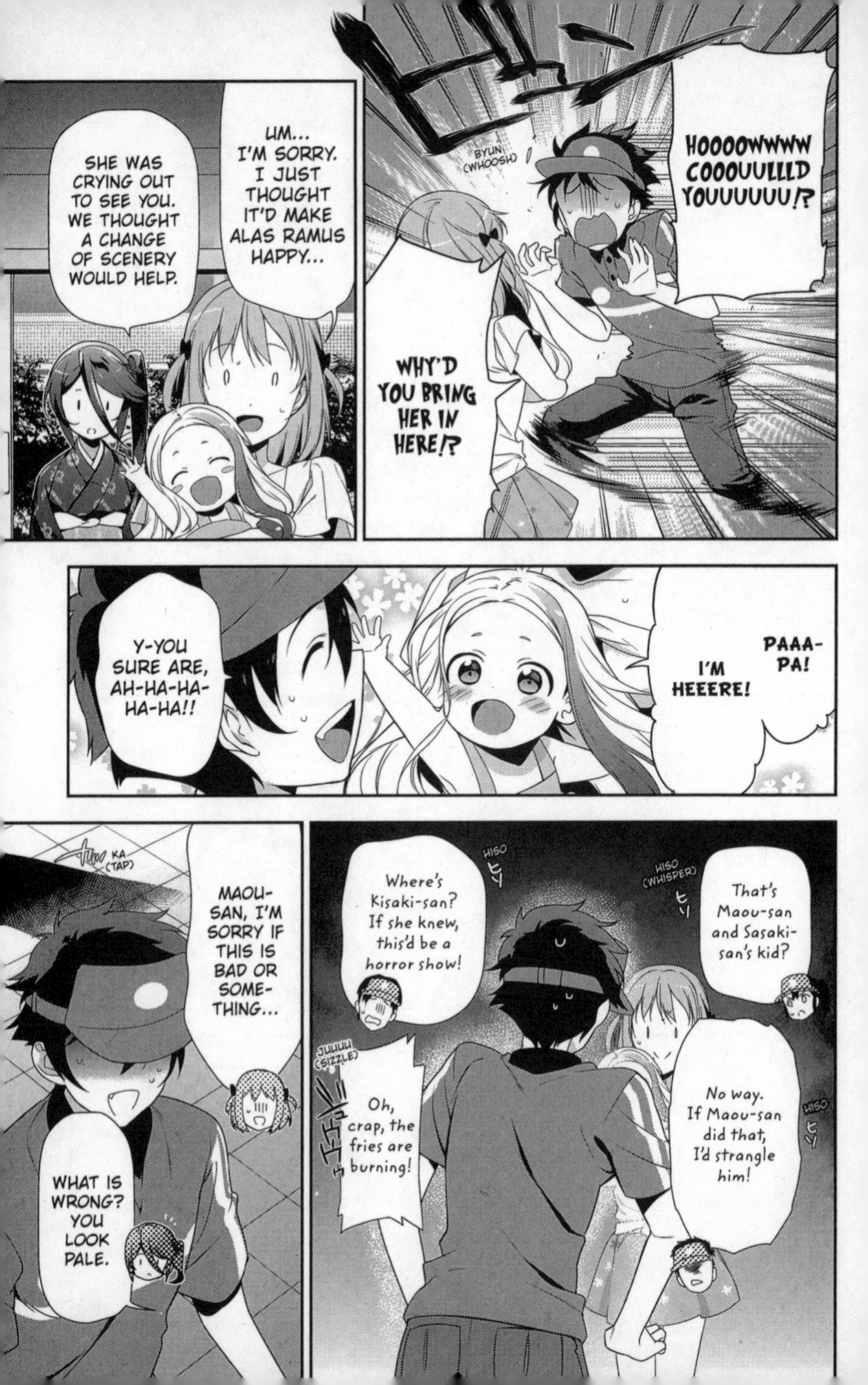
BYUN (WHOOSH)
HOOOOWWWW COOOUULLLD YOUUUUUU!?
WHY'D YOU BRING HER IN HERE!?
UM... I'M SORRY. I JUST THOUGHT IT'D MAKE ALAS RAMUS HAPPY...
SHE WAS CRYING OUT TO SEE YOU. WE THOUGHT A CHANGE OF SCENERY WOULD HELP.
PAAA-PA!
I'M HEEERE!
Y-YOU SURE ARE, AH-HA-HA-HA-HA!!
HISO (WHISPER)
That's Maou-san and Sasaki-san's kid?
HISO
Where's Kisaki-san? If she knew, this'd be a horror show!
HISO
No way. If Maou-san did that, I'd strangle him!
JUUUU (SIZZLE)
Oh, crap, the fries are burning!
KA (TAP)
MAOU-SAN, I'M SORRY IF THIS IS BAD OR SOMETHING...
WHAT IS WRONG? YOU LOOK PALE.

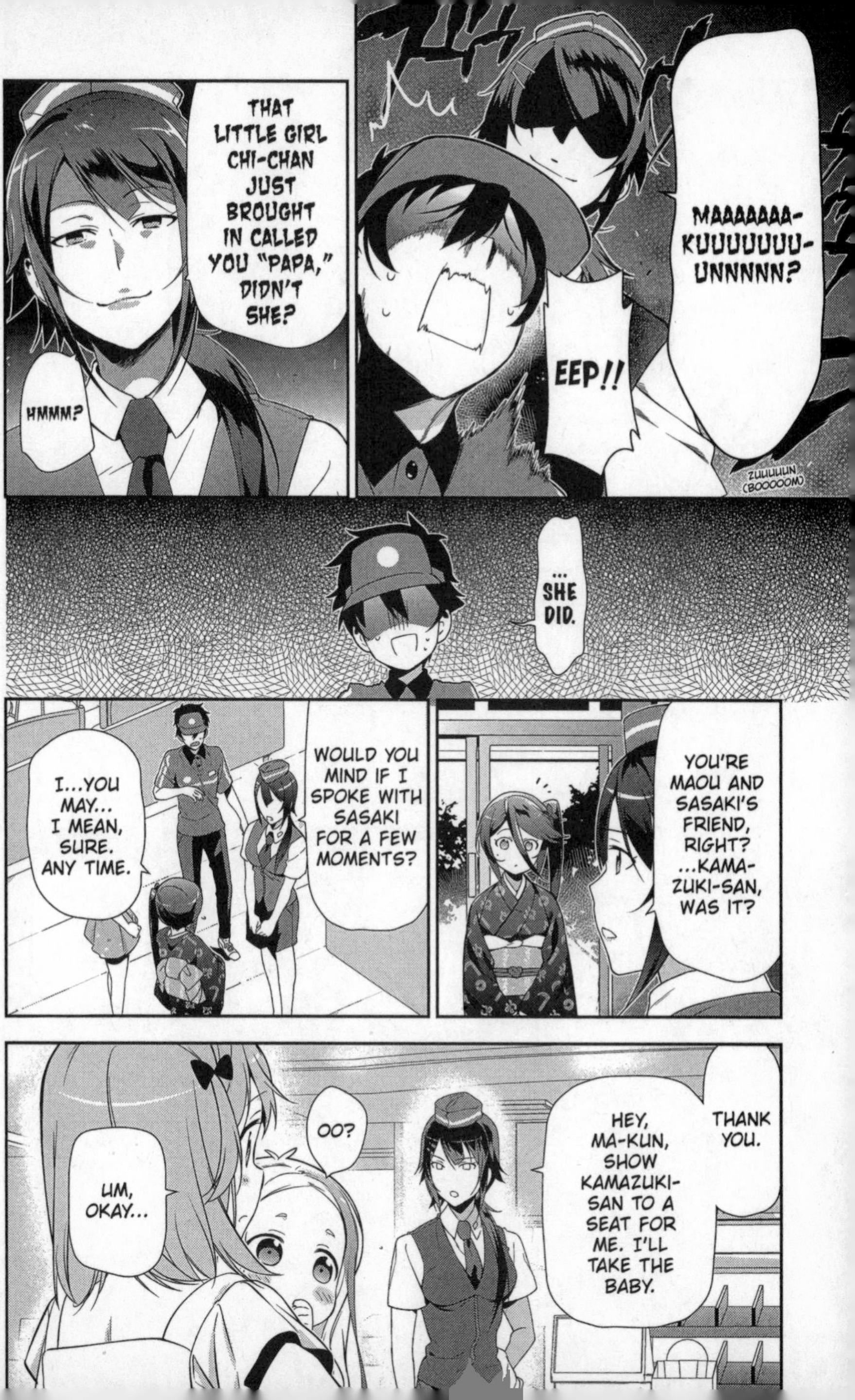
MAAAAAAA-KUUUUUUU-UNNNNN?
EEP!!
ZUUUUUUN (BOOOOOM)
THAT LITTLE GIRL CHI-CHAN JUST BROUGHT IN CALLED YOU "PAPA," DIDN'T SHE?
HMMM?
...SHE DID.
YOU'RE MAOU AND SASAKI'S FRIEND, RIGHT? ...KAMAZUKI-SAN, WAS IT?
WOULD YOU MIND IF I SPOKE WITH SASAKI FOR A FEW MOMENTS?
I...YOU MAY... I MEAN, SURE. ANY TIME.
THANK YOU.
HEY, MA-KUN, SHOW KAMAZUKI-SAN TO A SEAT FOR ME. I'LL TAKE THE BABY.
OO?
UM, OKAY...

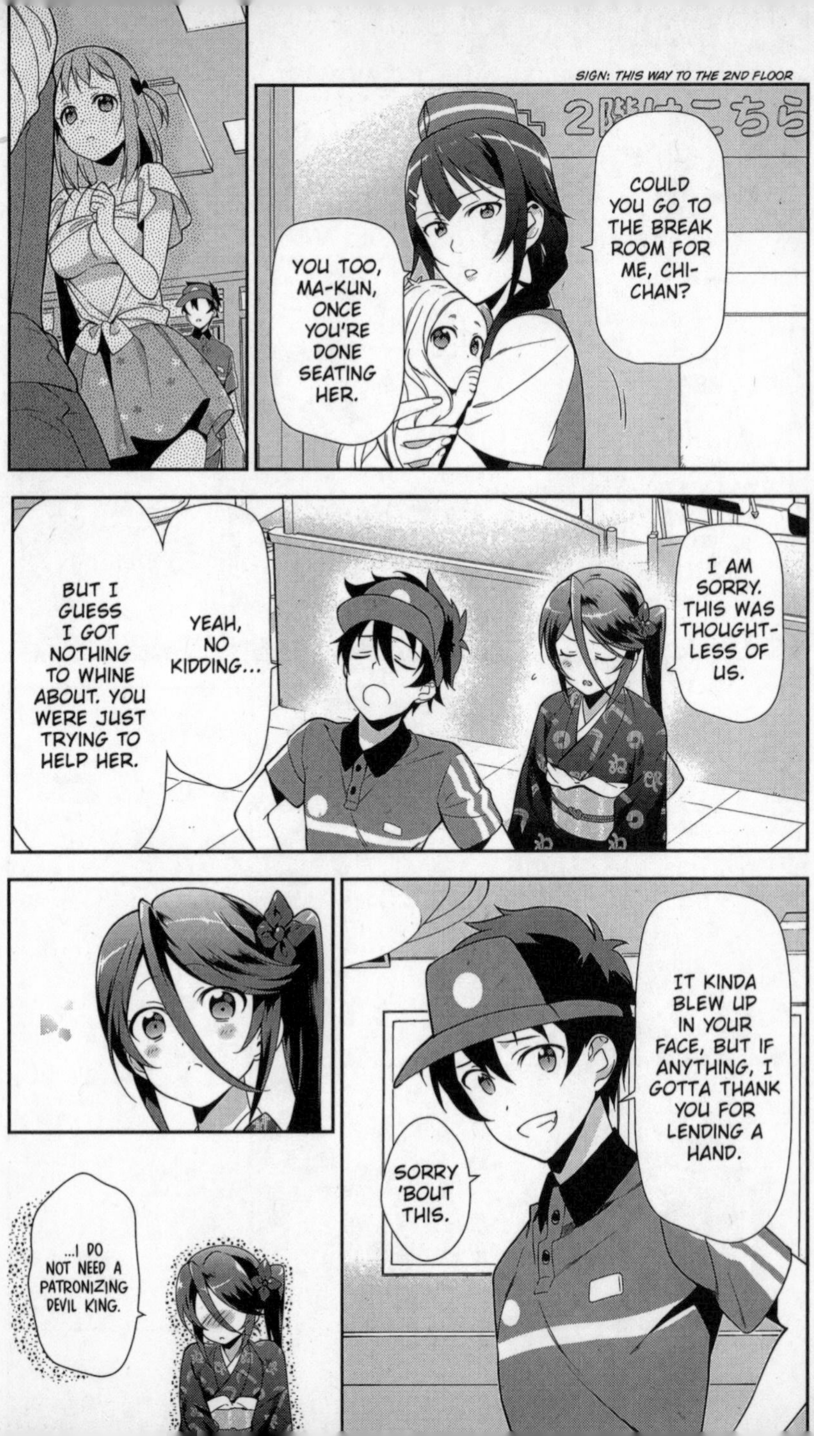
SIGN: THIS WAY TO THE 2ND FLOOR
COULD YOU GO TO THE BREAK ROOM FOR ME, CHI-CHAN?
YOU TOO, MA-KUN, ONCE YOU'RE DONE SEATING HER.
I AM SORRY. THIS WAS THOUGHTLESS OF US.
YEAH, NO KIDDING...
BUT I GUESS I GOT NOTHING TO WHINE ABOUT. YOU WERE JUST TRYING TO HELP HER.
IT KINDA BLEW UP IN YOUR FACE, BUT IF ANYTHING, I GOTTA THANK YOU FOR LENDING A HAND.
SORRY 'BOUT THIS.
...I DO NOT NEED A PATRONIZING DEVIL KING.

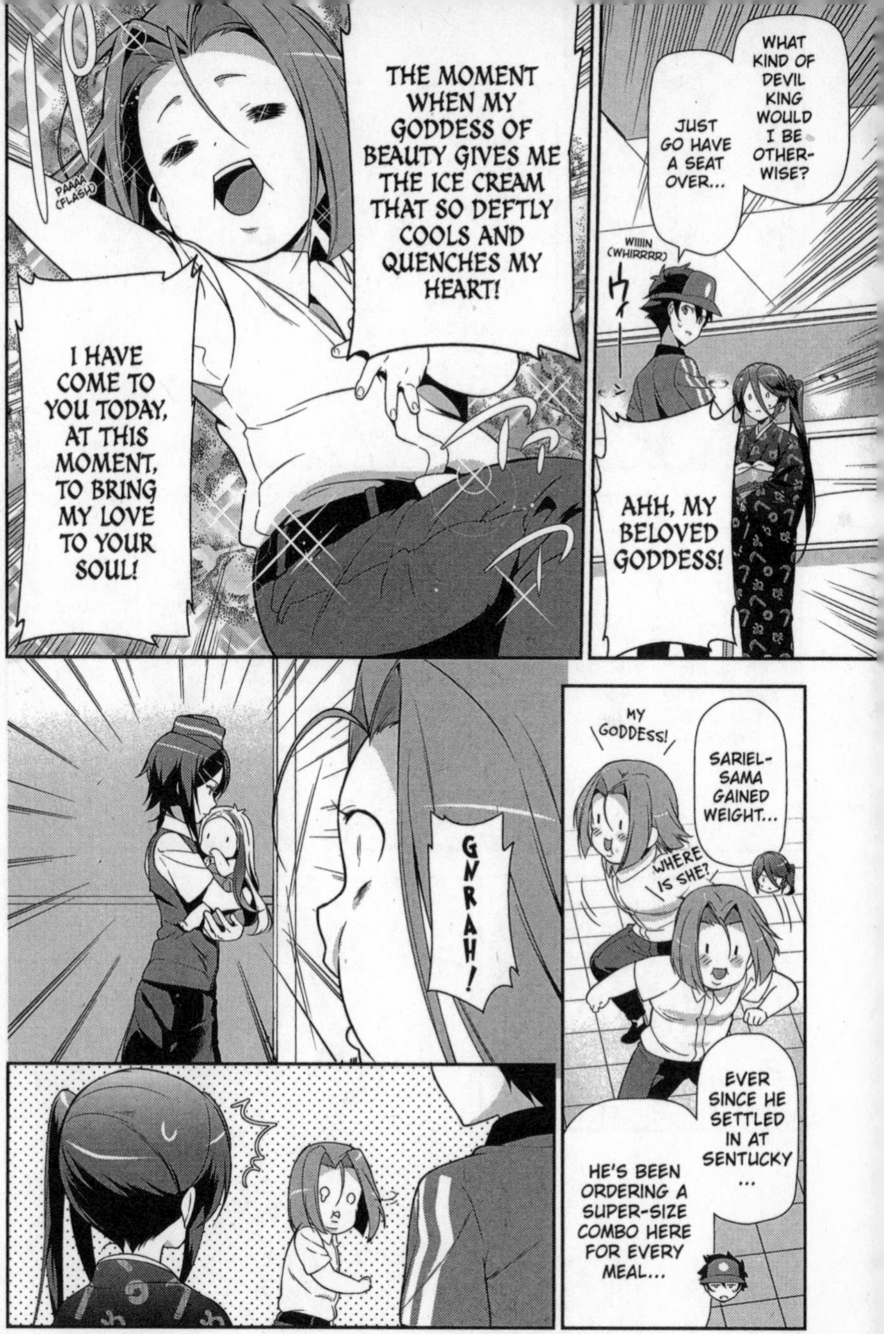
WHAT KIND OF DEVIL KING WOULD I BE OTHER-WISE?
JUST GO HAVE A SEAT OVER...
WIIIN (WHIRRRR)
AHH, MY BELOVED GODDESS!
THE MOMENT WHEN MY GODDESS OF BEAUTY GIVES ME THE ICE CREAM THAT SO DEFTLY COOLS AND QUENCHES MY HEART!
PAAAA (FLASH)
I HAVE COME TO YOU TODAY, AT THIS MOMENT, TO BRING MY LOVE TO YOUR SOUL!
SARIEL-SAMA GAINED WEIGHT...
MY GODDESS!
WHERE IS SHE?
EVER SINCE HE SETTLED IN AT SENTUCKY...
HE'S BEEN ORDERING A SUPER-SIZE COMBO HERE FOR EVERY MEAL...
GNRAH!

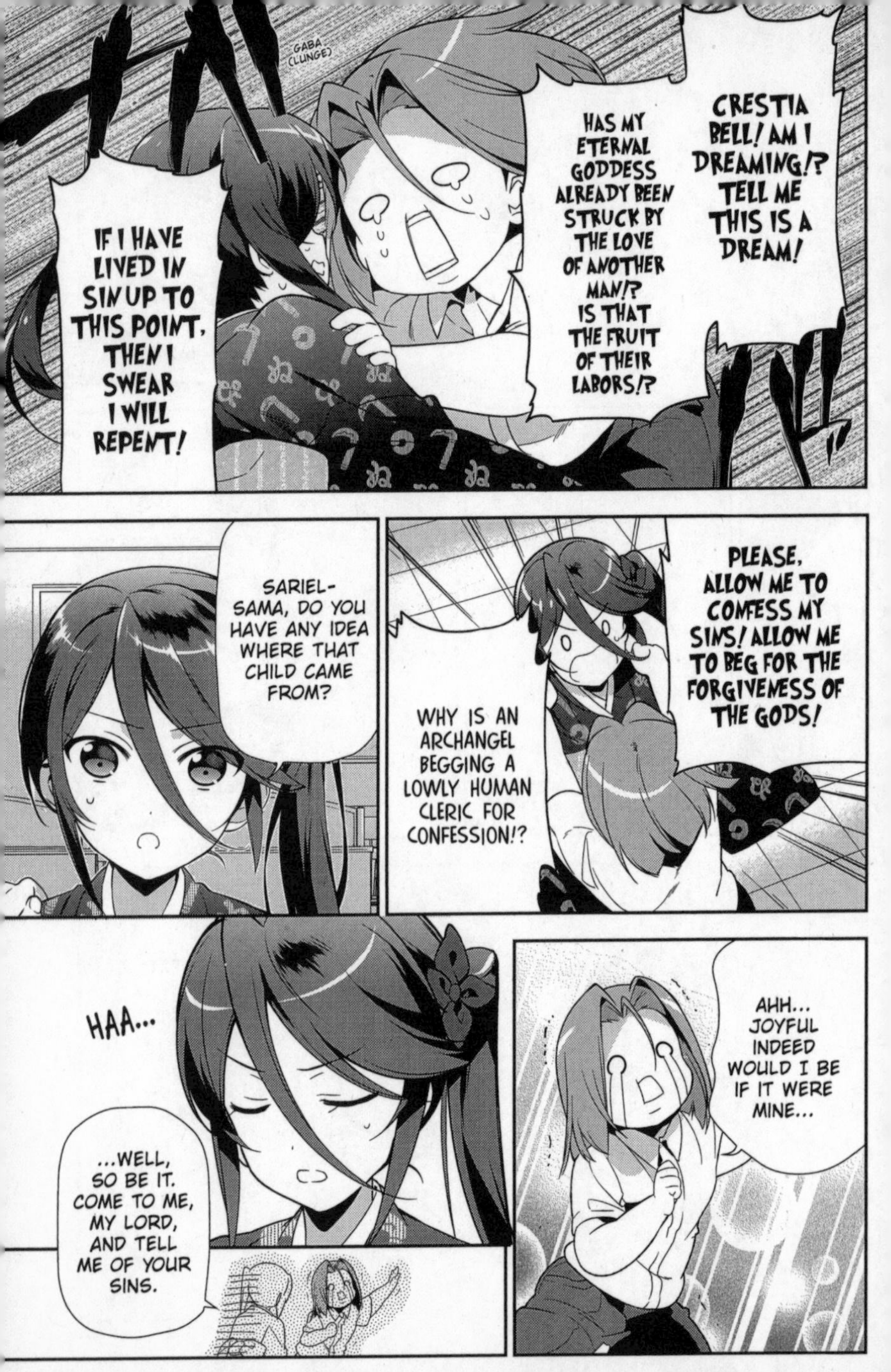
CRESTIA BELL! AM I DREAMING!? TELL ME THIS IS A DREAM!
HAS MY ETERNAL GODDESS ALREADY BEEN STRUCK BY THE LOVE OF ANOTHER MAN!? IS THAT THE FRUIT OF THEIR LABORS!?
GABA (LUNGE)
IF I HAVE LIVED IN SIN UP TO THIS POINT, THEN I SWEAR I WILL REPENT!
PLEASE, ALLOW ME TO CONFESS MY SINS! ALLOW ME TO BEG FOR THE FORGIVENESS OF THE GODS!
WHY IS AN ARCHANGEL BEGGING A LOWLY HUMAN CLERIC FOR CONFESSION!?
SARIEL-SAMA, DO YOU HAVE ANY IDEA WHERE THAT CHILD CAME FROM?
AHH... JOYFUL INDEED WOULD I BE IF IT WERE MINE...
HAA...
...WELL, SO BE IT. COME TO ME, MY LORD, AND TELL ME OF YOUR SINS.

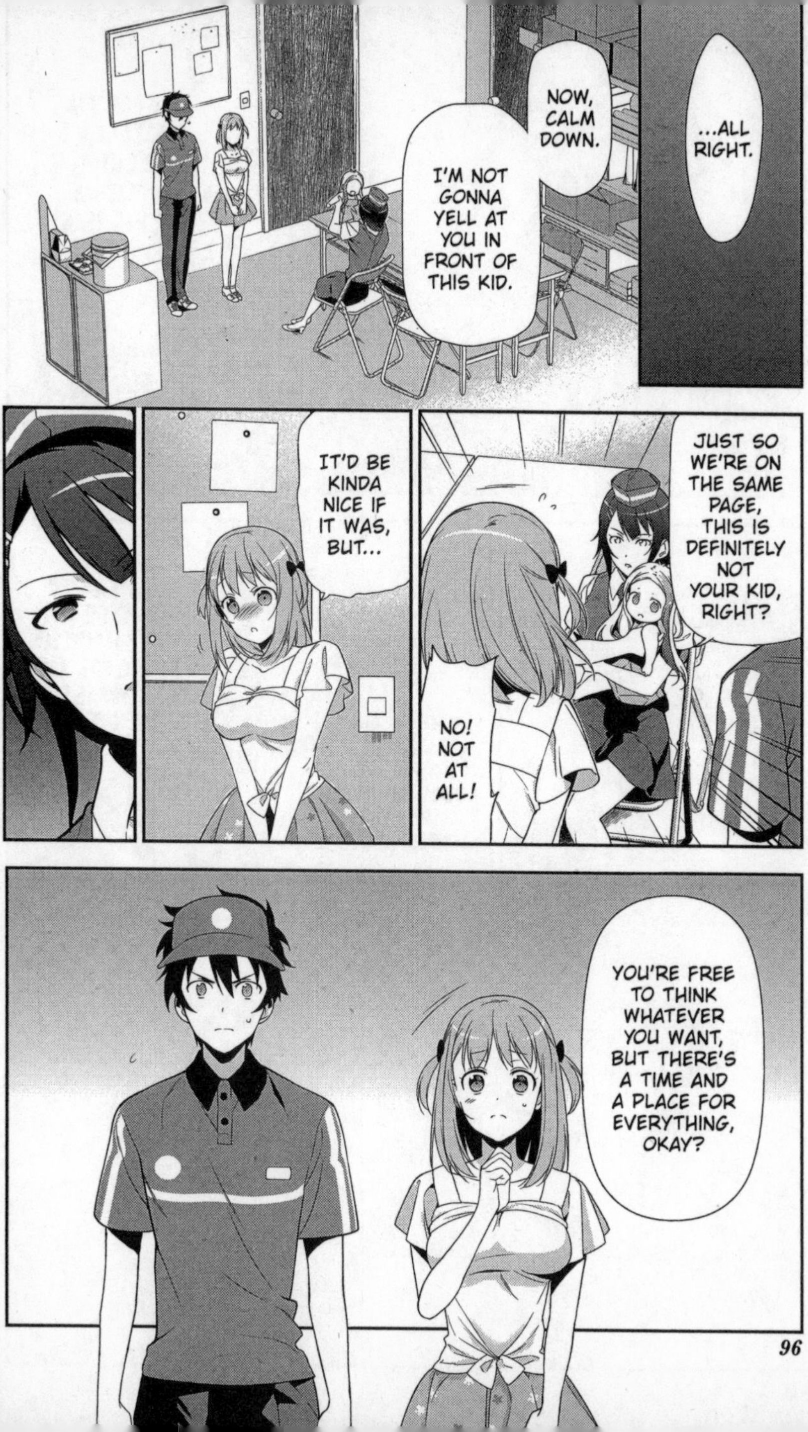
...ALL RIGHT.
NOW, CALM DOWN.
I'M NOT GONNA YELL AT YOU IN FRONT OF THIS KID.
JUST SO WE'RE ON THE SAME PAGE, THIS IS DEFINITELY NOT YOUR KID, RIGHT?
NO! NOT AT ALL!
IT'D BE KINDA NICE IF IT WAS, BUT...
YOU'RE FREE TO THINK WHATEVER YOU WANT, BUT THERE'S A TIME AND A PLACE FOR EVERYTHING, OKAY?

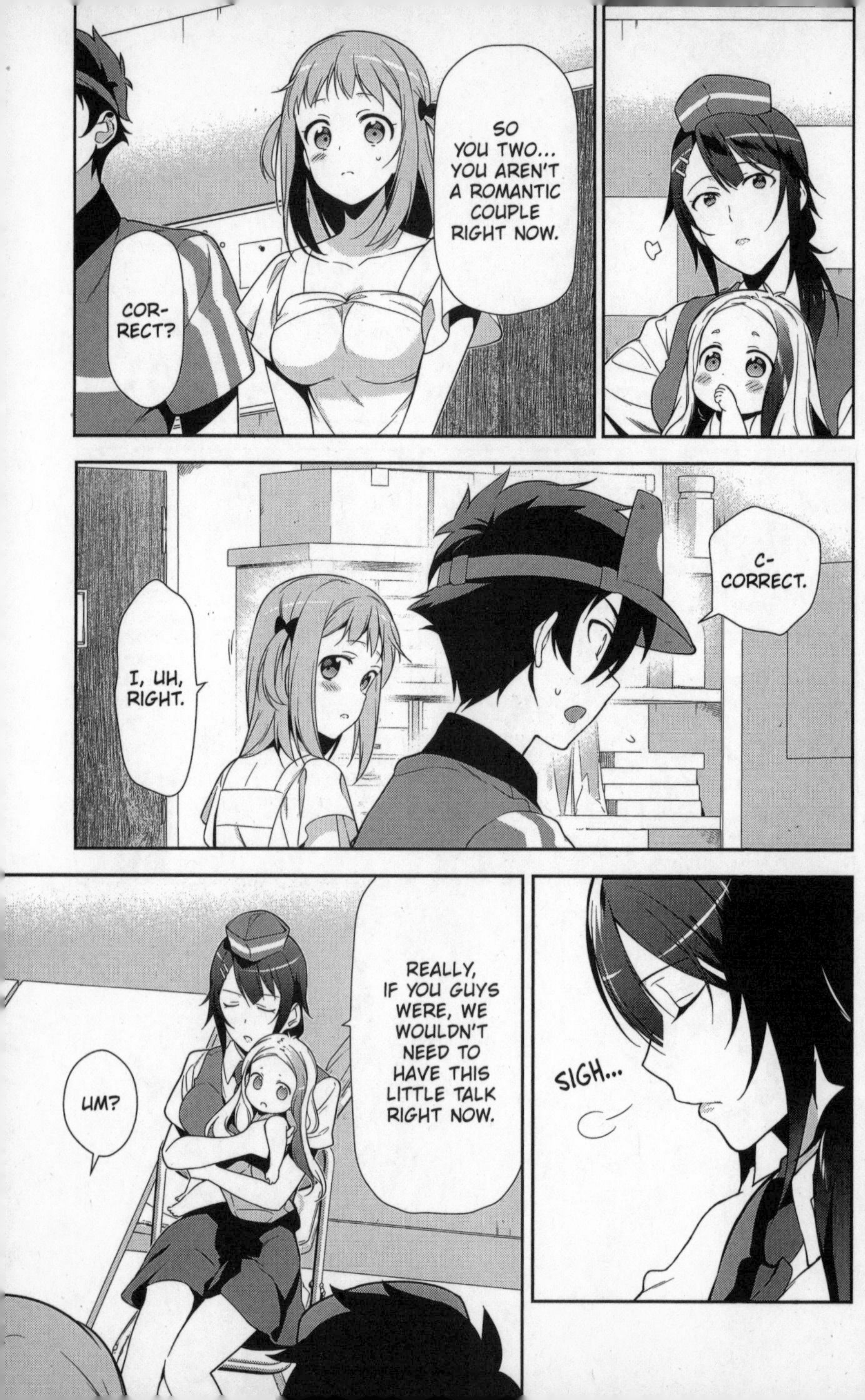
SO YOU TWO... YOU AREN'T A ROMANTIC COUPLE RIGHT NOW.
COR-RECT?
C-CORRECT.
I, UH, RIGHT.
SIGH...
REALLY, IF YOU GUYS WERE, WE WOULDN'T NEED TO HAVE THIS LITTLE TALK RIGHT NOW.
UM?

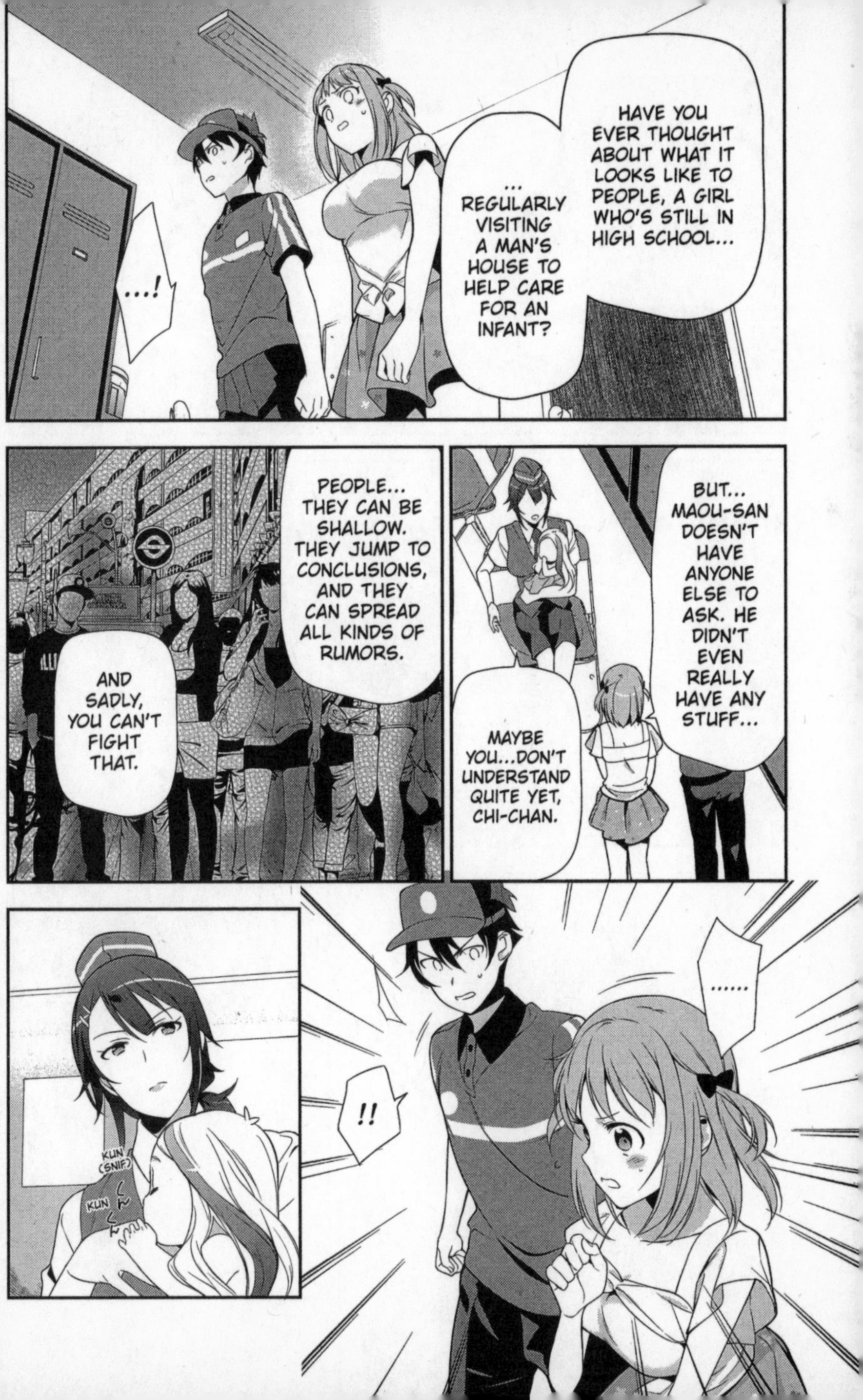
HAVE YOU EVER THOUGHT ABOUT WHAT IT LOOKS LIKE TO PEOPLE, A GIRL WHO'S STILL IN HIGH SCHOOL...
...REGULARLY VISITING A MAN'S HOUSE TO HELP CARE FOR AN INFANT?
...!
BUT... MAOU-SAN DOESN'T HAVE ANYONE ELSE TO ASK. HE DIDN'T EVEN REALLY HAVE ANY STUFF...
MAYBE YOU...DON'T UNDERSTAND QUITE YET, CHI-CHAN.
PEOPLE... THEY CAN BE SHALLOW. THEY JUMP TO CONCLUSIONS, AND THEY CAN SPREAD ALL KINDS OF RUMORS.
AND SADLY, YOU CAN'T FIGHT THAT.
......
!!
KUN (SNIF)
KUN

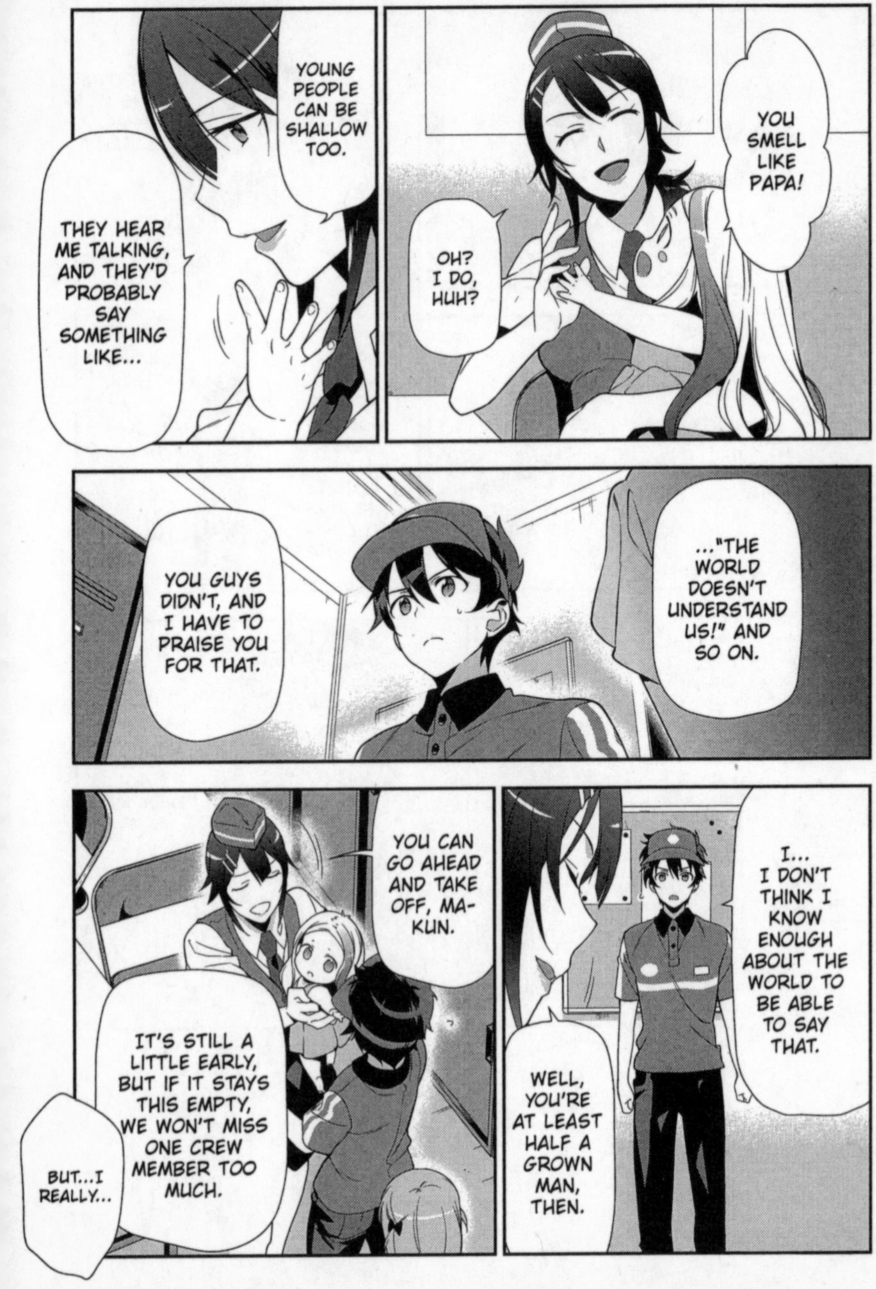
YOU SMELL LIKE PAPA!
OH? I DO, HUH?
YOUNG PEOPLE CAN BE SHALLOW TOO.
THEY HEAR ME TALKING, AND THEY'D PROBABLY SAY SOMETHING LIKE...
..."THE WORLD DOESN'T UNDERSTAND US!" AND SO ON.
YOU GUYS DIDN'T, AND I HAVE TO PRAISE YOU FOR THAT.
I... I DON'T THINK I KNOW ENOUGH ABOUT THE WORLD TO BE ABLE TO SAY THAT.
WELL, YOU'RE AT LEAST HALF A GROWN MAN, THEN.
YOU CAN GO AHEAD AND TAKE OFF, MA-KUN.
IT'S STILL A LITTLE EARLY, BUT IF IT STAYS THIS EMPTY, WE WON'T MISS ONE CREW MEMBER TOO MUCH.
BUT...I REALLY...

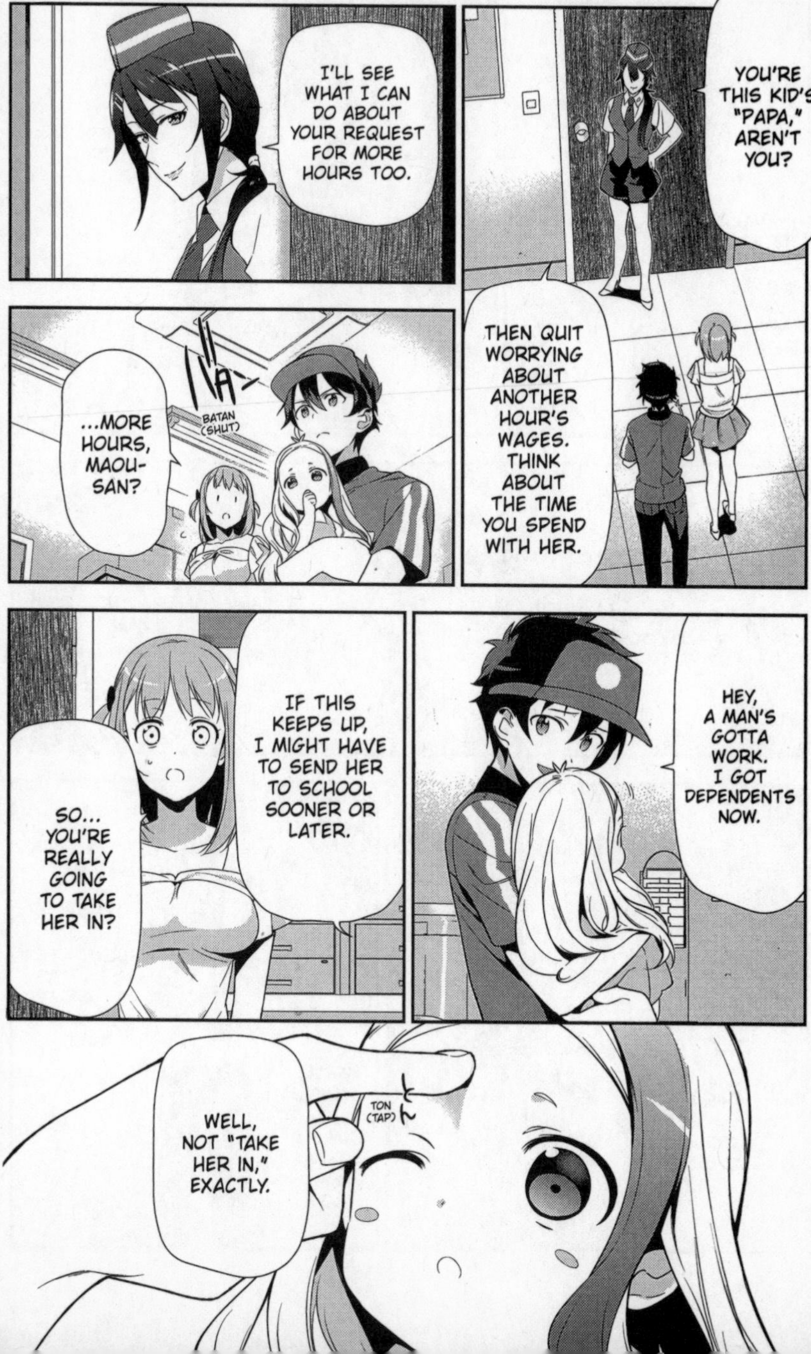
YOU'RE THIS KID'S "PAPA," AREN'T YOU?
THEN QUIT WORRYING ABOUT ANOTHER HOUR'S WAGES. THINK ABOUT THE TIME YOU SPEND WITH HER.
I'LL SEE WHAT I CAN DO ABOUT YOUR REQUEST FOR MORE HOURS TOO.
BATAN (SHUT)
...MORE HOURS, MAOU-SAN?
HEY, A MAN'S GOTTA WORK. I GOT DEPENDENTS NOW.
IF THIS KEEPS UP, I MIGHT HAVE TO SEND HER TO SCHOOL SOONER OR LATER.
SO... YOU'RE REALLY GOING TO TAKE HER IN?
とん
TON (TAP)
WELL, NOT "TAKE HER IN," EXACTLY.

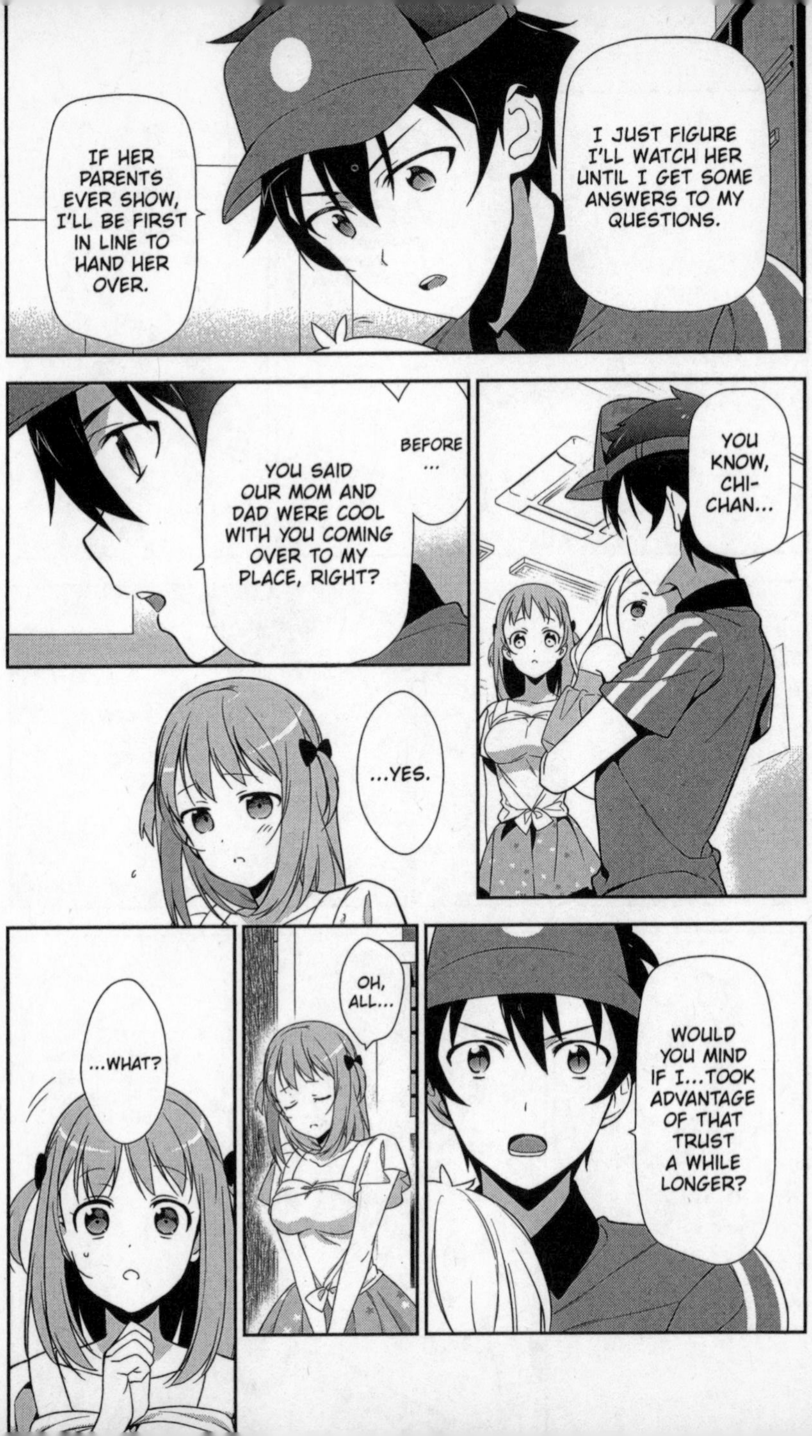
I JUST FIGURE I'LL WATCH HER UNTIL I GET SOME ANSWERS TO MY QUESTIONS.
IF HER PARENTS EVER SHOW, I'LL BE FIRST IN LINE TO HAND HER OVER.
YOU KNOW, CHI-CHAN...
BEFORE...
YOU SAID OUR MOM AND DAD WERE COOL WITH YOU COMING OVER TO MY PLACE, RIGHT?
...YES.
WOULD YOU MIND IF I...TOOK ADVANTAGE OF THAT TRUST A WHILE LONGER?
OH, ALL...
...WHAT?

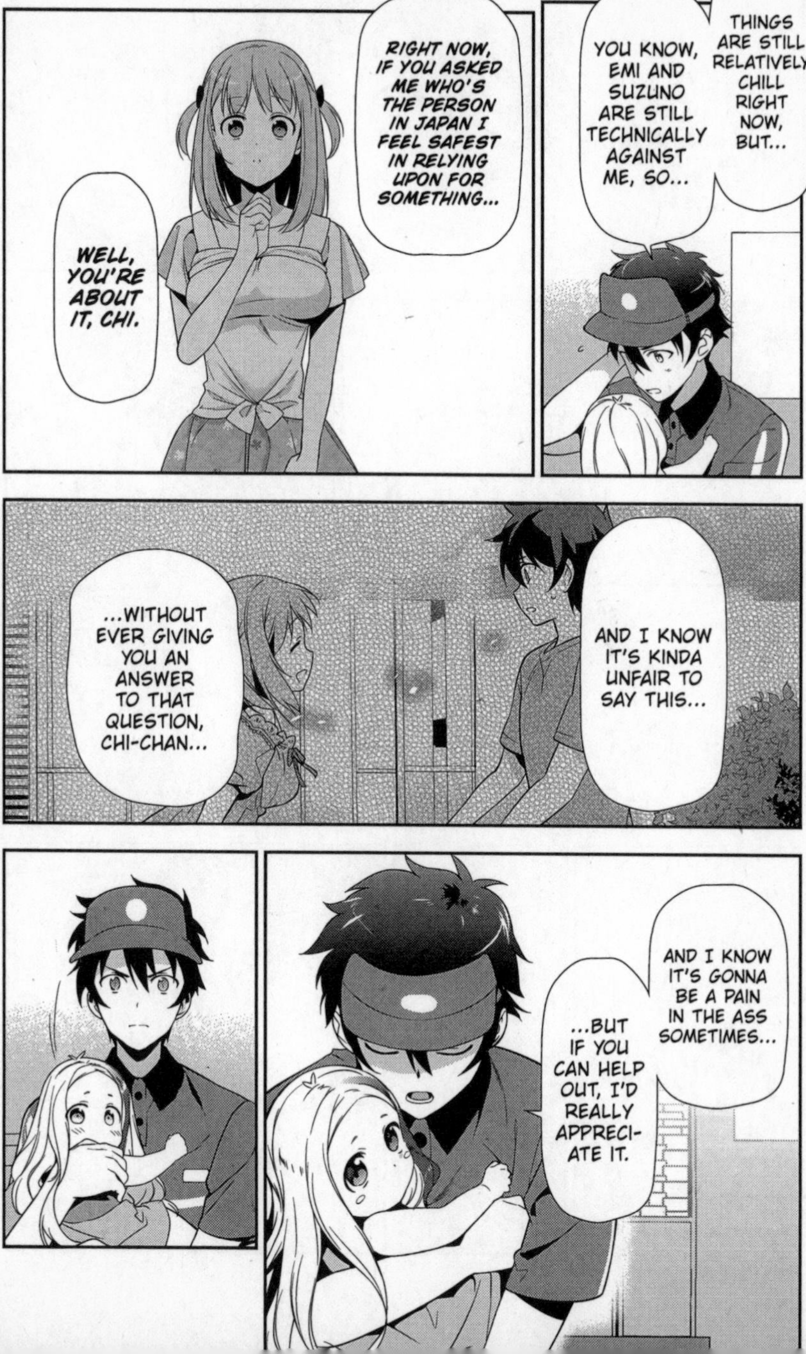
THINGS ARE STILL RELATIVELY CHILL RIGHT NOW, BUT...
YOU KNOW, EMI AND SUZUNO ARE STILL TECHNICALLY AGAINST ME, SO...
RIGHT NOW, IF YOU ASKED ME WHO'S THE PERSON IN JAPAN I FEEL SAFEST IN RELYING UPON FOR SOMETHING...
WELL, YOU'RE ABOUT IT, CHI.
AND I KNOW IT'S KINDA UNFAIR TO SAY THIS...
...WITHOUT EVER GIVING YOU AN ANSWER TO THAT QUESTION, CHI-CHAN...
AND I KNOW IT'S GONNA BE A PAIN IN THE ASS SOMETIMES...
...BUT IF YOU CAN HELP OUT, I'D REALLY APPRECIATE IT.

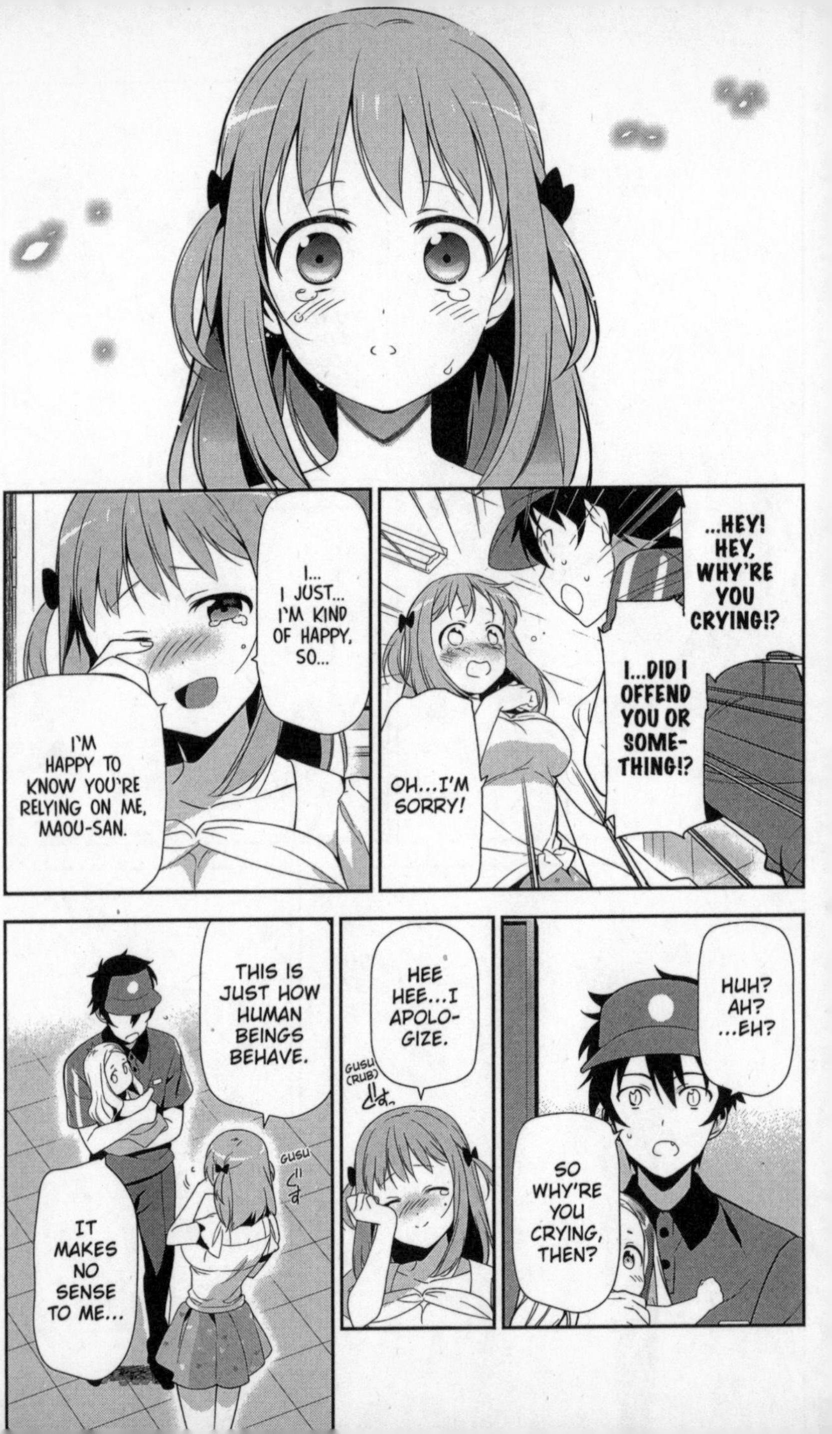
...HEY! HEY, WHY'RE YOU CRYING!?
I...DID I OFFEND YOU OR SOME-THING!?
OH...I'M SORRY!
I... I JUST... I'M KIND OF HAPPY, SO...
I'M HAPPY TO KNOW YOU'RE RELYING ON ME, MAOU-SAN.
HUH? AH? ...EH?
SO WHY'RE YOU CRYING, THEN?
HEE HEE...I APOLOGIZE.
GUSU (RUB)
THIS IS JUST HOW HUMAN BEINGS BEHAVE.
GUSU
IT MAKES NO SENSE TO ME...

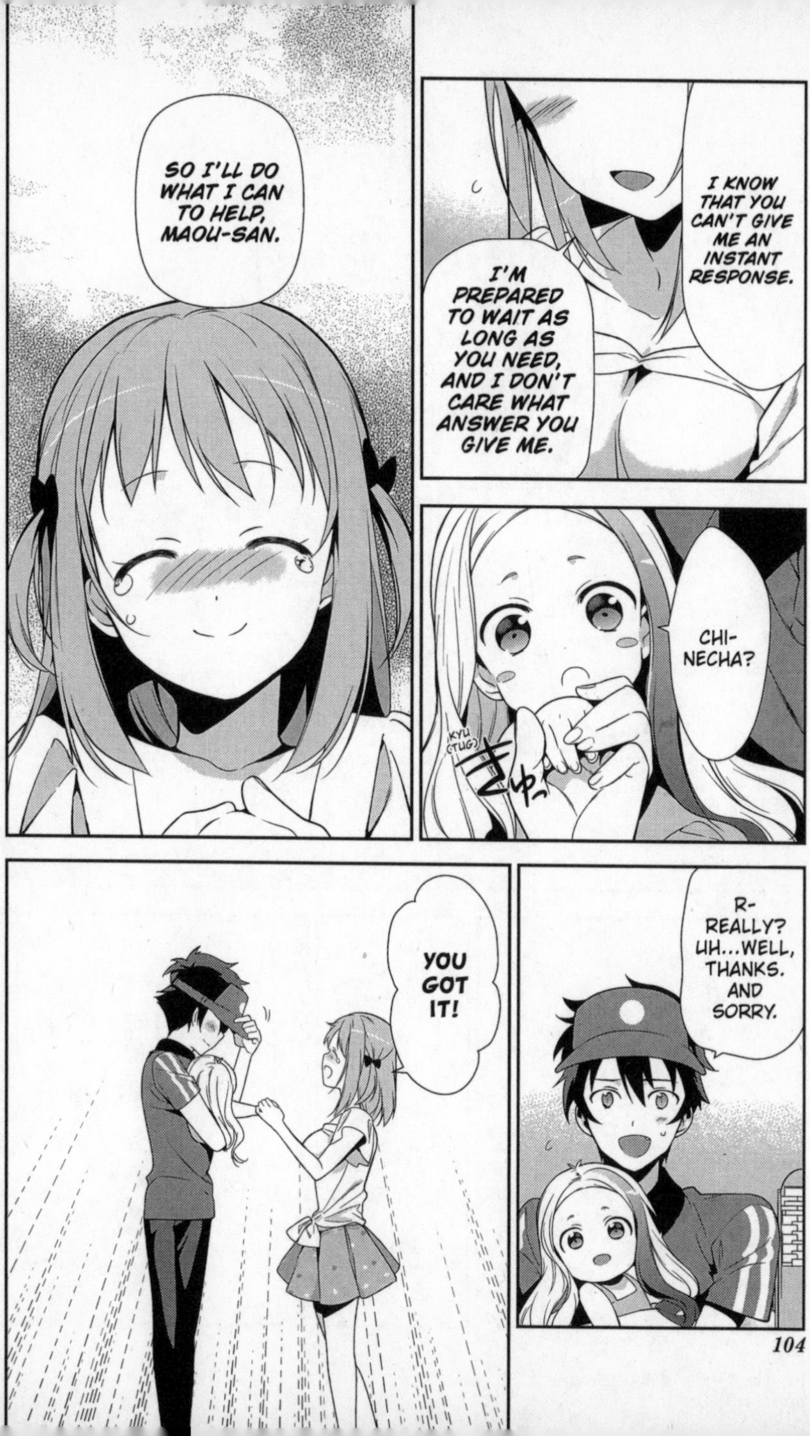
I KNOW THAT YOU CAN'T GIVE ME AN INSTANT RESPONSE.
I'M PREPARED TO WAIT AS LONG AS YOU NEED, AND I DON'T CARE WHAT ANSWER YOU GIVE ME.
CHI-NECHA?
KYU (TUG)
きゅっ
SO I'LL DO WHAT I CAN TO HELP, MAOU-SAN.
R-REALLY? UH...WELL, THANKS. AND SORRY.
YOU GOT IT!

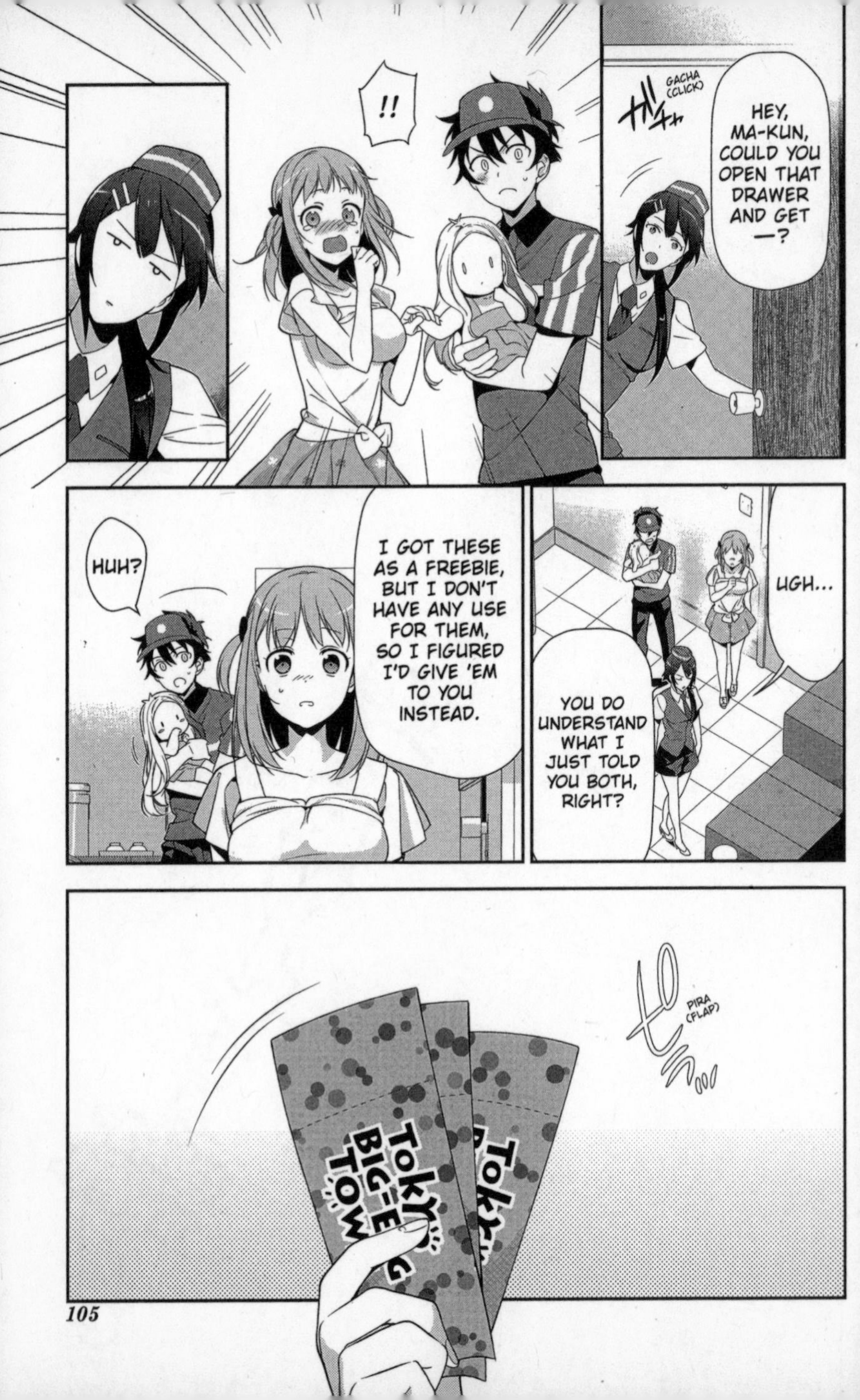
GACHA (CLICK)
HEY, MA-KUN, COULD YOU OPEN THAT DRAWER AND GET —?
!!
UGH...
YOU DO UNDERSTAND WHAT I JUST TOLD YOU BOTH, RIGHT?
I GOT THESE AS A FREEBIE, BUT I DON'T HAVE ANY USE FOR THEM, SO I FIGURED I'D GIVE 'EM TO YOU INSTEAD.
HUH?
PIRA (FLAP)

THE DEVIL IS A PART-TIMER!

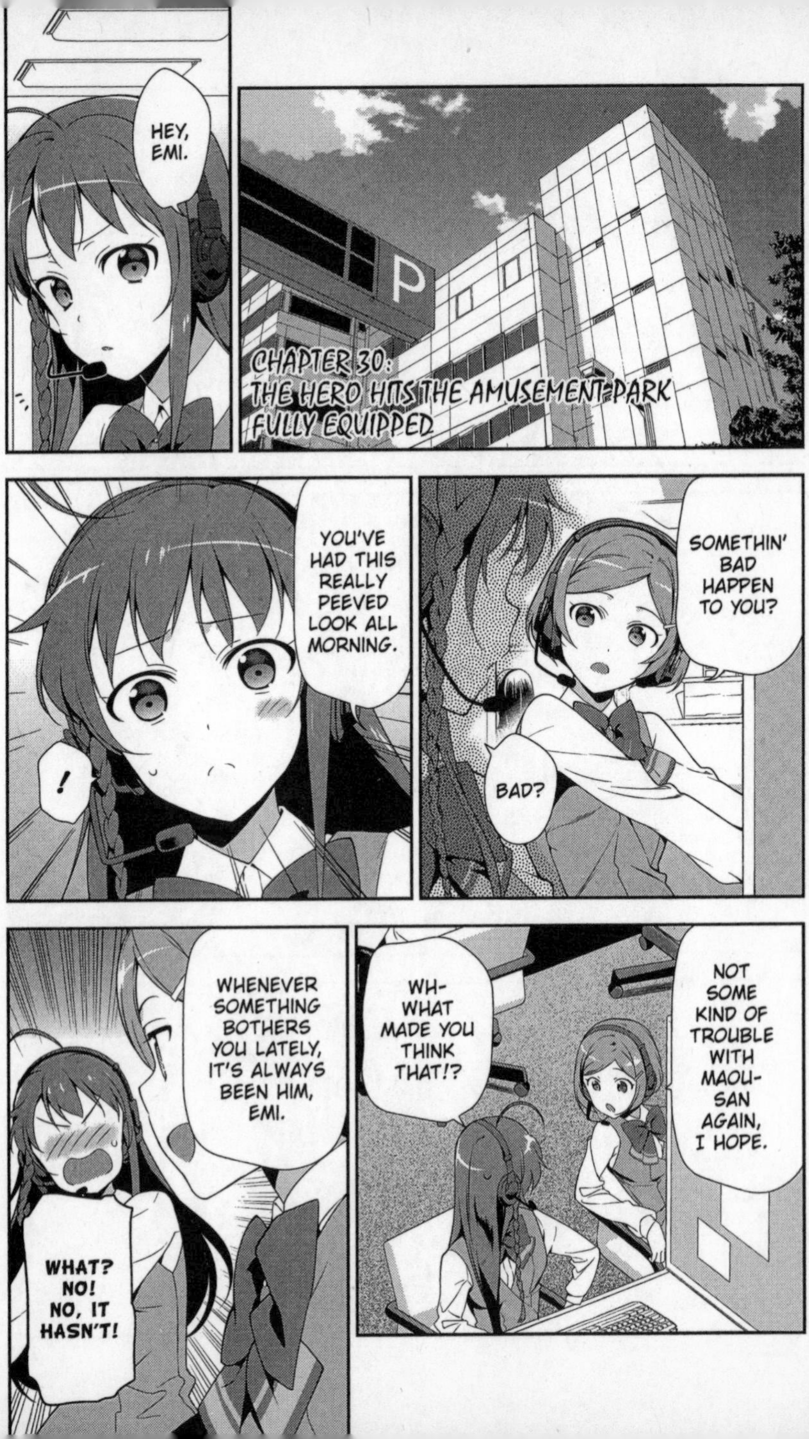
CHAPTER 30: THE HERO HITS THE AMUSEMENT PARK FULLY EQUIPPED
HEY, EMI.
SOMETHIN' BAD HAPPEN TO YOU?
BAD?
YOU'VE HAD THIS REALLY PEEVED LOOK ALL MORNING.
!
NOT SOME KIND OF TROUBLE WITH MAOU-SAN AGAIN, I HOPE.
WH-WHAT MADE YOU THINK THAT!?
WHENEVER SOMETHING BOTHERS YOU LATELY, IT'S ALWAYS BEEN HIM, EMI.
WHAT? NO! NO, IT HASN'T!

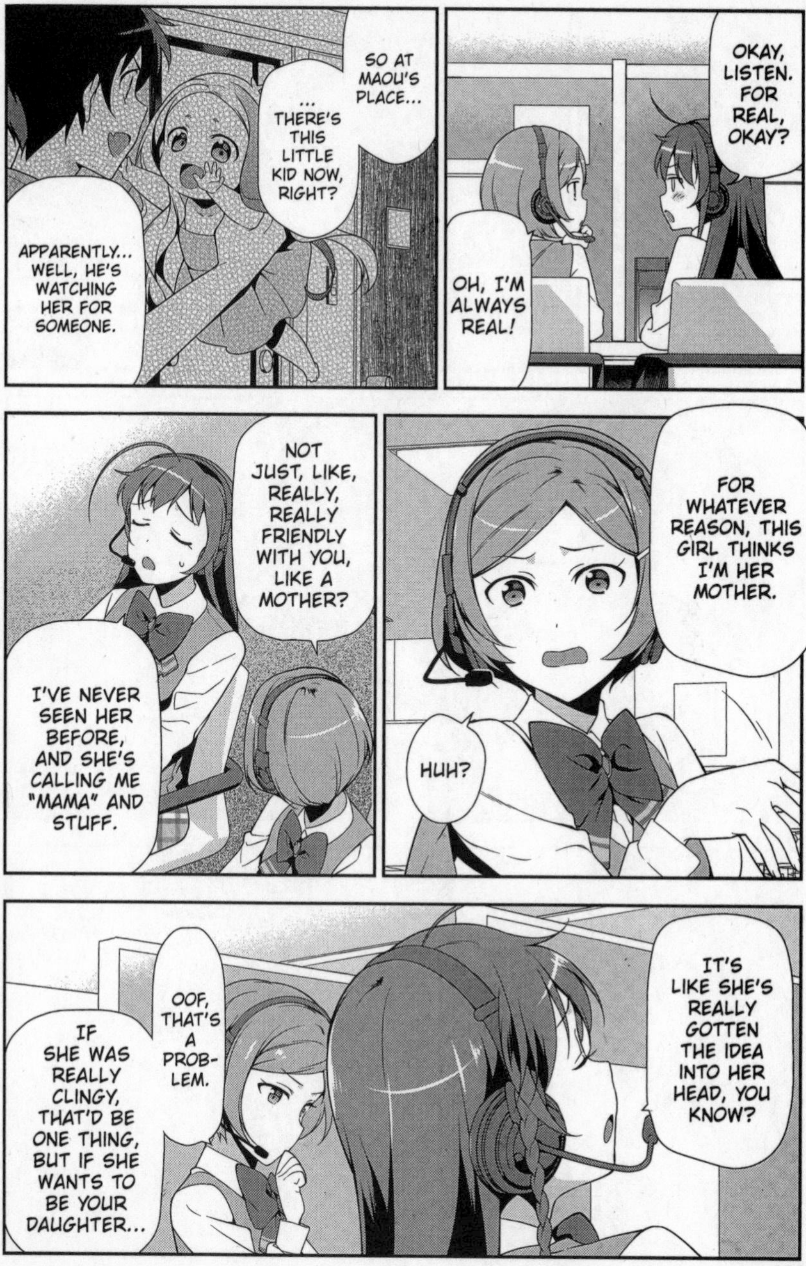
OKAY, LISTEN. FOR REAL, OKAY?
OH, I'M ALWAYS REAL!
SO AT MAOU'S PLACE...
... THERE'S THIS LITTLE KID NOW, RIGHT?
APPARENTLY... WELL, HE'S WATCHING HER FOR SOMEONE.
FOR WHATEVER REASON, THIS GIRL THINKS I'M HER MOTHER.
HUH?
NOT JUST, LIKE, REALLY, REALLY FRIENDLY WITH YOU, LIKE A MOTHER?
I'VE NEVER SEEN HER BEFORE, AND SHE'S CALLING ME "MAMA" AND STUFF.
IT'S LIKE SHE'S REALLY GOTTEN THE IDEA INTO HER HEAD, YOU KNOW?
OOF, THAT'S A PROB-LEM.
IF SHE WAS REALLY CLINGY, THAT'D BE ONE THING, BUT IF SHE WANTS TO BE YOUR DAUGHTER...

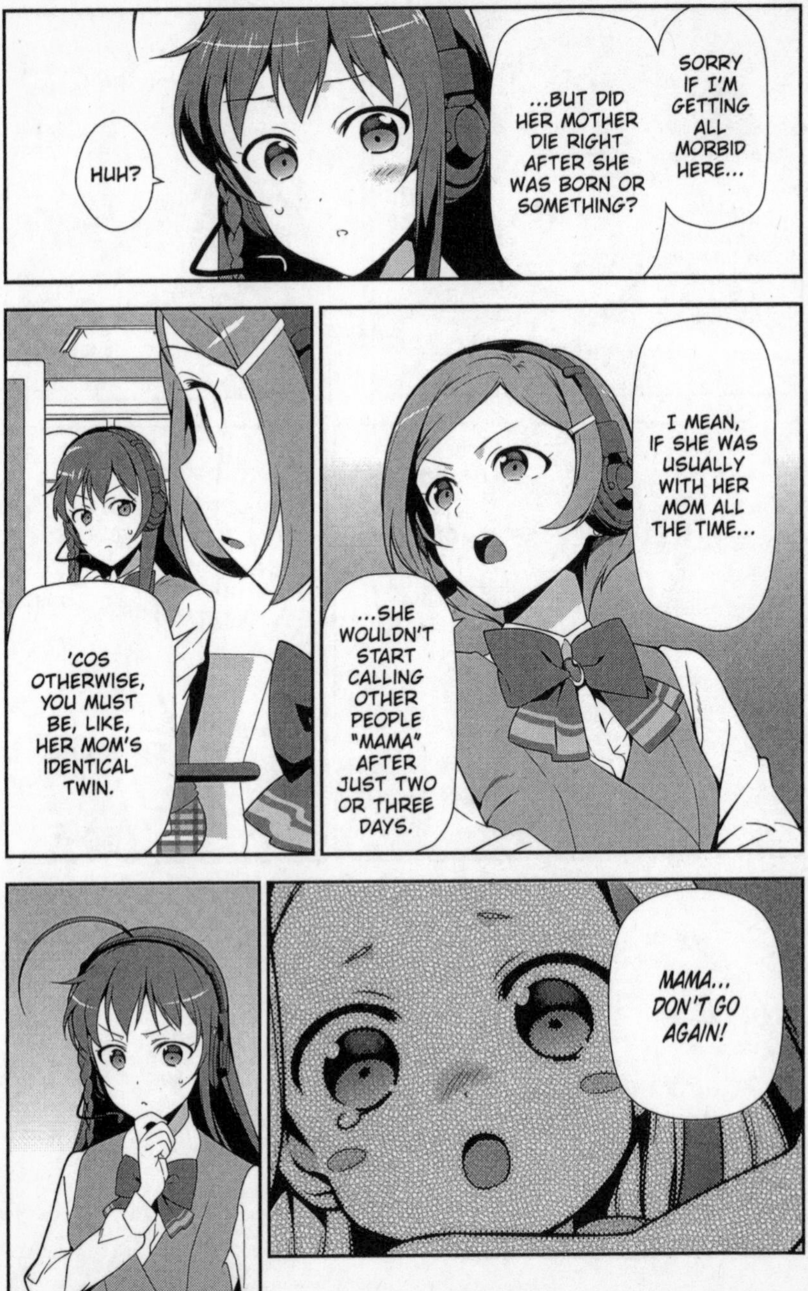
SORRY IF I'M GETTING ALL MORBID HERE...
...BUT DID HER MOTHER DIE RIGHT AFTER SHE WAS BORN OR SOMETHING?
HUH?
I MEAN, IF SHE WAS USUALLY WITH HER MOM ALL THE TIME...
...SHE WOULDN'T START CALLING OTHER PEOPLE "MAMA" AFTER JUST TWO OR THREE DAYS.
'COS OTHERWISE, YOU MUST BE, LIKE, HER MOM'S IDENTICAL TWIN.
MAMA... DON'T GO AGAIN!

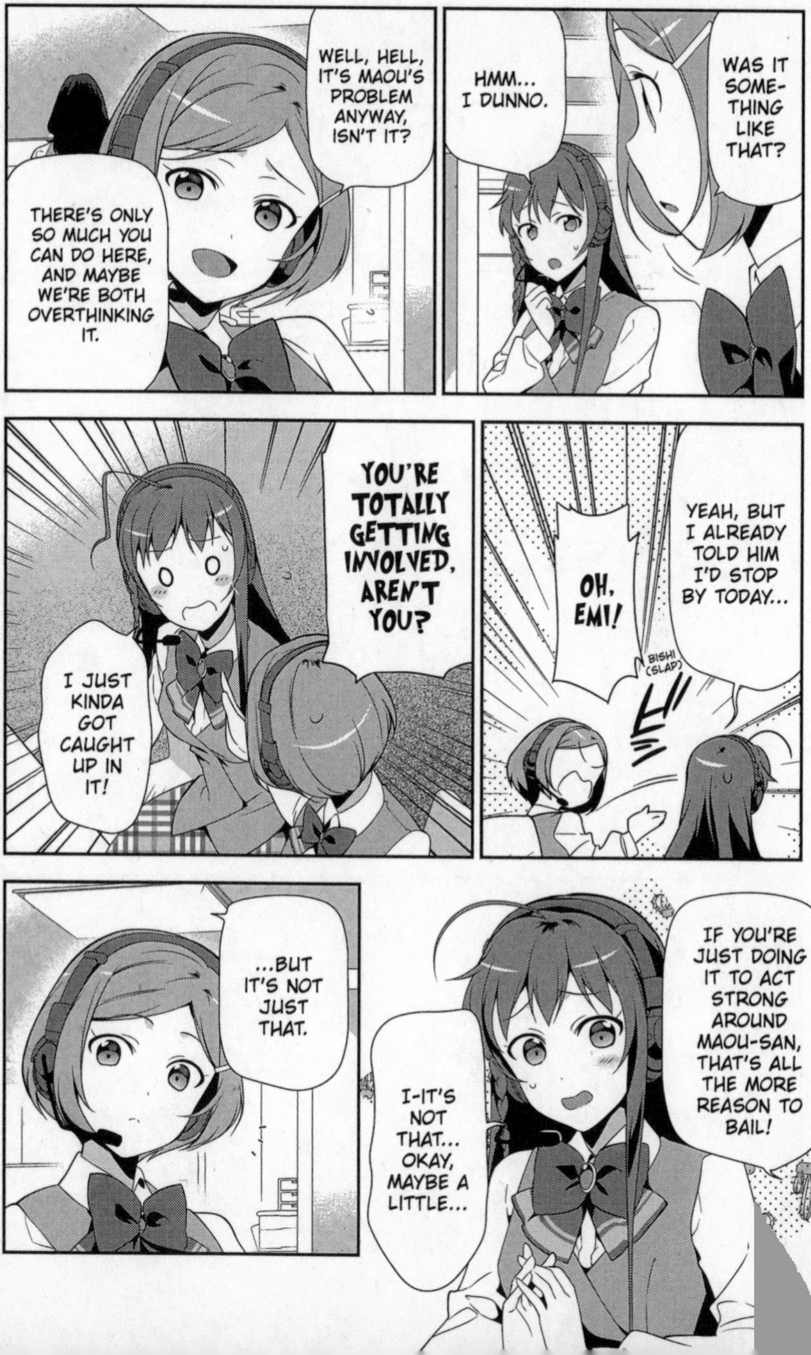
WAS IT SOMETHING LIKE THAT?
HMM... I DUNNO.
WELL, HELL, IT'S MAOU'S PROBLEM ANYWAY, ISN'T IT?
THERE'S ONLY SO MUCH YOU CAN DO HERE, AND MAYBE WE'RE BOTH OVERTHINKING IT.
YEAH, BUT I ALREADY TOLD HIM I'D STOP BY TODAY...
OH, EMI!
BISHI (SLAP)
YOU'RE TOTALLY GETTING INVOLVED, AREN'T YOU?
I JUST KINDA GOT CAUGHT UP IN IT!
IF YOU'RE JUST DOING IT TO ACT STRONG AROUND MAOU-SAN, THAT'S ALL THE MORE REASON TO BAIL!
I-IT'S NOT THAT... OKAY, MAYBE A LITTLE...
...BUT IT'S NOT JUST THAT.

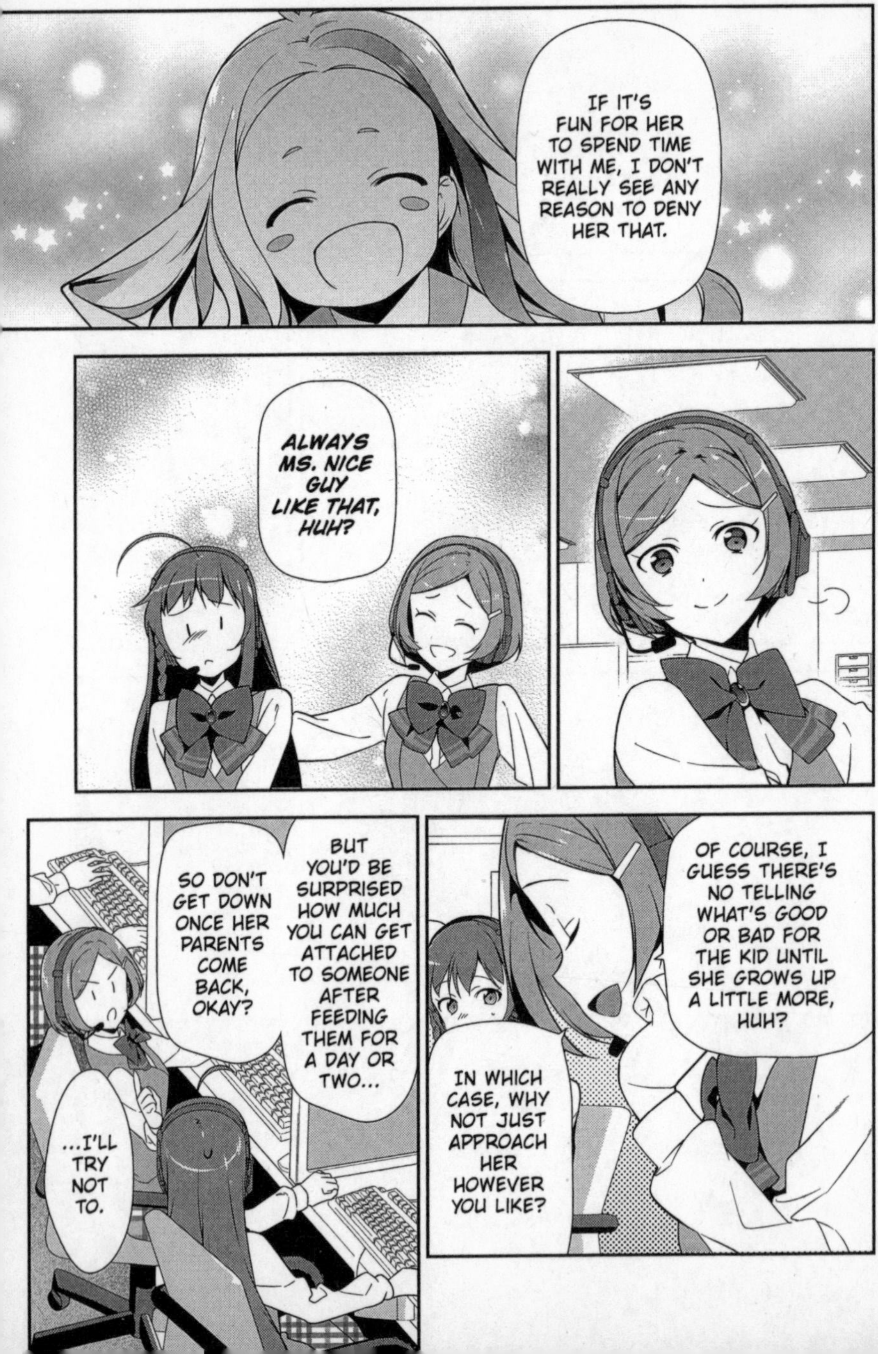
IF IT'S FUN FOR HER TO SPEND TIME WITH ME, I DON'T REALLY SEE ANY REASON TO DENY HER THAT.
ALWAYS MS. NICE GUY LIKE THAT, HUH?
OF COURSE, I GUESS THERE'S NO TELLING WHAT'S GOOD OR BAD FOR THE KID UNTIL SHE GROWS UP A LITTLE MORE, HUH?
IN WHICH CASE, WHY NOT JUST APPROACH HER HOWEVER YOU LIKE?
BUT YOU'D BE SURPRISED HOW MUCH YOU CAN GET ATTACHED TO SOMEONE AFTER FEEDING THEM FOR A DAY OR TWO...
SO DON'T GET DOWN ONCE HER PARENTS COME BACK, OKAY?
...I'LL TRY NOT TO.

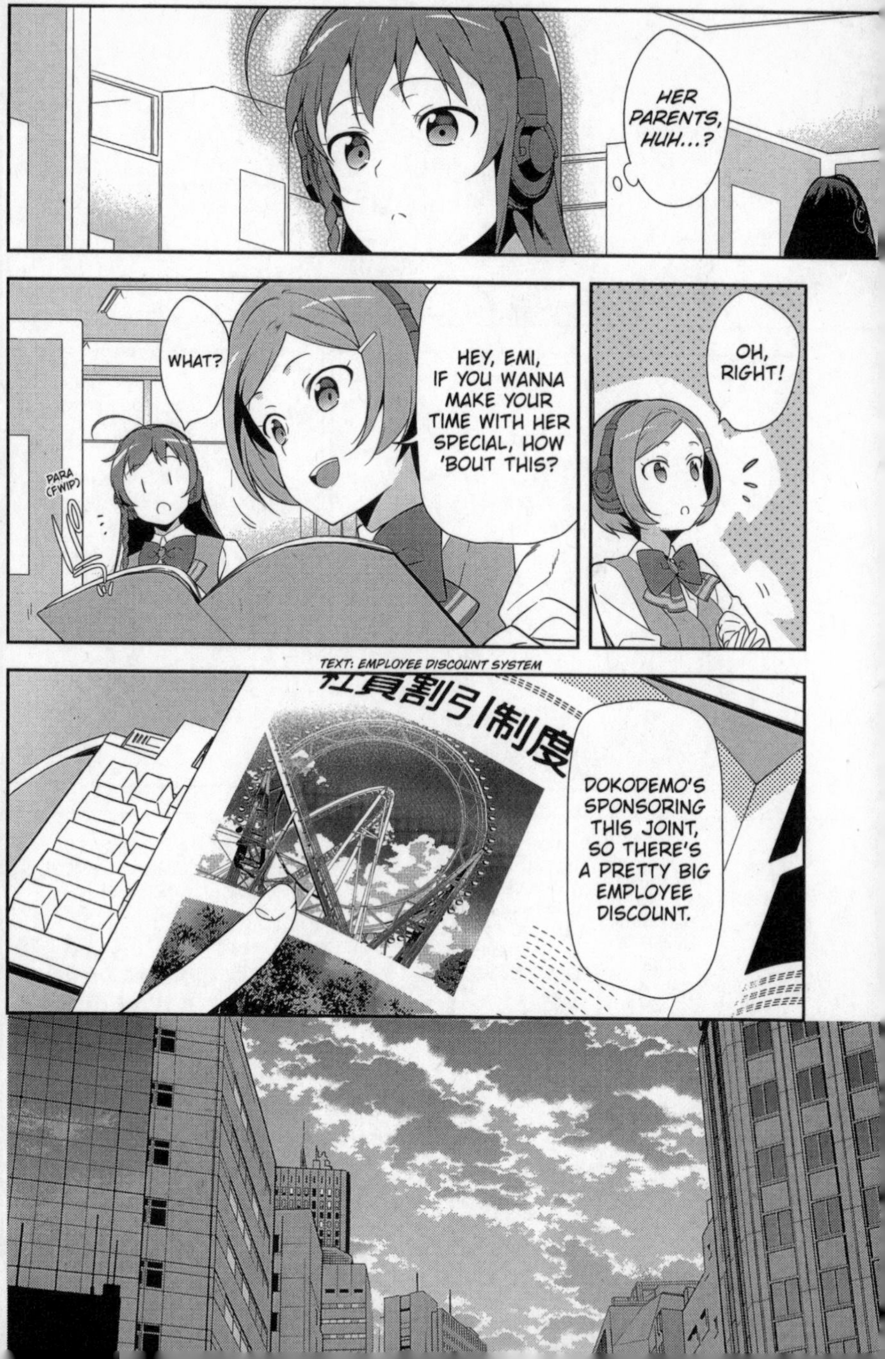
HER PARENTS, HUH...?
OH, RIGHT!
HEY, EMI, IF YOU WANNA MAKE YOUR TIME WITH HER SPECIAL, HOW 'BOUT THIS?
WHAT?
PARA (FWIP)
TEXT: EMPLOYEE DISCOUNT SYSTEM
社員割引制度
DOKODEMO'S SPONSORING THIS JOINT, SO THERE'S A PRETTY BIG EMPLOYEE DISCOUNT.

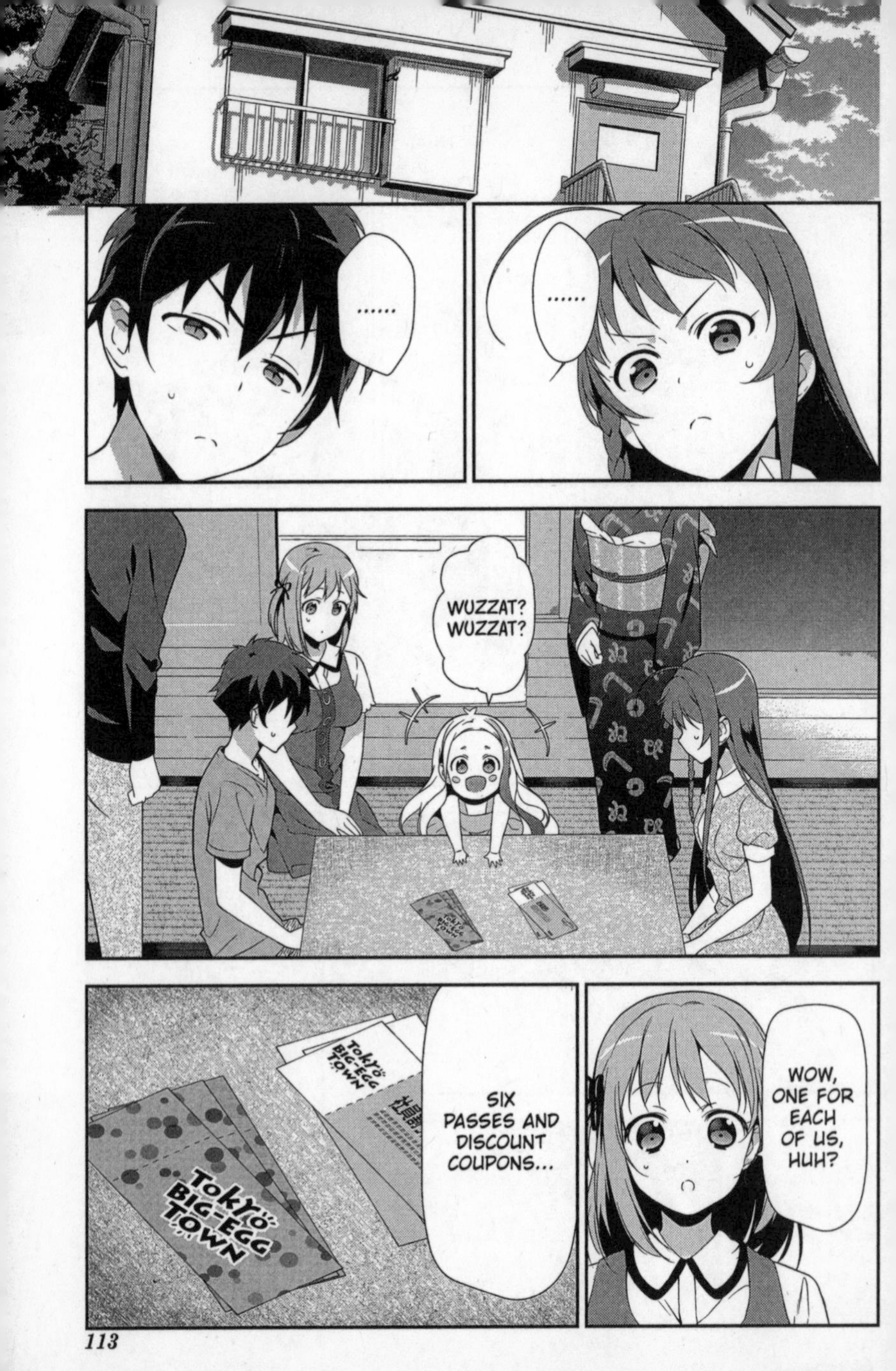
......
......
WUZZAT? WUZZAT?
WOW, ONE FOR EACH OF US, HUH?
SIX PASSES AND DISCOUNT COUPONS...
TOKYO BIG-EGG TOWN
TOKYO BIG-EGG TOWN

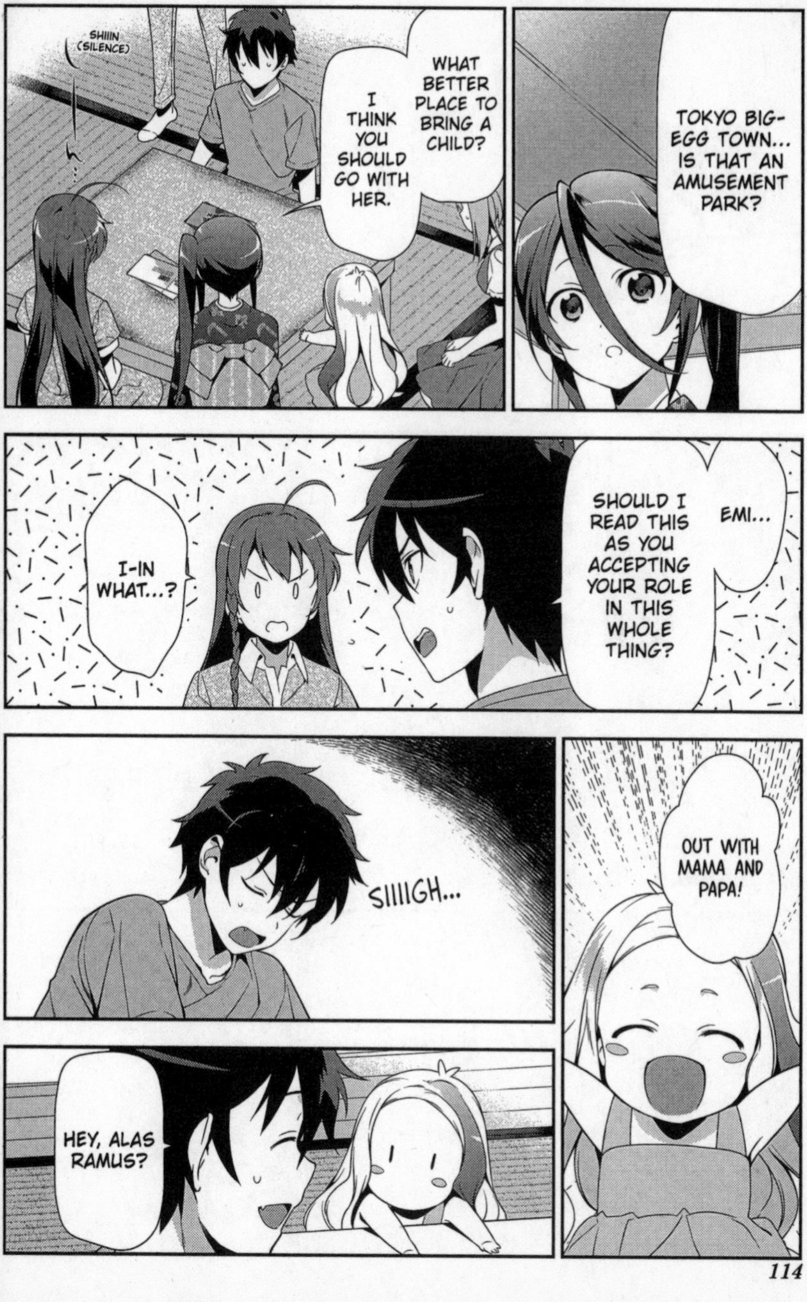
TOKYO BIG-EGG TOWN... IS THAT AN AMUSEMENT PARK?
WHAT BETTER PLACE TO BRING A CHILD?
I THINK YOU SHOULD GO WITH HER.
SHIIIN (SILENCE)
EMI...
SHOULD I READ THIS AS YOU ACCEPTING YOUR ROLE IN THIS WHOLE THING?
I-IN WHAT...?
OUT WITH MAMA AND PAPA!
SIIIGH...
HEY, ALAS RAMUS?

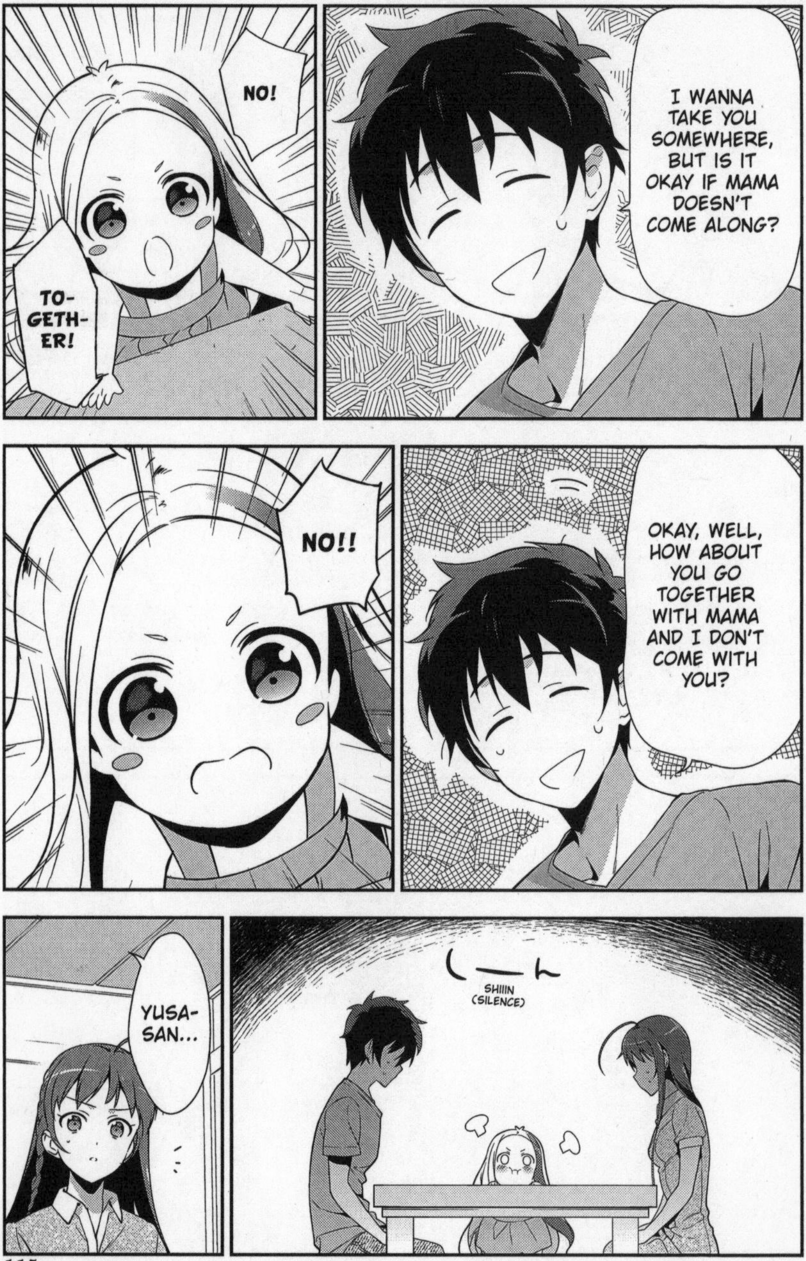

I WANNA TAKE YOU SOMEWHERE, BUT IS IT OKAY IF MAMA DOESN'T COME ALONG?
NO!
TO-GETH-ER!
OKAY, WELL, HOW ABOUT YOU GO TOGETHER WITH MAMA AND I DON'T COME WITH YOU?
NO!!
しーん
SHIIIN (SILENCE)
YUSA-SAN...

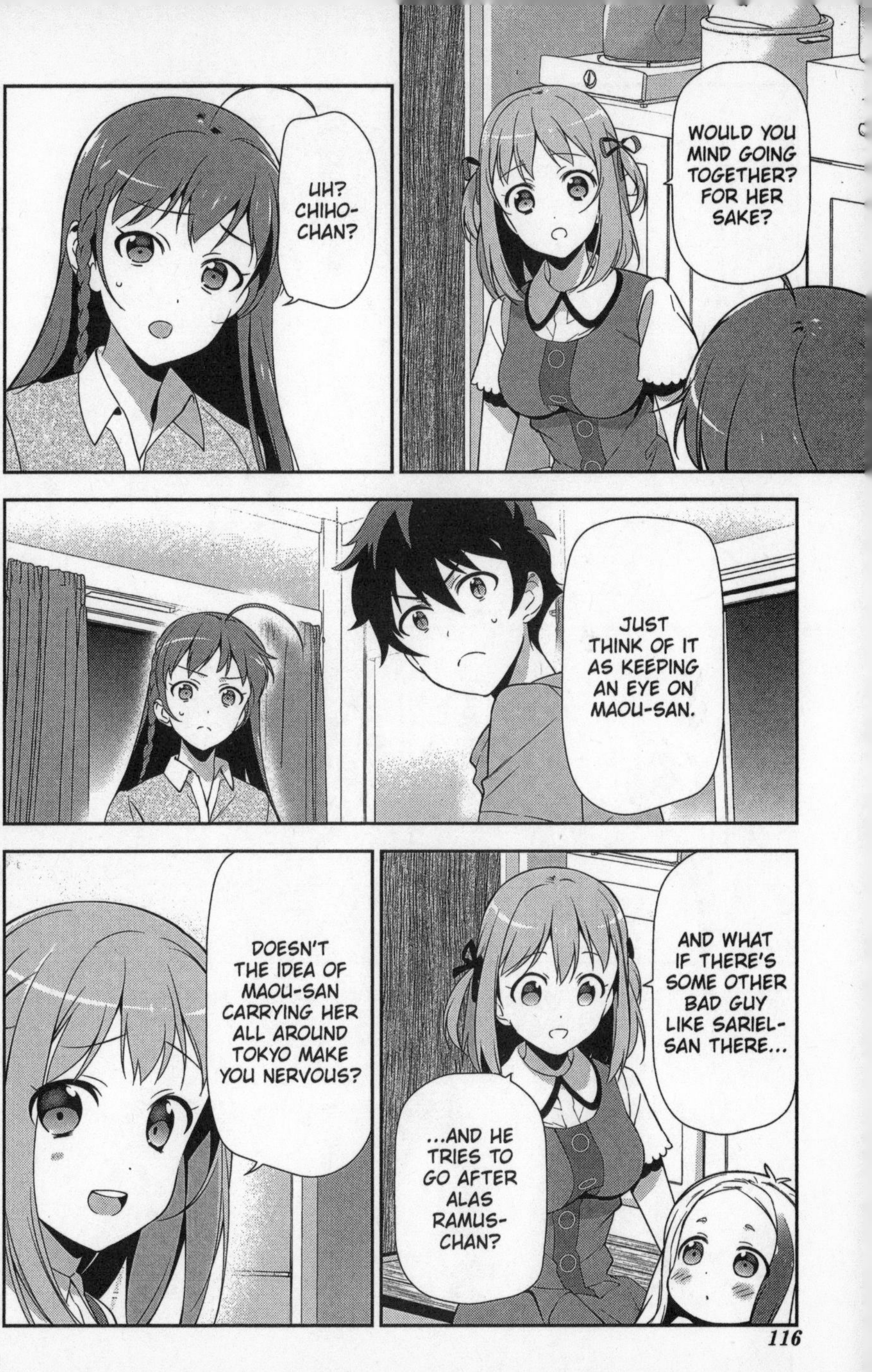
WOULD YOU MIND GOING TOGETHER? FOR HER SAKE?
UH? CHIHO-CHAN?
JUST THINK OF IT AS KEEPING AN EYE ON MAOU-SAN.
AND WHAT IF THERE'S SOME OTHER BAD GUY LIKE SARIEL-SAN THERE...
...AND HE TRIES TO GO AFTER ALAS RAMUS-CHAN?
DOESN'T THE IDEA OF MAOU-SAN CARRYING HER ALL AROUND TOKYO MAKE YOU NERVOUS?

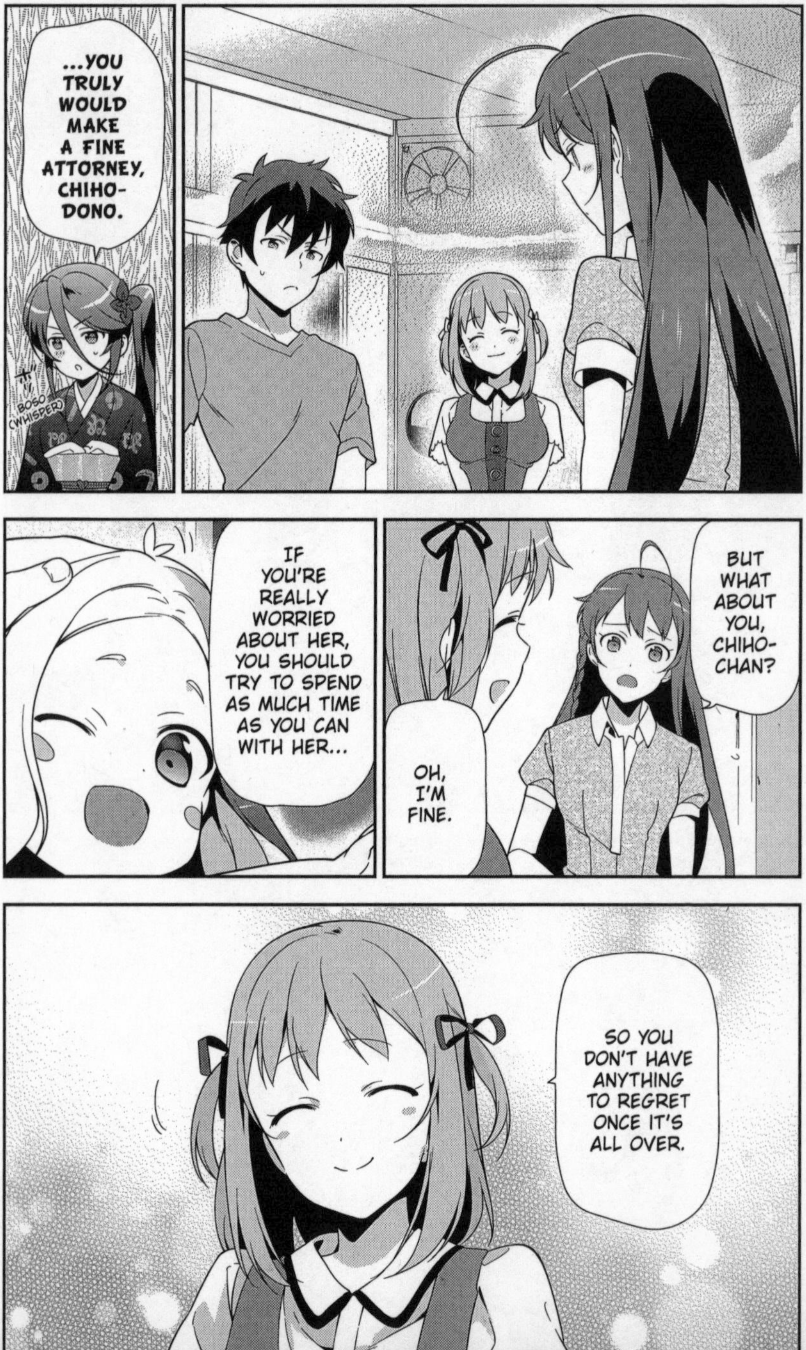
...YOU TRULY WOULD MAKE A FINE ATTORNEY, CHIHO-DONO.
BOSO (WHISPER)
BUT WHAT ABOUT YOU, CHIHO-CHAN?
OH, I'M FINE.
IF YOU'RE REALLY WORRIED ABOUT HER, YOU SHOULD TRY TO SPEND AS MUCH TIME AS YOU CAN WITH HER...
SO YOU DON'T HAVE ANYTHING TO REGRET ONCE IT'S ALL OVER.

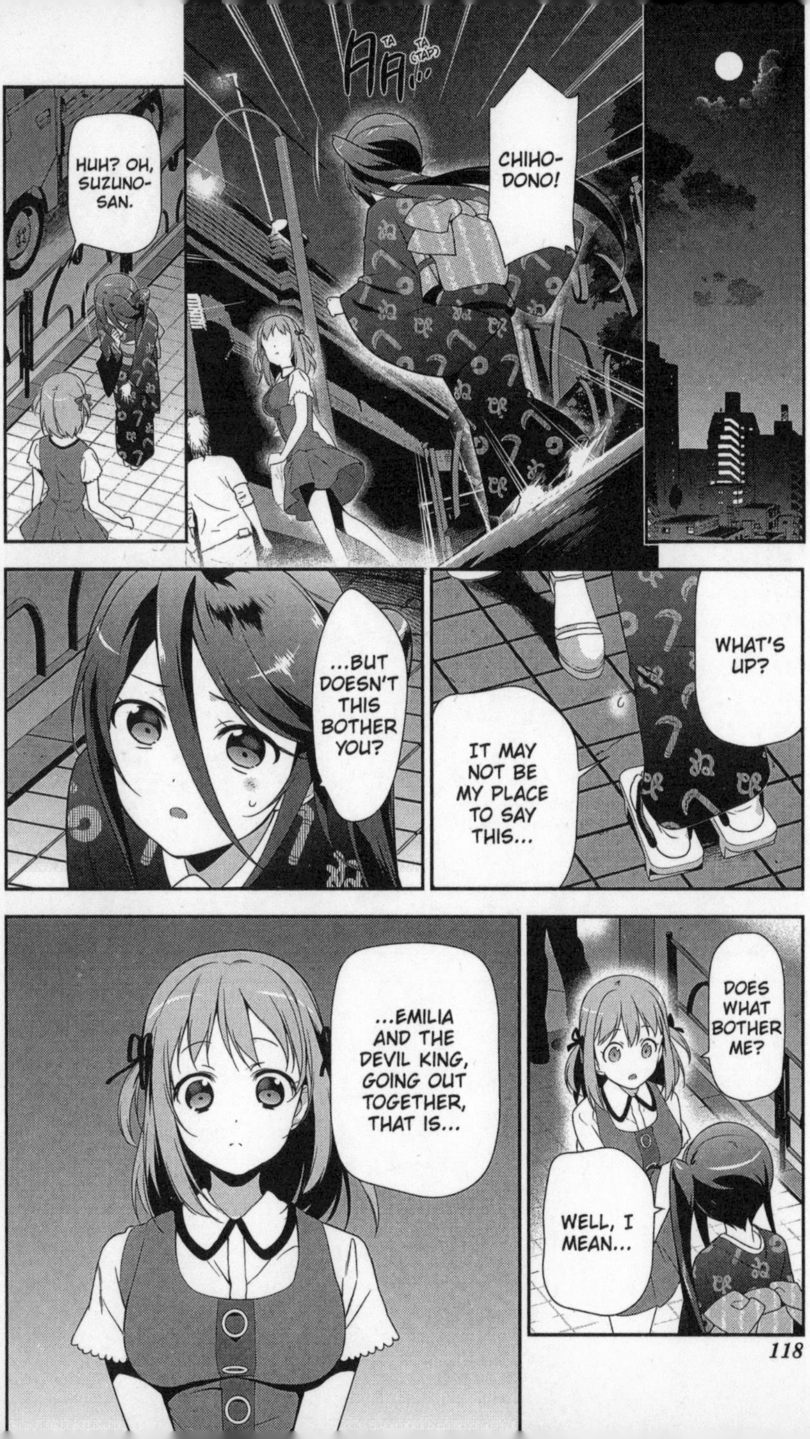
TA TA (TAP)...
CHIHO-DONO!
HUH? OH, SUZUNO-SAN.
WHAT'S UP?
IT MAY NOT BE MY PLACE TO SAY THIS...
...BUT DOESN'T THIS BOTHER YOU?
DOES WHAT BOTHER ME?
WELL, I MEAN...
...EMILIA AND THE DEVIL KING, GOING OUT TOGETHER, THAT IS...

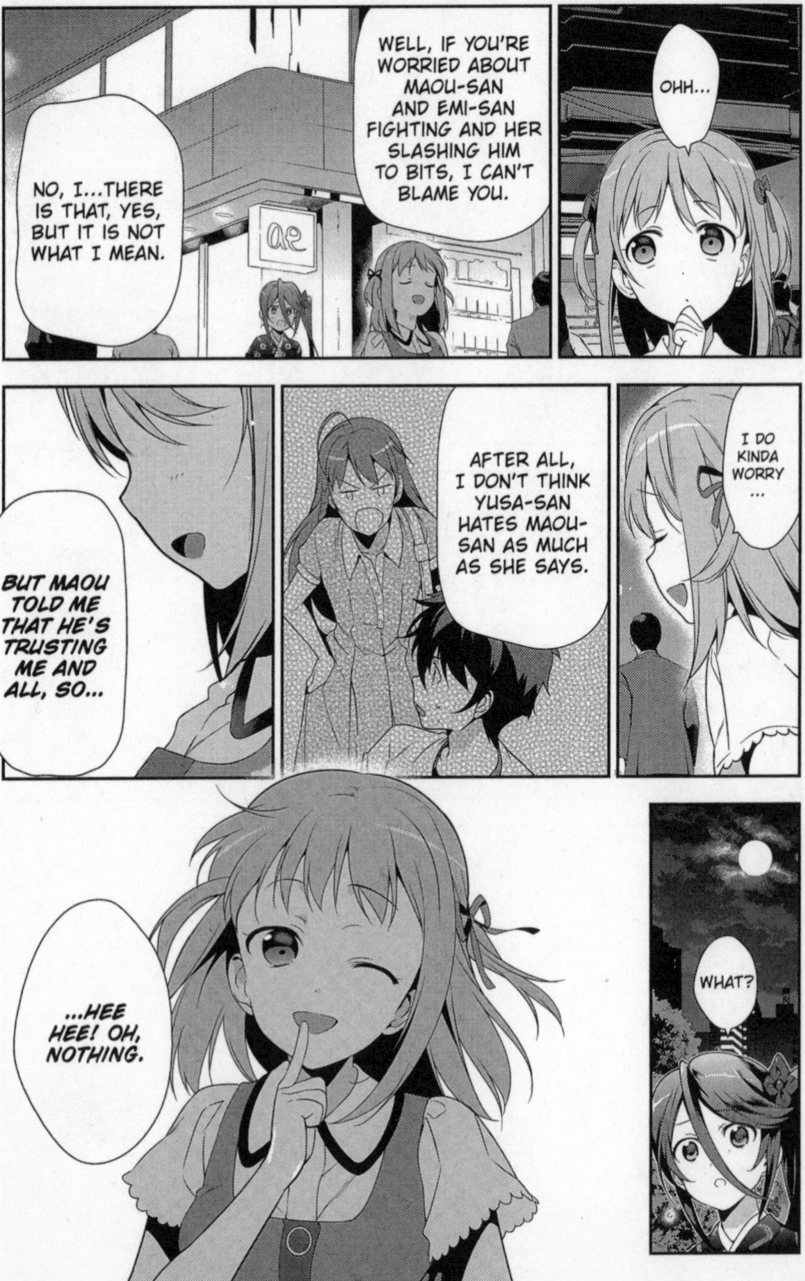
OHH...
WELL, IF YOU'RE WORRIED ABOUT MAOU-SAN AND EMI-SAN FIGHTING AND HER SLASHING HIM TO BITS, I CAN'T BLAME YOU.
NO, I...THERE IS THAT, YES, BUT IT IS NOT WHAT I MEAN.
I DO KINDA WORRY...
AFTER ALL, I DON'T THINK YUSA-SAN HATES MAOU-SAN AS MUCH AS SHE SAYS.
BUT MAOU TOLD ME THAT HE'S TRUSTING ME AND ALL, SO...
WHAT?
...HEE HEE! OH, NOTHING.

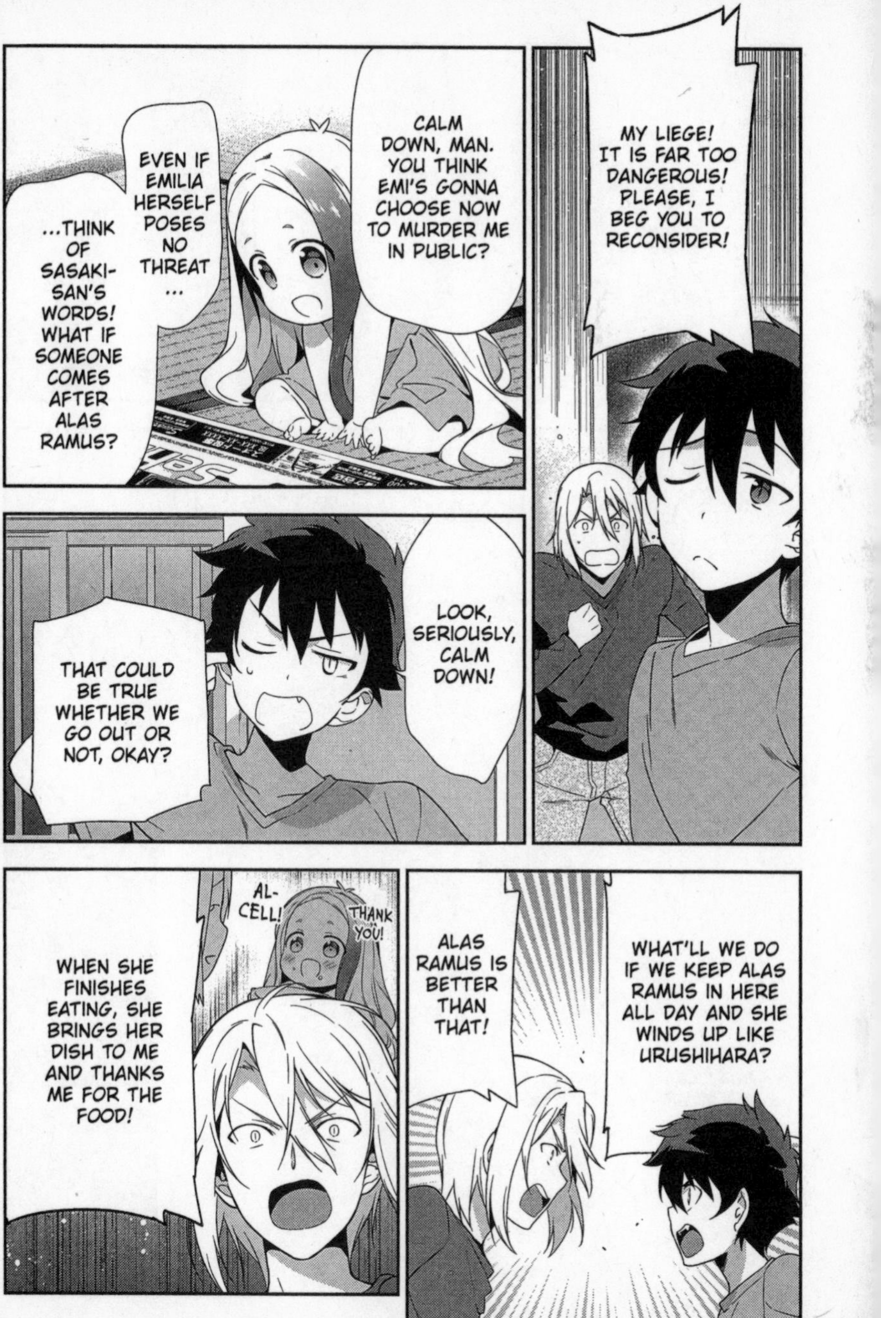
MY LIEGE! IT IS FAR TOO DANGEROUS! PLEASE, I BEG YOU TO RECONSIDER!
CALM DOWN, MAN. YOU THINK EMI'S GONNA CHOOSE NOW TO MURDER ME IN PUBLIC?
EVEN IF EMILIA HERSELF POSES NO THREAT...
...THINK OF SASAKI-SAN'S WORDS! WHAT IF SOMEONE COMES AFTER ALAS RAMUS?
LOOK, SERIOUSLY, CALM DOWN!
THAT COULD BE TRUE WHETHER WE GO OUT OR NOT, OKAY?
WHAT'LL WE DO IF WE KEEP ALAS RAMUS IN HERE ALL DAY AND SHE WINDS UP LIKE URUSHIHARA?
ALAS RAMUS IS BETTER THAN THAT!
THANK YOU!
AL-CELL!
WHEN SHE FINISHES EATING, SHE BRINGS HER DISH TO ME AND THANKS ME FOR THE FOOD!

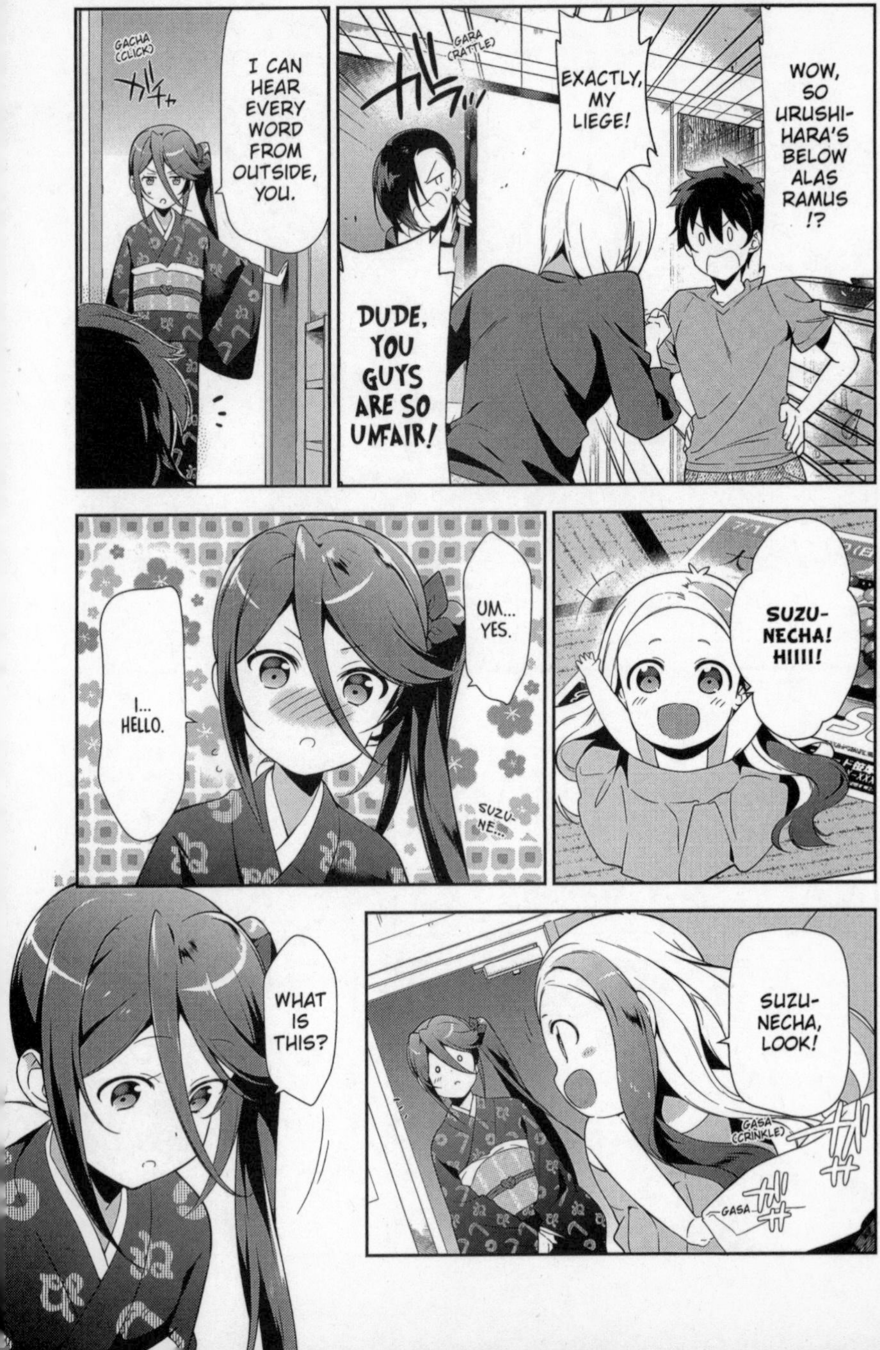
WOW, SO URUSHI-HARA'S BELOW ALAS RAMUS!?
EXACTLY, MY LIEGE!
GARA (RATTLE)
DUDE, YOU GUYS ARE SO UNFAIR!
I CAN HEAR EVERY WORD FROM OUTSIDE, YOU.
GACHA (CLICK)
SUZU-NECHA! HIIII!
UM... YES.
I... HELLO.
SUZU-NE...
SUZU-NECHA, LOOK!
GASA (CRINKLE)
GASA
WHAT IS THIS?

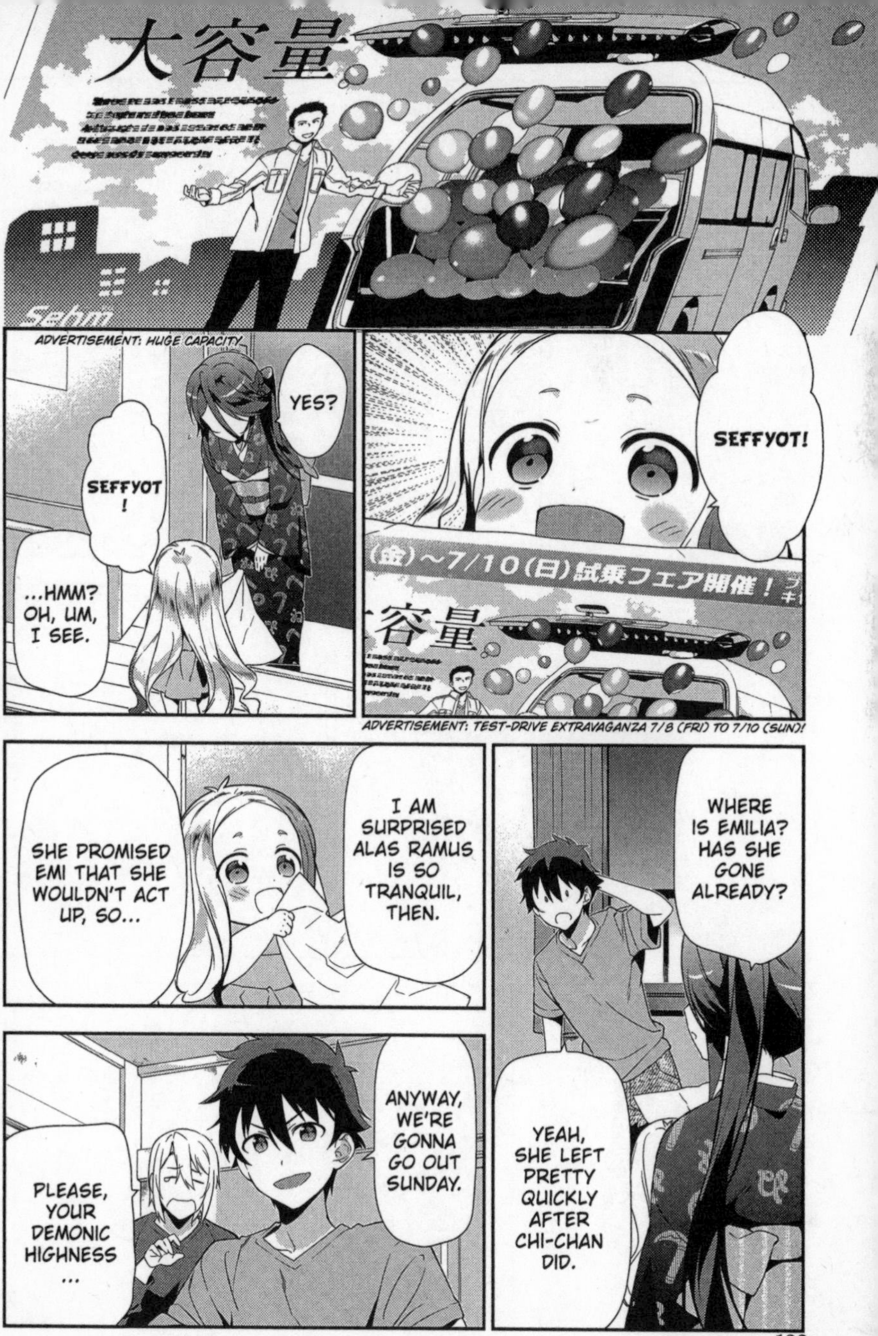

大容量
Sehm
ADVERTISEMENT: HUGE CAPACITY
SEFFYOT!
(金)~7/10(日)試乗フェア開催！
大容量
ADVERTISEMENT: TEST-DRIVE EXTRAVAGANZA 7/8 (FRI) TO 7/10 (SUN)!
YES?
SEFFYOT!
...HMM? OH, UM, I SEE.
WHERE IS EMILIA? HAS SHE GONE ALREADY?
YEAH, SHE LEFT PRETTY QUICKLY AFTER CHI-CHAN DID.
I AM SURPRISED ALAS RAMUS IS SO TRANQUIL, THEN.
SHE PROMISED EMI THAT SHE WOULDN'T ACT UP, SO...
ANYWAY, WE'RE GONNA GO OUT SUNDAY.
PLEASE, YOUR DEMONIC HIGHNESS...

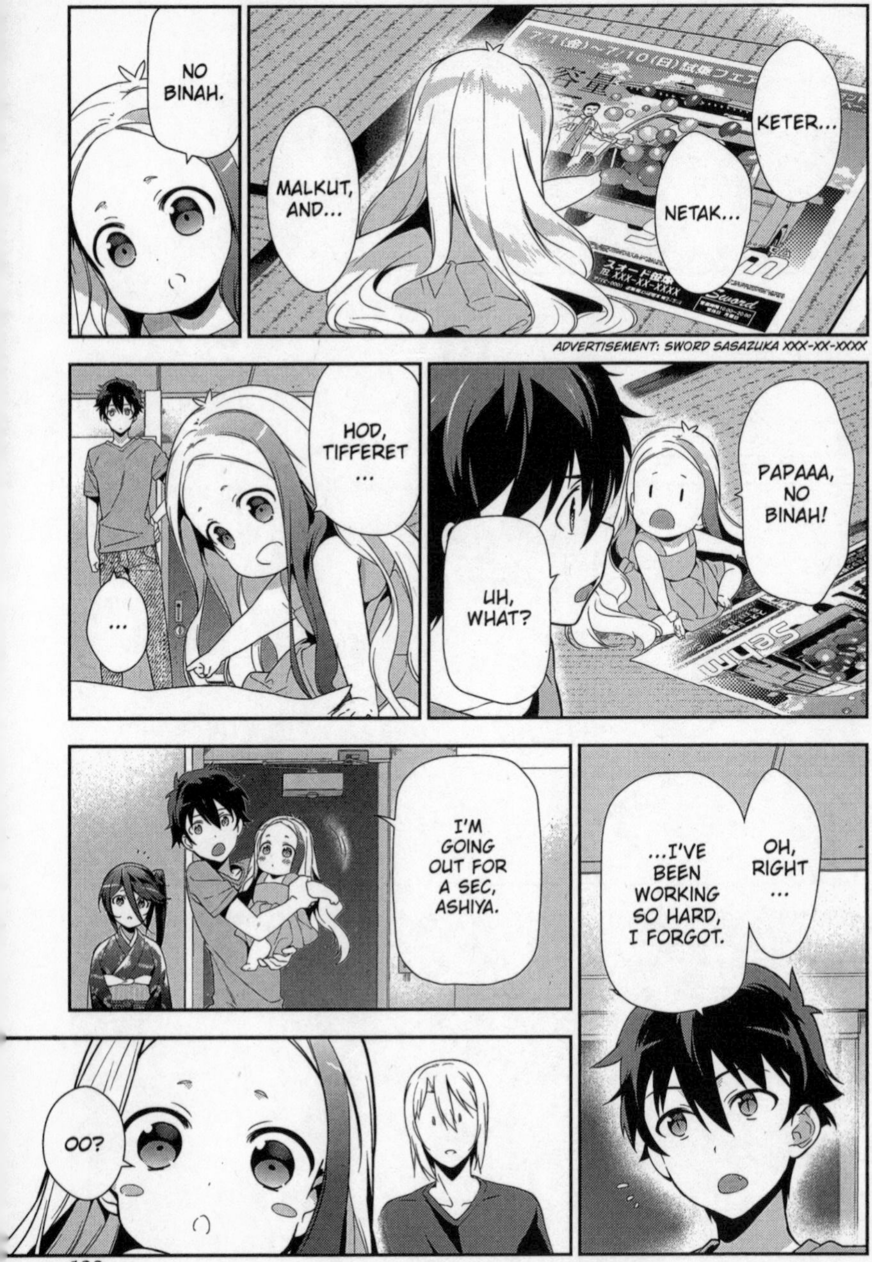
KETER...
NETAK...
MALKUT, AND...
NO BINAH.
ADVERTISEMENT: SWORD SASAZUKA XXX-XX-XXXX
PAPAAA, NO BINAH!
UH, WHAT?
HOD, TIFFERET ...
...
OH, RIGHT ...
...I'VE BEEN WORKING SO HARD, I FORGOT.
I'M GOING OUT FOR A SEC, ASHIYA.
OO?

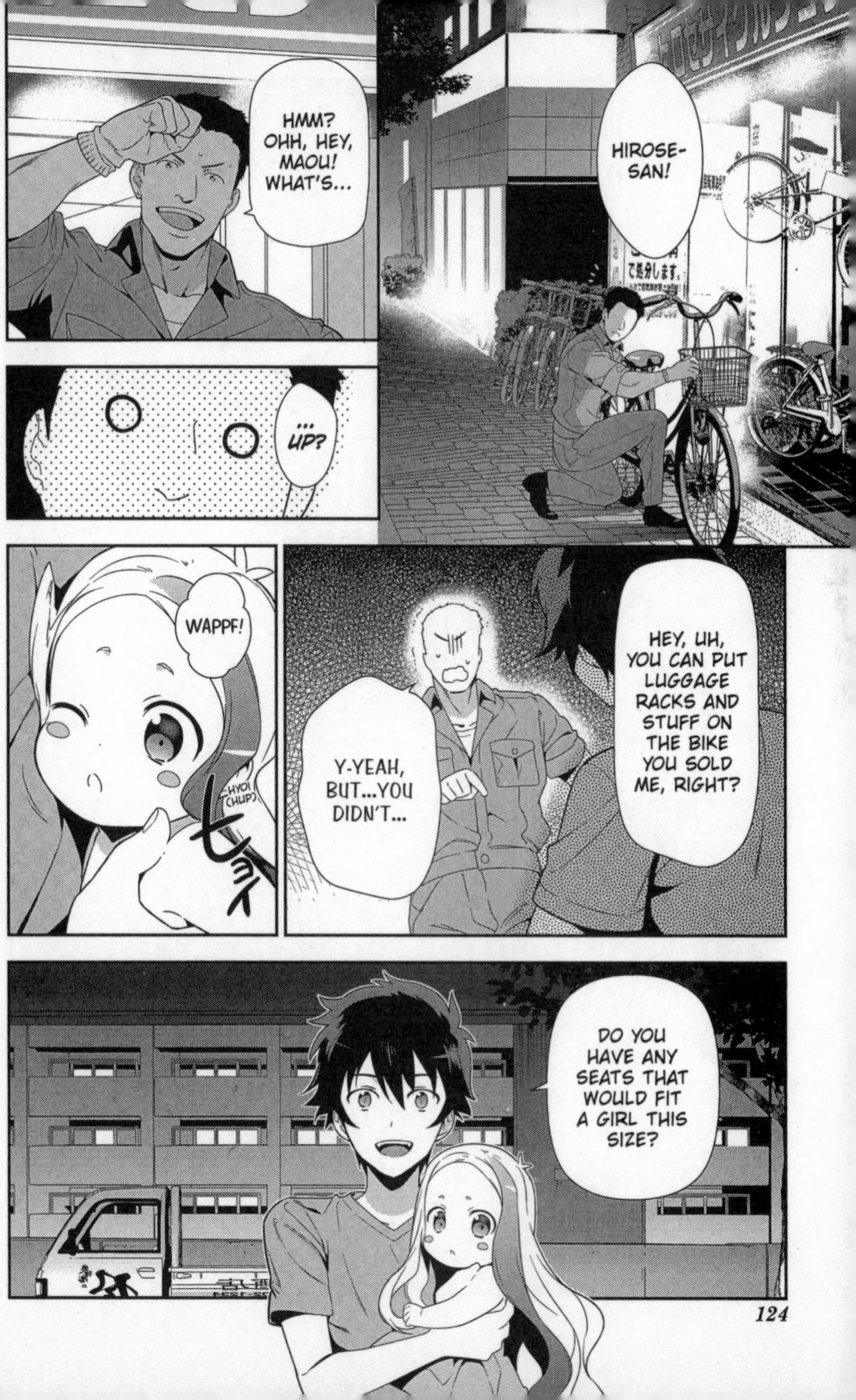
HIROSE-SAN!
HMM? OHH, HEY, MAOU! WHAT'S...
...UP?
HEY, UH, YOU CAN PUT LUGGAGE RACKS AND STUFF ON THE BIKE YOU SOLD ME, RIGHT?
Y-YEAH, BUT...YOU DIDN'T...
WAPPF!
HYOI (CHUP)
DO YOU HAVE ANY SEATS THAT WOULD FIT A GIRL THIS SIZE?

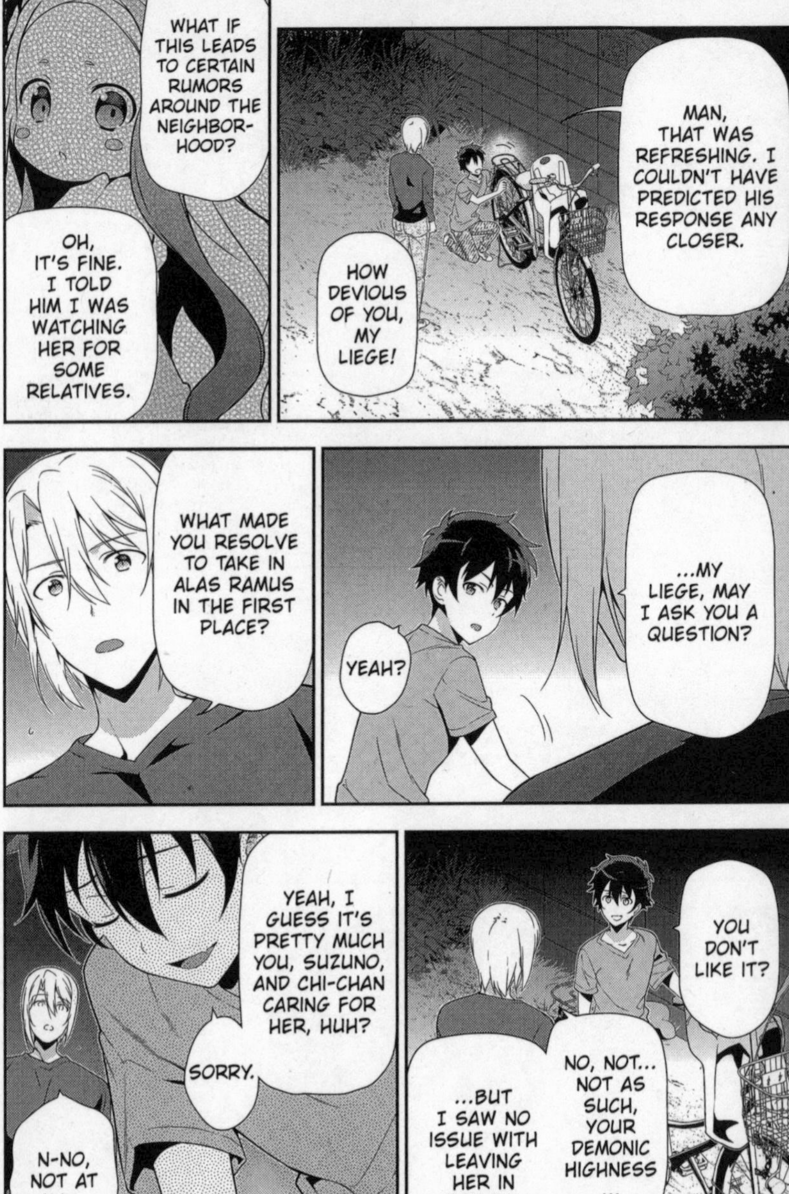
MAN, THAT WAS REFRESHING. I COULDN'T HAVE PREDICTED HIS RESPONSE ANY CLOSER.
HOW DEVIOUS OF YOU, MY LIEGE!
WHAT IF THIS LEADS TO CERTAIN RUMORS AROUND THE NEIGHBOR-HOOD?
OH, IT'S FINE. I TOLD HIM I WAS WATCHING HER FOR SOME RELATIVES.
...MY LIEGE, MAY I ASK YOU A QUESTION?
YEAH?
WHAT MADE YOU RESOLVE TO TAKE IN ALAS RAMUS IN THE FIRST PLACE?
YOU DON'T LIKE IT?
NO, NOT... NOT AS SUCH, YOUR DEMONIC HIGHNESS ...
...BUT I SAW NO ISSUE WITH LEAVING HER IN CRESTIA'S CARE...
YEAH, I GUESS IT'S PRETTY MUCH YOU, SUZUNO, AND CHI-CHAN CARING FOR HER, HUH?
SORRY.
N-NO, NOT AT ALL...

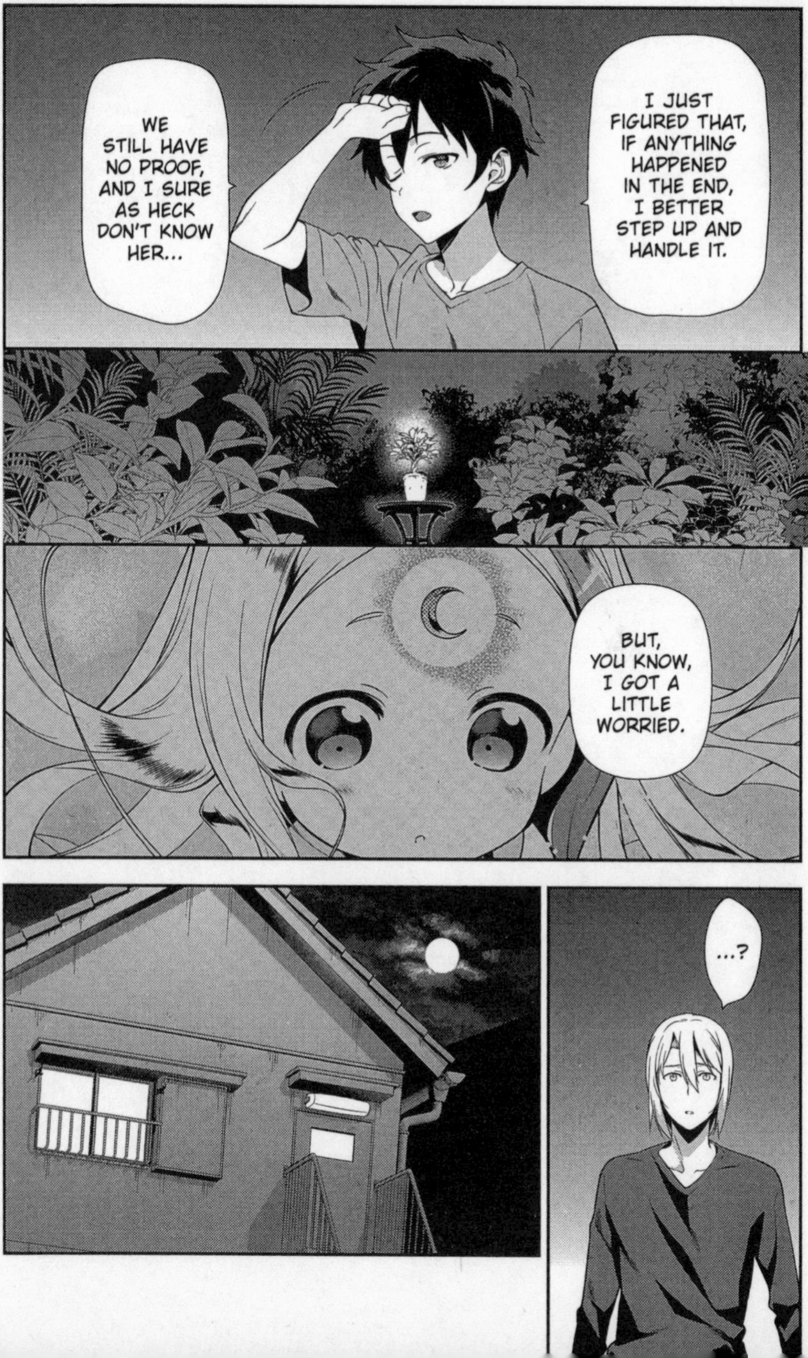
I JUST FIGURED THAT, IF ANYTHING HAPPENED IN THE END, I BETTER STEP UP AND HANDLE IT.
WE STILL HAVE NO PROOF, AND I SURE AS HECK DON'T KNOW HER...
BUT, YOU KNOW, I GOT A LITTLE WORRIED.
...?

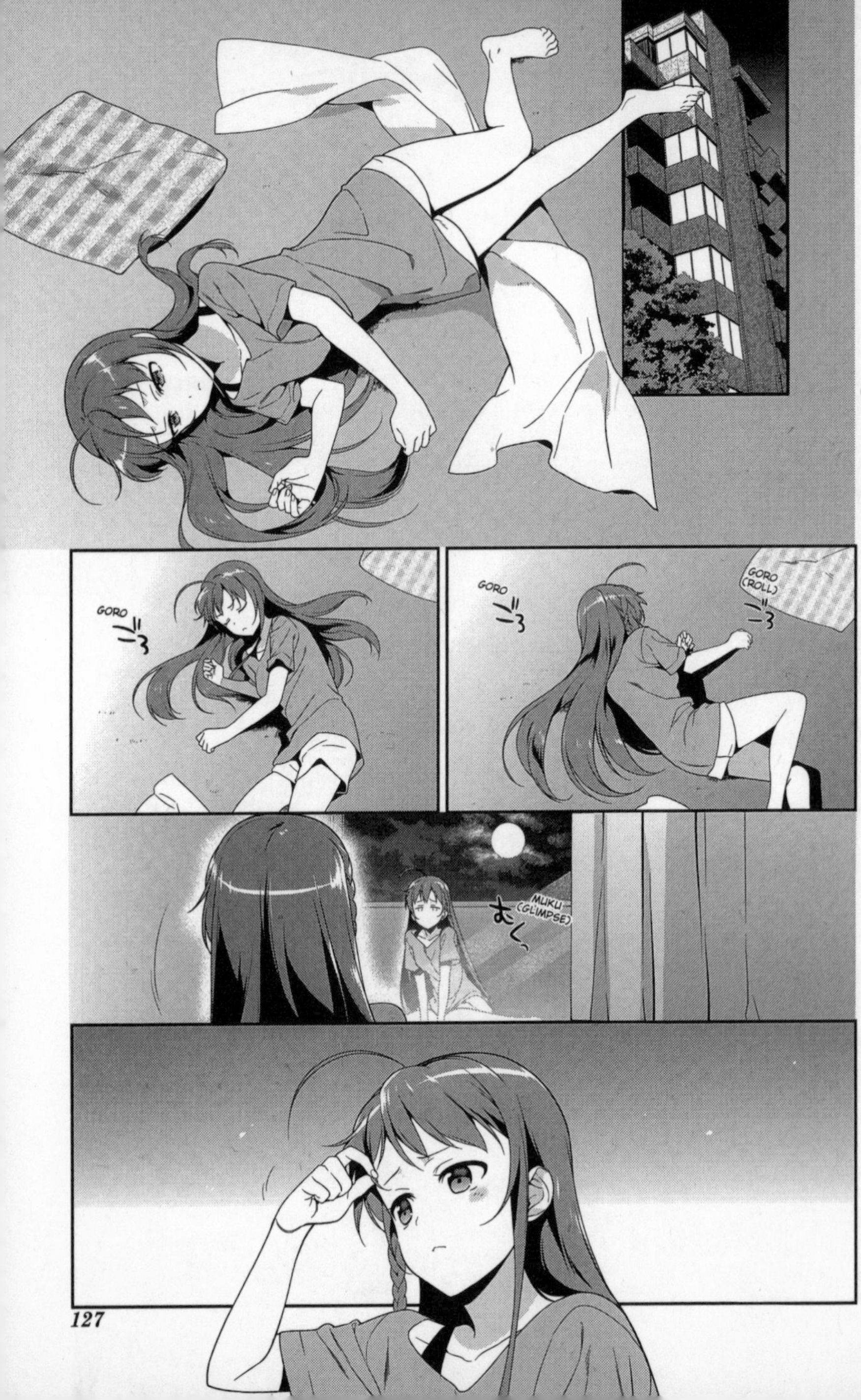
GORO (ROLL)
ごろ
GORO
ごろ
GORO
ごろ
MUKU (GLIMPSE)
むく

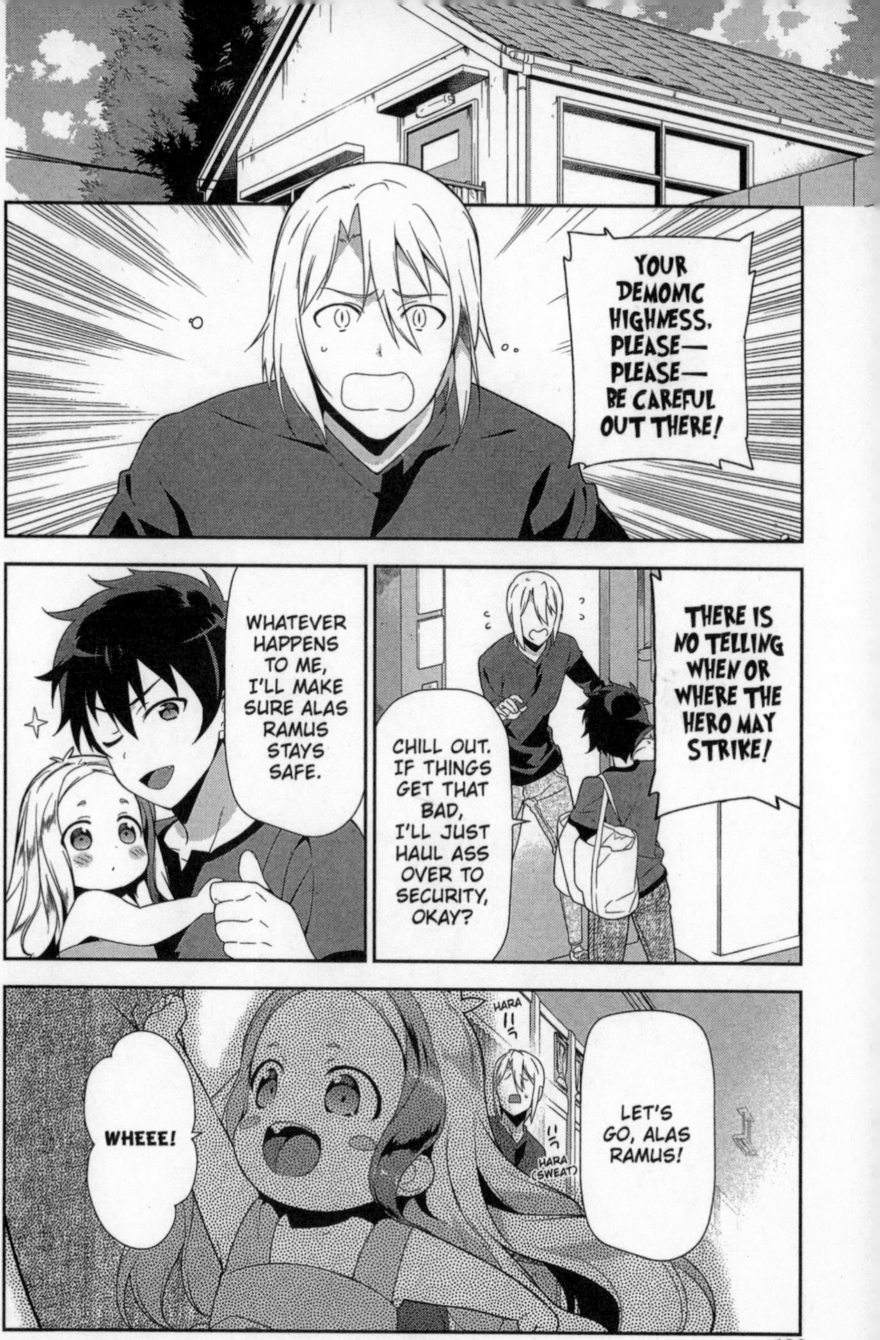
YOUR DEMONIC HIGHNESS. PLEASE—PLEASE—BE CAREFUL OUT THERE!
THERE IS NO TELLING WHEN OR WHERE THE HERO MAY STRIKE!
CHILL OUT. IF THINGS GET THAT BAD, I'LL JUST HAUL ASS OVER TO SECURITY, OKAY?
WHATEVER HAPPENS TO ME, I'LL MAKE SURE ALAS RAMUS STAYS SAFE.
LET'S GO, ALAS RAMUS!
HARA
HARA (SWEAT)
WHEEE!

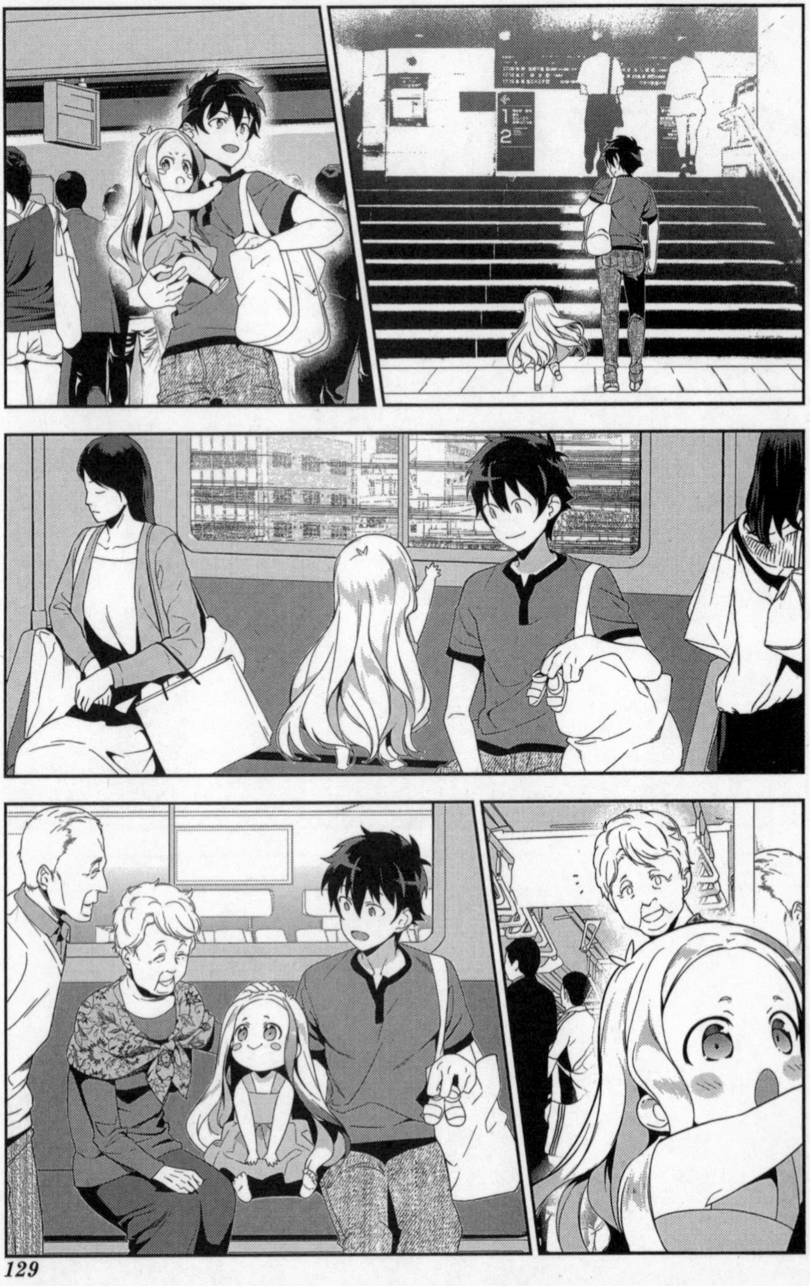

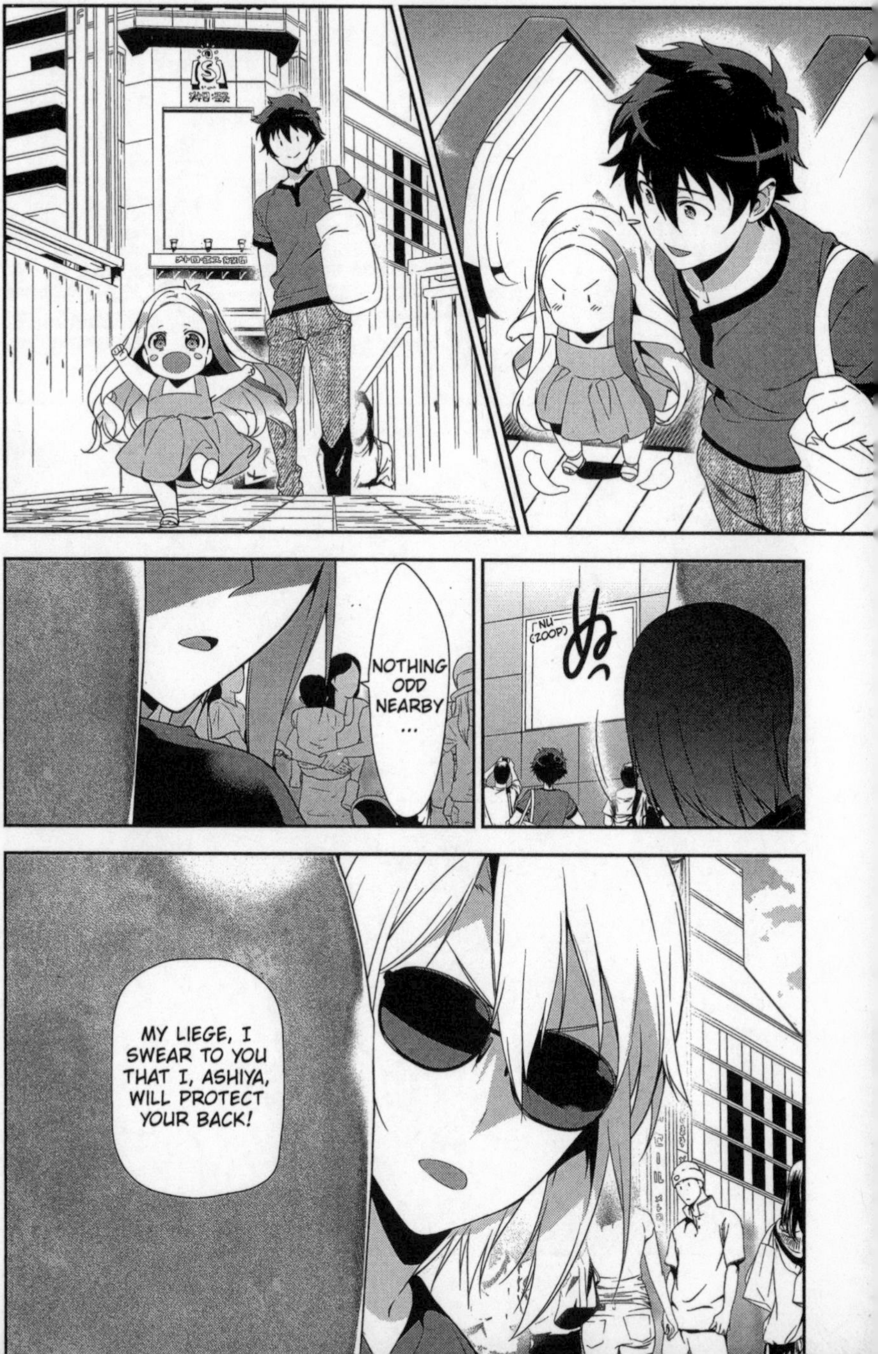

ぬっ
「NU」 (ZOOP)
NOTHING ODD NEARBY ...
MY LIEGE, I SWEAR TO YOU THAT I, ASHIYA, WILL PROTECT YOUR BACK!

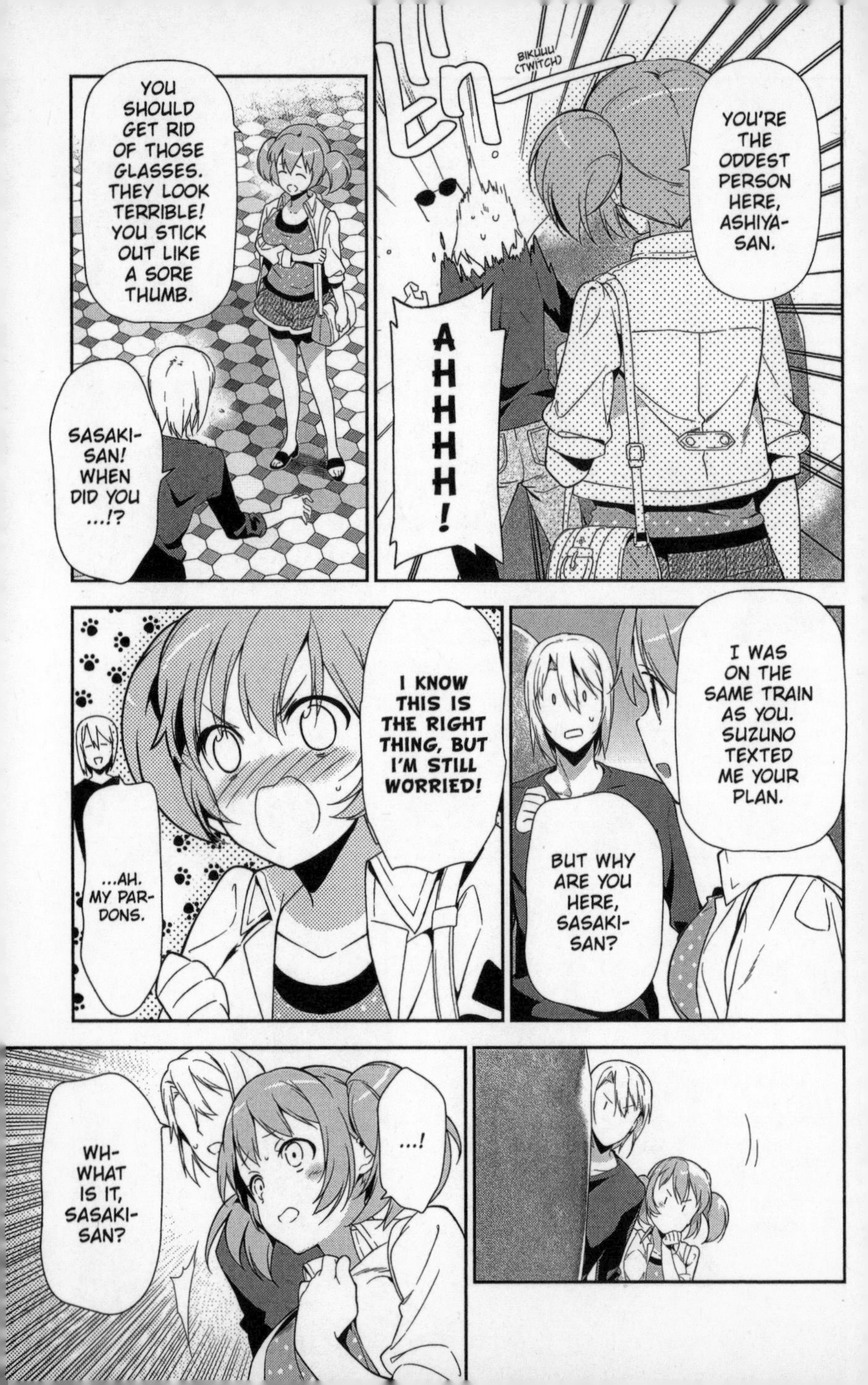
YOU'RE THE ODDEST PERSON HERE, ASHIYA-SAN.
BIKUUU (TWITCH)
AHHHHH!
YOU SHOULD GET RID OF THOSE GLASSES. THEY LOOK TERRIBLE! YOU STICK OUT LIKE A SORE THUMB.
SASAKI-SAN! WHEN DID YOU ...!?
I WAS ON THE SAME TRAIN AS YOU. SUZUNO TEXTED ME YOUR PLAN.
BUT WHY ARE YOU HERE, SASAKI-SAN?
I KNOW THIS IS THE RIGHT THING, BUT I'M STILL WORRIED!
...AH. MY PARDONS.
...!
WH-WHAT IS IT, SASAKI-SAN?

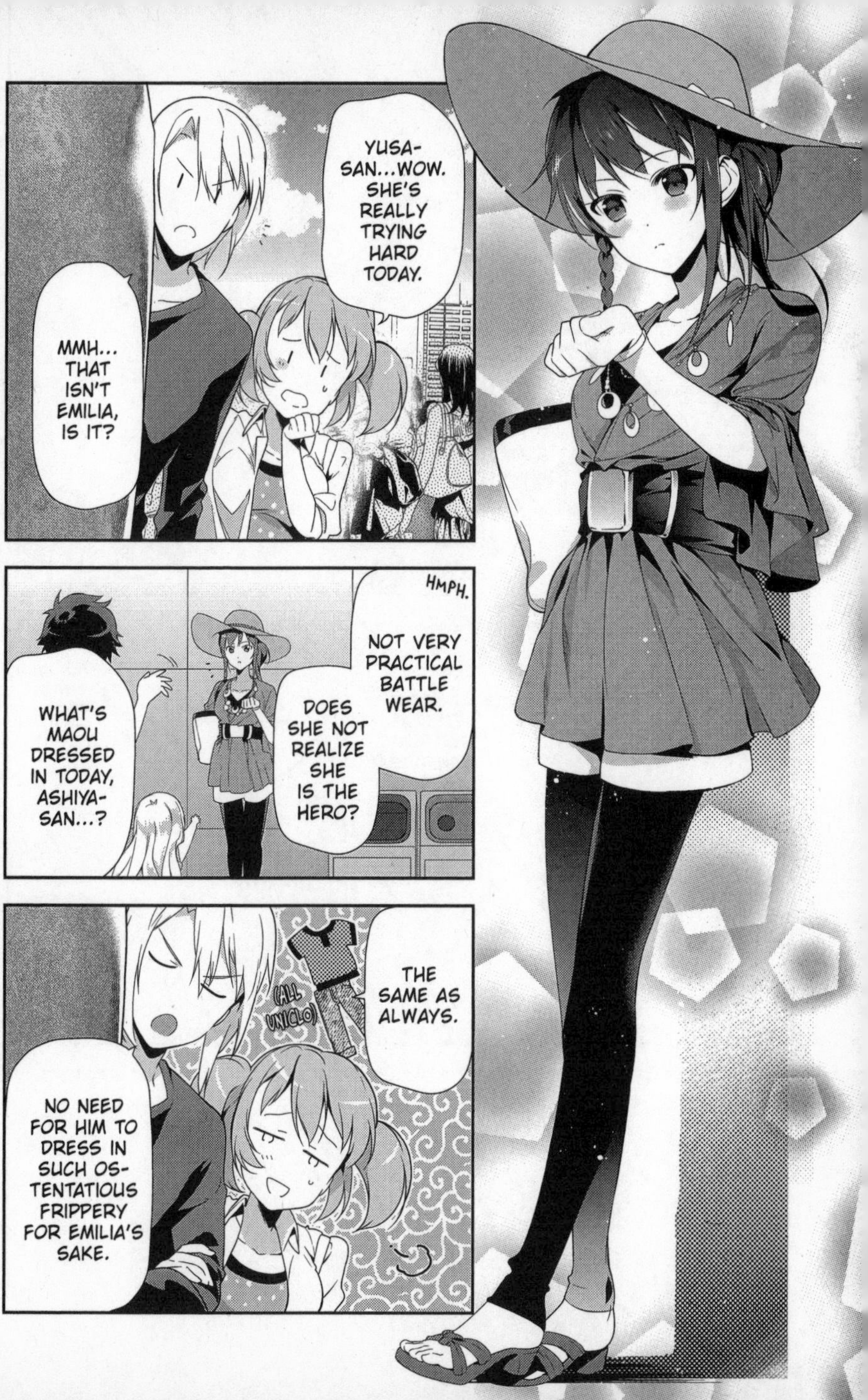
YUSA-SAN...WOW. SHE'S REALLY TRYING HARD TODAY.
MMH... THAT ISN'T EMILIA, IS IT?
HMPH.
NOT VERY PRACTICAL BATTLE WEAR.
DOES SHE NOT REALIZE SHE IS THE HERO?
WHAT'S MAOU DRESSED IN TODAY, ASHIYA-SAN...?
THE SAME AS ALWAYS.
(ALL UNICLO)
NO NEED FOR HIM TO DRESS IN SUCH OS-TENTATIOUS FRIPPERY FOR EMILIA'S SAKE.

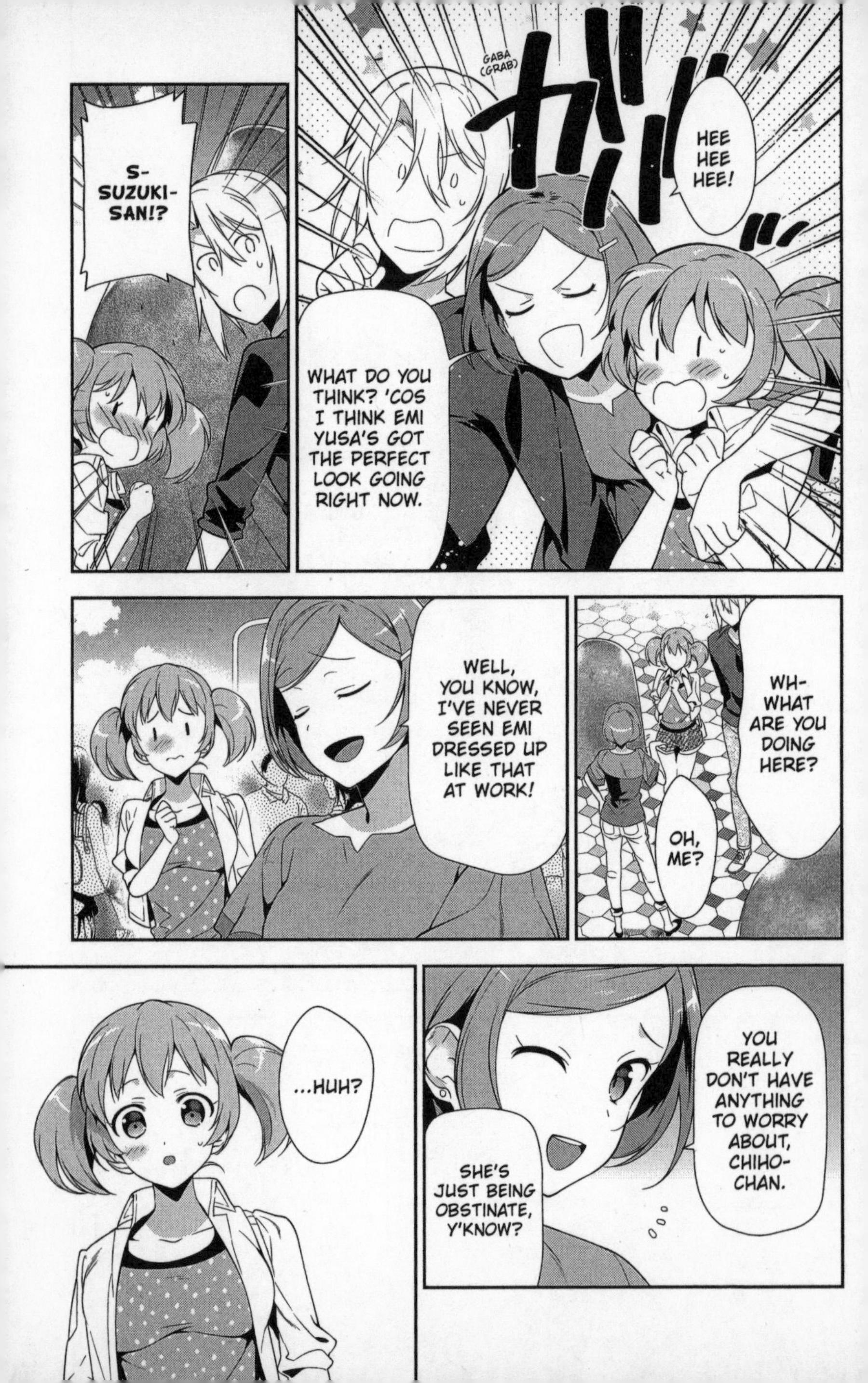
GABA (GRAB)
HEE HEE HEE!
WHAT DO YOU THINK? 'COS I THINK EMI YUSA'S GOT THE PERFECT LOOK GOING RIGHT NOW.
S-SUZUKI-SAN!?
WH-WHAT ARE YOU DOING HERE?
OH, ME?
WELL, YOU KNOW, I'VE NEVER SEEN EMI DRESSED UP LIKE THAT AT WORK!
YOU REALLY DON'T HAVE ANYTHING TO WORRY ABOUT, CHIHO-CHAN.
SHE'S JUST BEING OBSTINATE, Y'KNOW?
...HUH?

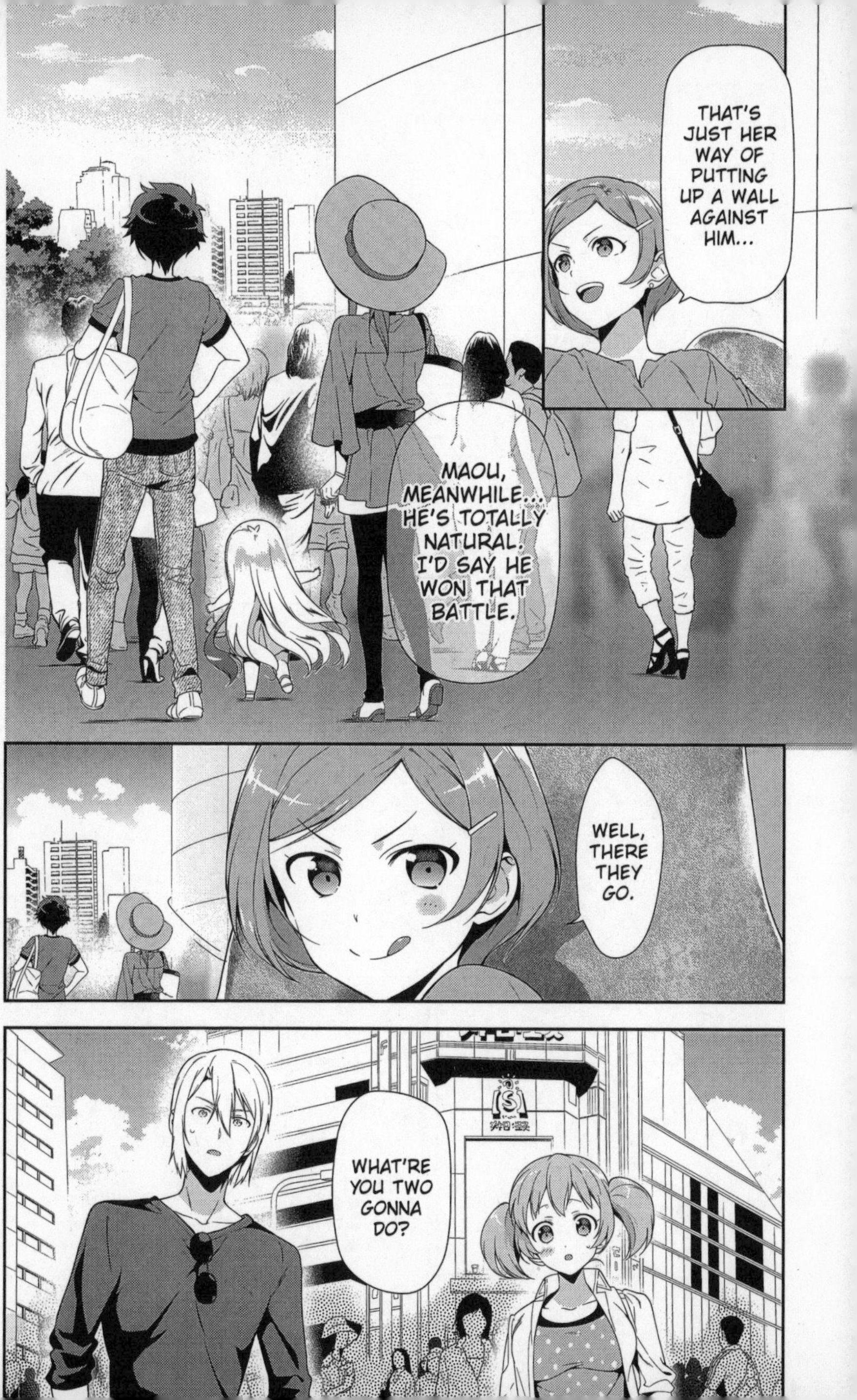
THAT'S JUST HER WAY OF PUTTING UP A WALL AGAINST HIM...
MAOU, MEANWHILE... HE'S TOTALLY NATURAL. I'D SAY HE WON THAT BATTLE.
WELL, THERE THEY GO.
WHAT'RE YOU TWO GONNA DO?

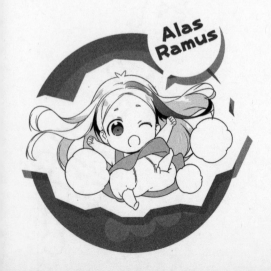
Alas Ramus

THE DEVIL IS A PART-TIMER!

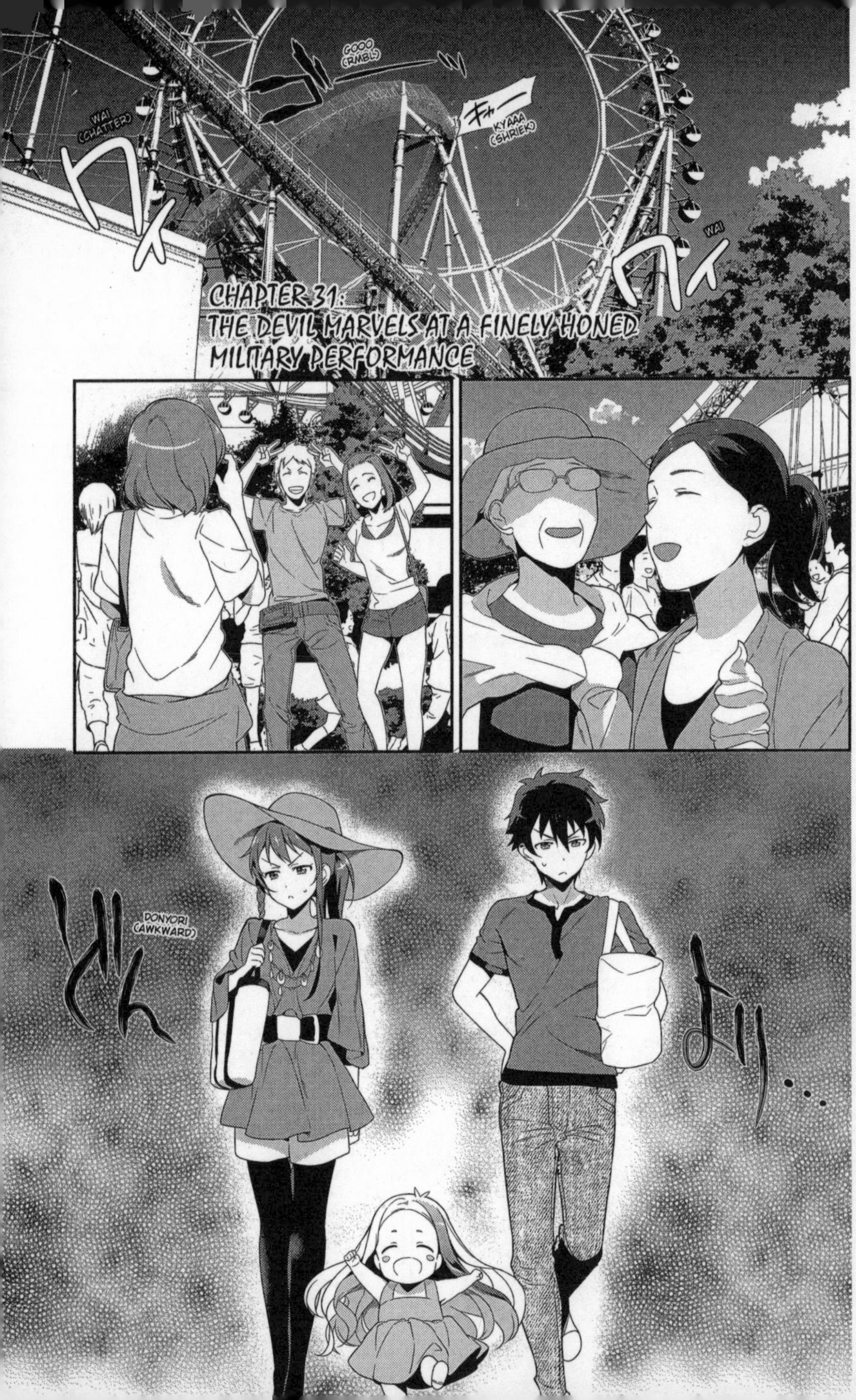
ワイ
WAI
キャー
KYAAA (SHRIEK)
GOOO (RMBL)
ワイ
WAI (CHATTER)
CHAPTER 31:
THE DEVIL MARVELS AT A FINELY HONED MILITARY PERFORMANCE
より...
どん
DONYORI (AWKWARD)

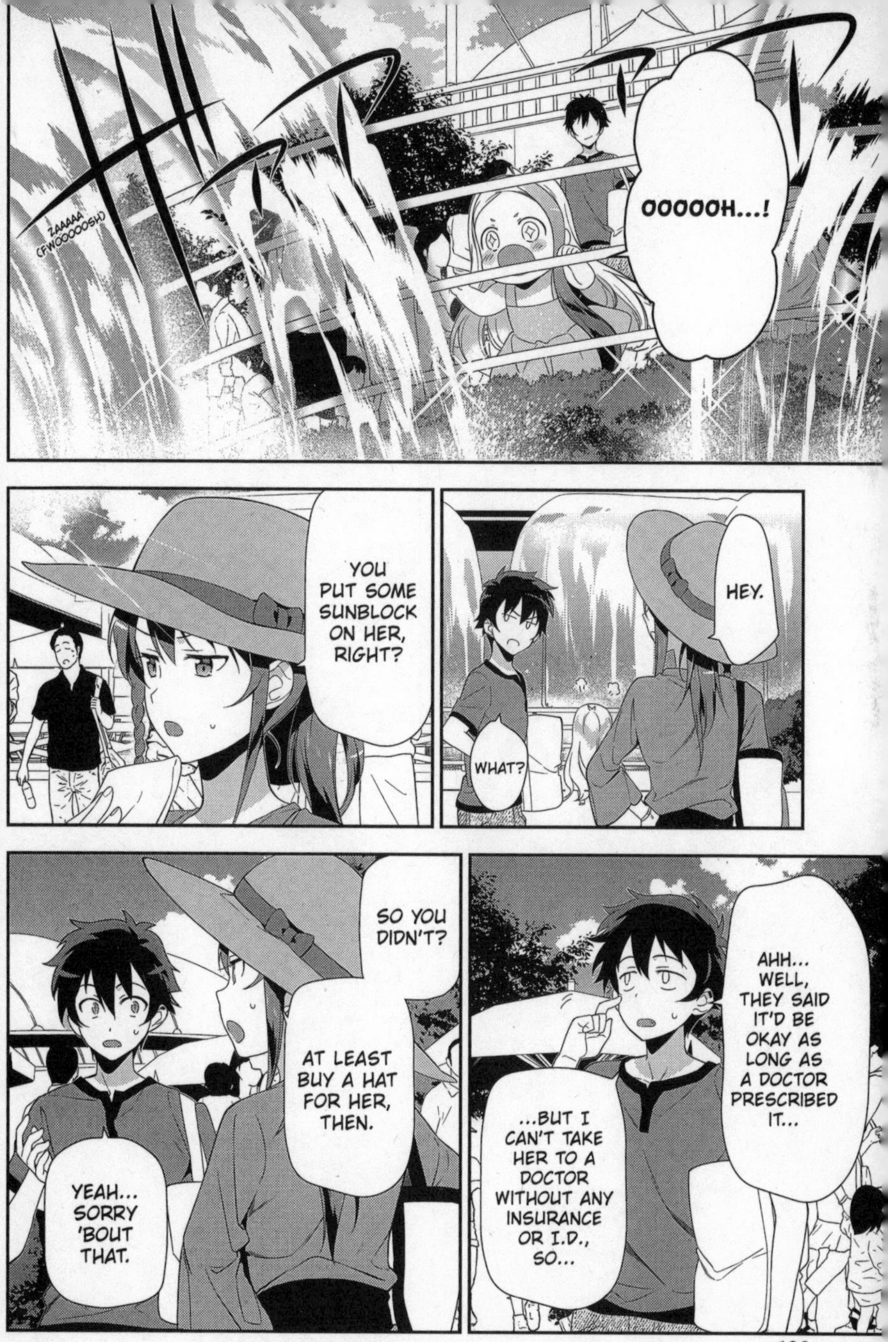
OOOOOH...!
ZAAAAA (FWOOOOOSH)
HEY.
WHAT?
YOU PUT SOME SUNBLOCK ON HER, RIGHT?
AHH... WELL, THEY SAID IT'D BE OKAY AS LONG AS A DOCTOR PRESCRIBED IT...
...BUT I CAN'T TAKE HER TO A DOCTOR WITHOUT ANY INSURANCE OR I.D., SO...
SO YOU DIDN'T?
AT LEAST BUY A HAT FOR HER, THEN.
YEAH... SORRY 'BOUT THAT.

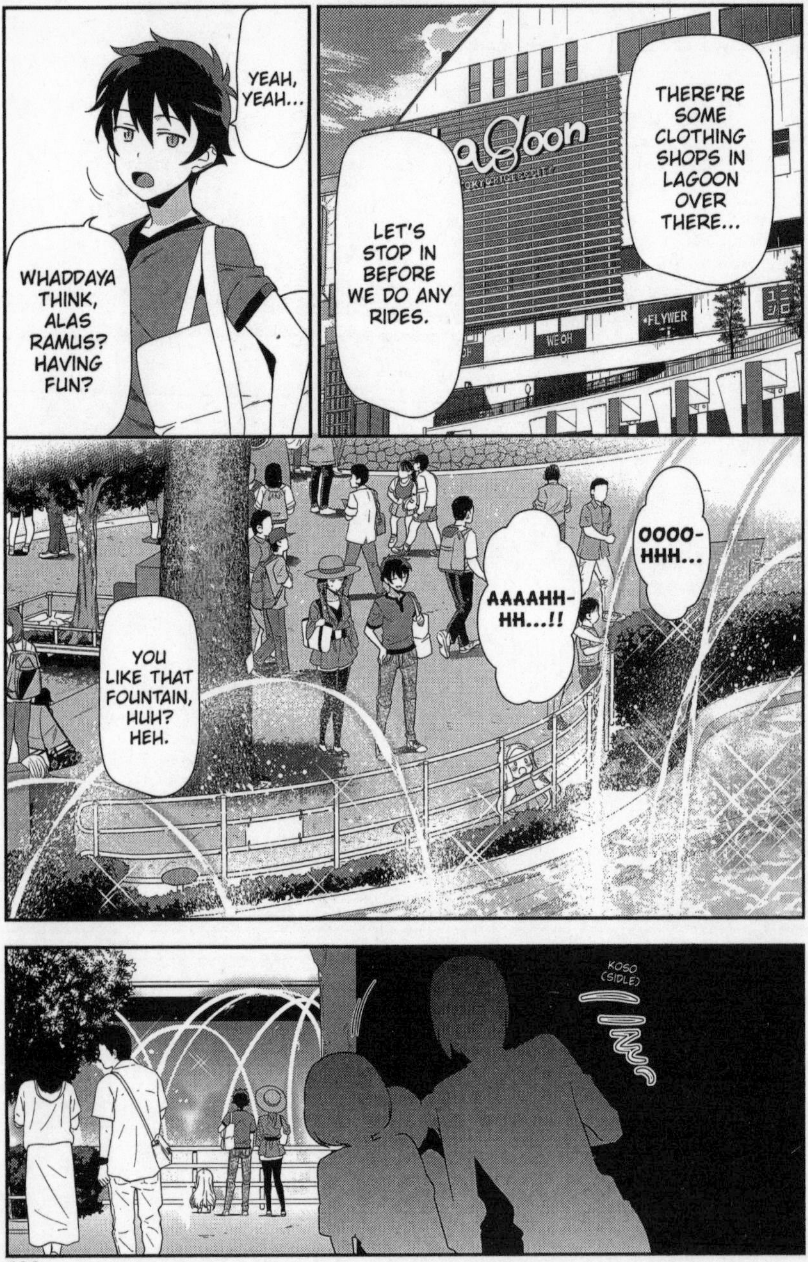
THERE'RE SOME CLOTHING SHOPS IN LAGOON OVER THERE...
LET'S STOP IN BEFORE WE DO ANY RIDES.
YEAH, YEAH...
WHADDAYA THINK, ALAS RAMUS? HAVING FUN?
OOOO-HHH...
AAAAHH-HH...!!
YOU LIKE THAT FOUNTAIN, HUH? HEH.
KOSO (SIDLE)

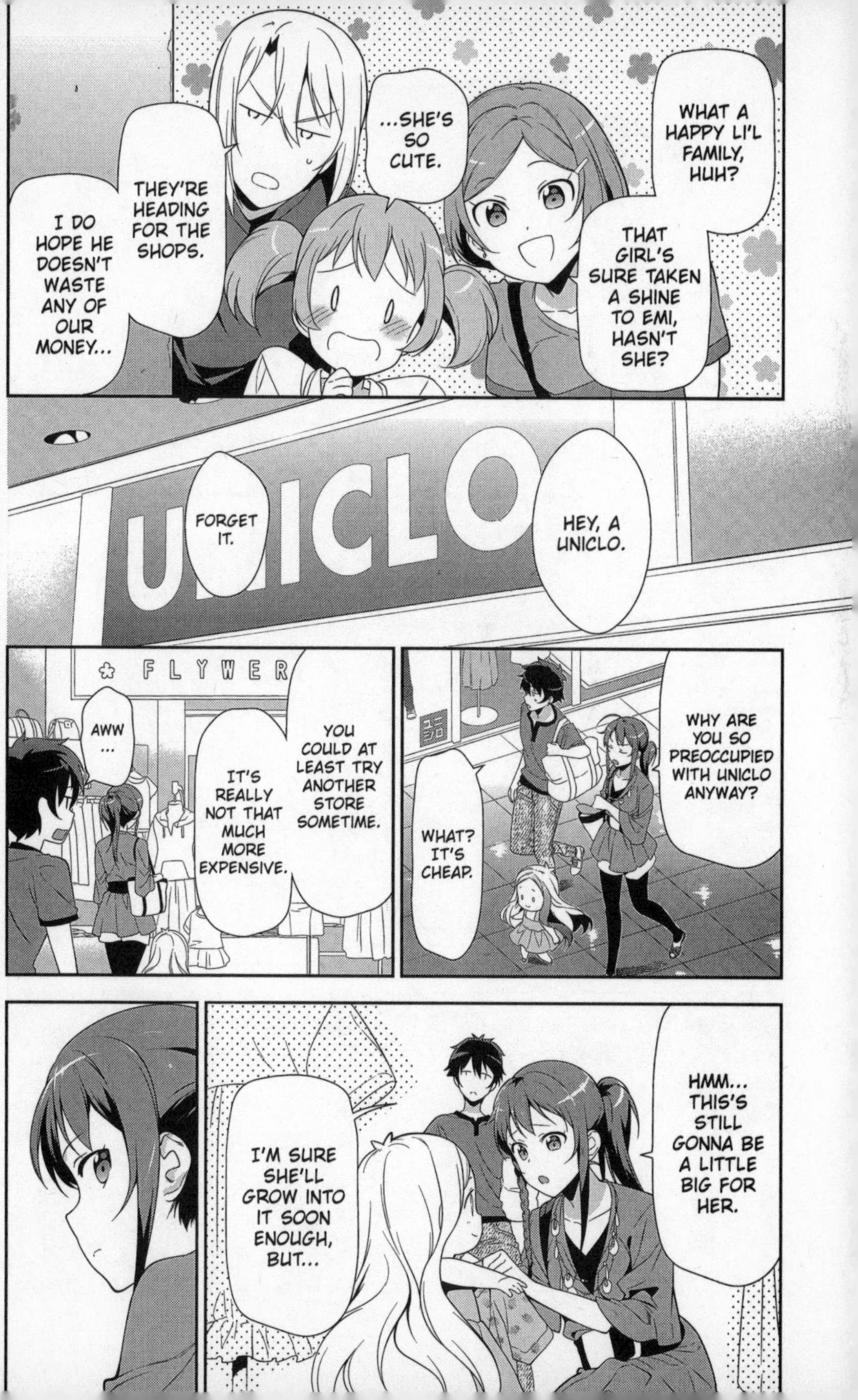
WHAT A HAPPY LI'L FAMILY, HUH?
THAT GIRL'S SURE TAKEN A SHINE TO EMI, HASN'T SHE?
...SHE'S SO CUTE.
THEY'RE HEADING FOR THE SHOPS.
I DO HOPE HE DOESN'T WASTE ANY OF OUR MONEY...
HEY, A UNICLO.
FORGET IT.
WHY ARE YOU SO PREOCCUPIED WITH UNICLO ANYWAY?
WHAT? IT'S CHEAP.
FLYWER
YOU COULD AT LEAST TRY ANOTHER STORE SOMETIME.
IT'S REALLY NOT THAT MUCH MORE EXPENSIVE.
AWW ...
HMM... THIS'S STILL GONNA BE A LITTLE BIG FOR HER.
I'M SURE SHE'LL GROW INTO IT SOON ENOUGH, BUT...

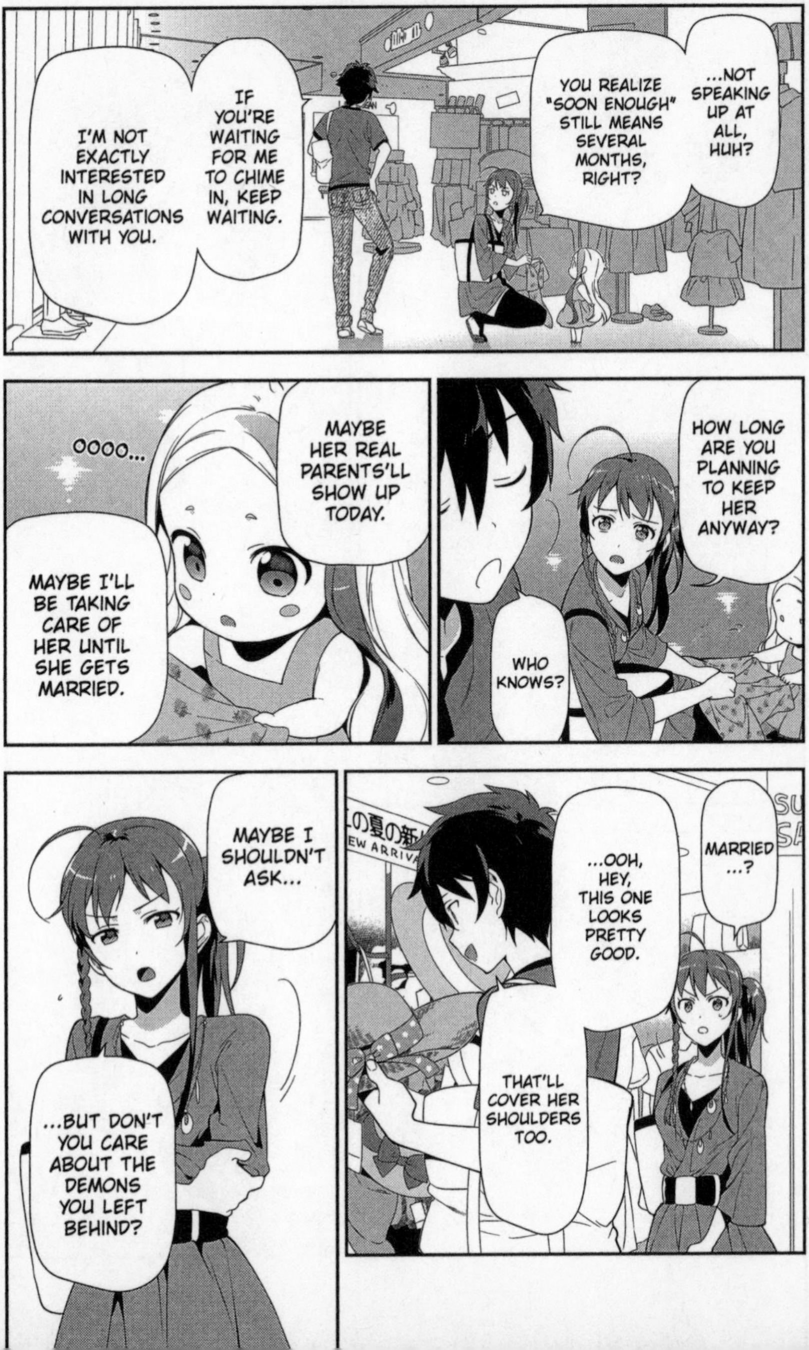
...NOT SPEAKING UP AT ALL, HUH?
YOU REALIZE "SOON ENOUGH" STILL MEANS SEVERAL MONTHS, RIGHT?
IF YOU'RE WAITING FOR ME TO CHIME IN, KEEP WAITING.
I'M NOT EXACTLY INTERESTED IN LONG CONVERSATIONS WITH YOU.
HOW LONG ARE YOU PLANNING TO KEEP HER ANYWAY?
WHO KNOWS?
MAYBE HER REAL PARENTS'LL SHOW UP TODAY.
OOOO...
MAYBE I'LL BE TAKING CARE OF HER UNTIL SHE GETS MARRIED.
MARRIED...?
...OOH, HEY, THIS ONE LOOKS PRETTY GOOD.
THAT'LL COVER HER SHOULDERS TOO.
MAYBE I SHOULDN'T ASK...
...BUT DON'T YOU CARE ABOUT THE DEMONS YOU LEFT BEHIND?

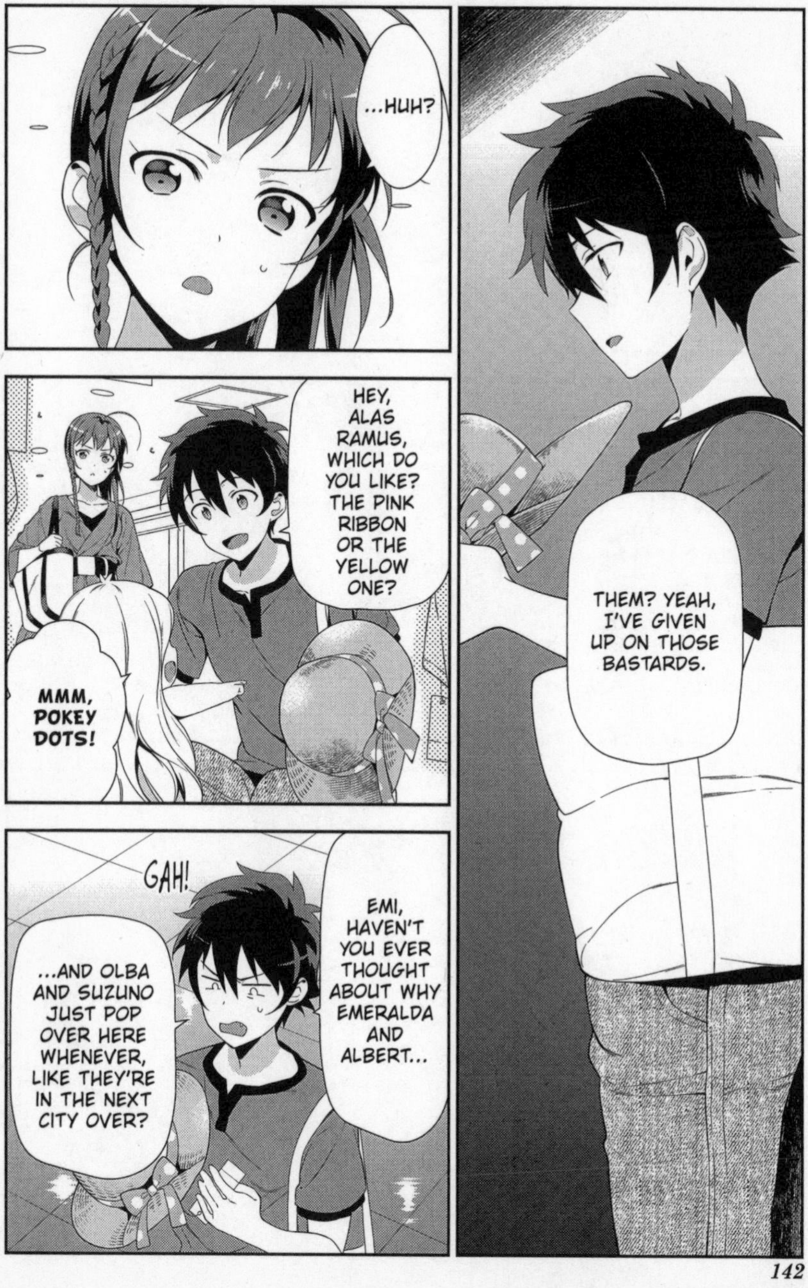
THEM? YEAH, I'VE GIVEN UP ON THOSE BASTARDS.
...HUH?
HEY, ALAS RAMUS, WHICH DO YOU LIKE? THE PINK RIBBON OR THE YELLOW ONE?
MMM, POKEY DOTS!
EMI, HAVEN'T YOU EVER THOUGHT ABOUT WHY EMERALDA AND ALBERT...
GAH!
...AND OLBA AND SUZUNO JUST POP OVER HERE WHENEVER, LIKE THEY'RE IN THE NEXT CITY OVER?

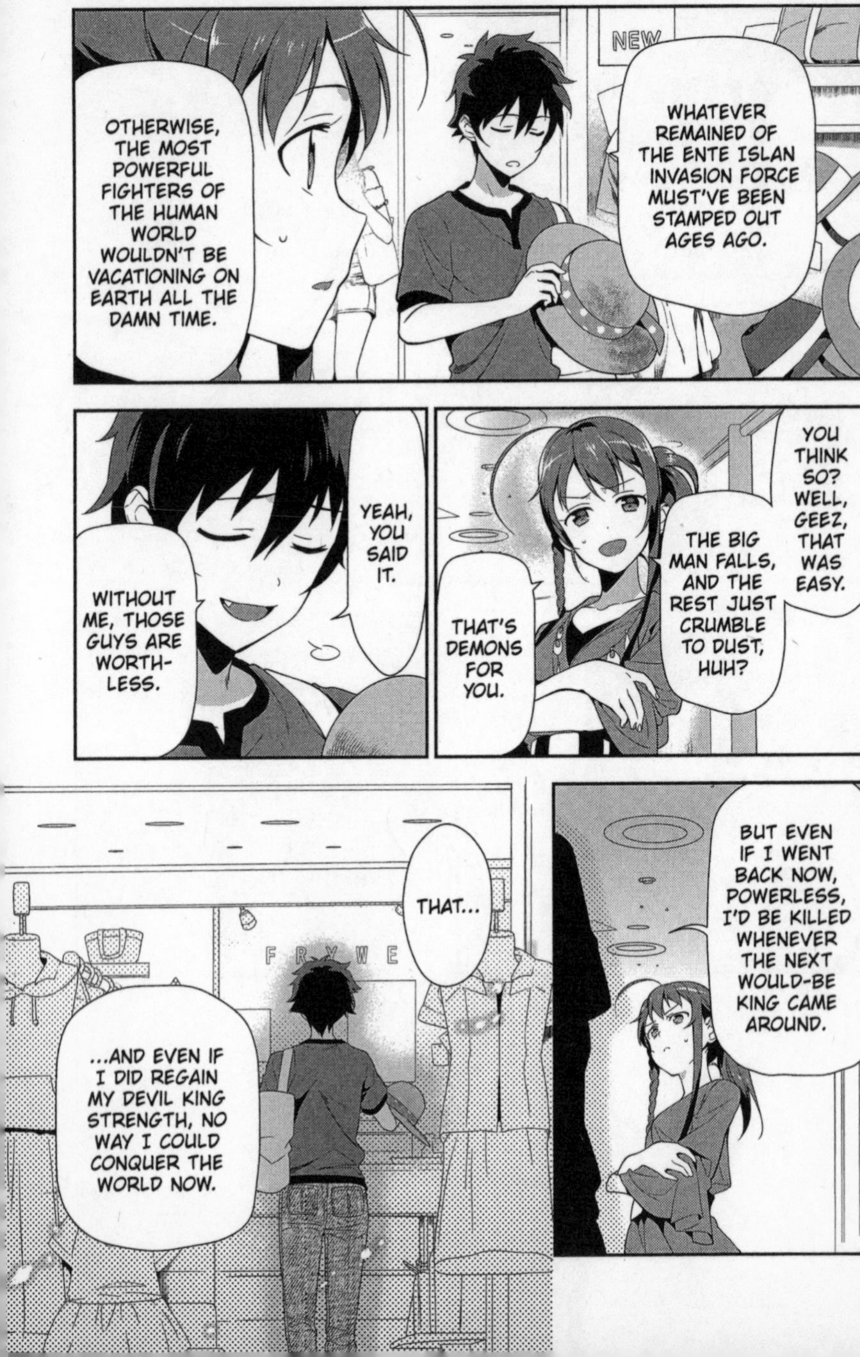
NEW
WHATEVER REMAINED OF THE ENTE ISLAN INVASION FORCE MUST'VE BEEN STAMPED OUT AGES AGO.
OTHERWISE, THE MOST POWERFUL FIGHTERS OF THE HUMAN WORLD WOULDN'T BE VACATIONING ON EARTH ALL THE DAMN TIME.
YOU THINK SO? WELL, GEEZ, THAT WAS EASY.
THE BIG MAN FALLS, AND THE REST JUST CRUMBLE TO DUST, HUH?
THAT'S DEMONS FOR YOU.
YEAH, YOU SAID IT.
WITHOUT ME, THOSE GUYS ARE WORTH-LESS.
BUT EVEN IF I WENT BACK NOW, POWERLESS, I'D BE KILLED WHENEVER THE NEXT WOULD-BE KING CAME AROUND.
THAT...
...AND EVEN IF I DID REGAIN MY DEVIL KING STRENGTH, NO WAY I COULD CONQUER THE WORLD NOW.

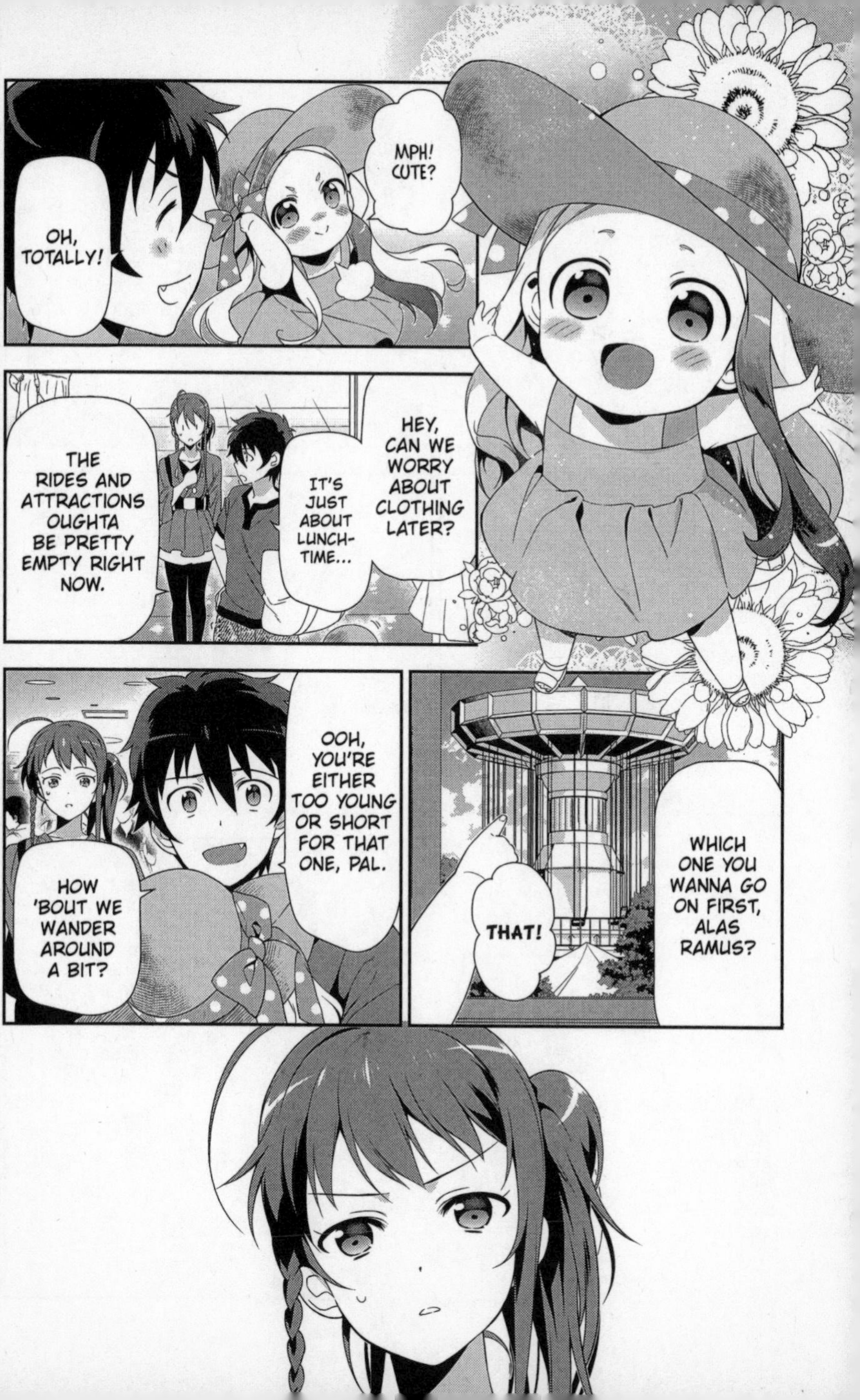
MPH! CUTE?
OH, TOTALLY!
HEY, CAN WE WORRY ABOUT CLOTHING LATER?
IT'S JUST ABOUT LUNCH-TIME...
THE RIDES AND ATTRACTIONS OUGHTA BE PRETTY EMPTY RIGHT NOW.
WHICH ONE YOU WANNA GO ON FIRST, ALAS RAMUS?
THAT!
OOH, YOU'RE EITHER TOO YOUNG OR SHORT FOR THAT ONE, PAL.
HOW 'BOUT WE WANDER AROUND A BIT?

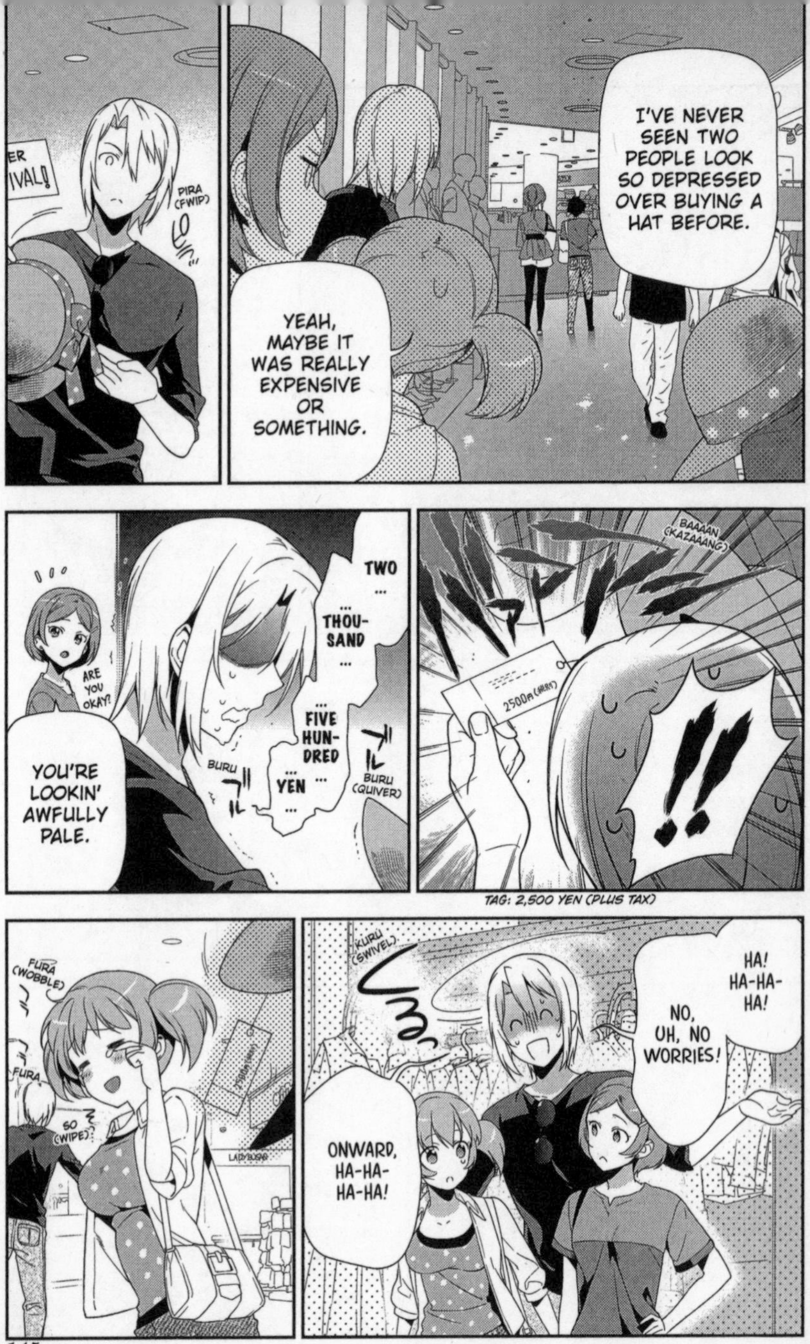
I'VE NEVER SEEN TWO PEOPLE LOOK SO DEPRESSED OVER BUYING A HAT BEFORE.
YEAH, MAYBE IT WAS REALLY EXPENSIVE OR SOMETHING.
PIRA (FWIP)
BAAAAN (KAZAAANG)
!!
TAG: 2,500 YEN (PLUS TAX)
TWO ... ... THOU-SAND ... ... FIVE HUN-DRED ... ... YEN ...
BURU BURU (QUIVER)
ARE YOU OKAY?
YOU'RE LOOKIN' AWFULLY PALE.
KURU (SWIVEL)
HA! HA-HA-HA!
NO, UH, NO WORRIES!
ONWARD, HA-HA-HA-HA!
FURA (WOBBLE)
FURA
SO (WIPE)

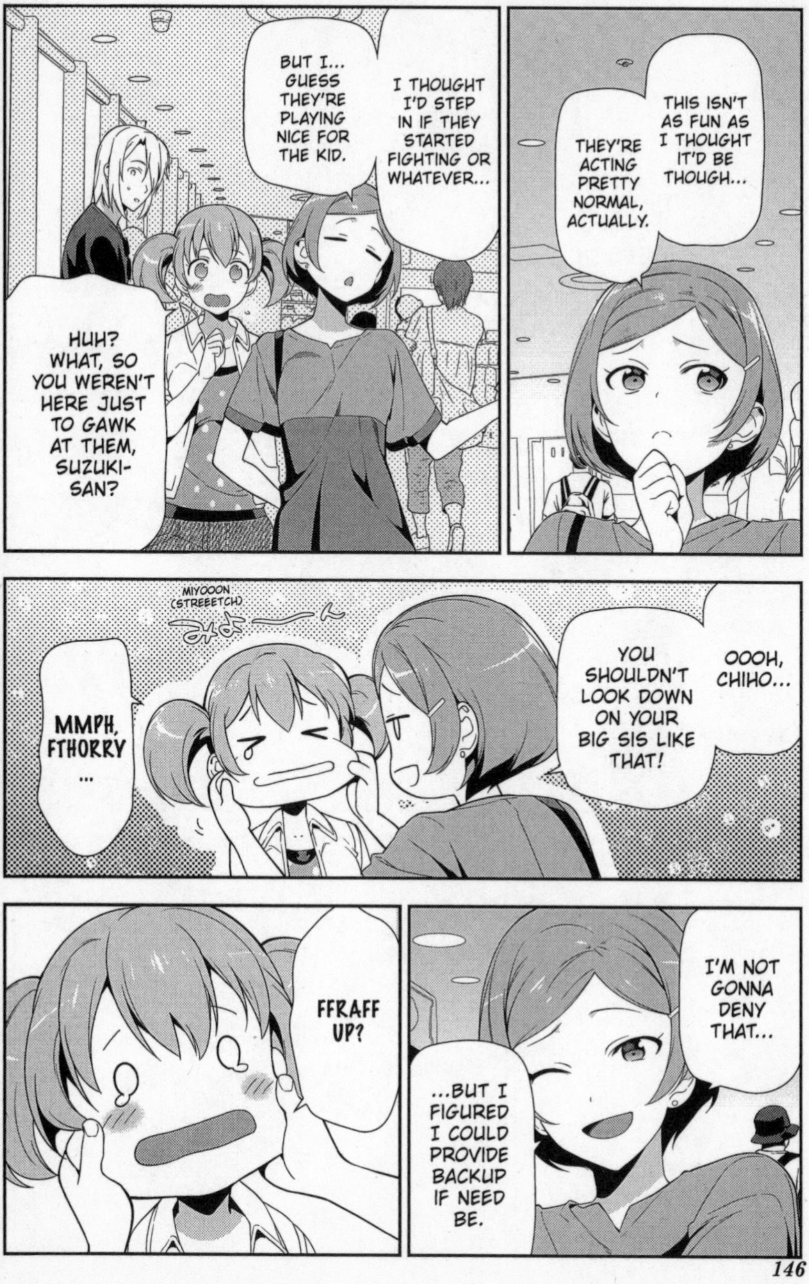
THIS ISN'T AS FUN AS I THOUGHT IT'D BE THOUGH...
THEY'RE ACTING PRETTY NORMAL, ACTUALLY.
I THOUGHT I'D STEP IN IF THEY STARTED FIGHTING OR WHATEVER...
BUT I... GUESS THEY'RE PLAYING NICE FOR THE KID.
HUH? WHAT, SO YOU WEREN'T HERE JUST TO GAWK AT THEM, SUZUKI-SAN?
OOOH, CHIHO...
YOU SHOULDN'T LOOK DOWN ON YOUR BIG SIS LIKE THAT!
MIYOOON (STREEETCH)
MMPH, FTHORRY ...
I'M NOT GONNA DENY THAT...
...BUT I FIGURED I COULD PROVIDE BACKUP IF NEED BE.
FFRAFF UP?

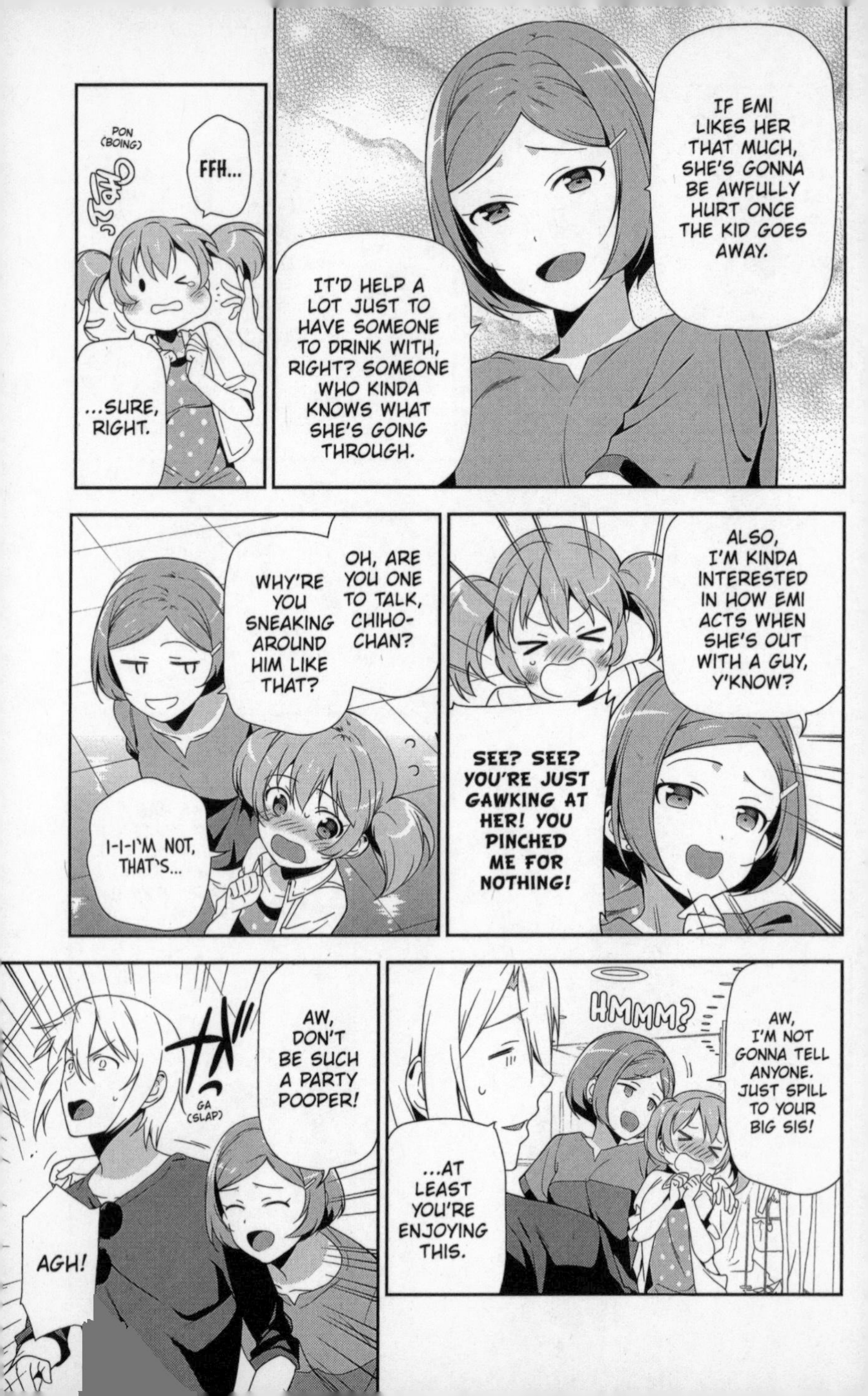
IF EMI LIKES HER THAT MUCH, SHE'S GONNA BE AWFULLY HURT ONCE THE KID GOES AWAY.
IT'D HELP A LOT JUST TO HAVE SOMEONE TO DRINK WITH, RIGHT? SOMEONE WHO KINDA KNOWS WHAT SHE'S GOING THROUGH.
PON (BOING)
FFH...
...SURE, RIGHT.
ALSO, I'M KINDA INTERESTED IN HOW EMI ACTS WHEN SHE'S OUT WITH A GUY, Y'KNOW?
SEE? SEE? YOU'RE JUST GAWKING AT HER! YOU PINCHED ME FOR NOTHING!
OH, ARE YOU ONE TO TALK, CHIHO-CHAN?
WHY'RE YOU SNEAKING AROUND HIM LIKE THAT?
I-I-I'M NOT, THAT'S...
HMMM?
AW, I'M NOT GONNA TELL ANYONE. JUST SPILL TO YOUR BIG SIS!
...AT LEAST YOU'RE ENJOYING THIS.
AW, DON'T BE SUCH A PARTY POOPER!
GA (SLAP)
AGH!

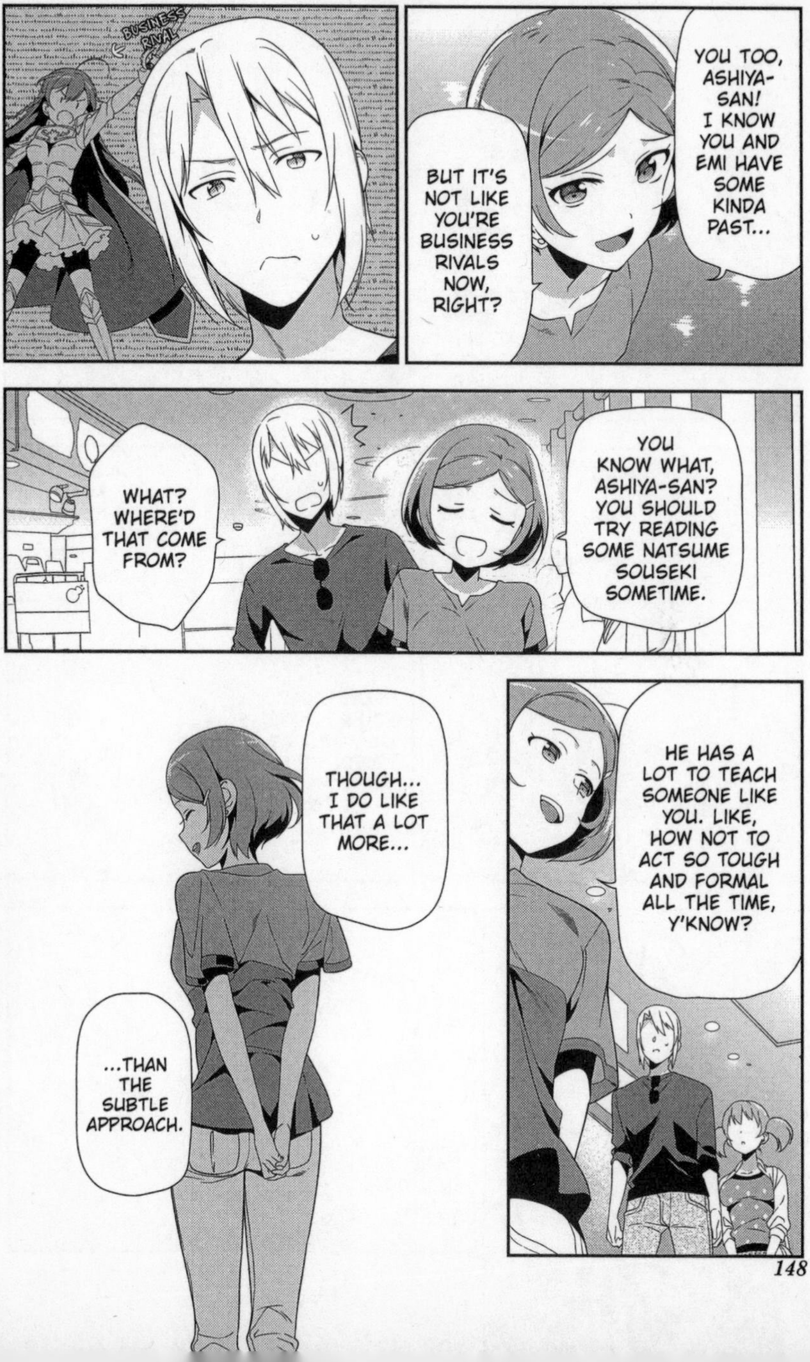
YOU TOO, ASHIYA-SAN! I KNOW YOU AND EMI HAVE SOME KINDA PAST...
BUT IT'S NOT LIKE YOU'RE BUSINESS RIVALS NOW, RIGHT?
BUSINESS RIVAL
YOU KNOW WHAT, ASHIYA-SAN? YOU SHOULD TRY READING SOME NATSUME SOUSEKI SOMETIME.
WHAT? WHERE'D THAT COME FROM?
HE HAS A LOT TO TEACH SOMEONE LIKE YOU. LIKE, HOW NOT TO ACT SO TOUGH AND FORMAL ALL THE TIME, Y'KNOW?
THOUGH... I DO LIKE THAT A LOT MORE...
...THAN THE SUBTLE APPROACH.

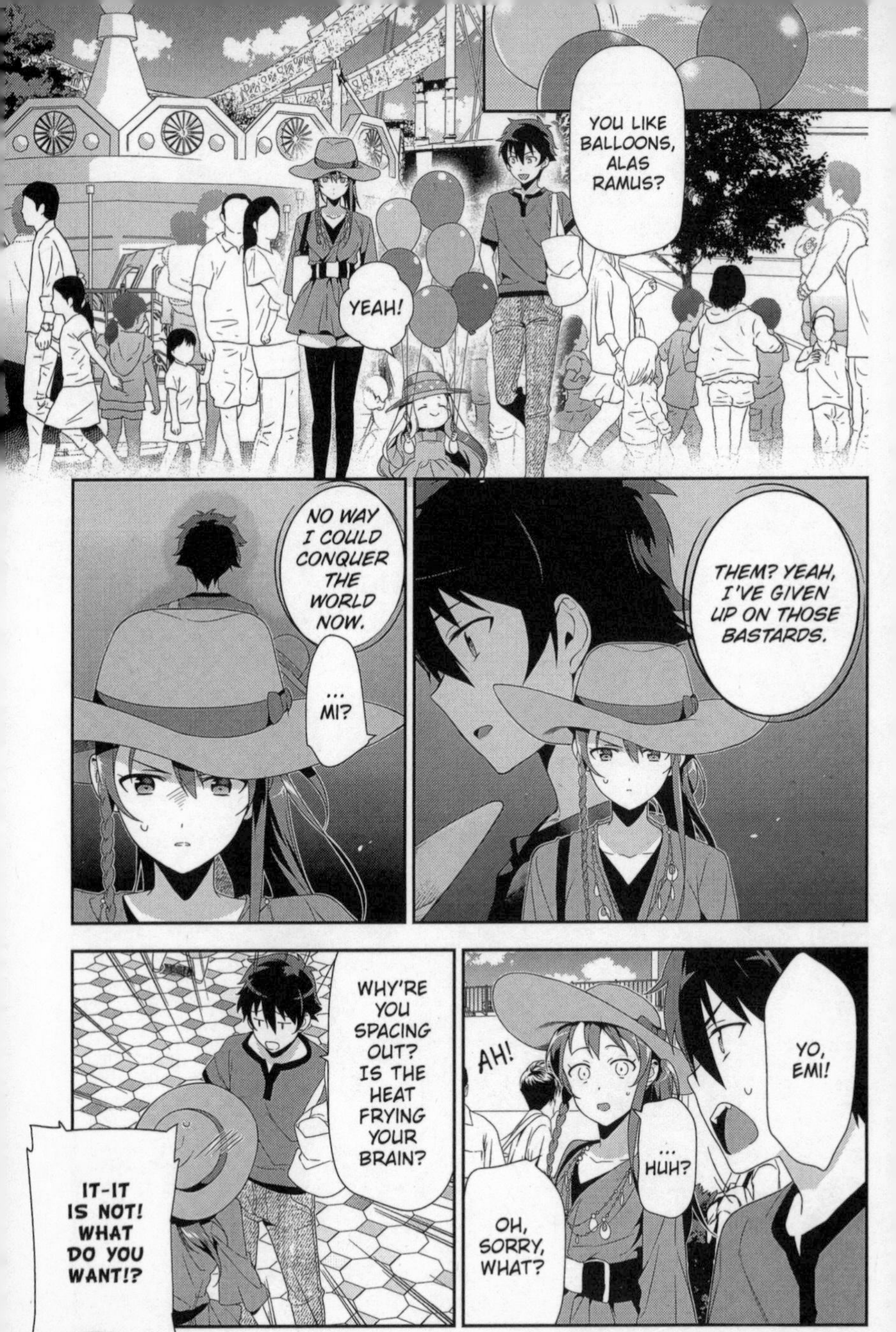
YOU LIKE BALLOONS, ALAS RAMUS?
YEAH!
THEM? YEAH, I'VE GIVEN UP ON THOSE BASTARDS.
NO WAY I COULD CONQUER THE WORLD NOW.
... MI?
YO, EMI!
AH!
... HUH?
OH, SORRY, WHAT?
WHY'RE YOU SPACING OUT? IS THE HEAT FRYING YOUR BRAIN?
IT-IT IS NOT! WHAT DO YOU WANT!?

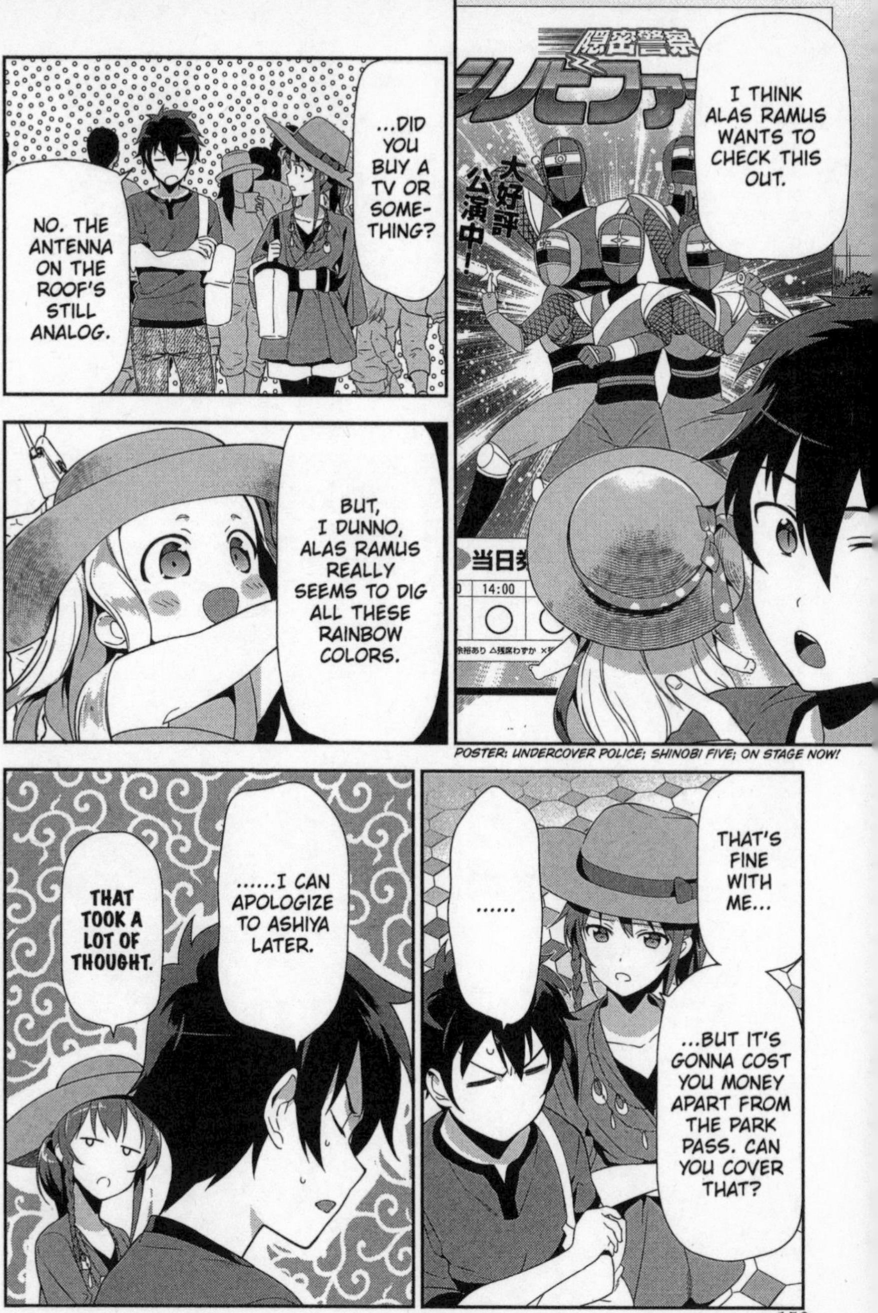
隠密警察
I THINK ALAS RAMUS WANTS TO CHECK THIS OUT.
大好評公演中！
14:00
...DID YOU BUY A TV OR SOME-THING?
NO. THE ANTENNA ON THE ROOF'S STILL ANALOG.
BUT, I DUNNO, ALAS RAMUS REALLY SEEMS TO DIG ALL THESE RAINBOW COLORS.
THAT'S FINE WITH ME...
......
...BUT IT'S GONNA COST YOU MONEY APART FROM THE PARK PASS. CAN YOU COVER THAT?
......I CAN APOLOGIZE TO ASHIYA LATER.
THAT TOOK A LOT OF THOUGHT.

POSTER: UNDERCOVER POLICE; SHINOBI FIVE; ON STAGE NOW!

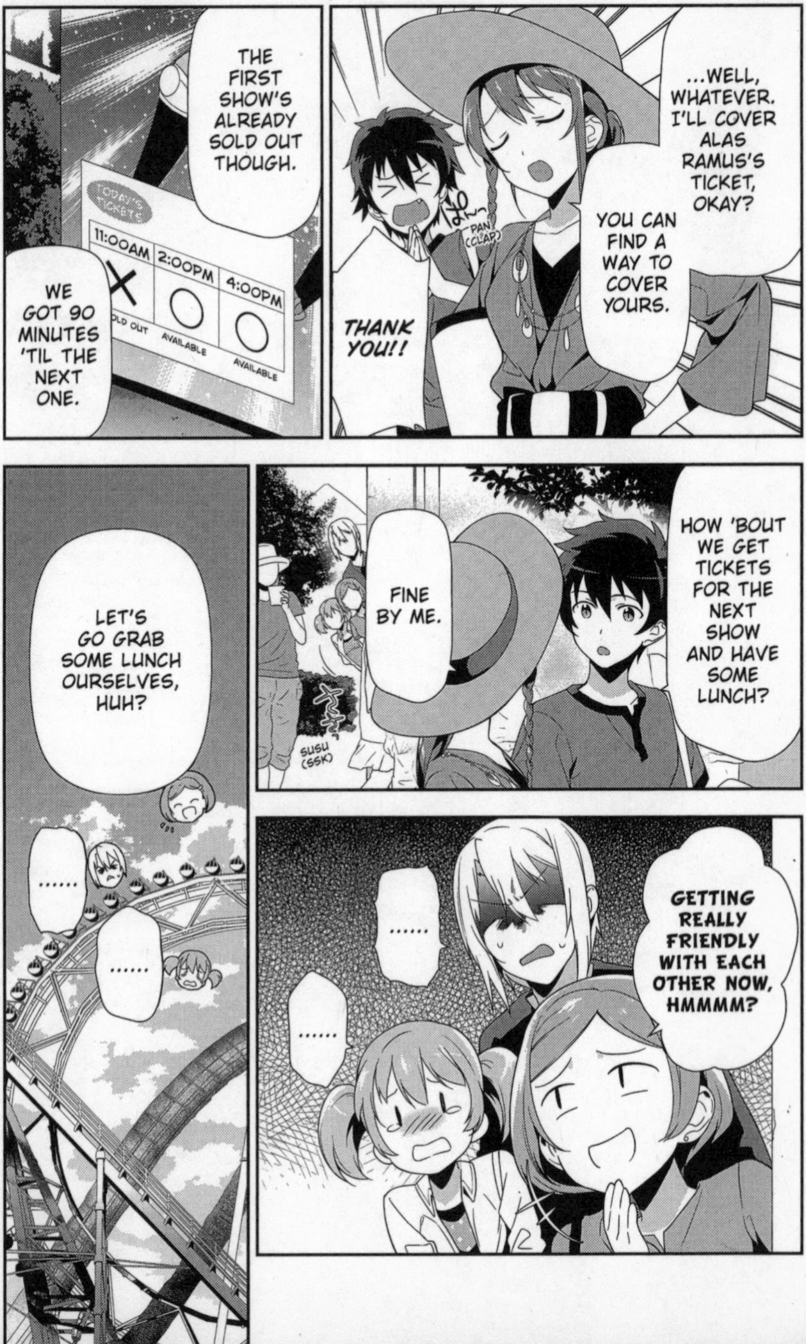
...WELL, WHATEVER. I'LL COVER ALAS RAMUS'S TICKET, OKAY?
YOU CAN FIND A WAY TO COVER YOURS.
PAN (CLAP)
THANK YOU!!
THE FIRST SHOW'S ALREADY SOLD OUT THOUGH.
TODAY'S TICKETS
11:00AM
SOLD OUT
2:00PM
AVAILABLE
4:00PM
AVAILABLE
WE GOT 90 MINUTES 'TIL THE NEXT ONE.
HOW 'BOUT WE GET TICKETS FOR THE NEXT SHOW AND HAVE SOME LUNCH?
FINE BY ME.
SUSU (SSK)
GETTING REALLY FRIENDLY WITH EACH OTHER NOW, HMMMM?
......
......
LET'S GO GRAB SOME LUNCH OURSELVES, HUH?
......
......

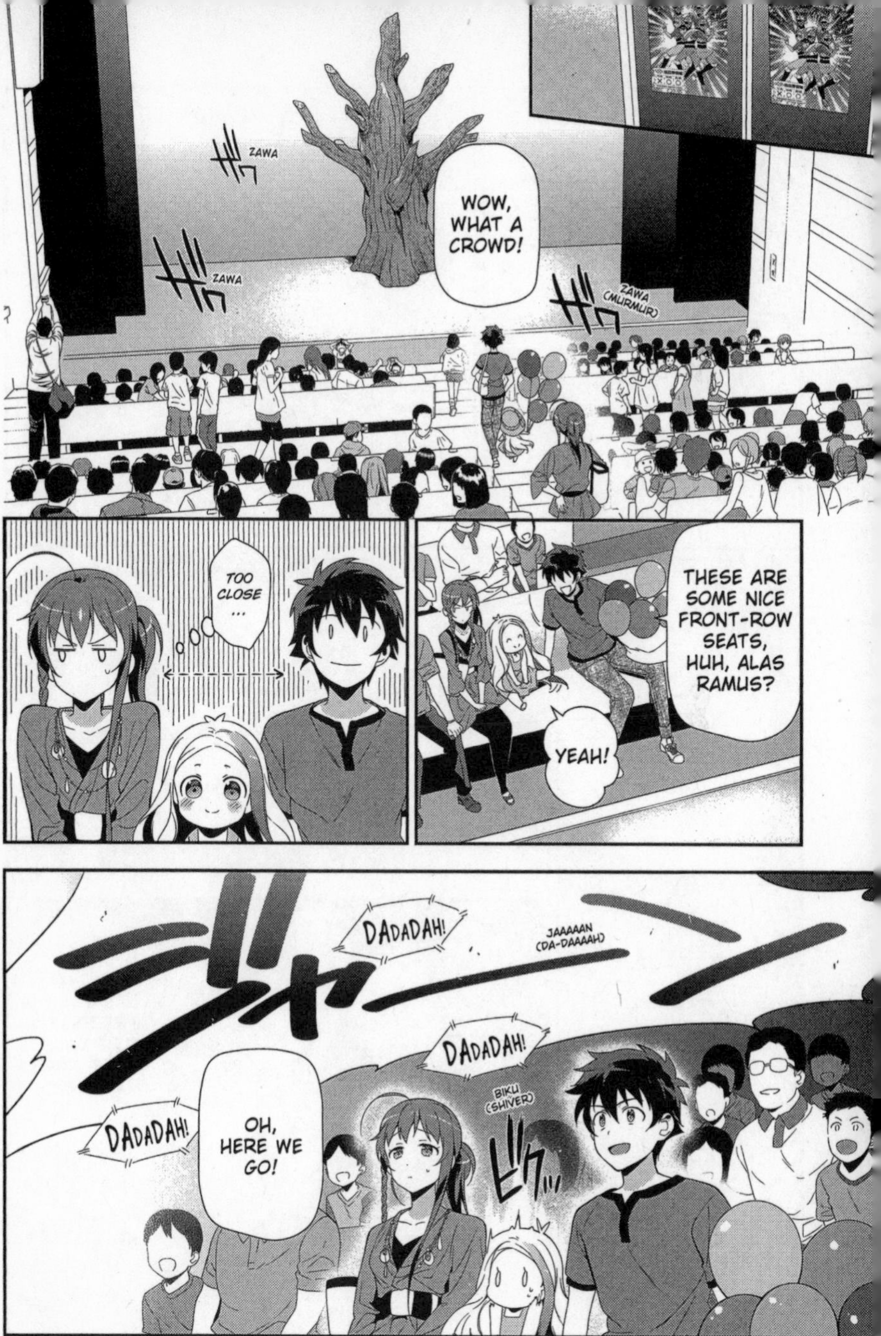
WOW, WHAT A CROWD!
ZAWA (MURMUR)
ZAWA
ZAWA
THESE ARE SOME NICE FRONT-ROW SEATS, HUH, ALAS RAMUS?
YEAH!
TOO CLOSE ...
JAAAAAN (DA-DAAAAH)
DADADAH!
DADADAH!
BIKU (SHIVER)
OH, HERE WE GO!
DADADAH!

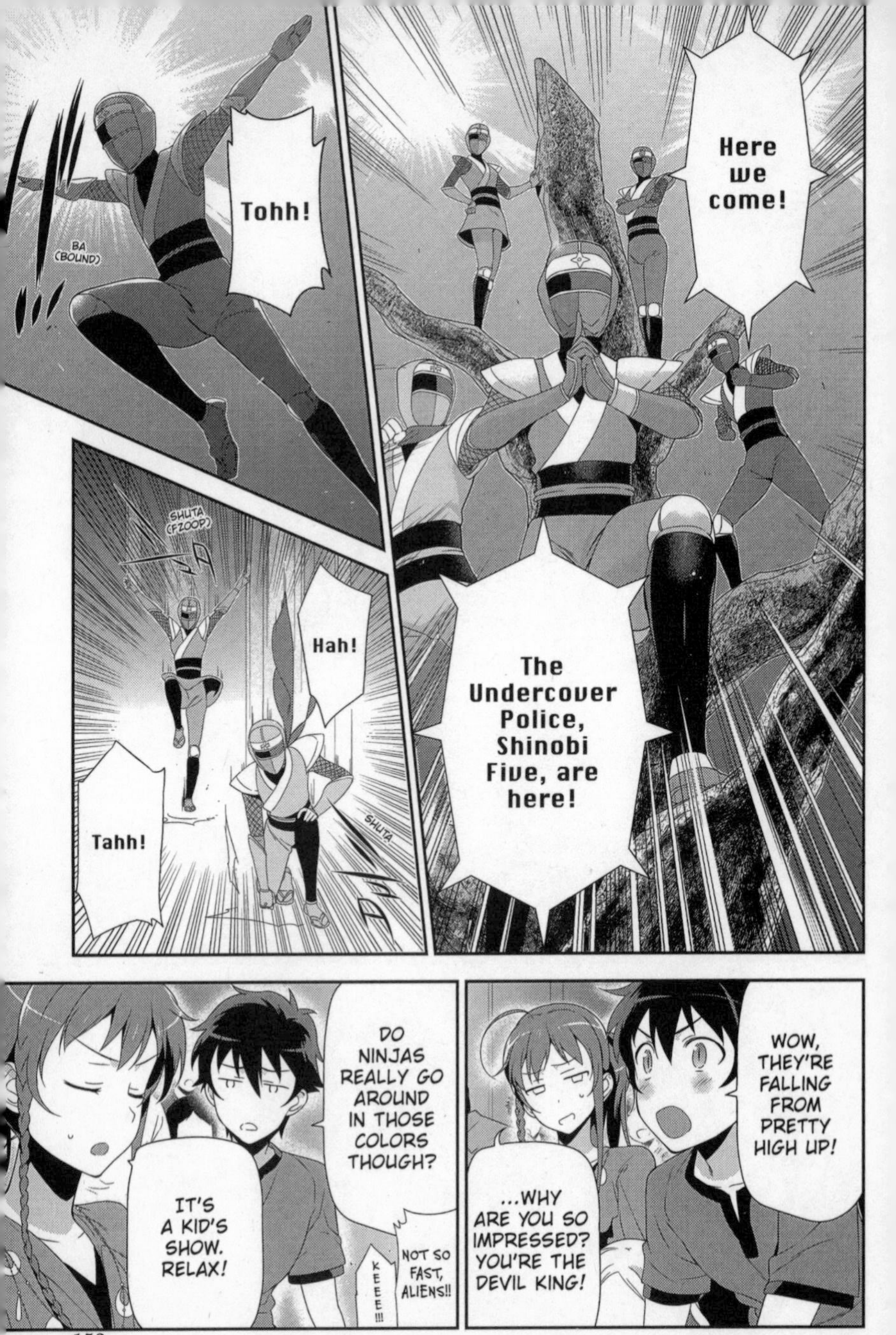
Here we come!
The Undercover Police, Shinobi Five, are here!
Tohh!
BA (BOUND)
SHUTA (FZOOP)
Hah!
SHUTA
Tahh!
WOW, THEY'RE FALLING FROM PRETTY HIGH UP!
...WHY ARE YOU SO IMPRESSED? YOU'RE THE DEVIL KING!
DO NINJAS REALLY GO AROUND IN THOSE COLORS THOUGH?
IT'S A KID'S SHOW. RELAX!
NOT SO FAST, ALIENS!!
KEEEE!!!

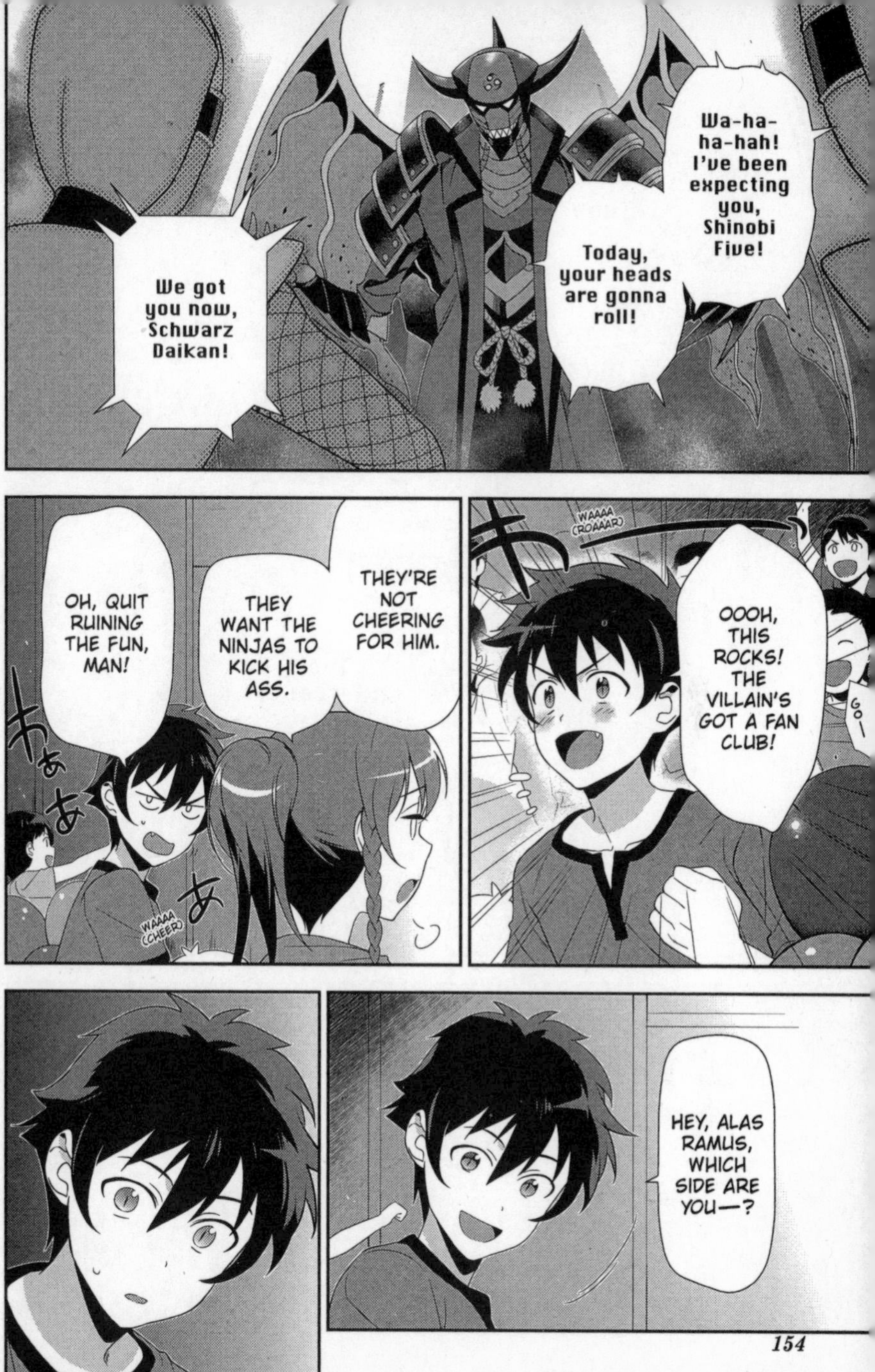
Wa-ha-ha-hah! I've been expecting you, Shinobi Five!
Today, your heads are gonna roll!
We got you now, Schwarz Daikan!
WAAAA (ROAAAR)
OOOH, THIS ROCKS! THE VILLAIN'S GOT A FAN CLUB!
THEY'RE NOT CHEERING FOR HIM.
THEY WANT THE NINJAS TO KICK HIS ASS.
OH, QUIT RUINING THE FUN, MAN!
WAAAA (CHEER)
HEY, ALAS RAMUS, WHICH SIDE ARE YOU—?

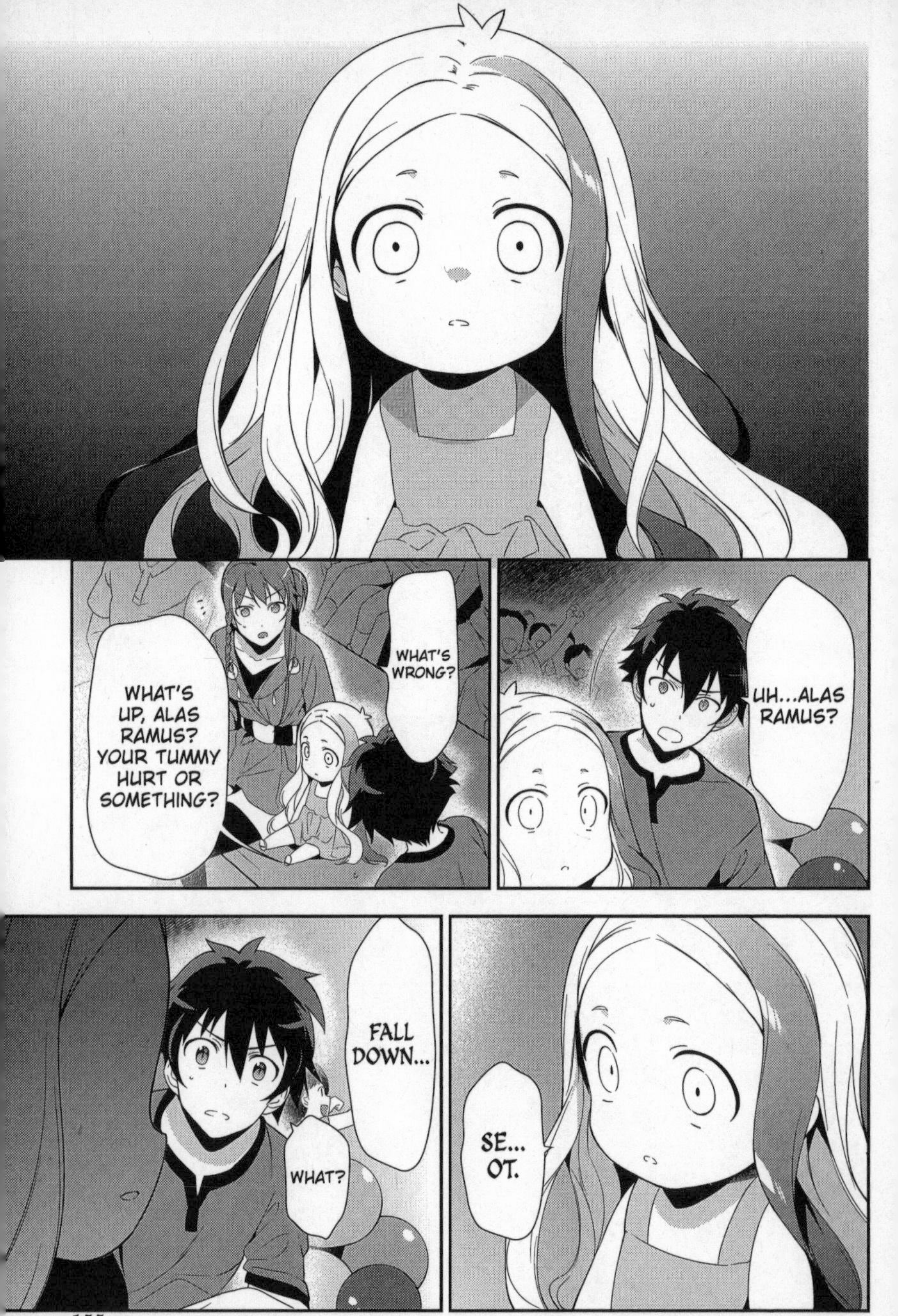
UH...ALAS RAMUS?
WHAT'S WRONG?
WHAT'S UP, ALAS RAMUS? YOUR TUMMY HURT OR SOMETHING?
SE... OT.
FALL DOWN...
WHAT?

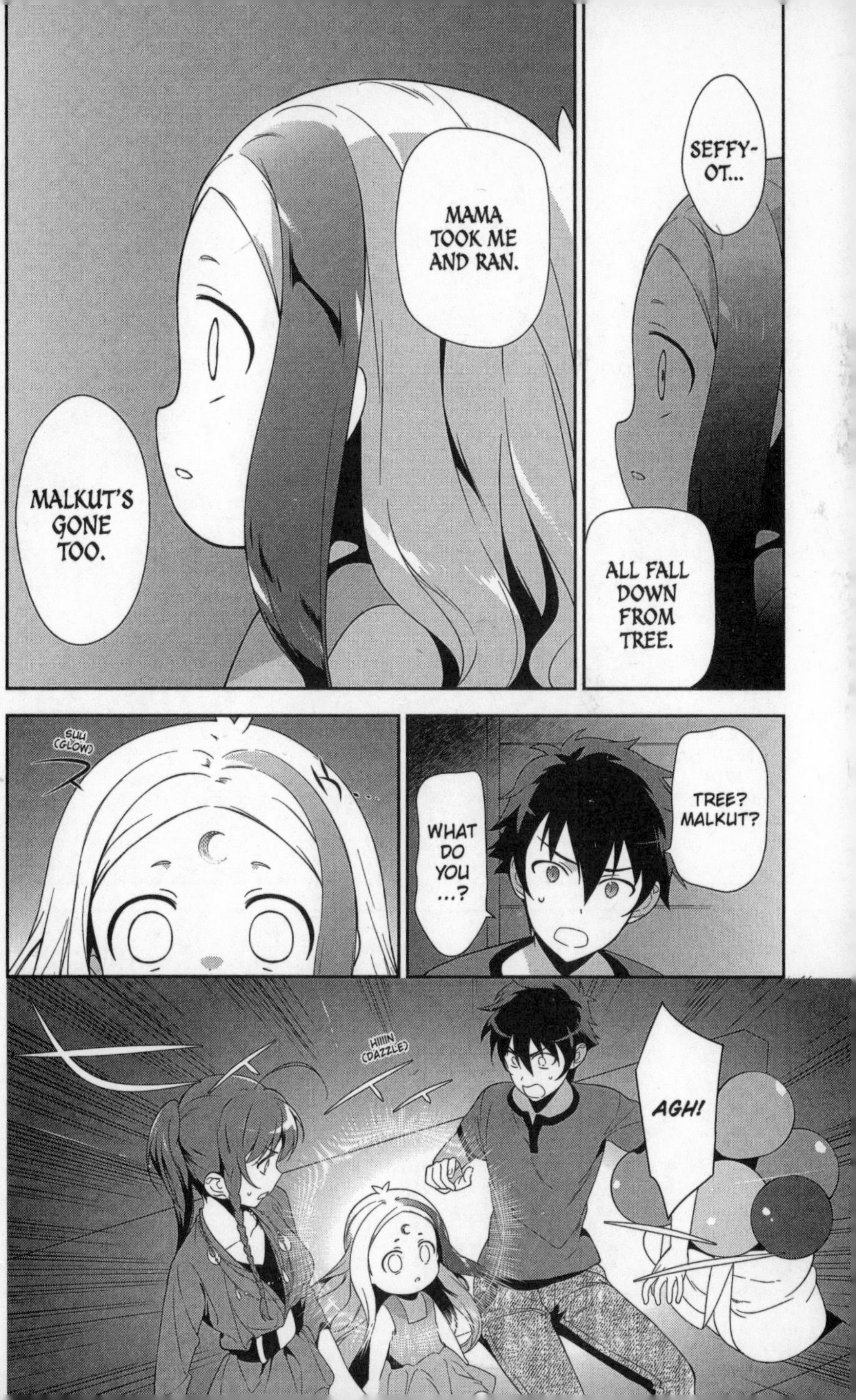
SEFFY-OT...
ALL FALL DOWN FROM TREE.
MAMA TOOK ME AND RAN.
MALKUT'S GONE TOO.
TREE? MALKUT?
WHAT DO YOU ...?
SUU (GLOW)
AGH!
HIIIN (DAZZLE)

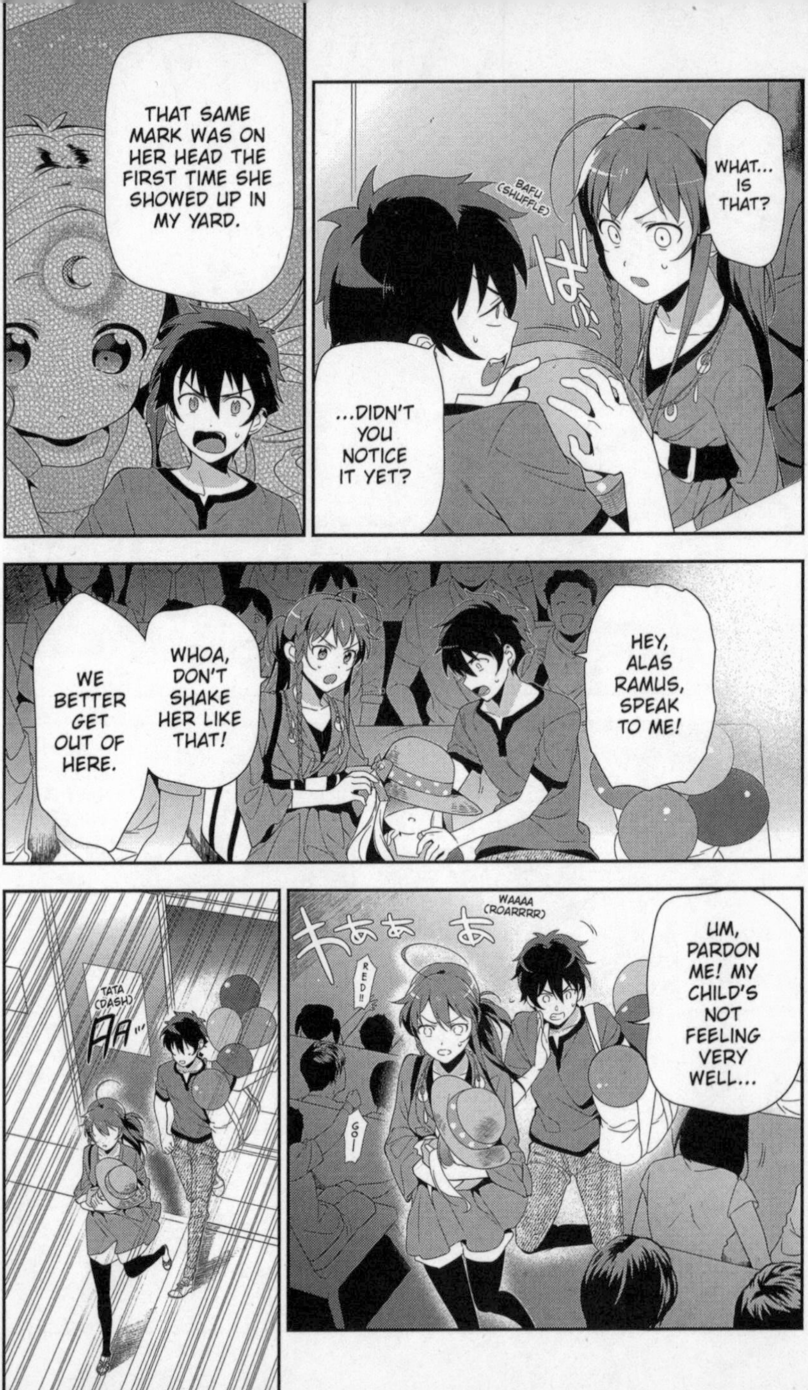
WHAT... IS THAT?
BAFU (SHUFFLE)
...DIDN'T YOU NOTICE IT YET?
THAT SAME MARK WAS ON HER HEAD THE FIRST TIME SHE SHOWED UP IN MY YARD.
HEY, ALAS RAMUS, SPEAK TO ME!
WHOA, DON'T SHAKE HER LIKE THAT!
WE BETTER GET OUT OF HERE.
WAAAA (ROARRRR)
UM, PARDON ME! MY CHILD'S NOT FEELING VERY WELL...
RED!!
GO!
TATA (DASH)

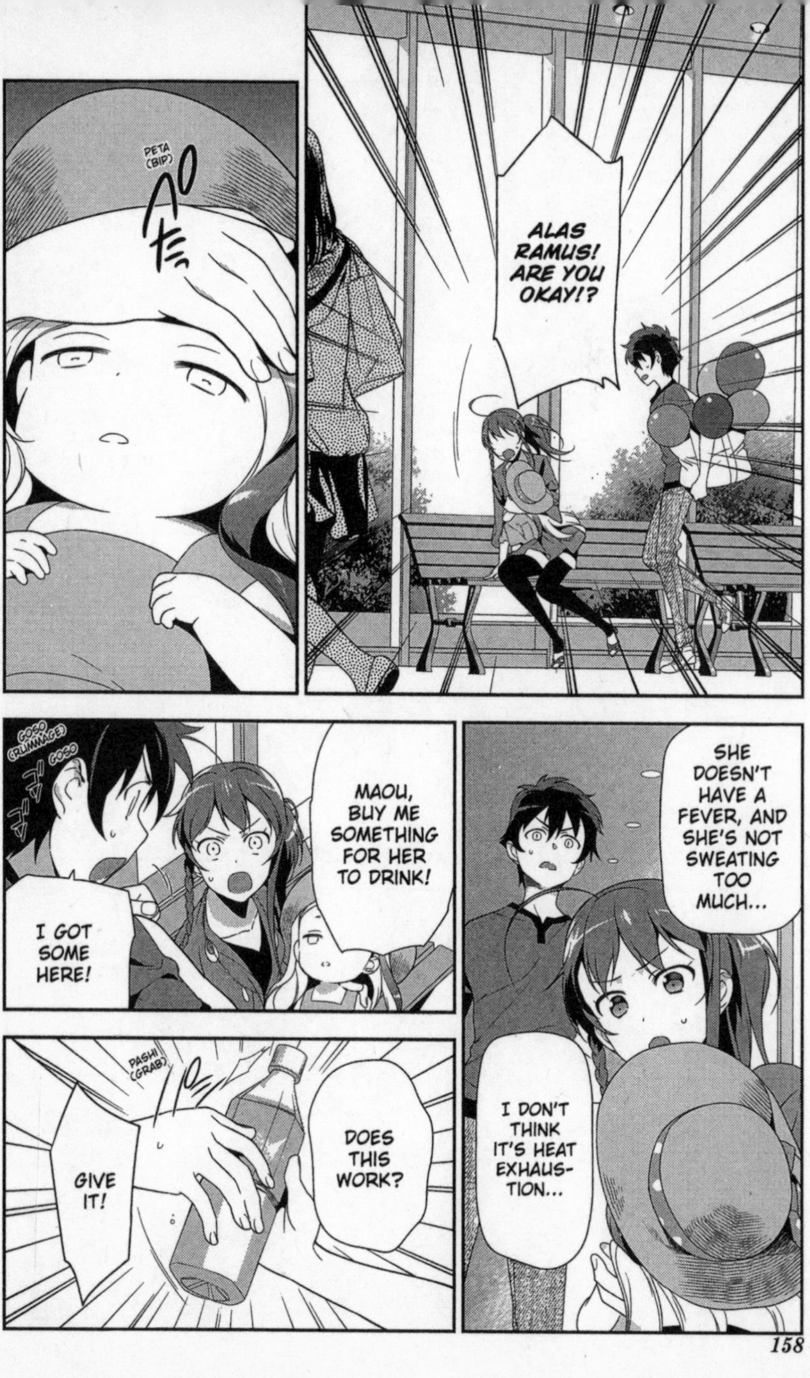
ALAS RAMUS! ARE YOU OKAY!?
PETA (BIP)
SHE DOESN'T HAVE A FEVER, AND SHE'S NOT SWEATING TOO MUCH...
I DON'T THINK IT'S HEAT EXHAUS-TION...
MAOU, BUY ME SOMETHING FOR HER TO DRINK!
GOSO (RUMMAGE) GOSO
I GOT SOME HERE!
DOES THIS WORK?
PASHI (GRAB)
GIVE IT!

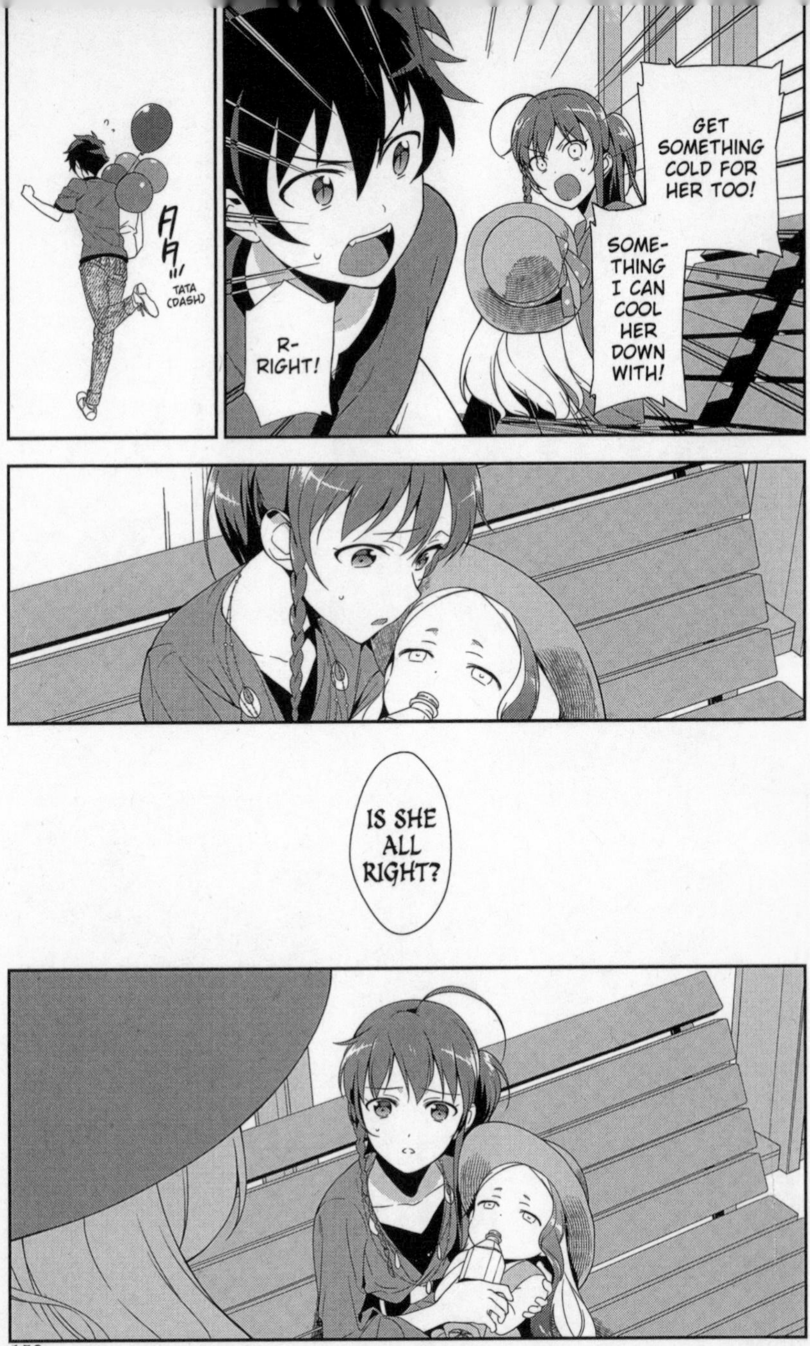
GET SOMETHING COLD FOR HER TOO!
SOME-THING I CAN COOL HER DOWN WITH!
R-RIGHT!
タタ
TATA (DASH)
IS SHE ALL RIGHT?

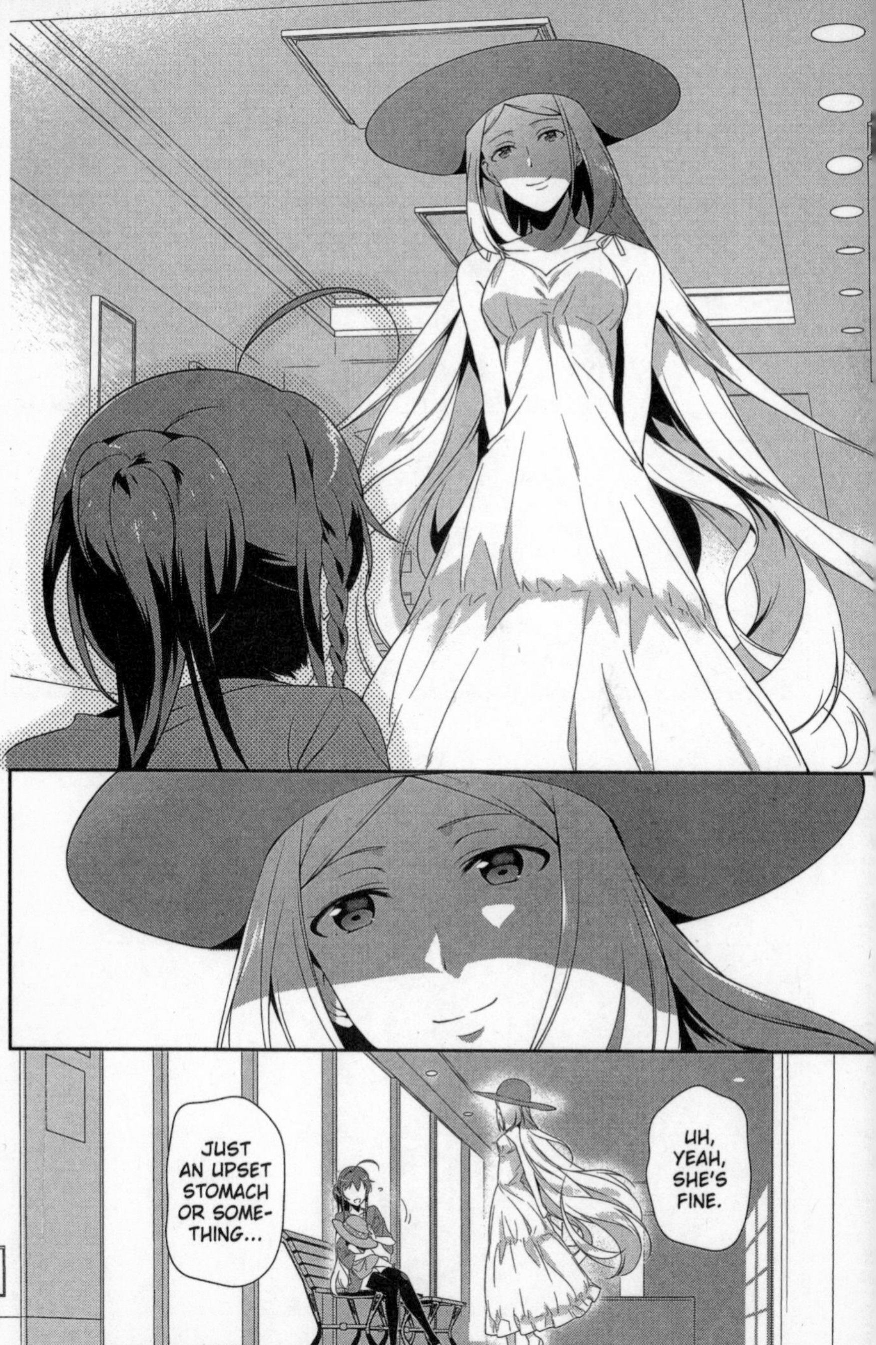
UH, YEAH, SHE'S FINE.
JUST AN UPSET STOMACH OR SOME-THING...

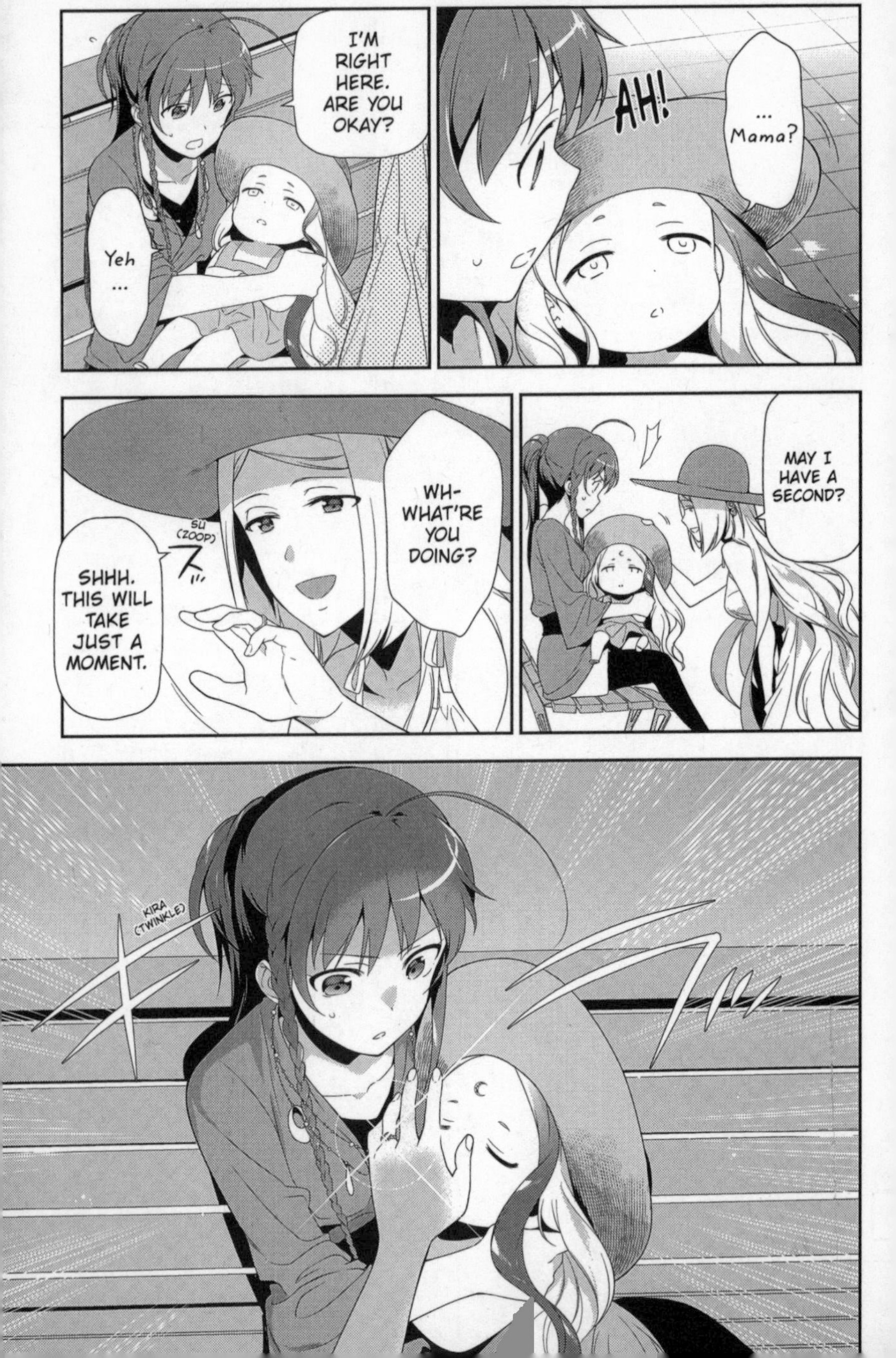
... Mama?
AH!
I'M RIGHT HERE. ARE YOU OKAY?
Yeh ...
MAY I HAVE A SECOND?
WH- WHAT'RE YOU DOING?
SU (ZOOP)
SHHH. THIS WILL TAKE JUST A MOMENT.
KIRA (TWINKLE)

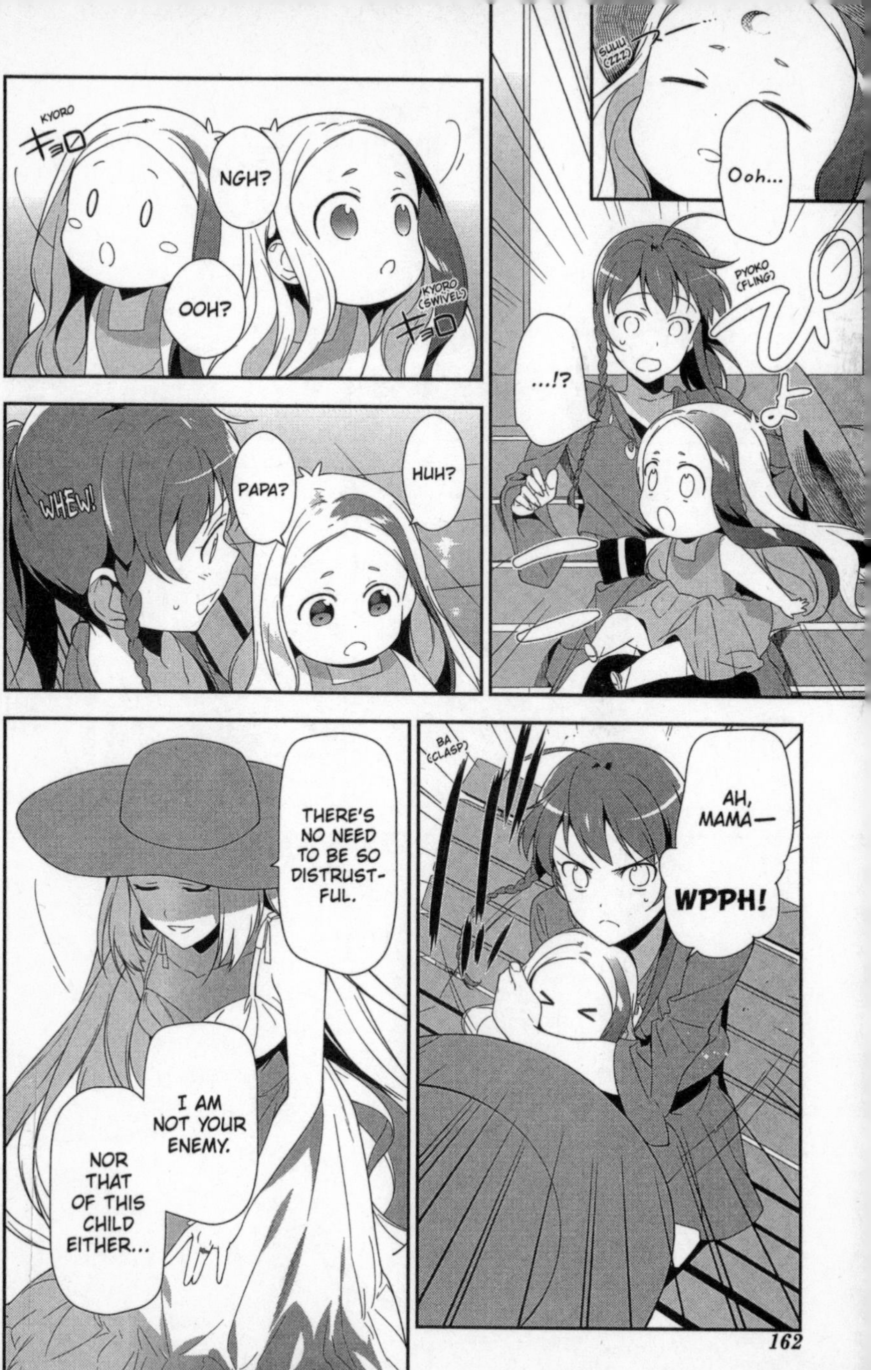
SUUU (ZZZ)
...
Ooh...
PYOKO (FLING)
...!?
KYORO
NGH?
KYORO (SWIVEL)
OOH?
HUH?
PAPA?
WHEW!
BA (CLASP)
AH, MAMA—
WPPH!
THERE'S NO NEED TO BE SO DISTRUST-FUL.
I AM NOT YOUR ENEMY.
NOR THAT OF THIS CHILD EITHER...

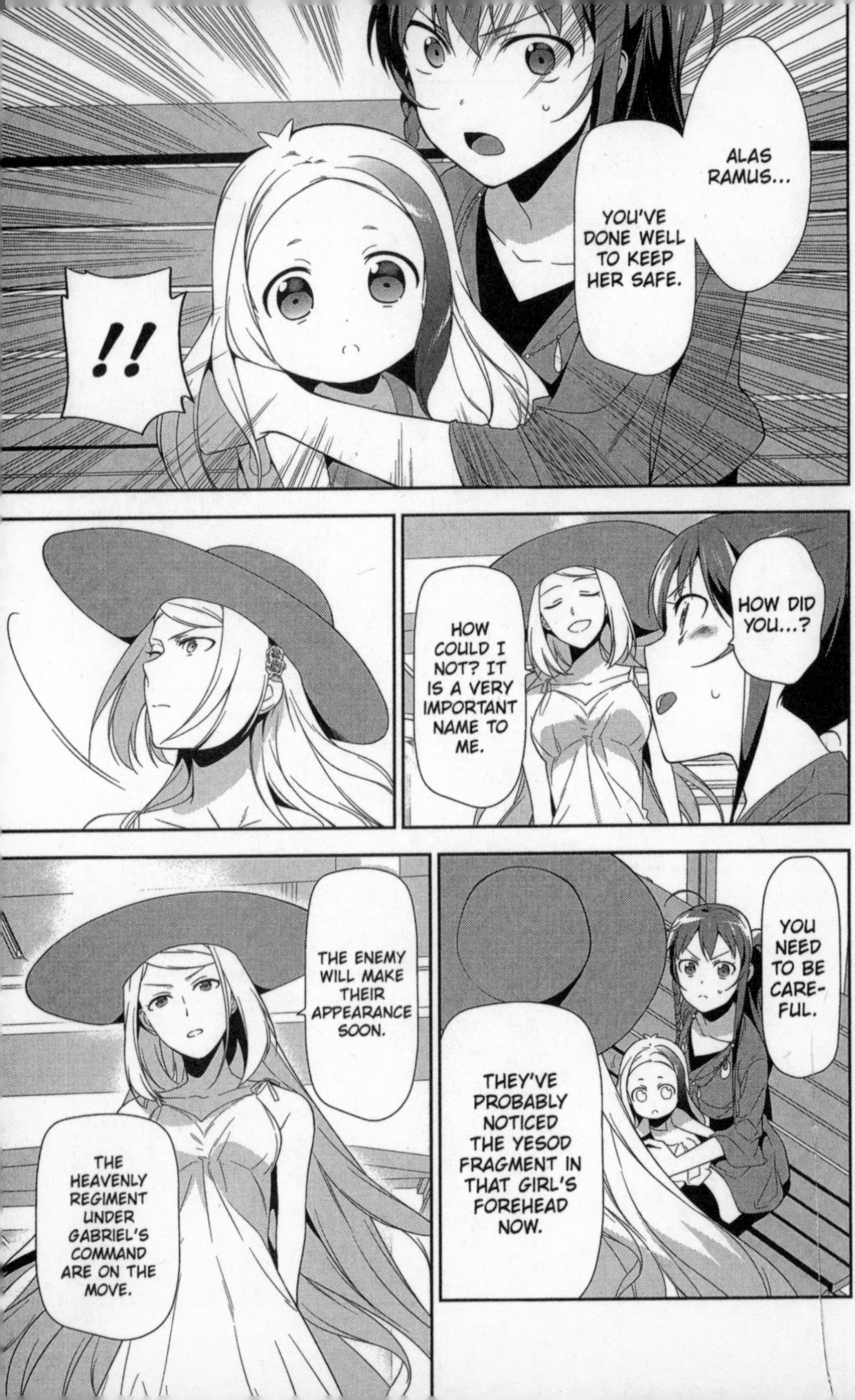
ALAS RAMUS...
YOU'VE DONE WELL TO KEEP HER SAFE.
!!
HOW DID YOU...?
HOW COULD I NOT? IT IS A VERY IMPORTANT NAME TO ME.
YOU NEED TO BE CARE-FUL.
THEY'VE PROBABLY NOTICED THE YESOD FRAGMENT IN THAT GIRL'S FOREHEAD NOW.
THE ENEMY WILL MAKE THEIR APPEARANCE SOON.
THE HEAVENLY REGIMENT UNDER GABRIEL'S COMMAND ARE ON THE MOVE.

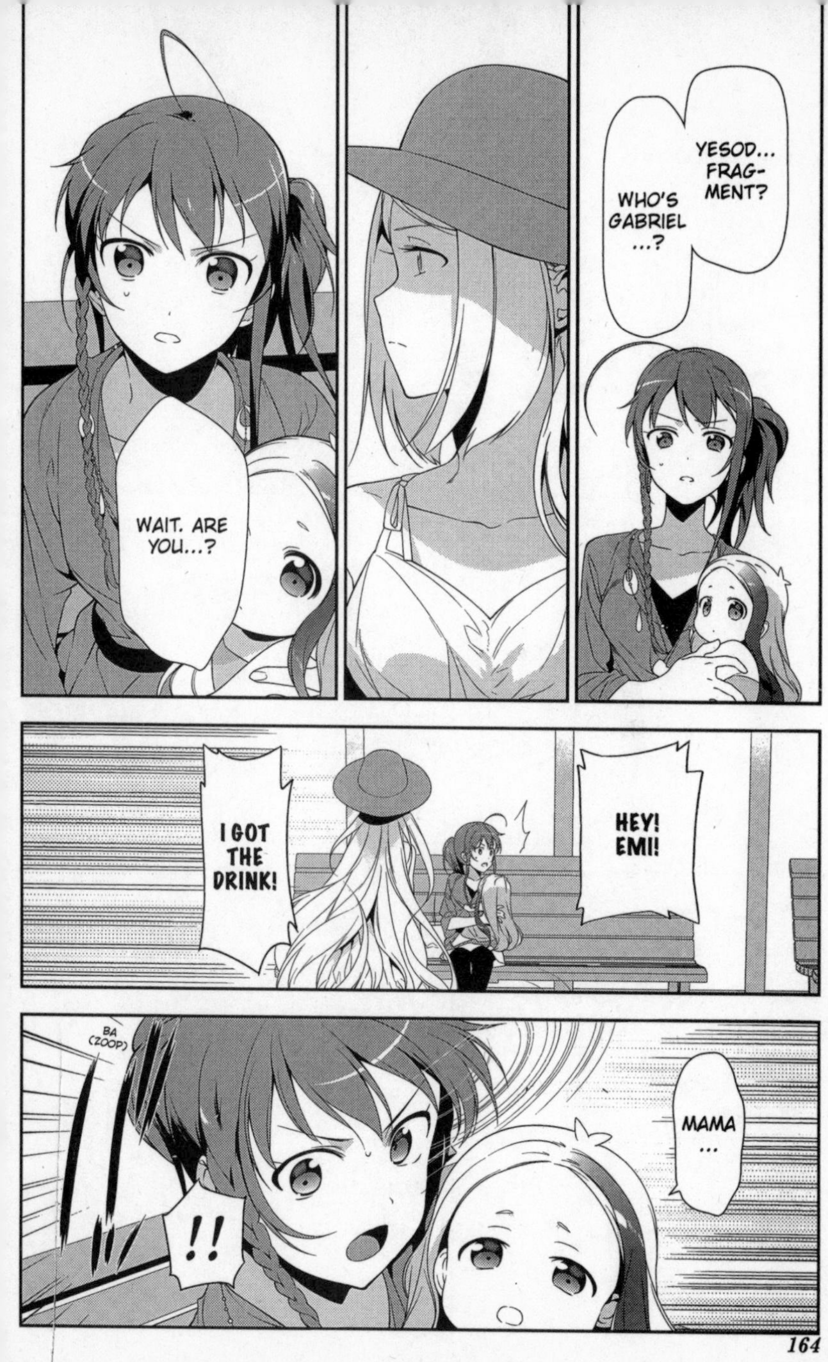
YESOD... FRAG-MENT?
WHO'S GABRIEL ...?
WAIT. ARE YOU...?
HEY! EMI!
I GOT THE DRINK!
MAMA ...
BA (ZOOP)
!!

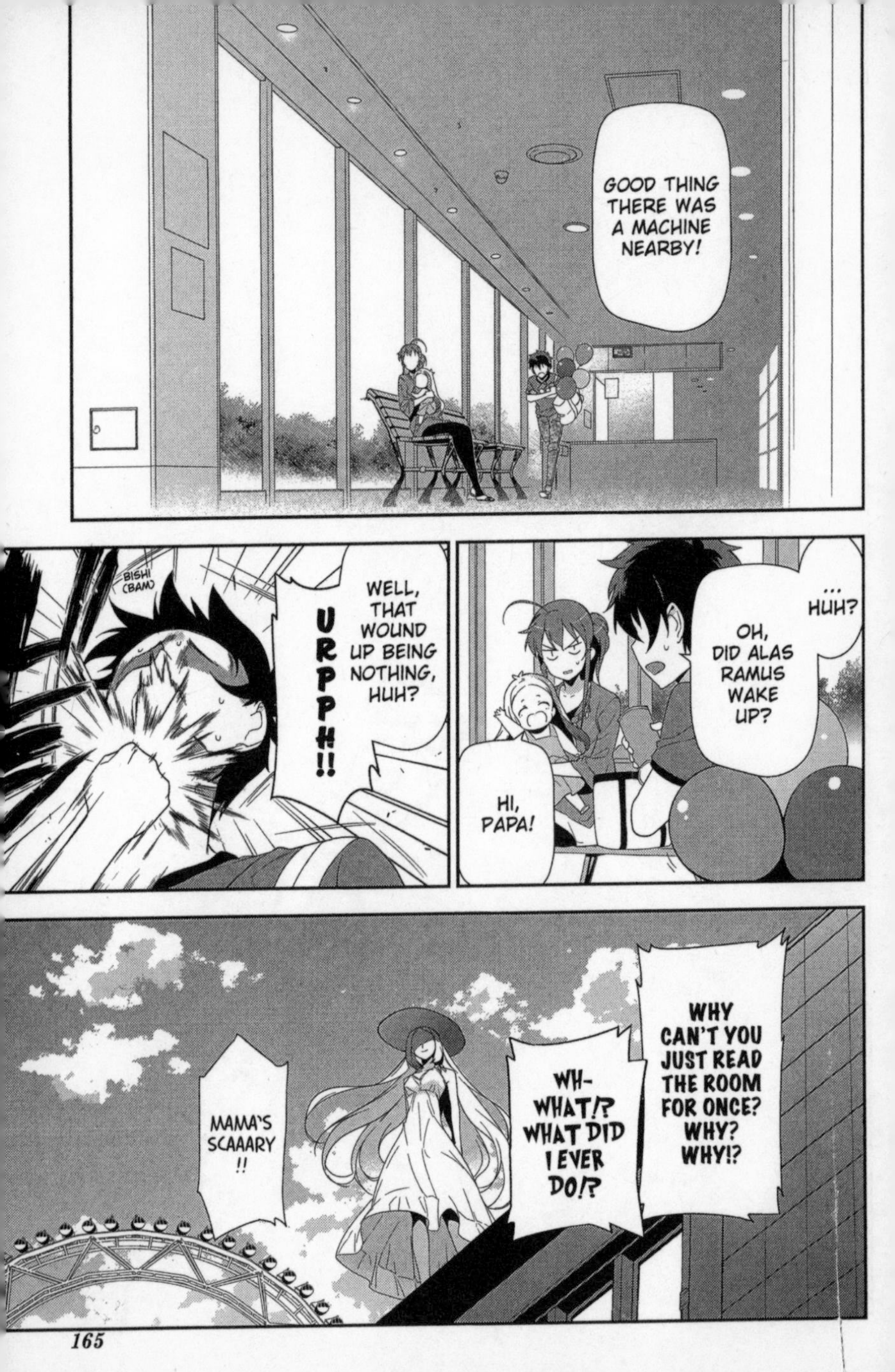
GOOD THING THERE WAS A MACHINE NEARBY!
... HUH?
OH, DID ALAS RAMUS WAKE UP?
HI, PAPA!
WELL, THAT WOUND UP BEING NOTHING, HUH?
URPPH!!
BISHI (BAM)
WHY CAN'T YOU JUST READ THE ROOM FOR ONCE? WHY? WHY!?
WH-WHAT!? WHAT DID I EVER DO!?
MAMA'S SCAAARY!!

THE DEVIL IS A PART-TIMER!

Laila

OMINOUS FLASHES IN THE NIGHT

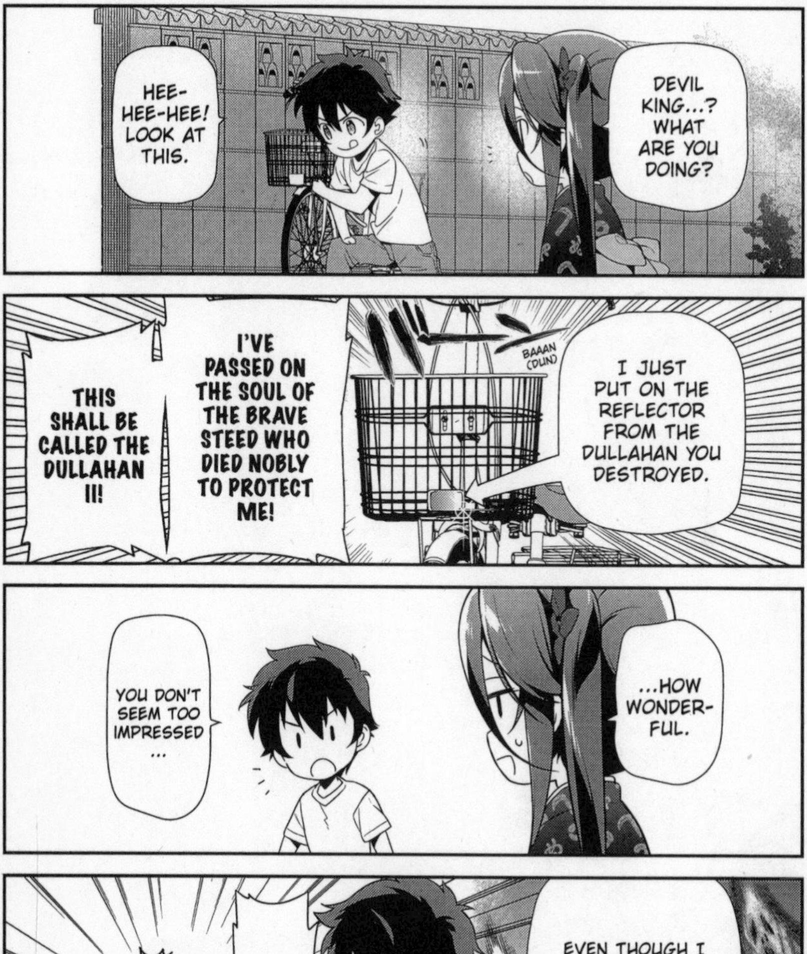
DEVIL KING...? WHAT ARE YOU DOING?
HEE-HEE-HEE! LOOK AT THIS.
I JUST PUT ON THE REFLECTOR FROM THE DULLAHAN YOU DESTROYED.
BAAAN (DUN)
I'VE PASSED ON THE SOUL OF THE BRAVE STEED WHO DIED NOBLY TO PROTECT ME!
THIS SHALL BE CALLED THE DULLAHAN II!
...HOW WONDERFUL.
YOU DON'T SEEM TOO IMPRESSED...
EVEN THOUGH I JUST APPLIED THE PUTRID FLESH OF MY HEADLESS WARRIOR ON A BARREN SOUL TO CREATE ANOTHER SLAVE TO DO MY BIDDING!
THAT'S SCARY!

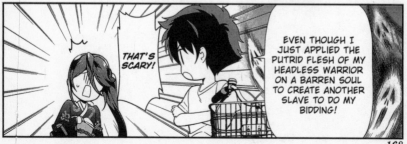

I AWAIT THEE, EMILIA, AT THE KOURAKUEN STATION EXIT...

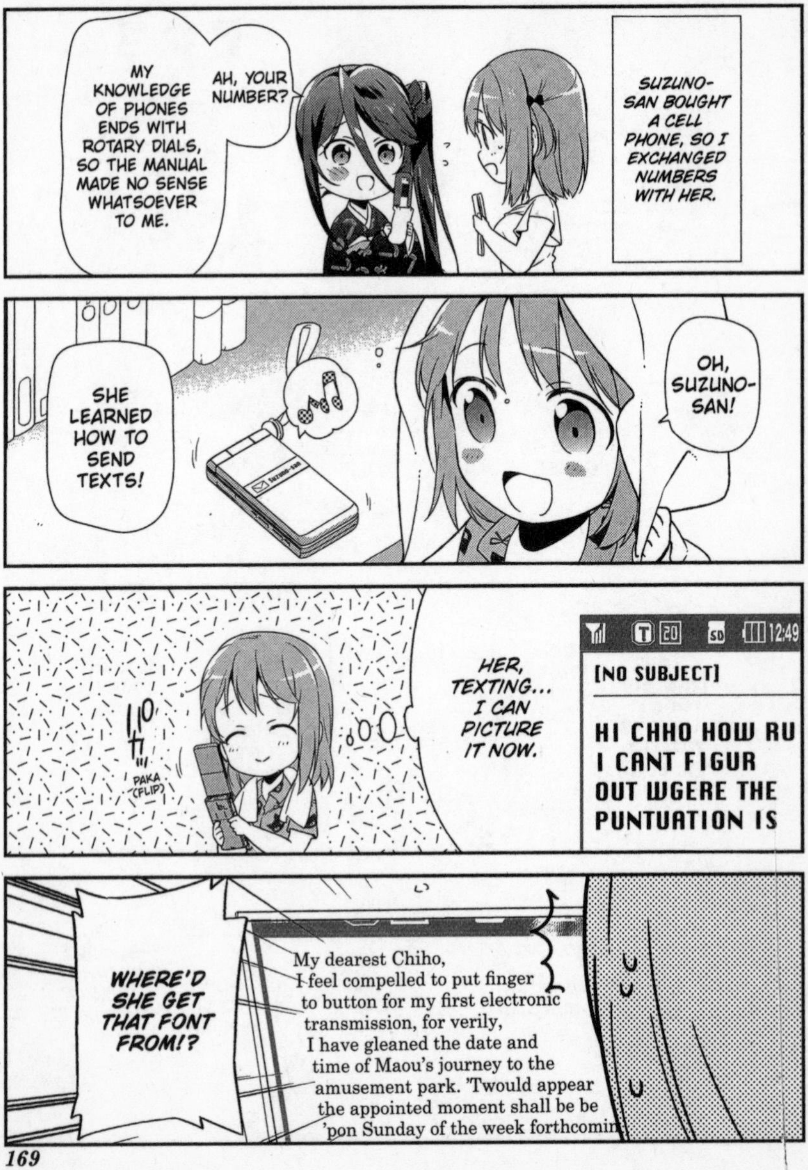
SUZUNO-SAN BOUGHT A CELL PHONE, SO I EXCHANGED NUMBERS WITH HER.
AH, YOUR NUMBER?
MY KNOWLEDGE OF PHONES ENDS WITH ROTARY DIALS, SO THE MANUAL MADE NO SENSE WHATSOEVER TO ME.
OH, SUZUNO-SAN!
SHE LEARNED HOW TO SEND TEXTS!
12:49
[NO SUBJECT]
HI CHHO HOW RU I CANT FIGUR OUT WGERE THE PUNTUATION IS
HER, TEXTING... I CAN PICTURE IT NOW.
PAKA (FLIP)
My dearest Chiho,
I feel compelled to put finger to button for my first electronic transmission, for verily, I have gleaned the date and time of Maou's journey to the amusement park. 'Twould appear the appointed moment shall be be 'pon Sunday of the week forthcomin
WHERE'D SHE GET THAT FONT FROM!?

DELUSIONAL SHOPPING

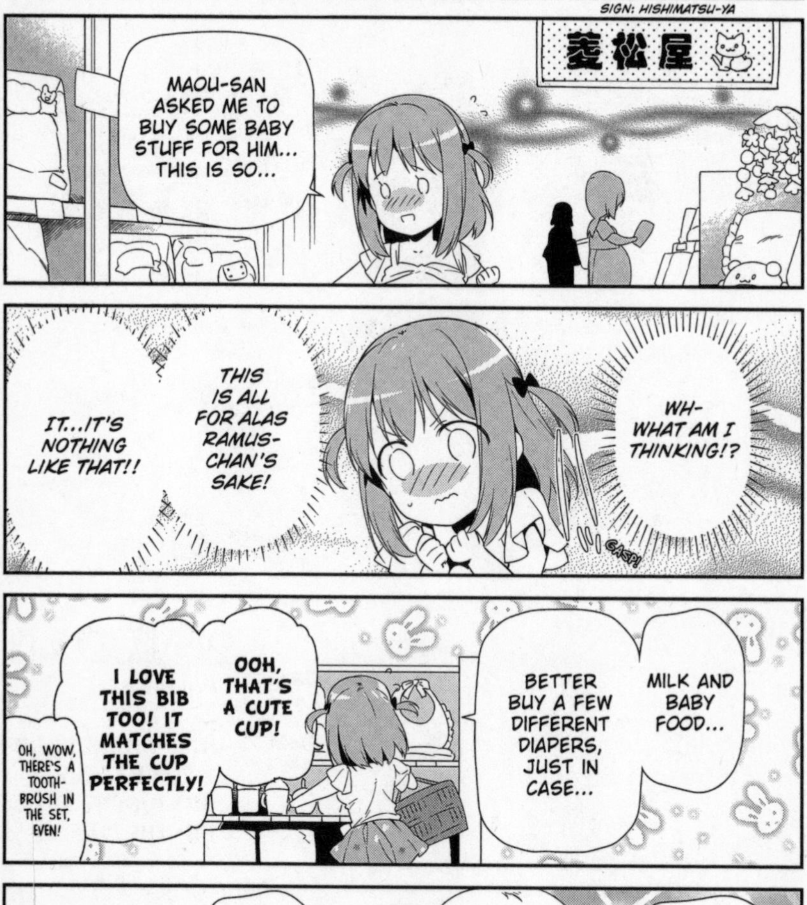
SIGN: HISHIMATSU-YA
菱松屋
MAOU-SAN ASKED ME TO BUY SOME BABY STUFF FOR HIM... THIS IS SO...
WH- WHAT AM I THINKING!?
GASP!
THIS IS ALL FOR ALAS RAMUS-CHAN'S SAKE!
IT...IT'S NOTHING LIKE THAT!!
MILK AND BABY FOOD...
BETTER BUY A FEW DIFFERENT DIAPERS, JUST IN CASE...
OOH, THAT'S A CUTE CUP!
I LOVE THIS BIB TOO! IT MATCHES THE CUP PERFECTLY!
OH, WOW, THERE'S A TOOTHBRUSH IN THE SET, EVEN!
YOU BOUGHT SO MANY THINGS FOR ME...
HOW COULD I EVER THANK YOU...!?
GUSU (SNIF)
ぐすっ
OH, UH, NO, JUST DOING SOME SHOPPING FOR MAOU-SAN!
DOSSARI (CLUTTER)
どっさり…

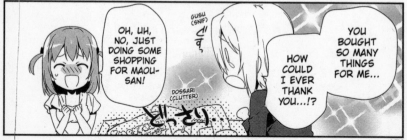

SOMEWHAT RELEVANT TO THE ARTIST TOO

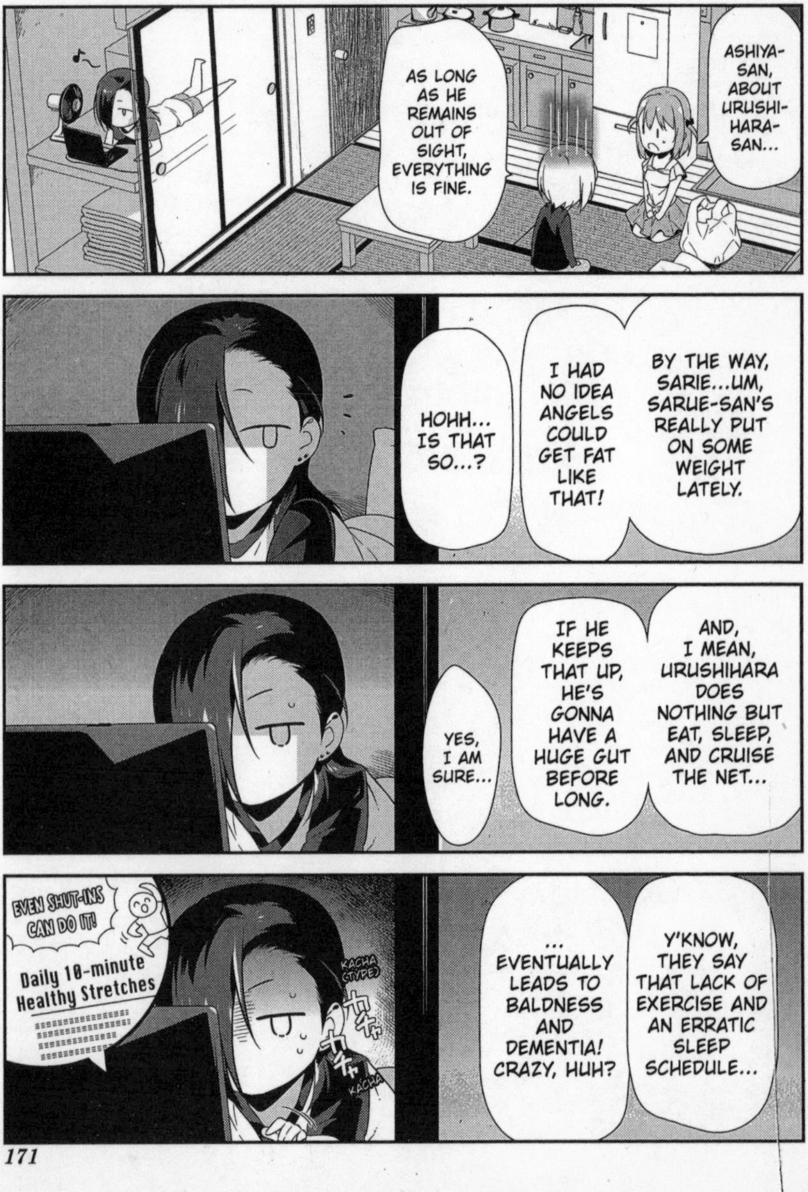
ASHIYA-SAN, ABOUT URUSHIHARA-SAN...
AS LONG AS HE REMAINS OUT OF SIGHT, EVERYTHING IS FINE.
BY THE WAY, SARIE...UM, SARUE-SAN'S REALLY PUT ON SOME WEIGHT LATELY.
I HAD NO IDEA ANGELS COULD GET FAT LIKE THAT!
HOHH... IS THAT SO...?
AND, I MEAN, URUSHIHARA DOES NOTHING BUT EAT, SLEEP, AND CRUISE THE NET...
IF HE KEEPS THAT UP, HE'S GONNA HAVE A HUGE GUT BEFORE LONG.
YES, I AM SURE...
Y'KNOW, THEY SAY THAT LACK OF EXERCISE AND AN ERRATIC SLEEP SCHEDULE...
...EVENTUALLY LEADS TO BALDNESS AND DEMENTIA! CRAZY, HUH?
KACHA (TYPED)
カチャ
カチャ
KACHA
EVEN SHUT-INS CAN DO IT!
Daily 10-minute Healthy Stretches

I'M MY OWN LIFE PRESERVER

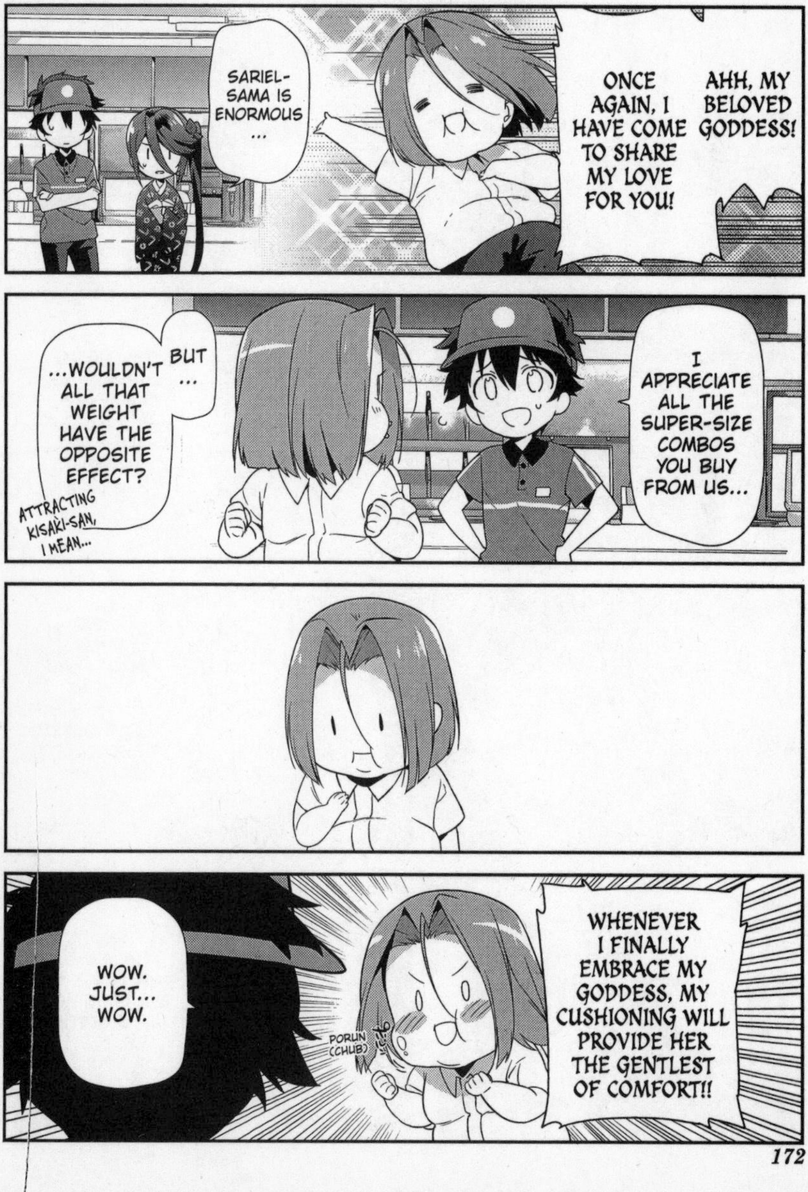
AHH, MY BELOVED GODDESS!
ONCE AGAIN, I HAVE COME TO SHARE MY LOVE FOR YOU!
SARIEL-SAMA IS ENORMOUS...
I APPRECIATE ALL THE SUPER-SIZE COMBOS YOU BUY FROM US...
BUT...
...WOULDN'T ALL THAT WEIGHT HAVE THE OPPOSITE EFFECT?
ATTRACTING KISAKI-SAN, I MEAN...
WHENEVER I FINALLY EMBRACE MY GODDESS, MY CUSHIONING WILL PROVIDE HER THE GENTLEST OF COMFORT!!
PORUN (CHUB)
WOW. JUST... WOW.

ME? LOSE TO A NINJA FROM EARTH?

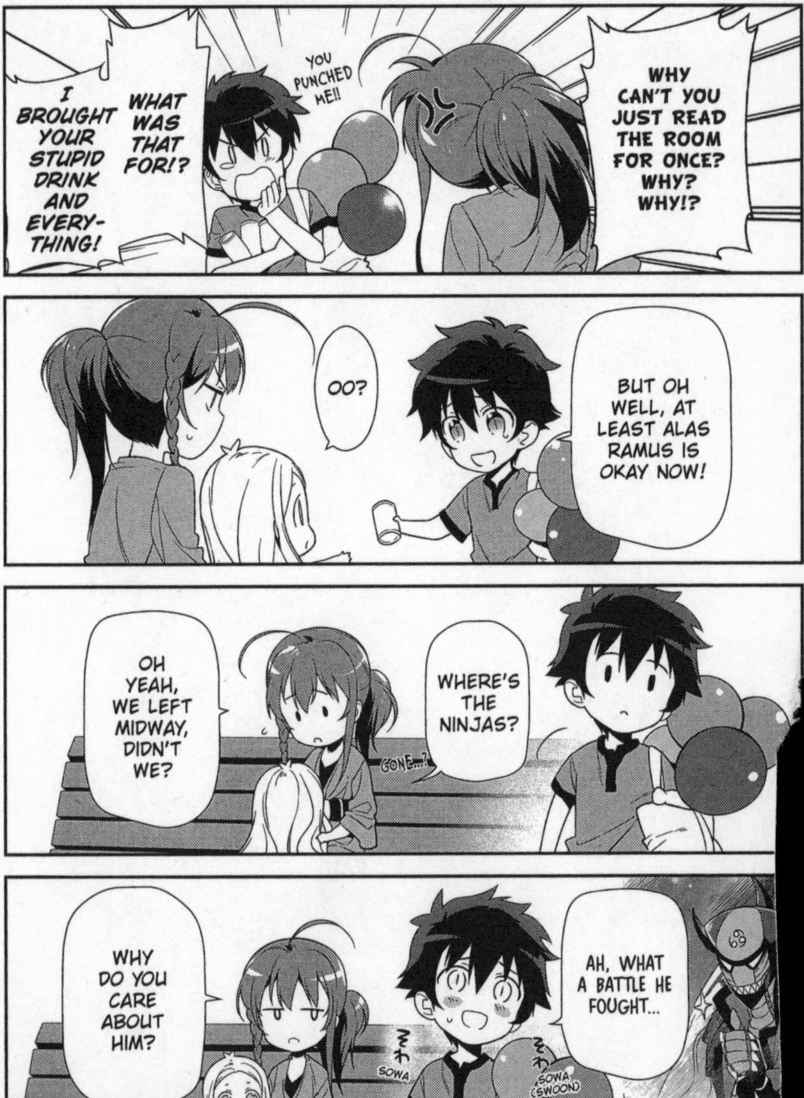
WHY CAN'T YOU JUST READ THE ROOM FOR ONCE? WHY? WHY!?
YOU PUNCHED ME!!
WHAT WAS THAT FOR!?
I BROUGHT YOUR STUPID DRINK AND EVERYTHING!
BUT OH WELL, AT LEAST ALAS RAMUS IS OKAY NOW!
OO?
WHERE'S THE NINJAS?
GONE...
OH YEAH, WE LEFT MIDWAY, DIDN'T WE?
AH, WHAT A BATTLE HE FOUGHT...
そわ
SOWA (SWOON)
そわ
SOWA
WHY DO YOU CARE ABOUT HIM?

AT LONG LAST, ALAS RAMUS HAS ESCAPED FROM THE WORLD OF THE NOVELS TO CAUSE A MAJOR RUCKUS. ALAS RAMUS'S STORY, WHICH BEGINS IN THIS VOLUME, WAS HONESTLY A TURNING POINT FOR THE WHOLE DEVIL IS A PART-TIMER! SERIES, ONE THAT DECIDED THE STORY'S DIRECTION ONCE AND FOR ALL. APPEARING BRISKLY AND WITH LITTLE WARNING TO BECOME THE SEVENTH REGULAR CHARACTER AFTER MAOU, EMI, CHIHO, ASHIYA, URUSHIHARA, AND SUZUNO, ALAS RAMUS WAS (AT ONE POINT) GOING TO BE SOME KIND OF SMALL ANIMAL FROM THE DEMON WORLD—ONE WHO SPARKED RUMORS OF ALIEN SIGHTINGS AT CHIHO'S HIGH SCHOOL BEFORE CREATING AN ENORMOUS ILLUSIONARY MIRAGE OF THE LANDLORD TO FIGHT ENEMIES. MANY THANKS TO THE EDITOR WHO SUGGESTED TO WAGAHARA THAT NOBODY WANTED A GIANT LANDLORD AND THAT I SHOULD THINK IT OVER A LITTLE BIT, AND THANKS TO 029-SAN FOR PAINTING PART OF VOLUME 1'S COVER ILLUSTRATION PURPLE WITHOUT ANY DIRECTION. THANKS TO THEM, WE NOW HAVE ALAS RAMUS, BELOVED OF THE ENTIRE CAST...AND, VIA THE DEFT HAND OF AKIO HIIRAGI-SAN, SHE'S NOW DARTING AROUND THE COMIC PAGES AS WELL. PLEASE ENJOY ALL OF MAOU'S (AND ASHIYA'S?) ANTICS STUFFED INTO THIS VOLUME, AS WELL AS QUITE POSSIBLY THE MOST DETAILED DEPICTION OF CHILD-RAISING EVER PRINTED BY DENGEKI COMICS!

SATOSHI WAGAHARA

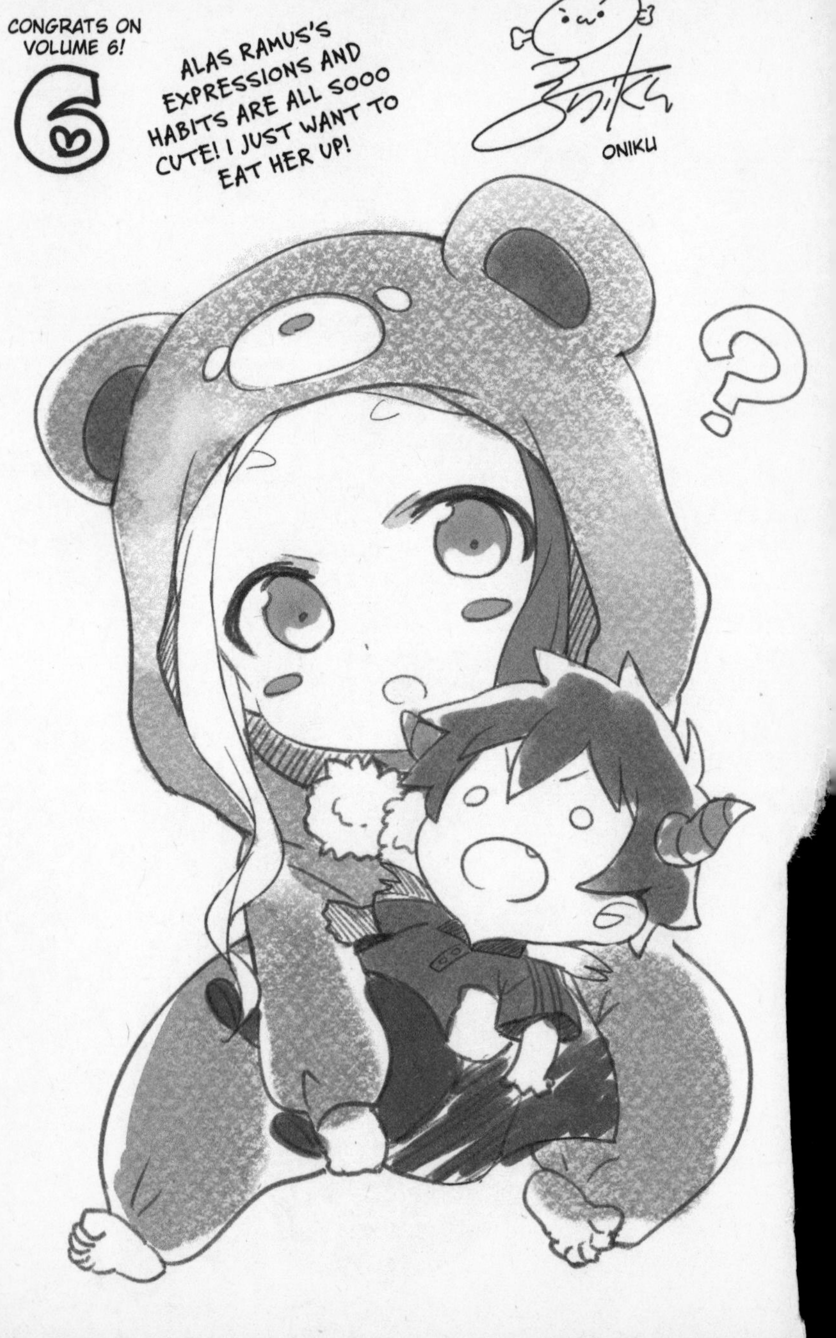
CONGRATS ON VOLUME 6!
6
ALAS RAMUS'S EXPRESSIONS AND HABITS ARE ALL SOOO CUTE! I JUST WANT TO EAT HER UP!
ONIKU

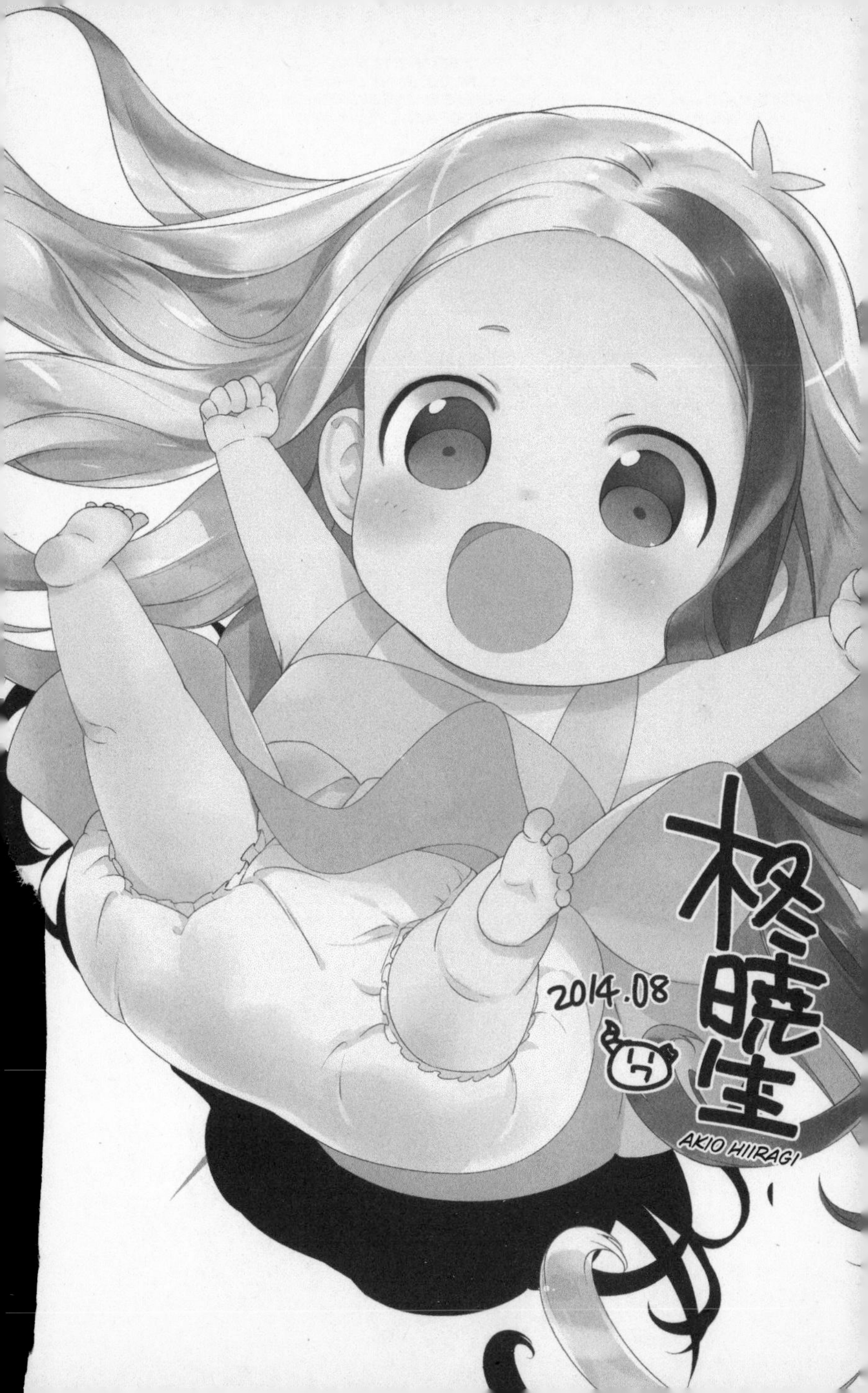
柊暁生
2014.08
AKIO HIIRAGI

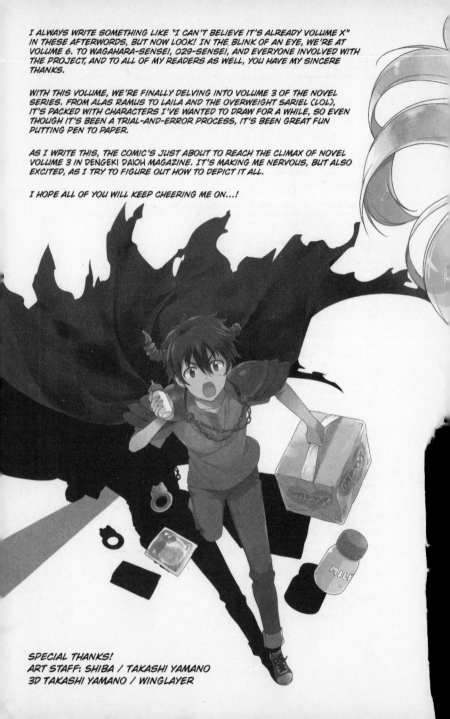

I ALWAYS WRITE SOMETHING LIKE "I CAN'T BELIEVE IT'S ALREADY VOLUME X" IN THESE AFTERWORDS, BUT NOW LOOK! IN THE BLINK OF AN EYE, WE'RE AT VOLUME 6. TO WAGAHARA-SENSEI, 029-SENSEI, AND EVERYONE INVOLVED WITH THE PROJECT, AND TO ALL OF MY READERS AS WELL, YOU HAVE MY SINCERE THANKS.

WITH THIS VOLUME, WE'RE FINALLY DELVING INTO VOLUME 3 OF THE NOVEL SERIES. FROM ALAS RAMUS TO LAILA AND THE OVERWEIGHT SARIEL (LOL), IT'S PACKED WITH CHARACTERS I'VE WANTED TO DRAW FOR A WHILE, SO EVEN THOUGH IT'S BEEN A TRIAL-AND-ERROR PROCESS, IT'S BEEN GREAT FUN PUTTING PEN TO PAPER.

AS I WRITE THIS, THE COMIC'S JUST ABOUT TO REACH THE CLIMAX OF NOVEL VOLUME 3 IN DENGEKI DAIOH MAGAZINE. IT'S MAKING ME NERVOUS, BUT ALSO EXCITED, AS I TRY TO FIGURE OUT HOW TO DEPICT IT ALL.

I HOPE ALL OF YOU WILL KEEP CHEERING ME ON...!

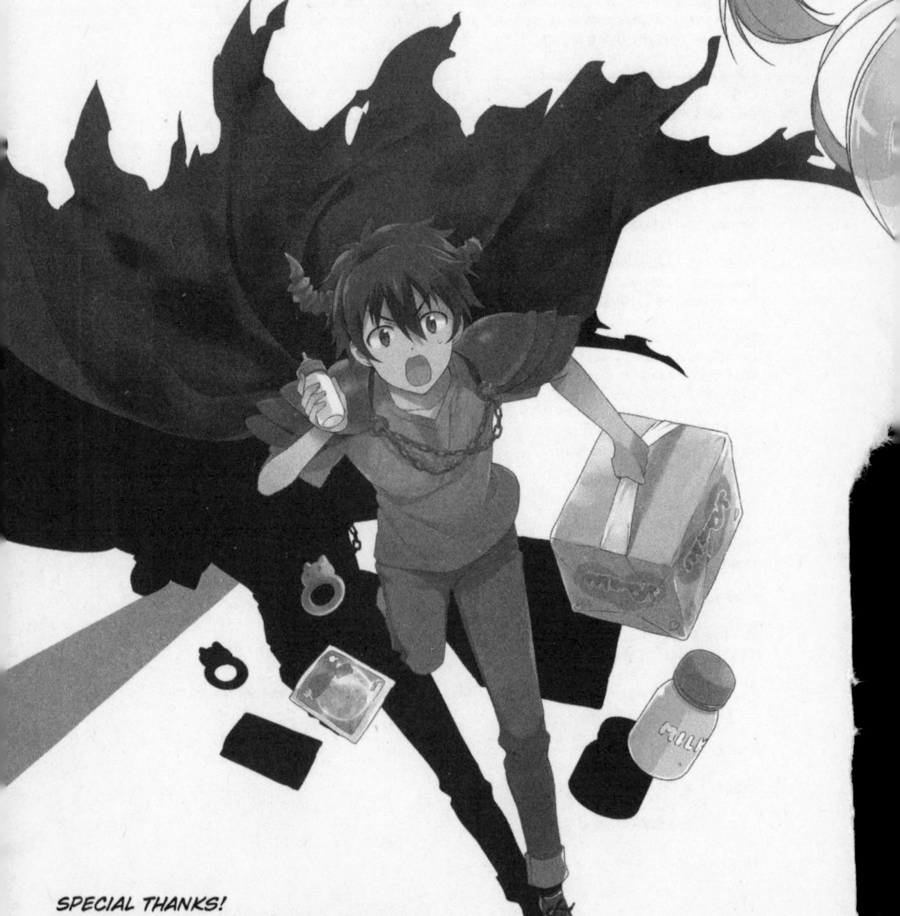

SPECIAL THANKS!
ART STAFF: SHIBA / TAKASHI YAMANO
3D TAKASHI YAMANO / WINGLAYER

THE DEVIL IS A PART-TIMER! ⑥

ART: AKIO HIIRAGI
ORIGINAL STORY: SATOSHI WAGAHARA
CHARACTER DESIGN: 029 (ONIKU)

Translation: Kevin Gifford

Lettering: Brndn Blakeslee

This book is a work of fiction. Names, characters, places, and incidents are the product of the author's imagination or are used fictitiously. Any resemblance to actual events, locales, or persons, living or dead, is coincidental.

HATARAKU MAOUSAMA! Vol. 6
© SATOSHI WAGAHARA / AKIO HIIRAGI 2014
All rights reserved.
Edited by ASCII MEDIA WORKS
First published in Japan in 2014 by KADOKAWA CORPORATION, Tokyo.
English translation rights arranged with KADOKAWA CORPORATION, Tokyo, through Tuttle-Mori Agency, Inc., Tokyo.

English translation © 2016 by Yen Press, LLC

Yen Press
1290 Avenue of the Americas
New York, NY 10104

Visit us at yenpress.com
facebook.com/yenpress
twitter.com/yenpress
yenpress.tumblr.com

First Yen Press Edition: July 2016

Yen Press is an imprint of Yen Press, LLC.
The Yen Press name and logo are trademarks of Yen Press, LLC.

The publisher is not responsible for websites (or their content) that are not owned by the publisher.

Library of Congress Control Number: 2014504637

ISBNs: 978-0-316-36014-2 (paperback)
        978-0-316-39820-6 (ebook)
        978-0-316-39821-3 (app)

10 9 8 7 6 5 4 3 2 1

BVG

Printed in the United States of America

W9-BUU-602